ANSWER KEY—END-OF-CHAPTER REVIEW QUESTIONS

Gaines and Coleman
POST-LICENSING EDUCATION FOR REAL ESTATE SALES ASSOCIATES,
5th edition (Update) by Edward J. O'Donnell

Chapter 1

1. d
2. a
3. c
4. b
5. c
6. c
7. d
8. b
9. c
10. d
11. a
12. b
13. c
14. d
15. b
16. c
17. d
18. a
19. d
20. b

Chapter 2

1. d
2. d
3. b
4. c
5. c
6. b
7. d
8. b
9. c
10. b
11. d

Chapter 2 (continued)

12. d
13. c
14. c
15. d
16. c
17. d
18. d
19. c
20. b

Chapter 3

1. c
2. d
3. c
4. d
5. d
6. b
7. a
8. d
9. d
10. c
11. b
12. b

Chapter 4

1. d
2. d
3. b
4. b
5. d

Chapter 4 (continued)

6. b
7. c
8. c
9. b
10. c

Chapter 5

1. c
2. b
3. d
4. d
5. c
6. a
7. d
8. a
9. b
10. d
11. c
12. c
13. b
14. b
15. c
16. a
17. a
18. d
19. c
20. a

Chapter 6

1. d
2. d

Chapter 6 (continued)

3. b
4. c
5. b
6. b
7. c
8. d
9. b
10. c
11. d
12. c
13. d
14. d
15. c
16. b
17. c
18. a
19. d
20. d

Chapter 7

1. b
2. d
3. a
4. c
5. b
6. c
7. c
8. a
9. d
10. b
11. d
12. c

Chapter 7 (continued)

13.	d
14.	b
15.	d
16.	b
17.	b
18.	d
19.	b
20.	a

Chapter 8

1.	b
2.	d
3.	d
4.	a
5.	c
6.	b
7.	b
8.	c
9.	c
10.	c
11.	a
12.	c
13.	d
14.	b
15.	d
16.	d
17.	c
18.	b
19.	d
20.	b

Chapter 9

1.	b
2.	c
3.	a

Chapter 9 (continued)

4.	a
5.	c
6.	b
7.	d
8.	a
9.	c
10.	a
11.	a
12.	c
13.	b
14.	c
15.	d
16.	a
17.	c
18.	d
19.	d
20.	b

Chapter 10

1.	b
2.	c
3.	c
4.	a
5.	d
6.	a
7.	c
8.	a
9.	b
10.	d
11.	a
12.	d
13.	d
14.	b
15.	b
16.	d
17.	d

Chapter 11

1.	d
2.	d
3.	c
4.	c
5.	c
6.	c
7.	a
8.	d
9.	c
10.	a

Chapter 12

1.	c
2.	a
3.	d
4.	d
5.	d
6.	a
7.	a
8.	c
9.	b
10.	d
11.	b
12.	c
13.	d
14.	c
15.	c
16.	d
17.	a
18.	b
19.	a
20.	d

Chapter 13

1.	c
2.	d
3.	b
4.	b
5.	c
6.	d
7.	b
8.	d
9.	c
10.	d
11.	b
12.	c
13.	b
14.	a
15.	a
16.	b
17.	d
18.	c
19.	b

Chapter 14

1.	d
2.	c
3.	b
4.	b
5.	b
6.	d
7.	c
8.	b
9.	d
10.	a
11.	b
12.	b
13.	b
14.	c
15.	d

ANSWER KEY—PRACTICE FINAL EXAM

Gaines and Coleman
POST-LICENSING EDUCATION FOR REAL ESTATE SALES ASSOCIATES,
5th edition (Update) by Edward J. O'Donnell

Note: Correct letter answer with textbook chapter.

1	c	(1)	21	d	(10)	41	b	(8)	61	d	(6)	81	b	(2)
2	b	(8)	22	d	(8)	42	c	(5)	62	b	(5)	82	b	(2)
3	d	(5)	23	c	(5)	43	b	(7)	63	d	(1)	83	a	(7)
4	c	(1)	24	a	(11)	44	a	(10)	64	a	(8)	84	d	(11)
5	c	(1)	25	a	(9)	45	d	(12)	65	a	(14)	85	b	(8)
6	b	(1)	26	d	(2)	46	a	(1)	66	d	(13)	86	b	(6)
7	a	(6)	27	a	(14)	47	d	(13)	67	b	(2)	87	c	(14)
8	b	(1)	28	b	(3)	48	d	(5)	68	c	(2)	88	a	(5)
9	c	(13)	29	b	(11)	49	a	(5)	69	c	(2)	89	b	(9)
10	a	(6)	30	b	(1)	50	a	(1)	70	c	(13)	90	a	(8)
11	d	(8)	31	d	(13)	51	d	(6)	71	b	(1)	91	b	(3)
12	b	(8)	32	b	(13)	52	b	(5)	72	c	(2)	92	d	(2)
13	a	(3)	33	d	(11)	53	d	(1)	73	d	(2)	93	a	(1)
14	b	(5)	34	c	(1)	54	d	(5)	74	d	(2)	94	d	(12)
15	b	(13)	35	a	(8)	55	b	(5)	75	b	(2)	95	c	(12)
16	a	(1)	36	a	(13)	56	c	(5)	76	c	(2)	96	c	(12)
17	b	(8)	37	c	(13)	57	c	(5)	77	a	(5)	97	a	(12)
18	c	(5)	38	a	(11)	58	c	(13)	78	c	(3)	98	a	(12)
19	a	(6)	39	b	(11)	59	b	(8)	79	a	(5)	99	b	(12)
20	c	(5)	40	c	(8)	60	c	(8)	80	c	(12)	100	d	(12)

GAINES & COLEMAN
POST-LICENSING EDUCATION
FOR REAL ESTATE SALES ASSOCIATES

5TH EDITION
UPDATE

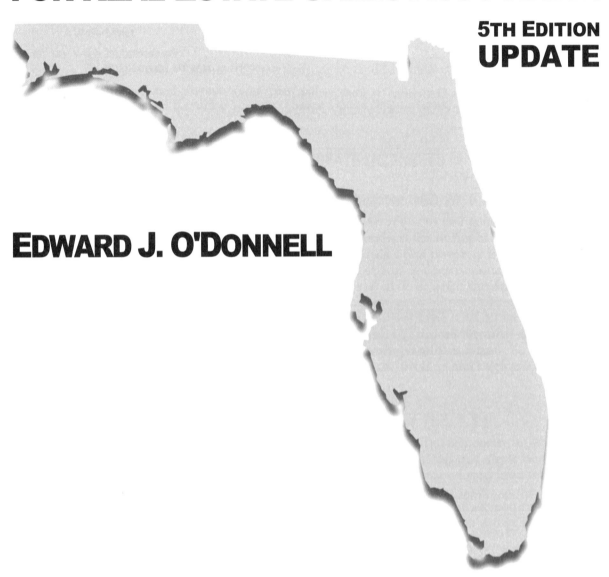

EDWARD J. O'DONNELL

Dearborn™
Real Estate Education

This publication is designed to provide accurate and authoritative information in regard to the subject matter covered. It is sold with the understanding that the publisher is not engaged in rendering legal, accounting or other professional service. If legal advice or other expert assistance is required, the services of a competent professional person should be sought.

President: Roy Lipner
Publisher: Evan Butterfield
Editorial Project Manager, Print Products: Louise Benzer
Production Coordinator: Daniel Frey
Typesetting: Janet Schroeder
Art and Design Manager: Lucy Jenkins

Published by Dearborn™ Real Estate Education
a division of Dearborn Financial Publishing, Inc.®
30 South Wacker Drive
Chicago, IL 60606-7481
312-836-4400
www.dearbornRE.com

Printed in the United States of America.

05 06 10 9 8 7 6 5 4 3

Library of Congress Cataloging-in-Publication Data

O'Donnell, Edward J. (Edward James), 1939-
    Post-licensing education for real estate salespersons / Edward J. O'Donnell,
George Gaines, David S. Coleman—5th ed.
        p. cm.
    Gaines's name appears first on the earlier edition.
    Includes index.
    ISBN 0-7931-4580-5
    1. Real estate business—Florida. 2. Real property—Florida.
3. Real estate agents—Licenses—Florida. 4. Real estate business—
Florida—Examinations, questions, etc. 5. Real property—Florida—
Examinations, questions, etc. I. Gaines, George. II. Coleman,
David S. III. Title.

HD266.F6G35 2001
333.33'09759—dc21
                                                        2001048258

CONTENTS

ACKNOWLEDGMENTS

The authors wish to express their appreciation to the following persons who were willing to provide their professional advice and the assistance necessary for the completion of this edition. Particular thanks go to Jerry Cox of Heritage Mortgage Company, Arthur Cody, and to Kitty Powl and Sandra Rodriguez of The Real Estate School, Inc., for help and suggestions, and to Sharon O'Donnell, for her creative ideas.

The authors are indebted to other Dearborn authors identified in this book, to the publisher's professional staff and especially to the editor of this edition, Louise Benzer. Her suggestions and prodding were done in a most agreeable way and helped make this a better book.

Special thanks go to those individuals who thoughtfully and thoroughly reviewed this edition of the text:

Cheri-Lynn Diamond, Gold Coast School of Real Estate; Richard T. Fryer, ABR, Institute of Florida Real Estate Careers, Inc., Andy Gray, Andy Gray Schools of Real Estate, Inc.; and Robert C. Gordon, Bob Hogue School of Real Estate.

We also would like to acknowledge those who reviewed previous editions of this book:

John F. Phillips, Ph.D., Curtis H. Wild, Donald L. Ross, John L. Greer, James Sweetin, Mary E. Sweetin, Anthony L. Griffon, Ron Guiberson, Linda Crawford, Audrey Van Vliet, Ronald O. Boatright, Terrance M. Fitzpatrick, Lawrence D. Greer, Robert L. Hogue, Michael Rieder, Roger L. Satterfield, Donald E. Tennant, and Audrey M. Conti.

INTRODUCTION

Florida real estate sales associates must complete the 45-hour post-licensing education course before their first license renewal, on subjects approved by the Florida Real Estate Commission. This book is approved by the Commission for use in meeting the post-licensing education requirement for sales associates.

This textbook is intended to provide licensees an opportunity to build on the principles and practices learned in the prelicensing course and to present new, hands-on training in many important subject areas.

Because many licensees work in residential real estate, the topics covered in this course book focus primarily on that part of the real estate industry. However, many of the principles and practices described in this book also apply to the commercial and investment sectors.

Learning objectives are listed at the beginning of each chapter as a guide to focusing on the most important points. Discussion questions are provided throughout each chapter to help the student acquire a more complete understanding of the material and to provide the instructor with feedback. A quiz has been included at the end of each chapter for additional review of the material.

The book is divided into seven sections, and the authors have attempted to arrange them in the logical sequence of real estate activities: learning the law, listing properties, marketing the properties, obtaining financing, closing the transaction, and working with investors.

Section I helps the licensee understand the many complex and important laws that regulate the licensee's daily activities. A complete understanding of these laws, from brokerage relationships to fair housing to lead-based paint disclosures, helps the licensee provide fair and honest service to consumers and reduce exposure to disciplinary action or civil damages.

Section II focuses on the primary building blocks of a successful career, such as ways to become more professional through ethics, education and planning. It also covers the changing world of information resources on the Internet, as well as technology.

Section III helps the licensee understand the process of listing real property. Preparing a comparative market analysis is covered in detail because of the importance of helping a seller establish market value for a property. The student will learn how to prepare a seller's net proceeds statement as well as explain important parts of the listing agreement.

Section IV shows the licensee how to work with buyers effectively. From the initial contact with a buyer to analysis of the buyer's needs and ability to purchase to showing the property, this is a real world discussion of selling real estate. A detailed section on sales and option contracts is included.

Section V concentrates on a key ingredient to a successful sale—financing. The coverage starts with an evaluation of current lending practices and programs, then continues with a step-by-step discussion of how a loan is processed after a contract is written.

Section VI provides the licensee with a step-by-step guide to getting the contract to closing. Responsibilities of each cooperating sales associate are covered in detail. The section ends with complete coverage of closing statements.

Section VII is an overview of investment in real estate, covering advantages and disadvantages of each property type. The student will have an opportunity to practice financial analysis techniques. The final chapter covers the management of investment property.

We have attempted to make this text as thorough and practical as possible and included many new features that we hope you find helpful.

Forms

A **"Forms-To-Go"** section is in the back of the book with symbols like the one on the left to show you when a form is available. The section has FREC registration forms, brokerage relationship disclosures, and other forms you might find useful in your daily practice.

www.

Web links are indicated throughout the book with an icon like the one shown on the left, so you can use the Internet to find more resource material.

At the end of this book are six items of interest:

1. Appendix of Resources, which lists books and articles appropriate for further study in each subject area;
2. Practice Final Exam of 100 multiple-choice questions similar to those in the end-of-course exam;
3. Glossary of key terms identified in the chapters, with definitions;
4. Index;
5. Forms-To-Go Section to provide the student with useful forms for real estate practice; and
6. Course Feedback Form, to be completed once the course has been taken.

While it is difficult for one book to meet all of the needs of every real estate sales associate entering the profession in Florida, it is the intention of the authors that this book provide a bridge from basic classroom knowledge to deeper understanding and practical hands-on experience in real estate.

Please complete the "Course Feedback Form" with your specific reactions and suggestions once you have completed the course and submit it so that the authors may improve the book for those who follow you.

We wish you well.

Edward J. O'Donnell

George Gaines, Jr.

David S. Coleman

SECTION I

LEGAL ISSUES IN REAL ESTATE PRACTICE

Chapter 1.   Brokerage Relationships and License Law Update

Chapter 2.   Federal and State Laws Affecting Real Estate

This section emphasizes the need for licensees to remain focused on the requirements of the law while listing and selling real estate.

The section will familiarize licensees with the important license law changes relating to the broker's relationships with customers. It will also describe the disclosure forms that licensees must give to persons with whom they come in contact, as well as list the situations when the disclosure requirements do not apply.

State and federal laws that affect real estate are also described to help the licensee stay current on important laws such as fair housing, property condition disclosure, federal income taxes, and lead-based paint disclosures.

CHAPTER 1—BROKERAGE RELATIONSHIPS AND LICENSE LAW UPDATE

LEARNING OBJECTIVES

Upon completion of this chapter, *you should be able to:*

1. list the differences between the duties of single agent brokers, transaction brokers, and brokers with "no representation" statuses;
2. distinguish between the terms *principal* and *customer;*
3. list the type of real property transactions that require licensees to disclose their brokerage relationship to customers;
4. list the different disclosure forms a licensee must give to buyers and sellers of residential property and understand the uses of each;
5. describe the required education for the first renewal and the required education for subsequent renewals;
6. describe the penalties for renewing a license without having completed the required education;
7. describe the legal requirements for including the personal name of a licensee in an advertisement; and
8. list the two recent exceptions to the rules for handling conflicting demands on escrow deposits.

CHAPTER 1

BROKERAGE RELATIONSHIPS AND LICENSE LAW UPDATE

THE REAL ESTATE LICENSE LAW

Students should be familiar with the Florida real estate license law and stay current on important changes to the law. This chapter covers brokerage relationships in detail and reviews and updates licensees on other requirements of the law.

The application of agency law to the real estate brokerage business is complex. This chapter updates licensees concerning a broker's relationships with the parties to a transaction and the disclosure requirements of Florida law.

Agency laws govern the dealings between single agent brokers and their principals. It is the product of common law, case law, and statute. To understand how we got where we are today, we must understand where we have been.

For years, brokers were usually single **agents** representing sellers. Buyers were unrepresented but were not always aware of the fact. A National Association of REALTORS® survey showed that 55 percent of buyers mistakenly believed that the seller's broker represented them. A later Federal Trade Commission survey put that figure at 72 percent. This led to legislation intended to provide better consumer disclosure.

Chapter 475 did not specifically address the issue of agency disclosure for many years because it was addressed in another statute. Florida's "Little FTC Act" (Ch 501, F.S.) required that licensees disclose to buyers before a contract was signed that the licensees were agents of the sellers, if that were the case. Often, the quality of the disclosures was less than perfect, and there was little documentation available to protect a broker from later claims of failure to disclose.

In 1994, Chapter 475, F.S., was amended with major changes to brokerage relationships. The law required that written **disclosures** be given to consumers in all real estate transactions, including nonresidential sales and leasing. The change allowed brokers to act as single agents, dual agents or transaction brokers. In the following years, certain problems in the law were identified, and in 1997, the *Brokerage Relationship Disclosure Act* became part of Chapter 475. The law was amended again in 2003.

BROKERAGE RELATIONSHIP DISCLOSURE ACT

The *Brokerage Relationship Disclosure Act*, effective October 1, 1997, was important to both licensees and consumers. The act specifically prohibited dual agency, intended or unintended, and removed the disclosure requirements from all transactions except residential property. It simplified the disclosure notices and required licensees in a residential transaction to give disclosure notices, including a *notice of nonrepresentation*, at "first contact" with a consumer.

In 1998, the law was changed to allow nonresidential brokers to appoint designated sales associates. The law was revised in 1999 to delete the notice of nonrepresentation form. In 2000, the legislature modified the law to require the *no brokerage relationship notice*. In 2003, the law was changed to add the presumption that all licensees are operating as a transaction broker unless a single agent or no brokerage relationship is established, in writing, with a customer. Licensees must give the notice to customers they do not represent before showing residential property. The law is important to licensees in two principal areas:

1. It describes the *type of brokerage relationship* a licensee may have with a customer. This section of the law applies to all licensees.
2. It requires *disclosure of the brokerage relationship* a licensee has with a customer. This section of the law applies only to licensees dealing in residential property sales.

AUTHORIZED BROKERAGE RELATIONSHIPS

A real estate licensee may have a brokerage relationship with potential buyers and sellers either as a single agent or as a transaction broker. It is illegal for a licensee to be a disclosed or undisclosed **dual agent.** A licensee may also work with a customer with no brokerage relationship, acting as a nonrepresentative.

There is a presumption that licensees are operating as transaction brokers unless the broker decides to have a different relationship with the customer. If a single agency relationship is established with a residential seller, all licensees in that brokerage firm have single agent duties to that seller. It is not legal for another sales associate in the firm to represent a buyer when selling that property, nor can that sales associate be a transaction broker. A sales associate may not decide the type of relationship without the broker's consent.

Once a single agent relationship is established, a licensee may change to a transaction broker relationship. The licensee must make the appropriate disclosure of duties to the buyer or seller, and the buyer or the seller, or both, must give written consent before the change. A **customer** is not required to enter a brokerage relationship with any real estate licensee [475.278(1)].

All licensees have the legal duties of:

- fair and honest dealing with customers;
- disclosure of known facts that materially affect the value of residential property, and that are not readily observable to the buyer; and
- accounting for all funds.

Additional duties are imposed on single agents and transaction brokers. A discussion of each type of relationship follows.

DISCLOSURE REQUIREMENTS FOR RESIDENTIAL PROPERTY TRANSACTIONS

The real estate licensee disclosure requirements of this section apply to all residential sales. As used in this subsection, the term *residential sale* means the sale of improved residential property of four units or fewer, the sale of unimproved residential property intended for use of four units or fewer, or the sale of agricultural property of ten acres or fewer.

The real estate disclosure requirements of this section do not apply:

- when a licensee knows that the potential seller or buyer already is represented by a single agent or a transaction broker.

- when an owner is selling new residential units built by the owner and the circumstances or setting should reasonably inform the potential buyer that the owner's employee or single agent is acting on behalf of the owner, whether because of the location of the sales office or because of office signage or placards or identification badges worn by the owner's employee or single agent.
- to nonresidential transactions.
- to the rental or leasing of real property, unless an option to purchase all or a portion of the property improved with four or fewer residential units is given.
- to a bona fide "open house" or model home showing that does not involve eliciting confidential information; the execution of a contractual offer or an agreement for representation, or negotiations concerning price, terms, or conditions of a potential sale.
- to unanticipated casual conversations between a licensee and a seller or buyer that do not involve eliciting confidential information; the execution of a contractual offer or agreement for representation; or negotiations concerning price, terms, or conditions of a potential sale.
- to responding to general factual questions from a potential buyer or seller concerning properties that have been advertised for sale.
- to situations in which a licensee's communications with a potential buyer or seller are limited to providing general factual information, oral or written, about the qualifications, background, and services of the licensee or the licensee's brokerage firm.
- to auctions, appraisals, and dispositions of any interest in business enterprises or business opportunities, except for property with four or fewer residential units.

Time for Disclosure of Brokerage Relationships in a Residential Transaction

If a licensee will be a single agent or a transaction broker, the licensee must provide disclosure before or at the time of entering into a **listing agreement** or an agreement for representation or before the showing of property, whichever occurs first. If a licensee will not be representing a customer in any capacity, the licensee must give the customer a No Brokerage Relationship Notice before showing a property. *Residential real estate* is defined as:

- improved residential property of four units or fewer;
- unimproved residential property intended for use as four units or fewer; or
- agricultural property of ten acres or fewer.

Licensees in a residential transaction may be required to give the customer some or all of the following four disclosure notices:

1. **No Brokerage Relationship Notice**
2. **Single Agent Notice**
3. **Transaction Broker Notice**
4. **Consent to Transition to Transaction Broker Notice**

These notices will be discussed in the following sections.

Retaining Brokerage Relationship Disclosure Documents

Brokers must keep copies of the disclosure notices for all residential transactions that result in a written sales contract for at least five years. It does not matter whether the sale closes. Brokerage relationship disclosure notices are checked by DBPR investigators during office inspection visits.

NO BROKERAGE RELATIONSHIP

Licensees working with a customer without a brokerage relationship owe the customer the following duties:

- dealing honestly and fairly;
- disclosing all known facts that materially affect the value of the residential real property that are not readily observable to the buyer; and
- accounting for all funds entrusted to the licensee.

A single agent for one party in a transaction may decide to work with the other party as a nonrepresentative. If a broker does not have a brokerage relationship with a customer, and is a single agent for the other party, the customer is at a disadvantage. It is the duty of the single agent to work diligently for his principal and to get the best price and terms for the principal.

DISCUSSION EXERCISE 1.1

Nonrepresentation

Broker Helen lists the Smith's home as a single agent. Later, Helen shows it to Mr. Jones. She gives him the No Brokerage Relationship Notice, disclosing the fact that she will be working as a nonrepresentative with him.

While writing an offer for the property, Mr. Jones says, "I'll pay the asking price of $200,000 if I have to, but I would like to start the negotiations at $185,000."

When Helen presents the offer, she must tell the Smiths that Jones has said he will pay up to the listed price. Failure to make this disclosure would expose her to disciplinary action and civil liability for violation of her fiduciary duties.

No Brokerage Relationship Notice

Forms

The duties of a licensee who has no brokerage relationship with a buyer or seller must be fully described and disclosed in writing to the buyer or seller. The No Brokerage Relationship Notice must be given to prospective buyers and sellers of residential property before showing a property. The notice need not be signed. The No Brokerage Relationship Notice is shown in the Forms-To-Go Appendix.

SINGLE AGENT RELATIONSHIP

A *single agent* represents, as a fiduciary, either the buyer or seller, but not both, in the same transaction. Being a single agent broker does not mean, however, that there must be two brokers in every transaction. A single agent broker who represents the seller may work with a buyer as a nonrepresentative.

Fiduciary Relationship

A *fiduciary relationship* is a position of trust and confidence. The **principal** relies on the real estate single agent to give skilled and knowledgeable advice and to help negotiate the best terms in dealings with the customer. Because only single agency creates a fiduciary relationship, only single agents may call their customers *principals*. Once a single agent relationship is created, the law requires the agent to place the interests of the principal above the interests of everyone else, including those of the agent. The principal is responsible for the acts of his single agent.

Creation of Single Agent Relationships

A single agent relationship results from mutual consent between the principal and the agent. The broker requires only the principal's specific authorization to represent him or her. Single agency is not created simply because a licensee performs a service for a customer. Payment of a commission is not a factor in creating a single agent relationship. A single agent does not need a written contract or compensation for an agency relationship to exist. Single agents can represent either the seller or the buyer.

Single Agent Duties

A single agent owes nine specific duties to a buyer or seller:

1. Dealing honestly and fairly
2. Loyalty
3. Confidentiality
4. Obedience
5. Full disclosure
6. Accounting for all funds
7. Skill, care, and diligence in the transaction
8. Presenting all offers and counteroffers in a timely manner, unless a party has previously directed the licensee otherwise in writing
9. Disclosing all known facts that materially affect the value of residential real property and are not readily observable

Single Agent Notice

The *Single Agent Notice* must be given before, or at the time of, entering into a listing agreement or an agreement for representation or before the showing of property, whichever occurs first. It may be a separate and distinct disclosure document or part of another document, but is most often made part of a listing agreement or a **buyer representation agreement.**

 The notice should be signed. If a principal who wants the single agent form of representation refuses to sign a Single Agent Notice, the licensee may still work as a single agent for that person, but should note on the licensee's copy that the principal declined to sign. The Single Agent Notice is shown in the Forms-To-Go Appendix.

Seller Agency

Property listings are extremely important to brokerage firms. Listings help make the phone ring. The only way a broker can collect a commission on both sides of a transaction is to start out with a listing. While **seller agency** formerly was the most common form of brokerage relationship in real estate, a broker who lists property is not automatically the single agent of the seller. Many brokers in Florida now choose to act as transaction brokers when listing property and do not become the agents of either sellers or buyers.

Role of sales associates. Real estate sales associates and broker associates cannot sell their services directly to the public but must work under a broker's direct supervision. Sales associates are agents of, and act for, the employing brokers.

If a seller's broker has a listing, that broker *and all the sales associates in that firm, including any of the firm's branch offices,* represent the seller.

1   Sellers' brokers may encounter problems with both in-house sales and cooperative
2 sales.

3 ***In-House Sales.***   It is the goal of most real estate firms to sell their own listings, not
4 only because the practice generates more income but because sellers seem more satis-
5 fied that they made good choices in listing with firms. When a firm sells its own listing,
6 it is called an *in-house sale*. While only one broker is involved in the transaction, it is pos-
7 sible that more than one sales associate from the firm may participate.

8   Florida law allows the in-house sale of a broker's own listing to a buyer, even if the
9 broker wishes to remain a single agent for the seller. If the transaction is residential
10 property, the licensee must disclose in writing (No Brokerage Relationship Notice) to
11 the buyer that the licensee's brokerage firm is a fiduciary of the seller and that the buyer
12 will be unrepresented.

13   The seller's broker has the following duties to the buyer:

14 • Honest and fair dealing
15 • Disclosure of known facts about the condition of the property that affect its value and
16   that are not readily observable by the buyer
17 • Accounting for all funds

18   The sales associate can discuss with the buyer all factual data and public information
19 available about the property and must answer questions dealing with this information
20 honestly and fairly. In other words, the sales associate can provide the buyer with a great
21 deal of customer service, although not in a representative capacity. A single agent bro-
22 ker may never take any action detrimental to his principal.

23 ***Cooperative Sales.***   In a **cooperative sale,** it is important to clarify early in the trans-
24 action whether the selling broker is a subagent for the seller, a single agent of the buyer,
25 a transaction broker not in a fiduciary relationship with either the seller or the buyer,
26 or acting in a no brokerage relationship role.

Subagency

28 A *subagent* is a real estate licensee employed by a single agent listing broker, under
29 authority granted by the principal, to act as a single agent on the principal's behalf. It
30 should be noted that a buyer's broker also can appoint a subagent to represent the
31 buyer.

32 **Disadvantages of Subagency to the Seller.**   Subagency increases the seller's expo-
33 sure to potential liability caused by the subagents. Sellers are bound by and responsible
34 for the conduct and representations of authorized subagents whom they may have
35 never met and over whom they have no practical control. For these reasons, subagency
36 is rarely offered by the listing broker.

Buyer Agency

38 **Buyer agency** exists when the broker represents the buyer exclusively in a real estate
39 transaction. Buyers receive the greatest benefits from single agent representation. In
40 practice, however, a licensee may begin a relationship as a buyer's agent, remaining in
41 that status when showing MLS listings, but later transition to transaction broker status
42 if the licensee is showing his or her firm's listing. This should be explained to the buyer
43 who enters into a single agent relationship. A single agent buyer's broker would ordi-
44 narily give the buyer a Single Agent Notice, a Consent to Transition to Transaction
45 Broker Notice, and a Transaction Broker Notice to allow for this situation.

In Florida today, the trend is for licensees working with buyers to act as transaction brokers rather than as single agents. Still, some buyers familiar with the law may feel more comfortable with a single agent relationship when possible because of the benefits of:

- undivided loyalty from the licensee;
- full disclosure to the principal of all the facts known by the licensee that are relevant to a transaction;
- confidentiality forever for facts disclosed by the principal; and
- stronger negotiating strategy.

Deciding To Represent the Buyer. Just because a prospective buyer enters a broker's office asking to see homes for sale, the broker does not automatically represent the buyer as a single agent, particularly if the buyer is interested in one of the broker's listings. The broker and the customer must agree on the appropriate brokerage relationship. This is true even if the broker specializes in representing buyers.

Factors To Consider. Brokers who represent buyers must clarify their roles early in the transactions. Licensees should decide and disclose whether they will act as a single agent for a buyer, as a transaction broker, or in a no brokerage relationship status. In deciding whether to become a single agent representing the buyer, the licensee should keep these points in mind:

- The broker, not the sales associate, is the agent. As with sellers' listings, if the sales associate who obtained the buyer's representation contract leaves the brokerage firm, the contract stays with the firm.
- Sellers' brokers cannot be buyers' brokers in the same transactions. However, a seller's broker can provide services to a buyer in a no brokerage relationship status.

TRANSACTION BROKER RELATIONSHIP

There is now a legal presumption that all licensees are operating as a transaction broker unless a single agent or no brokerage relationship is established, in writing, with a customer. A **transaction broker** provides limited representation to a buyer, a seller, or both in a real estate transaction, but does not represent either in a fiduciary capacity. The licensee can "work for the contract" without being an advocate for either party. Limited representation means that a buyer or seller is not responsible for the acts of the licensee. Additionally, parties are giving up their rights to the undivided loyalty of the licensee. This aspect of limited representation allows a licensee to facilitate a real estate transaction by assisting both the buyer and the seller, but a licensee will not work to represent one party to the detriment of the other party when acting as a transaction broker to both parties.

Creation of a Transaction Brokerage Relationship

Transaction brokerage relationships can begin in one of two ways:

1. The broker chooses to be a transaction broker in all transactions.
2. A single agent broker transitions to transaction broker to facilitate the transaction in order to sell one of the firm's listings.

Transaction Broker Duties

Being a transaction broker includes the following duties:

1. Dealing honestly and fairly
2. Accounting for all funds
3. Using skill, care, and diligence in the transaction

4. Disclosing all known facts that materially affect the value of residential real property and are not readily observable to the buyer
5. Presenting all offers and counteroffers in a timely manner, unless a party has previously directed the licensee otherwise in writing
6. Limited confidentiality, unless waived in writing by a party. The transaction broker may *not* reveal to either party
   - that the seller might accept a price less than the asking or list price;
   - that the buyer might pay a price greater than the price submitted in a written offer;
   - the motivation of any party for selling or buying property;
   - that a seller or buyer will agree to financing terms other than those offered; and
   - any other information requested by a party to remain confidential.
7. Any additional duties that are entered into by this or a separate agreement

Some brokers choose to be a transaction broker in all transactions.   Brokers face increased liability because of the complexities of the disclosure requirements and the need for their sales associates to remember which "hat" they are wearing in a specific transaction. Customers and licensees can become confused if a licensee is a single agent for a buyer until he shows the firm's own listings then transitions to being a transaction broker.

Consequently, many brokers have established the policy that their firm will be a transaction broker in every situation with every customer. (The only time the policy might change is the rare situation in which a customer wishes the broker to have "no brokerage relationship" status.) All licensees in the firm then have the same role in every transaction, reducing the chance of the licensees inadvertently violating a legal duty.

Transaction Broker Notice

The *Transaction Broker Notice* must be given to a customer before or at the time of entering into a listing agreement, agreement for representation, or showing a property, whichever occurs first. It may be a separate and distinct disclosure document or part of another document, but is most often made part of a listing agreement or a buyer's representation agreement. The notice itemizes the legal duties of the licensee and informs the customer that his or her representation is limited, allowing the licensee to facilitate a transaction.

The Transaction Broker Notice should be signed by the customer. If a customer refuses to sign it, the licensee may still work as a transaction broker for that customer, but should note on the form that the customer declined to sign. The Transaction Broker Notice is shown in the Forms-To-Go Appendix. After July 1, 2008, transaction broker notices will no longer be required because of the presumption that all licensees are transaction brokers.

Transitioning from Single Agent

When a single agent for one party begins working with the party on the other side of the transaction, it is likely that the agent will transition to transaction broker to treat both parties fairly. The single agent who transitions to transaction broker may not disclose to another party any information gained while he was a single agent.

Example: Broker James listed the Smith's house as their single agent. Sally, a licensee in Broker James' office, is working as the single agent for a buyer, Mr. Farley. Mr. Farley becomes interested in the Smith's house. Because the broker cannot represent both parties (dual agency), the broker obtains the informed written consent of both parties for him to transition to transaction broker status.

Consent to Transition to Transaction Broker Notice

The *Consent to Transition to Transaction Broker Notice* allows a single agent to change his or her brokerage relationship to that of a transaction broker. This notice must be provided before or at the time of changing the brokerage relationship from single agent to transaction broker.

The notice *must* be signed by the principal before the single agent may change to transaction broker status. This form is often included in a listing or representation agreement and is usually authorized at the beginning of the single agent relationship. The single agent broker must make disclosure before changing to transaction broker.

Forms In practice, many licensees who are single agents will have the principal sign the Transition Notice and the Transaction Broker Notice when the Single Agent Notice is given. The forms are usually included as part of listing agreements and buyer representation agreements. The Consent to Transition to Transaction Broker Notice is shown in the Forms-to-Go Appendix.

THE DESIGNATED SALES ASSOCIATE

Forms Florida law allows a brokerage firm to designate one sales associate in the firm to act as agent for the buyer (or lessee) and another sales associate in the firm to act as the agent for the seller (or lessor). This status may be used only in a nonresidential transaction. In this status, each **designated sales associate** is an advocate for the party she represents in the transaction, and can actively help in the negotiations. To meet the requirements of the law, buyers and sellers must have personal assets of at least $1 million, must sign disclosures that their assets meet the requirement, and must request this representation status. The licensees must give the parties a *Single Agent Notice* and a *Designated Sales Associate Notice.* The Designated Sales Associate Notice is shown in the Forms-to-Go Appendix.

DISCUSSION EXERCISE 1.2

Designated Sales Associate

FatBurgers, Inc., is searching for five store locations in Pompano. It engages Mary Stevens of Pompano Commerce Realty as single agent because of her knowledge and expertise in the Pompano fast-food field. Jack Wilson represents the seller in one of the potential sites.

Mary finds a site listed by another sales associate in her firm. FatBurgers, Inc., wants Mary to be its single agent, so the broker appoints Mary as a single agent for FatBurgers, Inc., and Jack as single agent for the seller. Mary and Jack are now designated sales associates.

BROKER COMPENSATION

In recent years, the traditional method of broker compensation, the percentage commission, has been changing, and experts expect the change to accelerate in the near future. As sellers and buyers become more knowledgeable (primarily because of the information available on the Internet), they are less willing to pay for services they don't need or want.

Brokers Who Work with the Seller

Listing brokers have traditionally been paid by the seller in the form of a percentage commission. If a property sells for $200,000 and the agreed commission rate is 7 percent, the broker is entitled to collect $14,000. The listing broker would then pay a cooperating broker, referral fees to other brokers, if any, and her sales associates. A cooperating broker who shows the property to the buyer is rarely a single agent for the seller (subagent) but may be a transaction broker or a single agent representing the buyer.

While the commission percentage of the sales price is still common, many brokers are experimenting with a "service menu," with fees associated with each service selected by the customer. This is often called *unbundling*, allowing customers to select only the services they want. A brokerage firm could have a low percentage listing fee, with additional charges for MLS insertion, signs, advertising, and other services.

Some sellers who feel a multiple-listing service (MLS) is the most important marketing tool could pay the listing broker a flat fee of $500 for placing his listing in the MLS and agree to pay the selling broker 3 percent of the sales price. The listing broker would provide little or no additional service, and any advertising would be reimbursed by the seller. Because the listing broker's sign would be on the property, the listing broker has a good chance to sell the property and earn the additional 3 percent. If typical commissions in the area were 6 percent, the seller could "save" $5,500 on a $200,000 sale. ($200,000 x 6% = $12,000 standard commission. $200,000 x 3% = $6,000 plus $500 = $6,500 unbundled fee. $12,000 - $6,500 = $5,500 "savings.")

There may be an ethical problem with advertising to sellers how much they could "save," however. The agreement would likely involve less marketing activity, and that could result in fewer offers and a lower sale price.

A profit center for many brokers is a "transaction processing fee," charged in addition to the commission. These fees typically range from $200 to $500 for customers of the brokerage firm, and are not split with cooperating brokers or the sales associates. The fees should be disclosed before the customer enters into a brokerage relationship. A surprise fee at the closing could result in charges of dishonest dealing against the licensee. A recent HUD ruling indicates that the fee should 1) be disclosed early, 2) be for actual services provided, and 3) be reasonably priced.

Brokers Who Work with the Buyer

Brokers who work with buyers are typically paid a commission split from the listing broker, but may also be paid by the buyer.

Compensating the Buyer's Broker.   A buyer's broker may be paid in a number of ways:

- Seller-paid fees—commission split
- Buyer-paid fee
- Retainer fee
- Hourly rate
- Percentage fee
- Flat fee

Seller-Paid Fee—Commission Split.   In residential sales, most buyer's broker commissions are paid by the sellers in the form of commission splits from the listing brokers. If the listing broker is not authorized to split the commission, the buyer's broker should inform the buyer that he will be responsible for paying the commission. The buyer may then decide to reduce the offering price to a net amount.

1 Sellers are concerned primarily with selling their property and netting a certain
2 amount of money from the sales proceeds. Sellers usually are much less concerned
3 about whether their brokers split commissions with someone labeled a *buyer's broker, a*
4 *transaction broker,* or a *subagent of the seller.*

5 ***Buyer-Paid Fee.***   The buyer may elect to pay the commission directly to the buyer's
6 broker. This avoids any implication of seller agency that may be present when the seller
7 pays the brokerage fee. An experienced buyer's broker may prefer to be paid directly
8 by the buyer rather than receiving a commission split from the listing broker or being
9 paid directly by the seller at closing. Before the transaction is structured, however, the
10 buyer's broker should check with the lender providing financing for the transaction to
11 determine whether the fee the buyer pays will be treated as part of the purchase price.
12 In most cases, the lender refuses to include it, so the buyer must pay extra cash at
13 closing.

DISCUSSION EXERCISE 1.3

A buyer has a lower down payment if the seller pays the entire commission
because many lenders do not finance the buyer's broker's commission. The difference to the buyer is shown below:

	With Seller Paying Full Commission	With Buyer Paying Half of the Commission
Price	$100,000	$97,000
Less 95% mortgage	− 95,000	−92,150
Cash down payment	$ 5,000	$ 4,850
Plus buyer commission	+ 0	+ 3,000 *
Buyer cash requirement	$ 5,000	$ 7,850

*Depending on the broker's agreement with the buyer, the commission could be
a percentage of the $100,000 or the $97,000, or it could be a flat fee.

---

14 ***Retainer Fee.***   Some brokers who specialize in representing buyers use retainer fees as
15 a screening device to determine whether a buyer is a genuine prospect or just shopping.

16 ***Hourly Rate.***   Under this arrangement, the broker is, in essence, a consultant,
17 charging a noncontingent hourly rate. A fee is due whether or not a title transfer is com-
18 pleted. A variation may be an hourly fee that is applied against an incentive fee if the
19 broker finds the right property for the buyer. This requires brokers to keep time sheets
20 and become diligent in their recordkeeping and billing practices. This method is not
21 recommended unless:

22 • time is going to be a major factor in finding the property, structuring the transaction,
23 and obtaining permits, such as with a large commercial development; or
24 • a risk exists that a sale will not take place because of the unusual nature of the prop-
25 erty desired.

Percentage Fee. The broker may charge a percentage fee based on the purchase price of the property. The obvious problem the percentage fee creates is the appearance of disloyalty because the higher the purchase price, the greater the fee. The percentage fee appears to be seller-oriented. It is commonly used because the seller's broker has agreed to split his percentage commission with the buyer's broker.

Flat Fee. Sometimes the buyer's broker is compensated on a flat fee payable if the buyer purchases a property located through the broker. The amount of the flat fee is based on the broker's estimate of the work and skills involved and the chance of success. A **fee** often is based on what the buyer expects to pay for the home, in contrast to a **commission,** which is based on a percentage of the sales price.

Some listing agreements provide that the buyer is obligated to pay a fee but is entitled to a credit for any amounts the seller agrees to pay. Thus, the buyer would not pay the buyer's broker's fee in the usual MLS sale. However, the buyer probably would pay the fee directly if the broker located an unlisted property such as a property for sale by owner. In either event, the buyer benefits because the broker is motivated to search all properties, even those not listed.

SELECTED LAWS REGULATING REAL ESTATE PRACTICE

Chapter 475, F.S., and Chapter 61J2, F.A.C., the rules of the Florida Real Estate Commission, are changed as the need arises. Licensees may stay current on the law by using the Division of Real Estate's Web site at http://www.state.fl.us/dbpr/re/dre.shtml.

License Renewal

The Department is required to send a notice of renewal to the last known address of the licensee at least 60 days before the expiration date. Licensees who do not receive a renewal notice should ensure that the Department has their current address on file or send a change of address to the Department using a Form DBPR 0080-1.

After the first renewal, the license will expire on the same date every two years. If a licensee fails to renew the license, the license will become *involuntarily inactive,* and the licensee may not perform real estate services.

Licensees should send the renewal notice and a check to the Department before the renewal date. The renewal request must be postmarked on or before the renewal date or there is a $45 late renewal fee. A licensee is advised to send renewal notices by certified mail with return receipt, and to retain a copy of all documents.

DBPR may waive license renewal fees when the Department determines that there is a surplus in the profession's trust funds. The Division of Real Estate currently has a surplus that will be used to reduce the renewal fees due from licensees until the surplus has been used.

Required Education for Renewing the Initial License

The first real estate license will be effective for at least 18 months, but not more than 24 months. It expires on the first of two dates after 18 months: March 31 or September 30.

A sales associate must successfully complete a 45-hour post-licensing course before the first renewal. A new broker must complete the 60-hour post-license course before the first renewal. If the licensee does not successfully complete the post-license course, the license becomes void. A sales associate wanting to continue in real estate would have to take the pre-license course again and pass the state exam. If a broker does not complete the post-license course, the broker will lose the broker's license. He may, however,

1 take a 14-hour continuing education course and apply for sales associate status. If the
2 licensee wishes to become a broker again, he must successfully complete the broker pre-
3 license course and pass the state exam.

4   Students failing a Commission-prescribed post-licensing education end-of-course
5 examination must wait at least 30 days from the date of the original examination to
6 again take the end-of-course examination. Within one year of the original end-of-course
7 examination, a student may retake the prescribed end-of-course examination a max-
8 imum of one time. Otherwise, students failing the Commission-prescribed end-of-
9 course examination must repeat the Commission prescribed course prior to being eli-
10 gible to again take the end-of-course examination. Students retaking the end-of-course
11 examination must be administered a different form of the end-of-course examination.

12   Makeup classes to enable a student to take the prescribed end-of-course examination
13 due to student or family illness may not extend more than 30 days beyond the class
14 scheduled end of course examination without approval of the Commission. Makeup
15 classes must be the classes missed by the student and must consist of the original Com-
16 mission-prescribed course material.

17   The Commission may allow an additional 6-month period after the first renewal fol-
18 lowing initial licensure for brokers and sales associates who cannot, due to individual
19 physical hardship as defined in Rule 61J2-3.013(2), complete the course or courses
20 within the required time [61J2-3.020].

21   Any licensee who has received a four-year degree in real estate from an accredited
22 institution of higher education is exempt from the post-license education requirements.

Required Education for Subsequent Renewals

24 After the first renewal, a real estate licensee must complete a FREC-approved 14-hour
25 continuing education course before all subsequent renewals. The course consists of
26 three hours of "core law" and 11 hours of "specialty" education. Licensees may take the
27 course in a classroom with no examination, or by distance education with a final exam-
28 ination.

29   The core law portion updates licensees on Florida real estate license law, agency law,
30 other state and federal laws, and taxes. FREC gives credit for six hours of core law if the
31 licensee takes the three-hour core law class in each year of the renewal period.

32   The FREC-approved specialty education course must focus on real estate issues rele-
33 vant to Chapter 475. The FREC grants up to three hours of specialty education to a li-
34 censee who attends a FREC meeting on disciplinary cases. The licensee must make an
35 appointment, and must stay for the entire day [61J2-3.009].

36   Brokers are no longer required to ensure that their sales associates complete the
37 required continuing education, but must see that each of their sales associates per-
38 forming brokerage services have a current, valid license.

39   The licensee should not send proof of the required education with the renewal appli-
40 cation. The licensee, by applying for renewal, is acknowledging that the required edu-
41 cation was successfully completed. The licensee must retain the original grade report
42 for the FREC-approved education course for at least two years following the end of the
43 renewal period. If audited by the Department, the licensee must furnish the original
44 grade report.

Disciplinary Action for Failure to Complete the Required Education

46 If a licensee renewed the license without having completed the required education,
47 there is a range of penalties, depending on the circumstances. (See Table 1.1.)

TABLE 1.1   VIOLATIONS AND PENALTIES

VIOLATION	PENALTY
Renewed license without having complied with Rule 61J2-3.009 and voluntarily notified the BPR within 30 days after the renewal cycle ended.	Notice of noncompliance. Licensee has 15 days to comply with the Rule.
Renewed a license without completing the continuing education requirement and the act is discovered by the BPR, but the licensee has completed the continuing education within 30 days after his renewal date.	$200 fine and completion of the continuing education requirement for the previous renewal cycle.
Renewed a license without completing the continuing education requirement and the act is discovered by the BPR, but the licensee has completed the continuing education within 90 days after his renewal date.	$500 fine and completion of the continuing education requirement for the previous renewal cycle.
Renewed license without having complied with Rule 61J2-3.009 and voluntarily notified the BPR more than 90 days after the renewal cycle ended.	$500 fine and completion of the continuing education requirement for the previous renewal cycle.
Renewed a license without completing the continuing education requirement and the act is discovered by the BPR, and the licensee has not completed the required continuing education within 90 days after the renewal cycle has ended.	Revocation

Broker Applicants

Broker applicants must have held an active sales associate license for six months within the preceding five years before enrolling for the broker education course. A person who applies for a broker's license must hold:

- an active real estate sales associate's license for at least 12 months during the preceding five years in the office of one or more real estate brokers licensed in this state or any other state, territory, or jurisdiction of the United States or in any foreign national jurisdiction;
- a current and valid real estate sales associate's license for at least 12 months during the preceding five years in the employ of a governmental agency for a salary and performing the duties authorized for real estate licensees; or
- a current and valid real estate broker's license for at least 12 months during the preceding five years in any other state, territory, or jurisdiction of the United States or in any foreign national jurisdiction.

A person who has been licensed as a real estate sales associate in Florida may not be licensed as a real estate broker unless, in addition to the other requirements of law, she or he has completed the sales associate post licensure educational requirements.

TABLE 1.2   MUTUAL RECOGNITION STATES

Alabama Real Estate Commission 1201 Carmichael Way Montgomery, AL 36106-3672 (334) 242-5544 www.arec.state.al.us	**Arkansas** Real Estate Commission 612 S. Summit Street Little Rock, AR 72201 (501) 683-8010 www.state.ar.us/arec/arecweb.html
Colorado Real Estate Commission 1900 Grant Street, Suite 600 Denver, CO 80203 (303) 894-2166 www.dora.state.co.us/real-estate	**Georgia** Real Estate Commission 229 Peachtree St. NE Atlanta, GA 30303-1605 (404) 656-3916 www.state.ga.us/Ga.Real_Estate/
Indiana Real Estate Commission 302 W. Washington Street, #E034 Indianapolis, IN 46204 (317) 232-2980 www.in.gov/pla/bandc/estate	**Kentucky** Real Estate Commission 10200 Linn Station Rd., Suite 200 Louisville, KY 40223 (502) 425-4273 www.krec.net
Mississippi Real Estate Commission 5176 Keele St. Jackson, MS 39206 (601) 987-3969 www.mab.state.ms.us/	**Nebraska** Real Estate Commission 1200 N Street, Suite 402 Lincoln, NE, 68508 (402) 471-2004 www.state.ne.us/
Oklahoma Real Estate Commission 4040 N. Lincoln Blvd., Suite 100 Oklahoma City, OK 73105 (405) 521-3387 www.oklaosf.state.ok.us/	**Tennessee** Real Estate Commission 500 James Robertson Parkway Nashville, TN 37243-1151 (615) 741-2273 www.state.tn.us/commerce/trec

Mutual Recognition Agreements

The Commission has reached **mutual recognition agreements** with ten states: Alabama, Arkansas, Colorado, Georgia, Indiana, Kentucky, Mississippi, Nebraska, Oklahoma, and Tennessee. Florida has ongoing negotiation with other states as well. Applicants holding a real estate license in one of these states may become a Florida licensee by passing a 40-question exam on Florida Real Estate Law. Thirty correct answers (75 percent) is passing. Any Florida licensee has the same opportunity to become licensed in one of those states and may contact the appropriate state regulatory agency for an application. (See Table 1.2.)

Nonresident licensees, whether or not they have qualified under mutual recognition, must successfully complete the same post-licensing and continuing education required for Florida resident licensees.

UNIFORM STANDARDS OF PROFESSIONAL APPRAISAL PRACTICE

A broker or sales associate may prepare a comparative market analysis (CMA) in the normal course of his or her listing and selling activities. Brokers may not call the results

1   of the CMA an appraisal; it should be called an *opinion of value*. A licensee may charge
2   a fee for preparing a CMA.

3   Mortgage loans that are federally related transactions require that the appraisal be
4   performed by a certified or licensed appraiser. For this reason, real estate brokers and
5   sales associates make fewer appraisals than in years past. The law does not prohibit bro-
6   kers from performing appraisals for a fee. A 1998 change to the law, however, requires
7   that brokers comply with the **Uniform Standards of Professional Appraisal Practice**
8   when making appraisals. The Standards are strict and detailed, and a violation of the
9   Standards is a violation of Chapter 475. An opinion of value or broker price opinion is
10 not considered an appraisal [475.25(1)(t)].

11 CURRENT MAILING ADDRESS

12 Licensees who change their personal mailing address must notify the Division of Real
13 Estate within ten days on Form DBPR 0080-1. Violations of this rule may result in a cita-
14 tion and a $100 fine [61J2-24.002].

15 FORMS MAY BE SENT TO THE DBPR BY FAX

16 The Division of Real Estate will now accept documents, such as Form DBPR 0080-1, by
17 fax at (407) 999-5482. This method would not, of course, work for initial applications or
18 renewals that require that payment be included [475.5018, F.S.].

19 LICENSEE'S PERSONAL NAME IN ADVERTISING

20 If a licensee wants his personal name to appear in a brokerage firm's ad, the licensee's
21 last name as registered with the Division of Real Estate must be included at least once
22 in the ad. The brokerage firm's name must be included to avoid charges of "blind"
23 advertising. For example, Joseph J. Perkins, a sales associate, could place an advertise-
24 ment with "call Joe for more information" provided the ad includes the brokerage firm's
25 name and Joe's last name somewhere in the ad [61J2-10.025(2)].

26 EXCEPTIONS TO CONFLICTING DEMANDS ON ESCROW DEPOSITS

27 Normally, if a buyer and seller make demands for escrowed funds held by a broker, the
28 broker must notify the Florida Real Estate Commission within 15 days, then follow one
29 of the prescribed escrow settlement procedures. Recent changes to Chapter 475 pro-
30 vide for two exceptions to those requirements.

31 Condominium Exception

32 If the buyer of a residential condominium unit delivers to a licensee written notice of
33 the buyer's intent to cancel the contract for sale and purchase as authorized by F.S.
34 718.503, the broker may return the escrowed property to the purchaser without noti-
35 fying the Commission or initiating any of the escrow settlement procedures. If the
36 broker disburses the funds, the broker is not subject to disciplinary action but may have
37 civil liability to the seller if the seller sues and is successful.

Financing Contingency Exception

If the buyer of a residential property with a financing contingency delivers notice of the buyer's intent to cancel the contract for sale and purchase because the buyer is unable to obtain the required financing, the broker may return the escrowed deposit to the buyer without notifying the Commission or initiating any of the escrow settlement procedures. If the broker disburses the funds, the broker is not subject to disciplinary action, but may have civil liability to the seller if the seller sues and is successful.

SALES ASSOCIATES MAY BE PAID DIRECTLY BY THE CLOSING AGENT

Brokerage firms may allow a sales associate to receive his or her commissions directly from the closing agent immediately after closing if the broker gives specific written instructions to the closing agent for each closing. This authorization was given under Chapter 475.42(1)(d), and simplifies the process of a closing agent's issuing a check to the brokerage firm, with the brokerage firm then issuing a check to the sales associate.

FREC Handbook

To stay up to date on the real estate license law, Chapter 475, F.S., and the rules of the Florida Real Estate Commission, Chapter 61J2, F.A.C., you can print them from the following Web page:

www.

Web Link

http://www.state.fl.us/dbpr/re/frectoc.shtml

THE "CLEAN SLATE" BILL

A licensee who has committed a minor violation may petition the DBPR to reclassify the violation as "inactive." The petition will be granted if two years have passed since the final order imposing discipline and the licensee has not been disciplined for any subsequent minor violation of the same nature. After the department has reclassified the violation as inactive, it is no longer considered to be part of the licensee's disciplinary record. Thereafter, the licensee may lawfully deny or fail to acknowledge the incident as a disciplinary action.

Under the law, the Department may establish a schedule to automatically make the records of minor offenses inactive. This would eliminate the need for an individual to petition the Department to do so. So far, the Department has not adopted rules to implement this subsection [F.S. 455.225].

SUMMARY

Licensees selling residential property may work with their customers in several ways:

- Single agent brokers represent either the buyer or the seller, but not both, in a transaction. Only single agent brokers may call their customers *principals*. Principals are responsible for the acts of their single agent. The broker must give a single agent notice before showing property or before entering a representation agreement. The notice should be signed, but if the principal declines to sign the notice, the licensee may note the fact on the form and work with the principal.
- Transaction brokers provide limited representation but do not have a fiduciary relationship with the customer. The customer is not responsible for the acts of the trans-

action broker. A transaction broker must give a Transaction Broker Notice before showing property, or before entering an agreement for limited representation. The notice should be signed, but if the customer declines to sign the notice, the licensee may note the fact on the form and work with the customer. A single agent may enter into a transaction broker relationship by having the principal sign a Consent to Transition to Transaction Broker Notice.

- Brokers who will not represent the customer as a single agent or a transaction broker must give the customer a No Brokerage Relationship Notice before showing property. The notice need not be signed.

Brokers in nonresidential transactions may work with a customer in one of the ways shown above, but are not required to give a brokerage relationship notice. Nonresidential brokers may appoint one sales associate in the firm to represent the seller and one sales associate to represent the buyer. They are called *designated sales associates*, and act as single agents for their principal. The buyer and seller must each have at least $1 million in assets and agree to the relationship. A Designated Sales Associate Notice and a Single Agent Notice must be given to each party.

Dual agency is specifically forbidden by the law.

When a licensee renews a license for the first time, the licensee must complete a post-license course, or the license will be void. After the first renewal, a licensee must complete 14 hours of continuing education before renewing. If a licensee fails to complete the required education, the licensee may be faced with a fine or license revocation.

Florida has mutual recognition of education with ten states. This allows nonresidents to become Florida licensees by passing a 40-question exam on the Florida license law. Florida licensees may become licensed in one of the mutual recognition states in the same manner.

While Florida licensees are not prohibited from performing appraisals for a fee, the appraisal must be completed in conformance with the Uniform Standards of Professional Appraisal Practice. A licensee's opinion of value or broker's price opinion generated by a comparative market analysis is not considered an appraisal.

DEFINE THESE KEY TERMS

agency
agent
buyer agency
buyer representation agreement
commission
Consent to Transition to Transaction
   Broker Notice
cooperative sale
customer
designated sales associate
disclosure
dual agent

fee
fiduciary relationship
listing agreement
mutual recognition agreements
No Brokerage Relationship Notice
principal
seller agency
single agent
Single Agent Notice
transaction broker
Transaction Broker Notice
Uniform Standards of Professional
   Appraisal Practice

CHAPTER 1 PRACTICE EXAM

1. Before showing homes to a customer she has just met, a transaction broker must:

   a. have the customer sign a buyer broker agreement.
   b. give the customer a No Brokerage Relationship Notice.
   c. give the customer a No Brokerage Relationship Notice and a Transaction Broker Notice.
   d. give the customer a Transaction Broker Notice.

2. The only broker who may refer to a customer as his or her *principal* is:

   a. a single agent.
   b. a dual agent.
   c. a transaction broker.
   d. both a and c.

3. Nancy is a seller's broker who listed and then sold Dave's townhouse. She did not tell Dave that a pending zoning change would allow businesses to open in the area, thus increasing property values. Nancy:

   a. had a fiduciary duty to disclose the pending change because zoning laws require such notice.
   b. did not have to disclose the pending change because Dave received his full asking price.
   c. had fiduciary duties requiring that she disclose the change.
   d. was not required to mention the change because Dave never asked about it.

4. Whom does a broker legally represent?

   a. The party who pays the commission
   b. The party who authorizes the broker to act on his behalf in a transaction as a single agent
   c. The person who has a single agent or transaction brokerage relationship with the broker
   d. The person who buys a house through the broker

5. Which of the following is not an authorized status for a broker to take in dealing with customers?

   a. Transaction broker
   b. Single agent
   c. Dual agent
   d. No brokerage relationship

6. A principal is responsible for the acts of her:

   a. transaction broker.
   b. dual agent.
   c. single agent.
   d. broker, if the broker has no official brokerage relationship with the customer.

7. A transaction broker tells a buyer that a seller is under pressure to sell because of a pending divorce and possible foreclosure. Such disclosure is:

   a. acceptable if it results in a sale.
   b. acceptable if none of the details of the foreclosure is disclosed.
   c. unacceptable because the listing broker is the agent of the buyer.
   d. unacceptable because of the limited confidentiality requirements of the law.

8. If a transaction broker agrees to prepare a CMA for the seller, but does not offer to prepare one for the buyer, the broker:

   a. must offer the same services to all customers in a transaction.
   b. is legally able to offer one party additional services not offered to the other, providing that the services do not work to the other party's detriment.
   c. is not civilly liable to the buyer, but he has violated the license law.
   d. must, by law, provide CMAs to all parties to a transaction before the party enters into an agreement to sell or buy residential property.

9. What is true about the Consent to Transition to Transaction Broker Notice?

   a. It must be provided at first contact with a customer.
   b. A signature is desirable but not required.
   c. The principal must sign the Notice before the single agent may become a transaction broker.
   d. It is used when a transaction broker wishes to become a single agent.

10. Jacqueline and Samuel are sales associates for Able Realty. Jacqueline takes a listing as a single agent. Samuel is working with a buyer as a single agent, and the buyer becomes interested in Jacqueline's listing. What statement is correct?

   a. Both the buyer and the seller must sign a Consent to Transition to Transaction Broker Notice and agree that the broker may become a transaction broker.
   b. Either or both of the parties may agree to have no official brokerage relationship in the transaction and may proceed on that basis.
   c. Jacqueline and Samuel should represent each of their principals as well as possible in the transaction.
   d. Either a or b is correct.

11. A single agent seller's broker owes which duties to the prospective buyer?

   a. Disclosure of known facts affecting the value of the property
   b. Obedience
   c. Loyalty
   d. All of the above

12. Licensed sales associates working at the seller's single agent brokerage firm:

   a. may represent either the seller or the buyer in a transaction.
   b. are legally bound to represent the seller.
   c. may have another principal in the transaction.
   d. may be transaction brokers for the buyer to ensure limited confidentiality.

13. A single agent broker who wishes to remain loyal to the principal:

   a. may be a transaction broker for the other party.
   b. may become a dual agent with the written approval of both parties.
   c. must work with the other party in a no official brokerage relationship role.
   d. cannot remain loyal if he works with the other party in a transaction.

14. If Jill sells commercial property exclusively, she:

    a. need not give the customer a No Brokerage Relationship Notice before showing property.
    b. may be a single agent, a transaction broker, a designated sales associate, or have no brokerage relationship with the customer.
    c. must give the customer a No Brokerage Relationship Notice before showing property.
    d. Both a and b

15. What is the penalty if a licensee renews his license without having completed the required continuing education, and voluntarily notifies the BPR within 30 days after the renewal cycle has ended?

    a. His license will be revoked.
    b. A notice of noncompliance will be issued to the licensee.
    c. His license will be suspended.
    d. His license will be involuntarily inactive until the education has been completed.

16. Which require(s) disclosure of brokerage relationship to a customer?

    I. Sale of improved property with four units or fewer
    II. Leasing of property with four units or fewer, unless the owner occupies one of the units
    III. Sale of agricultural property with 10 acres or less
    a. I only
    b. I and II only
    c. I and III only
    d. I, II, and III

17. A broker must disclose known facts that materially affect the value of residential property when she is a:

    a. licensee with no official brokerage relationship.
    b. single agent.
    c. transaction broker.
    d. All of the above

18. A broker has no brokerage relationship with a buyer because the broker is a single agent for the seller. The buyer agrees to pay up to the listed price, if necessary, but first wants to submit an offer 10 percent below that price. What should the broker do?

    a. Tell the seller, "The buyer said he will pay up to the listed price."
    b. Refuse to disclose the statement because of the broker's duty of limited confidentiality.
    c. Suggest that the seller counteroffer, if desired.
    d. Tell the seller, "The buyer is qualified."

19. A broker must retain required brokerage relationship disclosures used in transactions that result in a contract for how many years?

    a. One
    b. Three
    c. Four
    d. Five

20. John and Bill are sales associates working for Southland Commercial brokers. Their broker allows John to act as a single agent for the buyer and Bill to act as a single agent for the seller. Both the buyer and the seller have assets of more than $1 million and each agrees to this form of representation. The situation describes a:

    a. transaction broker relationship.
    b. designated sales associate.
    c. single agency.
    d. dual agency.

CHAPTER 2—FEDERAL AND STATE LAWS AFFECTING REAL ESTATE

LEARNING OBJECTIVES

Upon completion of this chapter, *you should be able to:*

1. describe the difference between fraudulent misrepresentation and negligent misrepresentation;
2. state the requirements for a consumer to have a successful misrepresentation case against a licensee;
3. list at least five careless statements a broker should never make;
4. list the nine steps a licensee can take to decrease the risk of misrepresentation claims;
5. list at least six questions that should be asked of sellers in a property condition disclosure form;
6. explain the major differences between the Civil Rights Acts of 1866, 1964, and 1968;
7. list the persons protected under the amended Fair Housing Act;
8. list the acts prohibited under the Fair Housing Act;
9. describe the major requirement under Regulation Z of the Truth-in-Lending Act and the five triggers that require disclosure;
10. list at least three activities prohibited by antitrust legislation;
11. list the six major areas of the Real Estate Settlement Procedures Act;
12. explain the required lead-based paint hazard disclosures for residential properties built before 1978;
13. understand the risks involved when listing and selling property that may be contaminated with toxic substances;
14. list the two major income tax benefits of owning a personal residence;
15. describe the Federal income tax requirements that a sales associate and broker must meet in order for the sales associate to qualify as an independent contractor;
16. define and explain the term *concurrency* as it relates to real estate practices in Florida;
17. list the documents required by law to be provided to buyers of condominiums;
18. list two required disclosures to buyers of new time-share units and two required disclosures to buyers of resale time-share units;
19. apply the requirements of the Florida Americans with Disabilities Act;
20. explain the disclosure statement regarding radon gas;
21. list the duties performed for a community association that would require a community association manager's license; and
22. list at least ten disclosures a licensee must provide to buyers of real property in Florida.

CHAPTER 2

FEDERAL AND STATE LAWS AFFECTING REAL ESTATE

1　In the early part of this century, the Florida real estate industry was a free-for-all of
2　unregulated business practices. Many unscrupulous individuals brought the profession
3　into disrepute by selling properties that were under water for six months of the year or
4　buildings that had substantial structural damage. Sellers and brokers operated under
5　the doctrine *caveat emptor* (let the buyer beware).

6　　Leaders of the real estate industry understood only too well that these fraudulent
7　practices needed to stop, or consumers would attribute them to every broker. Ethical
8　brokers, as well as consumer advocates, pushed hard for reforms. Florida's legislature
9　has responded to the call to stop unfair practices of real estate owners and licensees by
10　requiring disclosures about material items that might affect consumers. Some practi-
11　tioners oppose the increased disclosure requirements because of the difficulties in
12　keeping up with the new laws and the confusion buyers and sellers experience when
13　faced with many pages of disclosure statements to sign. Florida real estate laws are
14　intended to ensure a standard of quality that protects consumers and tends to build
15　their confidence in purchasing property. This chapter examines many of the required
16　disclosures and details methods of avoiding charges of misrepresentation.

17　MISREPRESENTATION AND CONDITION DISCLOSURE

18　While the legal definition is much broader, the common definition of **misrepresenta-**
19　**tion** is the act of a licensee who, either intentionally or unintentionally, fails to disclose
20　a **material fact** or makes a **false or misleading statement** that is justifiably relied on by
21　another, resulting in damage. Intentional misrepresentation is actionable as fraud.
22　Unintentional misrepresentation is negligence.

23　　A common complaint of buyers against listing brokers are based on misrepresen-
24　tation by the brokers. Listing brokers have a duty to disclose material facts con-
25　cerning the value and desirability of property. Buyers frequently ask brokers to
26　describe a property and to make representations about the condition of the prop-
27　erty or other facts associated with the sale. Some complain about the listing broker
28　concealing material defects.

29　　To bring a successful fraudulent misrepresentation case against a broker, a plaintiff
30　(complaining party) must prove that the:

31　• broker made an error in giving information, oral or written, to the buyer or failed to
32　　disclose a material fact to the buyer;

1 • broker knew that the statement was not accurate or that the information should have
2   been disclosed;
3 • buyer reasonably relied on such statement; and
4 • buyer was damaged as a result.

5   Courts have held that the buyer is entitled to relief if the representation was a mate-
6 rial inducement to the contract. This also applies in cases where the buyer may have
7 made efforts to discover the truth and did not rely on the representation. The seller has
8 a duty not to misrepresent, and the broker's duty stems from the seller's duty. The
9 licensee who wishes to be professional should attempt to verify information she receives
10 from the seller.

11   In establishing liability or in applying remedies, it does not make a difference whether
12 the misrepresentation was fraudulent (intentional) or negligent (unintentional). The
13 most common remedies available to the offended party include monetary damages,
14 rescission of the contract, forfeiture of the broker's commission, and possible FREC
15 penalty assessments.

Careless or Negligent Statements

17 Brokers must consider carefully their statements to buyers and sellers. A broker is con-
18 sidered a real estate expert; therefore, the consumer relies on what the broker says, even
19 when the broker does not act as the buyer's agent. A short list follows of some state-
20 ments brokers should never make:

21 • "No need to get a title search. I sold this same property last year, and there was no
22   title problem."
23 • "Don't worry, the seller told me by phone I could sign the contract for her."
24 • "I won't be able to present your offer until the seller decides on the offer submitted
25   yesterday."
26 • "Don't worry about the due-on-sale clause. The lender will never find out about the
27   sale."

Avoiding Misrepresentation

29 A real estate licensee can take nine practical steps to decrease the risk of misrepresen-
30 tation claims:

Forms 31   1. Question the seller thoroughly regarding the property. Use a **property condition**
32   **disclosure** form, such as the one shown in the Forms-To-Go Section, and discuss:

33   • owners and interests;
34   • condition of improvements and utility systems;
35   • history of repairs, warranties;
36   • easements: where, purpose, restrictions on use;
37   • boundaries and encroachments, stakes visible;
38   • nonconforming or illegal uses;
39   • lease restrictions, permitted uses;
40   • current and future zoning;
41   • special ordinances concerning height limits, design standards;
42   • state and municipal improvements, assessments;
43   • outstanding building permits and violations, citations;
44   • financing restrictions;
45   • any declaration of covenants, conditions, and restrictions;
46   • on income properties, accuracy of expense and income projections, any signifi-
47   cant neighborhood trends;
48   • termite or rodent problems; and
49   • any other matters that might affect the property's value.

2. Investigate the property independently. Remember that a real estate licensee's job is not simply to pass on information. The licensee can keep himself and the seller out of trouble by verifying that information is complete and accurate. The licensee owes the duty of care to the seller and the buyer. Keeping in mind that a disgruntled buyer may prefer to sue a stationary broker rather than a moving seller, the licensee should do the following:

   - Check out the items under step 1 above, especially those you find to be sensitive or suspect.
   - Pay attention to decorative improvements that might conceal defects, such as new plaster over a cracked wall.
   - If a matter is technical and important, suggest to the seller that it might be wise to bring in expert assistance, such as a soil engineer or a swimming pool contractor.

3. With respect to condominium sales, check into the following common problem areas:

   - House rules regarding children, pets, waterbeds, and barbecuing
   - Location of lockers and parking stalls
   - Existence of special assessments (for what and how much)
   - Maintenance fee(s) (what is included, proposed increases)

4. Check into factors external to the property that might influence its value and affect a person's decision to buy, including the following:

   - Abutting and nearby uses (present and proposed), for example, a rock band next door
   - Highway expansion, rerouting of a bus line

5. Do not make statements concerning matters about which you do not have first-hand knowledge or that are not based on expert opinion or advice. For example, avoid statements that begin "A neighbor told me that. . . ." It would be safer to say: "According to Mr. Jones at the Building Department, who handles these matters. . . ." If you do not know the answer to a buyer's question, it is better to concede, "I don't know, but I'll research it or find someone who does know."

6. Have a list of government agencies you can call to get further information. Use the list to investigate the seller's information and find out things for the buyer. Urge the buyer to check things out, too, by giving the buyer the proper departments and numbers to call. Offer to assist the buyer, but don't volunteer highly technical information. This information should come directly to the buyer from the government agency.

7. Do not participate with the seller in nondisclosure of information. If the seller refuses to disclose such things as citations for building code violations, decline the listing. Taking a listing of this nature is not worth damage claims, loss of reputation, and loss of license.

8. Avoid exaggeration, and be circumspect with opinions. Exaggeration is unethical and could even be considered misrepresentation, depending on the statement's context and the listener's background. If you wish to venture a "quick" opinion, make sure the buyer understands that it is only a guess, that it is not necessarily an educated guess, and that the buyer should not rely on it in making her decision. While it is permissible to give factual sales data, try to avoid giving an opinion of value increases. If you feel compelled to give such an opinion, it is best to do so in writing and with proper caveats and disclaimers. Some disclaimers may not be effective, however. The law does not allow certain consumer protections to be eliminated simply by having the consumer sign a disclaimer of liability form.

9. Obtain and disclose certain pertinent information in writing, such as a Property Condition Disclosure form from the seller. Get a signed receipt from the buyer

1 when it is given to him. Give a fact sheet, memo, or tactful letter to the buyer when-
2 ever disclosures are appropriate. For example, such a letter would confirm earlier
3 discussions in which you pointed out a leaky roof or the need to consult with a soil
4 engineer, and would affirm that neither you nor the seller makes any warranty as
5 to the condition of the roof or the foundation. Keep copies of these documents in
6 the transaction file as part of the paper trail you create, in the event you must later
7 testify.

Home Inspection

9   One of the most effective risk management tools available to licensees is a home inspec-
10 tion prepared for the buyer by a qualified home inspector. When performed properly,
11 the inspection should disclose material defects in a building that buyers, sellers, and real
12 estate licensees might miss. From the licensee's perspective, it is far better that a
13 problem is identified before the closing so the parties can negotiate a settlement. If a
14 material defect is discovered after closing, it is easier for the buyer to sue the licensee
15 rather than the seller, who may now live in a distant city.

16   Florida does not regulate or license home inspectors. To become a home inspector,
17 a person need only call himself one. Home inspectors rarely guarantee their work, and
18 most have a disclaimer limiting damages to the amount of their fee.

19   The buyer should be encouraged to select his or her own inspector; otherwise, or the
20 buyer may infer collusion between the sales associate and the inspector if the inspector
21 misses one or more important defects. Many excellent home inspectors are members of
22 the American Society of Home Inspectors.

Web Link

24 www.ashi.com
25   American Society of Home Inspectors

Stigmatized Property

27 In the past, residential licensees have had no clear direction about the requirement to
28 make disclosures when a murder, suicide, or death occurs in a house. The property is
29 said to be "stigmatized" or "psychologically impacted." Changes in 2003 to Chapter 689
30 (Conveyances of Land and Declarations of Trust) have resolved the issue; disclosure is
31 not required.

32   "The fact that a property was, or was at any time suspected to have been, the site of
33 a homicide, suicide, or death is not a material fact that must be disclosed in a real estate
34 transaction. A cause of action shall not arise against an owner of real property, his or
35 her agent, an agent of a transferee of real property, or a person licensed under
36 Chapter 475 for the failure to disclose to the transferee that the property was or was sus-
37 pected to have been the site of a homicide, suicide, or death or that an occupant of the
38 property was infected with human immunodeficiency virus or diagnosed with acquired
39 immune deficiency syndrome." [689.25(1)(b)]

Megan's Law

41 *Megan's Law* is named for 7-year-old Megan Kanka of Hamilton Township, New Jersey.
42 Megan was killed by a convicted sex offender who lived across the street from Megan's
43 family. The family was unaware of his past. In May 1996, a federal law was passed
44 requiring public law enforcement agencies to register and disclose the address of con-
45 victed sex offenders. On July 1, 1996, Chapter 97.299, F.S., required that the Florida
46 Department of Law Enforcement (FDLE) maintain an updated list of Registered Sexual
47 Predators in this state.

FIGURE 2.1   "MEGAN'S LAW" SUGGESTED DISCLOSURE

Megan's Law is designed to protect the public by notifying communities when a convicted sex offender moves into an area. Information including photos, identities, and addresses is available from the Florida Department of Law Enforcement (FDLE) at (850) 410-7000, or on the Internet at the site shown below.

The buyer is encouraged to contact the FDLE for further information, and by signature below acknowledges that the real estate licensee has provided this notification.

 www.fdle.state.fl.us/sexual_predators/
        FDLE's List of Registered Sexual Predators

---

1   The law does not require that licensees disclose the address of convicted sex
2   offenders. While the licensee could possibly be sued for failure to reveal such informa-
3   tion, providing outdated or wrong information could also result in substantial liability.
4   FDLE cautions that positive identification of a person believed to be a sexual predator
5   or sex offender cannot be established unless a fingerprint comparison is made.

6   Some licensees may wish to use a disclosure statement that recommends that the
7   buyers contact local law enforcement agencies for the information. (See Figure 2.1.)

---

8 FEDERAL LAWS AFFECTING REAL ESTATE LICENSEES

9 Civil Rights and Fair Housing

10   The Civil Rights Act of 1866, passed just after the Civil War, was designed to prevent
11   discrimination based on race. The law was not widely observed, although in 1968, the
12   Supreme Court upheld the law in the case of *Jones v. Mayer*. Subsequent to that decision,
13   court actions requiring compliance with the law have been numerous and successful.

14   The Civil Rights Act of 1964 prohibits racial discrimination in any residential trans-
15   action that uses federal funds or in any Federal Housing Administration (FHA) or
16   Department of Veterans Affairs (VA) transaction.

17   The Civil Rights Act of 1968 included Title VIII, the **Fair Housing Act.** The act, which
18   has been amended several times to more broadly protect against discrimination in
19   housing, now covers:

20   • race,
21   • color,
22   • religion,
23   • sex,
24   • national origin,
25   • handicap, and
26   • familial status (presence of children or pregnant women).

1   The law applies to persons who own four or more homes, multifamily properties
2 (except for properties with fewer than four units, one of which the owner occupies),
3 owners who sell two or more homes in a year, and transactions in which brokers are
4 involved. It should be noted that while it would seem that a private owner may discrim-
5 inate, the 1866 act clearly prohibits racial discrimination in any real estate transaction.

6   The following acts by the owners or brokers listed above are specifically prohibited:

7 • **Steering** in real estate ads or in showing properties
8 • **Blockbusting** a neighborhood by attempting to frighten homeowners into selling
9 • **Redlining** by lenders that have different conditions and terms for loans made in cer-
10   tain areas
11 • Refusing to rent to, sell to or negotiate with a party
12 • Quoting different terms or conditions for buying or renting
13 • Making false statements about the availability of housing
14 • Denying membership in any real estate service (See Figure 2.2.)

15   The U.S. Department of Housing and Urban Development (HUD) has provided a list
16 of catchwords that should be avoided in advertising. They include:

17 • *traditional* (neighborhood, not architecture),
18 • *exclusive,*
19 • *integrated neighborhood,* and
20 • *restricted.*

21   See Figure 2.3 for examples of words that may or may not be used in advertising.

22   Licensees must avoid placing ads for homes located in minority areas in publications
23 intended only for those minority groups, unless the broker advertises other nonminor-
24 ity-area properties in the same publications.

25   Adult-only designations are outlawed by the familial status provision; however, cer-
26 tain age-55-and-older communities are exempt if they meet the following requirements:

27 • at least 80 percent of the households have at least one occupant who is at least 55
28   years old.
29 • the communities offer amenities, specific programs, and activities designed for the
30   mature adult, unless such facilities are not practicable.

31   A Florida community claiming an exemption from the Fair Housing Act with respect
32 to familial status for housing for older persons must register with the Florida Commis-
33 sion on Human Relations and affirm compliance with the specified requirements. The
34 Commission is required to maintain a database of exempt communities.

35   Apartment properties must not set up particular areas in the complexes for families
36 with children or for any other protected class. Owners may set reasonable rules for max-
37 imum occupancy in an apartment building (excluding families with 20 children from
38 occupying one two-bedroom apartment, for instance). Legal advice should be obtained.

Forms 39   Brokers should post the Equal Housing Opportunity poster in all offices. Failure to
40 do so shifts the burden of proof in discrimination actions to the brokers. (You can find
41 a copy of the Equal Housing Opportunity Poster in the Forms-To-Go Section.) It is a
42 broker's responsibility to provide training and supervision to ensure compliance with
43 the law.

FIGURE 2.2   EXAMPLES OF FAIR HOUSING VIOLATIONS

PROHIBITED ACTION	EXAMPLE OF VIOLATION
Refusing to sell, rent, or negotiate the sale or rental of housing.	John is the property manager of an apartment building with 125 units. When a minority family asks to look at some of the apartments, he tells them to go away.
Changing the terms or conditions or services for different individuals as a method of screening.	Linda is the owner of a 20-unit apartment building. She is very religious, and when a non-Christian family asks to look at a $300 apartment, she tells them that the $300 price is a discount for Christians, and their rent would be $340.
Advertising any discriminatory preference or limitation in housing or making any inquiry or reference that is discriminatory in nature.	Broker Bill places the following advertisement in the *Miami Herald:* "Just listed! Beautiful 3-bedroom home with Spanish barrel-tile roof. Perfect for Cuban families!" Developer Jean has an ad that says: "Be a happy homeowner in Bellair Gardens." The ad has a photo of several African American families.
Falsely representing that a property is not for sale.	Mildred, a disabled person, looks at a single-family home, and is told that the home is no longer available. The next day, Mildred sees the home advertised and a "for rent" sign in front of the house.
Profiting by inducing property owners to sell or rent based on the prospective entry into the neighborhood of persons of a protected class.	Sales associate Josie sends a newsletter to homeowners in a predominantly white neighborhood. The newsletter features Josie's real estate achievements, and a request to call her to list property. On the cover of the newsletter is a photo showing several racial minorities. The title of the newsletter is "The Changing Face of Sunland Station."
Altering the terms or conditions of a home loan, or denying a loan, as a means of discrimination.	A lender requires Mary, a divorced mother of three children, to pay for a credit report and to have her father cosign her application. A male friend who worked with her had lower income than she did and also poor credit. He told her that he was not required to do either of those things.
Denying membership or participation in a multiple-listing service, a real estate organization, or another facility related to the sale or rental of housing as a means of discrimination.	The Orange County Realty Council meets weekly to market available properties. The Council has restricted membership to Caucasian males, rejecting applications from women and African Americans.

Adapted from *Modern Real Estate Practice*, 15th Edition, by Galaty, Allaway, and Kyle. Dearborn™ Real Estate Education, Chicago, 1999.

FIGURE 2.3   HUD ADVERTISING GUIDELINES

Protected Status	Rule	Green Light Permitted	Red Light Not Permitted
Race Color National Origin	No discriminatory limitation or preference may be expressed	"master bedroom" "good neighborhood"	"white neighborhood" "no Oriental"
Religion	No religious preference or limitation	"chapel on premises" "kosher meals available" "Merry Christmas"	"no Muslims" "nice Christian family" "close to Catholic school"
Sex	No explicit preference based on sex	"mother-in-law suite" "master bedroom" "female roommate wanted"	"great house for a man" "wife's dream kitchen"
Handicap	No exclusions or limitations based on handicap	"wheelchair ramp" "walk to shopping"	"no wheelchairs" "able-bodied tenants only"
Familial status	No preference or limitations based on family size or nature	"two-bedroom home" "family room" "quiet neighborhood"	"married couple only" "no more than two children" "retiree's dream house"
Photographs or illustrations of people	People should be clearly representative and nonexclusive	Illustrations showing ethnic races, family groups, singles, etc.	Illustrations showing only singles, African American families, elderly white adults, etc.

Adapted from *Modern Real Estate Practice*, 15th Edition, by Galaty, Allaway, and Kyle. Dearborn™Real Estate Education, Chicago, 1999.

CASE STUDY

Discrimination Based on a Familial Status

This case study was excerpted from the records of the United States Department of Housing and Urban Development, Office of Administrative Law Judges. The names have been removed and made generic. The case was decided February 9, 1995.

Facts: Complainants ("Prospect") were a single woman and her two sons, aged two years and two months, respectively. Respondent ("Broker") is the owner of a property management company and a licensed real estate broker. The subject property was advertised as a "spacious two-bedroom apartment" in a four-unit building.

Prospect was helped in her search by a housing association but also looked at newspaper ads herself. She responded to a rental ad for the subject property by calling the number in the ad. Broker answered the call and asked her, among other things, how many children she had. When she told him she had two children, he told her she had "too many children" and hung up. Prospect thought Broker was rude.

Prospect was in shock after speaking to Broker. His statement made her feel she had made a mistake by having two children. She was discouraged from looking further for housing based on his rude behavior. Later, she searched for two months for adequate housing.

Prospect called the housing association the same day to report what had happened. Her complaint was tested the next day by an Equal Opportunity Specialist and a HUD Fair Housing Investigator.

The first tester called Broker and made inquiries about the subject unit that was being advertised. She, too, was asked how many children she had. She responded she had twins, 12 months old. Broker responded that was a problem, but perhaps an exception could be made because they were so young. "If they were two or three years old," he said, "that would definitely be a 'no.'" The tester said she would call back the next day. When she did, Broker told her the owner said "no."

Tester number 2 called and spoke to Broker later that day. When he asked about children, she told him she was calling on behalf of herself, her husband, and a six-year old son. Broker said he only showed apartments by appointment. Tester 2 said she would call back for an appointment later.

Questions: Did Broker refuse to "rent to, sell to, or negotiate with" a party based on discrimination?

Did Broker make any statement about the rental of a dwelling that suggests any preference, limitation, or discrimination based on race or an intention to act on any such preference, limitation, or discrimination?

Your Response:

_____

_____

Determination of Violation: The administrative law judge found that Broker caused Prospect and her two sons to suffer considerable damages, including economic loss, emotional distress, and loss of housing opportunity.

She stated in her opinion: It is well established that the damages that may be awarded under the Act include damages for embarrassment, humiliation, and emotional distress caused by acts of discrimination. Such damages can be inferred from the circumstances, as well as proven by testimony. Because these intangible type injuries cannot be measured quantitatively, courts do not demand precise proof to support a reasonable award of damages for such injuries.

Penalty: The administrative law judge awarded Prospect $280 for actual out-of-pocket expenses, $6,000 for emotional distress, and $500 for lost housing opportunity, for a total of $6,780.

Broker was permanently enjoined from discriminating with respect to housing. Additionally, to "vindicate the public interest and meet the goal of deterrence," Broker was ordered to pay a civil penalty to the Secretary, United States Department of Housing and Urban Development, in the amount of $5,000.

Web Links

www.fairhousing.com/legal_research/index.htm
National Fair Housing Advocate Online

www.hud.gov/fairhsg1.html
U.S. Dept. of Housing and Urban Development: Fair Housing Assistance Providers

www.hud.gov/bshelf7.html
Fair Housing Bookshelf

www.hud.gov/hdiscrim.html
U.S. Department of Housing and Urban Development: Housing Discrimination

---

Truth in Lending

The **Truth-in-Lending Act** requires lenders to inform consumers of exact credit costs before they make their purchases. It also sets up standard disclosures so that consumers can better compare loan costs. The Federal Reserve's **Regulation Z** implements the law and requires lenders to disclose the annual percentages rate of interest on loans, including the yields on fees the lenders charge.

Of particular interest to real estate licensees is the portion of the law relating to advertising of credit terms to be granted by an institutional lender. When an advertisement provides certain credit information, a trigger, Regulation Z requires that the ad supply additional information. The five triggers are:

1. quotation of the interest rate;
2. amount or percentage of any down payment;
3. number of payments or period of repayment;
4. amount of any payment; and
5. amount of any finance charge.

When the ad supplies any of the trigger information, it must include the following additional information:

- purchase price;
- amount financed;
- amount or percentage of any down payment;
- monthly payment;
- terms of repayment;
- annual percentage rate; and
- deferred payment price.

Antitrust Legislation

Brokers risk their assets and careers by attempting to get other brokers to charge a standard commission. **Antitrust** laws prohibit any action by a party to fix prices or inhibit competition by using unfair practices. Some of the prohibited actions include:

- conspiracy to set prices,
- splitting up competitive market areas,

DISCUSSION EXERCISE 2.1

You have been appointed to the MLS committee of the Board of REALTORS®. Henry West is the committee's new chairperson. When the committee meets for the first time under Henry, he talks about the goals for the committee and asks for discussion. After everyone talks about the coming year, Henry predicts that mortgage interest rates will increase and tells the committee that he intends to raise his commission rate to 7 percent due to diminishing sales. He recommends that others would be smart to do the same, then calls for discussion.

What is your position?

- conspiring to boycott cut-rate brokers or otherwise interfering with their business, and
- requiring a minimum commission before allowing listings to be circulated in any service, such as through the MLS.

DISCUSSION EXERCISE 2.2

Gloria, President of Big Tree Realty, Inc., had a luncheon meeting with Samuel, President of Statewide Residential Brokers, Inc. The subject of the meeting was Southern Discount Realty and the increased market share it had achieved since it announced its new discount fee structure. Big Tree and Statewide had previously had a 47 percent market share between them, but their combined share was now 39 percent.

They agreed to tell their sales associates not to show Southern Discount Realty listings to their buyers. Also, they agreed to call several other brokers in the area to do the same.

"A broker simply cannot give good service by charging that little. It's unprofessional," Gloria said.

If you were a sales associate for Statewide Realty, and your sales manager suggested that you boycott Southern Discount listings, what would your response be?

Real Estate Settlement Procedures Act (RESPA)

Before 1974, persons buying property experienced many levels of service and a myriad of documents. In 1974, the *Real Estate Settlement Procedures Act* (**RESPA**) was enacted to provide protection to buyers with respect to the amount and type of charges they pay at closing. Residential property is included in the act unless the existing loan is assumed or the property is purchased subject to the loan. Not all property types fall under RESPA requirements, including commercial property and large tracts of land.

Florida licensees are most interested in six major areas of the law:

1. **Uniform closing statement.** The HUD-1 settlement statement is the closing statement used in most transactions. The lender has primary responsibility for preparing the statement, and the closing agent must use the form. The fiduciary duties of skill, care and diligence include the agent asking that the statement be ready one business day before the closing and carefully ensuring that it is complete and correct. It is important for licensees to be familiar with the closing statement, which will be covered in detail in Chapter 12.

2. **Borrower's special information booklet.** *Settlement Costs: A HUD Guide* must be provided by the lender within three business days of loan application. It describes closing costs and the duties of each service provider in the transaction.

3. **Good-faith estimate of settlement costs.** This estimate, required from the lender at the time of loan application, or within 72 hours of loan application, details costs such as survey fees, title insurance, discount points, origination fees, and recording fees. Any settlement charges known to the lender must be included.

4. **Selection of the closing agent.** The lender must disclose the business relationship and the charges of any closing agent if the lender requires that agent to close the loan. If the borrower does not pay any of the title agent's charges, such disclosure is unnecessary.

5. **No kickbacks.** Persons or businesses may not give or accept anything of value in exchange for business relating to a real estate loan transaction unless all persons involved in the transaction have been informed before the exchange of valuable consideration. Service fees may not be paid unless a service actually was performed by a person licensed to do so and all parties are informed. In addition to some other exceptions, referral fees between brokers are permitted. Violations of this section carry criminal and civil penalties (triple damages).

6. **Purchase of title insurance.** No seller of real property can require that title insurance be purchased from any particular company. Triple damages may be awarded for violation of this provision.

Web Links

www. www.hud.gov/fha/sfh/res/respa_hm.html
   U.S. Department of Housing and Urban Development: RESPA

www.hud.gov/fha/sfh/res/respafaq.html
   U.S. Department of Housing and Urban Development: FAQs about RESPA

Federal Residential Lead-based Paint Hazard Reduction Act

Because of the danger of neurological damage, the *Residential Lead-based Paint Hazard Reduction Act* requires that disclosure be made to purchasers of residential buildings constructed before 1978. The law requires that the seller, landlord, or licensee provide the following before the contract is signed:

* A lead hazard information pamphlet
* Information about the presence of any known lead-based paint or lead-based paint hazard
* A ten-day period to conduct an inspection

Forms The lead warning statement shown in the Forms-To-Go Section must be attached to the contract.

Web Links

www.epa.gov/lead/
   U.S. Department of Environmental Protection: National Lead Information Clearing-
   house

http://www.hud.gov/lea/leahome.html
   U.S. Department of Housing and Urban Development: Office of Healthy Homes and
   Lead Hazard Control

Comprehensive Environmental Response, Compensation and Liability Act of 1980 (CERCLA)

The Comprehensive Environmental Response, Compensation, and Liability Act of 1980 imposes substantial liability on owners of real property that has been contaminated with toxic or hazardous substances. The liability also extends to other parties in a transaction, such as attorneys, developers, lenders, and real estate brokers. The liability in the act is joint and several, which means that all present or former property owners may be forced to pay (joint) or only one owner may be required to pay (several).

A purchaser who wishes to avoid liability under the statute must do intensive research, usually in the form of an environmental audit. The audit is expensive and time-consuming. The statute allows the purchaser to defend against any later action by claiming **innocent purchaser status,** provided that the purchaser exercised due diligence to investigate the property. Licensees should be particularly careful when listing or selling sites such as former gas stations or dry cleaning establishments. Residential properties built on former farm land have been found to be contaminated by pesticide use (Dioxin, DDT) or old farm gas tanks that have leaked. Other problem areas for residential licensees are old, leaking heating oil tanks buried in the ground.

In *Johnson v. Davis,* the Florida Supreme Court decreed that sellers must disclose material facts concerning a residential property's value and desirability. A recent court case in Florida found that sellers in nonresidential transactions do not fall under defect-disclosure requirements of *Johnson v. Davis.* If this decision becomes a precedent for the entire state, licensees will not be required to make condition disclosures on nonresidential property. Licensees should, however, assess the amount of risk they bear, not only legally but from loss of business reputation, when they fail to disclose everything.

Income Tax Regulations Affecting Residential Real Property

Real estate licensees are not expected to be income tax experts, but they should be knowledgeable about basic provisions of the Internal Revenue Code (IRC) as they relate to real estate transactions. The information included in this section is designed to help licensees provide general information about advantages and disadvantages of taking certain actions. Licensees always should advise consumers to seek professional tax advice. An important benefit to homeowners is that interest and property taxes are deductible. Additionally, all or part of the gain on sale of the property is exempt from taxes.

A homeowner can buy and sell many homes over a lifetime without, in most cases, having to pay taxes on the profits. The Taxpayer Relief Act of 1997 changed the need for homeowners to purchase another home to postpone taxes on their gains. It also eliminated the once-in-a-lifetime $125,000 exclusion on gain on the sale of a personal residence.

A taxpayer currently may exclude up to $250,000 ($500,000 for a married couple filing jointly) of gain on the sale of a personal residence if the taxpayer owned and occupied the residence for at least two of the previous five years. If the taxpayer held the home less than two years, a prorata portion of the exclusion applies. The number of times a homeowner may use this exclusion is unlimited except that the **exclusion can be used only once every two years.** While the change is extremely **advantageous to most** families because it allows them to earn large profits on their residences **tax free, owners** of more expensive homes may find it to be a mixed bag.

If the owners of very expensive residences have gains greater than $500,000, **they must pay capital gains taxes of 15 percent on the excess. (Under the previous law, they could **roll over** the gains into new homes and postpone paying taxes.) This may help the real estate industry because it encourages owners with gains approaching $500,000 to list and sell their properties to escape paying taxes on the gains.

Example: The Wilsons bought their home in 1982 for $250,000. In 1992, they added a family room, deck, and pool for a total of $50,000. They lived in the home until they sold it for $900,000 in March of this year. Selling costs were $60,000. They would calculate their taxes as follows:

Selling price		$900,000
Less selling expenses		– 60,000
Equals net selling price		$840,000
Basis		
Original cost	$250,000	
Plus improvements	+ 50,000	
Equals cost basis		300,000
Gain on sale ($840,000 – $300,000)		$540,000
Less exclusion on sale of residence		–500,000
Taxable capital gain		**$ 40,000**
Long-term capital gains rate (15%)		× .15
Taxes due on sale		**$ 6,000**

Lower Capital Gains Tax Rates on Investment Property

The rates for long-term (holding period more than 12 months) capital **gains have been** reduced from 20 percent to a maximum of 15 percent (5 percent for **persons in the** 10 percent ordinary income tax rate). When investment property is sold, **any deprecia-**tion taken must be "recaptured" and is taxed at 25 percent.

Example: An apartment property was purchased in 1994 for $300,000. **The building** represented 80% of the total. The property is sold in 2003 for $510,000, **with** selling costs of $10,000. Depreciation, using a 27½-year life, is approximately $78,545 ($300,000 × 80% ÷ 27.5 × 9 years). What is the tax liability?

To Calculate Taxes on Gain:

Selling price	$510,000
Less selling costs	–10,000
Amount realized	500,000
Deduct purchase price	–300,000
Gain on sale	$200,000
× Tax rate	× 15%
Taxes on gain	**$ 30,000**

To Calculate Taxes on Depreciation:

Depreciation taken	$ 78,545
× Recapture rate	× 25%
Taxes on recapture	$ 19,636

Add Taxes on Gain to Taxes on Depreciation:

Taxes on gain	$ 30,000
Taxes on depreciation	19,636
Total taxes due on sale	**$ 49,636**

1   Owners of moderately priced homes who expect never to have gains of $500,000 find
2 in the new law an advantage beyond tax savings: The owners need not maintain such
3 careful tax records showing small improvements made to the properties.

Shorter Life for Depreciating Furniture

5 IRS had set a seven-year recovery rate for depreciating furniture, appliances, and car-
6 peting used in residential rental property. In a 1999 policy change, IRS decreased the
7 recovery period to five years. This change will result in a 40 percent increase in depre-
8 ciation deductions for these items! For furniture placed in use before 1999, owners may
9 use Form 3115 to change the accounting method. Furniture and equipment used in
10 commercial and office properties are not affected by this change.

Reporting Cash Payments Greater Than $10,000

12 If a broker receives more than $10,000 in cash, either for a single real estate transaction
13 or for two or more related transactions, the broker must report the event to the IRS
14 within 15 days on Form 8300. Cash is either U.S. or foreign currency. Brokers selling
15 real property need not report funds received by bank check or wire transfer when cash
16 was not physically transferred. The purpose of the report is to prevent money laun-
17 dering.

18   Cash equivalents such as money orders, travelers' checks, cashiers' checks, and bank
19 drafts with a face value of $10,000 or less are treated as cash only in sales of consumer
20 durables, collectibles, travel, and entertainment. Consumer durables include items such
21 as boats, cars, and jewelry.

Deducting the Home Office

23 Many brokers are legally able to work from their homes and may benefit from recent tax
24 law changes related to home offices. These changes are called Section 179 deductions,
25 and they are particularly beneficial for deducting office equipment. Home-based busi-
26 nesses may also deduct part of their expenses for heating, cooling, and maintenance of
27 the office proportionate to the space used relative to the size of the home. However, the
28 home office must be an area used exclusively for business activity, and it must be the only
29 major location used to conduct business or meet with customers. Brokers should seek
30 professional advice or review IRS publication 587.

INDEPENDENT CONTRACTOR RELATIONSHIPS

32 Most real estate brokerage firms contract with their sales associates as independent con-
33 tractors. If the broker meets all requirements, this results in substantial savings, primar-
34 ily from employer's share of Social Security taxes, worker's compensation insurance,
35 unemployment taxes, and other fringe benefits. There are three major requirements for
36 a sales associate to qualify as an independent contractor:

37   1. The sales associate must hold an active real estate license.
38   2. The sales associate's gross income must be based on production rather than on the
39   number of hours worked.
40   3. The sales associate's work must be done based on a written contract that states,
41   among other things, that the sales associate will not be considered an employee for
42   federal tax purposes.

43   The IRS may review the status based on the degree of behavioral control of the sales
44 associate by the broker. The broker may not dictate to the sales associate how his or her
45 work is to be done. The IRS will deny the status if an audit reveals that the broker directs
46 how the sales associates should do their job, requires sales associates to take a floor duty

FIGURE 2.4   EMPLOYEE OR INDEPENDENT CONTRACTOR? IRS CONSIDERATIONS

FACTORS INDICATING CONTROL*	EMPLOYEE	INDEPENDENT CONTRACTOR
Is the worker required to comply with employer instructions about when, where, and how work is to be performed?	Yes	No
Is the worker required to undergo training?	Yes	No
Does the worker hire, supervise, and pay others to perform work for which he or she is responsible?	No	Yes
Must the worker's job be performed during certain set hours?	Yes	No
Must the worker devote full time to the job?	Yes	No
Must the work be performed on the employer's property?	Yes	No
Must tasks be performed in a certain order set by the employer?	Yes	No
Is the individual required to submit regular written or oral reports to the employer?	Yes	No
Is payment by the hour, week, or month?	Yes	No
Is payment in a lump sum?	No	Yes
Are the worker's business and travel expenses paid by the employer?	Yes	No
Does the employer furnish the tools and materials required for the job?	Yes	No
Does the worker rent his or her own office or working space?	No	Yes
Will the worker realize a profit or loss as a result of his or her services?	No	Yes
Does the individual work for more than one firm at a time?	No	Yes
Does the worker make his or her services available to the general public?	No	Yes
Does the employer have the right to fire the worker?	Yes	No
Does the worker have the right to quit the job at any time, whether or not a particular task is complete?	Yes	No
* **Note:** These factors are only possible indicators of a worker's status. Each case must be determined on its own facts, based on all the information.		

Source: *Modern Real Estate Practice*, 15th Edition, by Galaty, Allaway, and Kyle, Dearborn™ Real Estate Education®.

time, or makes attendance at company meetings mandatory. Figure 2.4 is a table showing the indications of broker control.

Financial control is another problem area for brokers. If the broker reimburses the sales associate for business expenses, such as automobile expenses or pays for business cards, insurance plans, licensing, or board dues, the IRS may determine that the sales associate is an employee. The broker would then be liable for Social Security and Medicare taxes and income taxes.

These rules are also applicable to sales associates who employ personal assistants. Because an unlicensed assistant is paid by salary and controlled by the employer, he or she would not be an independent contractor.

Web Links

www.irs.ustreas.gov
U.S. Internal Revenue Service

http://ftp.fedworld.gov/pub/irs-pdf/p587.pdf
U.S. Internal Revenue Service **(Home Office Regulations).**

STATE LAWS AFFECTING REAL ESTATE LICENSEES

Coastal Zone Management Act (Chapter 380.20, F.S.)

Although the federal *Coastal Zone Management Act* requires that coastal states develop and implement management plans, the major interest for licensees is Florida's restrictions in response to the act. A great deal of Florida's real property is located in coastal areas (24 of 67 counties). Florida's plan places significant restrictions on oceanfront development. Licensees who list and sell property in those areas should be familiar with permitted land uses. Sellers must provide to buyers, at or before closing, an affidavit or a survey delineating the **Coastal Construction Control Line (CCCL)** location (50-foot setback line). A buyer may waive this requirement, but the waiver must be in writing. Many transactions have resulted in buyers purchasing land that cannot be developed as represented by the sales associates. This exposes the brokers and sales associates to disciplinary action and substantial civil damages.

Florida Growth Management Act (Chapter 163, F.S.)

Florida's Growth Management Act requires that every city and county in Florida prepare a comprehensive plan of land use, together with controls that implement the plan. The comprehensive plan affects nearly every parcel of undeveloped land and many buildings that need renovation or enlargement. **Concurrency** is one of the significant requirements of the act. It requires that a minimum level of infrastructure be present before development can take place. **Infrastructure** includes such things as transportation systems, schools, and utilities.

Licensees must become knowledgeable about the comprehensive plans in their areas so that they can act competently with sellers and buyers. A licensee takes on substantial liability when representing that a site can be used for a specific purpose. Properties outside the urban services area are more difficult to subdivide, and the number of homes per acre is limited. This has affected the ability of licensees to market property for development. Most licensees, even after investigating the possible uses of an undeveloped commercial parcel, insert a **land-use contingency clause** into the contract for purchase. In this way, the buyer has the right to cancel the contract for property that cannot be used as represented.

1 Many cities and counties in Florida now require land-use disclosures before a pur-
2 chaser signs a contract. Such disclosures may cover items such as:

3 • restrictive covenants for the neighborhood;
4 • the buyer's responsibility to investigate whether the anticipated land use conforms to
5   comprehensive plan, zoning, building codes, and so on; and
6 • whether streets and drainage are publicly maintained or are the homeowner's
7   responsibility.

DISCUSSION EXERCISE 2.3

You have just shown your listing, a home in Killearn Estates, to Savannah Cooley,
and she seems prepared to make an offer. She feels that the garage could be
enclosed to make a wonderful art studio with northern exposure. You believe that
the restrictive covenants prohibit garage conversions, but have seen several others
done without any problems.

How should you handle this situation?

---

8 ## Condominium Act (Chapter 718, F.S.)

9 Some describe the concept of condominiums as a "cube in the sky." The cube has a spe-
10 cific legal description, much like a lot and block description in a subdivision. The buyer
11 of a condominium purchases title to a unit, usually in fee simple. The owner's property
12 generally extends to the inside of the wall coverings of the apartment. The cube rests
13 on a structure that is a common element along with the land and other facilities. (See
14 Figure 2.5.) Each apartment can be bought, sold, leased, or mortgaged. Real estate taxes
15 are separately assessed on each unit.

FIGURE 2.5   CONDOMINIUM OWNERSHIP

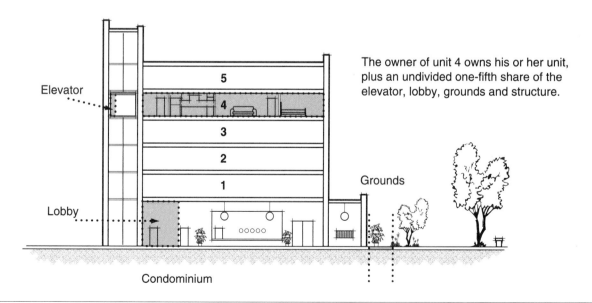

The owner of unit 4 owns his or her unit,
plus an undivided one-fifth share of the
elevator, lobby, grounds and structure.

SOURCE: *Modern Real Estate Practice*, 15th Edition, by Galaty, Allaway, and Kyle. Dearborn™Real Estate Education, Chicago, 1999.

1   The *Florida Condominium Act* prescribes the process by which condominiums are
2   created, marketed, and operated. It defines common elements, describes the mainte-
3   nance and assessment of common expenses, and requires full disclosure of information
4   before the sale of the property. Strong controls govern advance payments and deposits.
5   Developers must warrant the roof, the structural components, and the mechanical, and
6   plumbing components for three years after completion of construction. Other com-
7   ponents must be warranted for at least one year. For residential condominiums estab-
8   lished after April 1, 1992, each unit's share of common elements maintenance must be
9   related to the unit's total square footage or on an equal fractional basis.

10 The Division of Florida Land Sales, Condominiums and Mobile Homes, DBPR, is the
11 agency charged with carrying out the law. The Division requires detailed disclosures
12 before the sale of any units. Developers of residential condominiums having more than
13 20 units must prepare a prospectus and file it with the Division. The prospectus must
14 contain several bold-faced warnings to consumers, and must be given to every buyer. If
15 a developer publishes false or misleading information relied on by a purchaser, the pur-
16 chaser may rescind a contract if it has not yet closed or collect damages from the devel-
17 oper.

18 Buyers may rescind a purchase contract within 15 days for a new condominium, or
19 three business days for a resale unit. The time period begins when the buyer signs the
20 contract or is given the required condominium documents, whichever is later. The
21 required documents include the declaration of condominium, articles of incorporation,
22 bylaws, rules of the association, a copy of the association's "Question and Answer
23 Sheet," and a (new) copy of the most recent year-end financial statement.

INTERPRETING THE FINANCIAL STATEMENTS

Licensees should use caution if asked to interpret the most recent year-end
financial information. The sales associate could be guilty of misrepresentation in
case he or she is incorrect. Instead, the buyer should be referred to a CPA or
accountant.

---

24 **Web Link**

25 Go to **myflorida.com**, then click on Business & Industry > Learn > Real Estate > Condominiums/Coop-
26 eratives
27 Florida DBPR—Bureau of Condominiums

The Florida Vacation Plan and Timesharing Act (Chapter 721, F.S.)

29 Because of Florida's reputation for great weather, beautiful beaches, and family enter-
30 tainment, the time-share industry has continued to thrive and bring new properties to
31 market. With time-sharing, persons can own, for a short time, vacation property they
32 could not otherwise afford. Typically, time-sharing gives the buyer the right to occupy
33 a condominium apartment for one week each year. The price of the time-share depends
34 upon its size, location, and time of year.

35 The *Florida Vacation Plan and Timesharing Act* prescribes the procedures for the cre-
36 ation, sale, exchange, promotion, and operation of timeshare plans. The Division of
37 Florida Land Sales, Condominiums and Mobile Homes, DBPR, administers the law.
38 The law requires that the seller provide, among other things, specific information about
39 maintenance charges and management, an explanation of any exchange plan, and a

public offering statement (prospectus). The buyer has a ten-day "cooling off" period to cancel the contract after receiving all required documents from the developer.

The Florida Real Estate Commission has established very strict rules for real estate licensees who list or sell time-share units.

Disclosure Required When Listing a Resale Time-Share Period.   When listing a resale time-share period, a licensee must place the following statement in conspicuous type just above the owner's signature:

> There is no guarantee that your timeshare period can be sold at any particular price or within any particular period of time.

Any written advertising material for solicitation of time-share listings must also contain the same statement in conspicuous type.

Many other disclosures are required, including the amount of fees, the term of agreement, promotional efforts if any advance fee is to be paid, and a description of the service to be provided by the broker.

Disclosures Required When Selling a Resale Time-Share Period.   Licensees must place the following statement immediately above the signature of the buyer of a resale time-share condominium:

> The current year's assessment for common expenses allocable to the time-share period you are purchasing is _____. This assessment, which may be increased from time to time by the managing entity of the time-share plan, is payable in full each year on or before_____. This assessment (includes/ does not include) yearly ad valorem real estate taxes, which (are/are not) billed and collected separately.

If ad valorem real property taxes are not included in the current year's assessment for common expenses, the following statement must be included:

> The most recent annual assessment for ad valorem real estate taxes for the time-share period you are purchasing is $_____. Each owner is personally liable for the payment of his assessments for common expenses and failure to timely pay these assessments may result in restriction or loss of your use and/or ownership rights.

Disclosures Required When Selling New Time-Share Units

> You may cancel this contract without any penalty or obligation within 10 days from the date you sign this contract and until 10 days after you receive the public offering statement, whichever is later.

> The purchase of a time-share period should be based on its value as a vacation experience or for spending leisure time and not considered for purposes of acquiring an appreciating investment or with an expectation that the time-share period may be resold.

It is a serious offense if a licensee fails to disclose all material aspects of a time-share sale or fails to have a current license as a broker or sales associate while listing or selling one or more time-share periods per year. The Florida Real Estate Commission guidelines for disciplinary action show that the usual penalty of the commission will be revocation.

Web Link

www.   http://www.myflorida.com/myflorida/business/learn/realestate/timeshare/index.html
       Bureau of Timeshare

FIGURE 2.6 SAMPLE RATING FORM

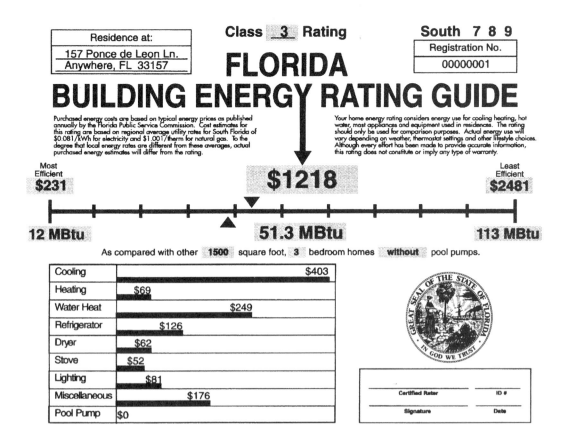

The Florida Building Energy-Efficiency Rating Act (Chapter 553.990, F.S.)

The *Florida Building Energy-Efficiency Rating Accessibility Implementation Act* creates an energy-efficiency rating and provides for disclosure of the rating system for residential and commercial buildings. Disclosure must be made affirming that such a rating system exists, and a pamphlet explaining the system must be given to buyers. Pamphlets may be obtained from the Department of Community Affairs. A rating need not be given. A sample rating form is shown in Figure 2.6.

Florida Americans with Disabilities Accessibility Implementation Act (Chapter 553.501, F.S.)

The *Florida Americans with Disabilities Accessibility Implementation Act* was passed because many buildings contain barriers that restrict access and use by disabled persons. The restrictions on use affect employment, training and consumer services and are prohibited. The act implements portions of the *Americans with Disabilities Act (ADA)* and includes other important provisions.

All new residential construction must have at least one bathroom that is accessible, as defined by law. Any new or renovated building frequented by the public must comply in the areas of landings, curb ramps, low-pull-force doors, seating spaces, aisles and public restrooms.

1   Licensees must be familiar with ADA requirements, especially when selling existing
2   commercial buildings. The cost of renovation to bring a building up to code may be sub-
3   stantial, and the purchaser should be made aware of the fact early in the presentation.

AIDS Victims and Housing (Chapter 760.50, F.S.)

5   The fact that an occupant of real property is infected with the HIV virus or has
6   been diagnosed with AIDS is not material and may not be disclosed in a real estate trans-
7   action.

8   No cause of action arises against an owner of real property or against his agent for
9   failing to disclose to the buyer or tenant that an occupant of the property was infected
10   with the HIV virus or with AIDS. A licensee does not have the duty to investigate
11   whether a person is HIV-positive or has AIDS to disclose the fact if known. F.S. 760.50,
12   as well as federal statutes, prohibits such discussions.

Radon Gas Protection Act (Chapter 404.056, F.S.)

14   Some authorities say that **radon gas** is the second most common source of lung cancer
15   in the United States. Radon is produced by uranium in the soil that decays and creates
16   a gas. While radon gas is all around us, it is not usually a problem because of very
17   low concentrations in the atmosphere. When uranium decays under a home the gas
18   seeps into the home through foundation cracks and plumbing lines. Improved building
19   techniques and insulation intended to provide energy-efficient homes have the unin-
20   tended side effect of trapping the gas inside the home.

21   Testing is the only way to learn if radon levels are a health hazard. The EPA recom-
22   mends intervention if testing shows radon levels at four **picocuries** per liter of air. This
23   would be a concentration approximately ten times that of outdoor air. Exposure to
24   radon inside the home can be reduced to an acceptable level by sealing foundation
25   cracks and other openings.

26   The radon levels in a building can also be reduced by mitigation systems. Such sys-
27   tems use PVC pipes installed through the slab with a fan that draws air from beneath
28   the building and vents it above the roof line. Such systems may cost from $1,000 to
29   $3,500. The electric cost for running the fan is only about five dollars per month.

Forms 30   Florida has enacted the *Radon Protection Act,* which requires disclosure of the charac-
31   teristics of the gas but does not require an inspection. The wording must be on every
32   sale contract and on every lease contract for more than 45 days (see Figure 2.7) and is
33   part of the Comprehensive Buyer's Disclosures seen in the Forms-To-Go Section.

Web Link

www. 35   www.epa.gov/iedweb00/radon/pubs/citguide.html
↖ 36   *A Citizen's Guide to Radon*, 2d ed. (U.S. EPA)

Community Association Management (Chapter 468, F.S.)

38   A **community association** is a residential homeowners' association in which member-
39   ship is required. Because Florida consumers had suffered losses from incompetent or
40   even criminal management activities, the Florida Legislature passed the *Community Asso-*
41   *ciation Management Act* to regulate managers of such associations.

42   The act requires community association managers to obtain a license from the DBPR.
43   A community association is defined as "a residential homeowners' association in which
44   membership is a condition of ownership of a unit in a **planned unit development,** or of
45   a lot for a home or a mobile home or of a town house, villa, condominium, cooperative

---

FIGURE 2.7 RADON GAS DISCLOSURE STATEMENT

Radon Gas—radon gas is a naturally occurring radioactive gas that, when it has
accumulated in a building in sufficient quantities, may present health risks to persons
who are exposed to it over time. Levels of radon gas that exceed federal and state
guidelines have been found in buildings in Florida. Additional information regarding
radon and radon testing may be obtained from your County Public Health Unit.
Pursuant to §404.056(7), Florida Statutes.

_____   _____
Buyer or Lessee Signature   Date

---

1 or other residential unit that is part of a residential development, and that is authorized
2 to impose a fee that may become a lien on the parcel."

3   The term *community association* under this law includes any association that has 50 or
4 more units, or has an annual budget greater than $100,000. A person must have a com-
5 munity association manager's license if he performs the following functions for com-
6 pensation: controlling or disbursing funds, preparing budgets or other financial
7 documents, helping in sending notices of meetings or conducting meetings, and coor-
8 dinating maintenance and other services for the association. A person need not have a
9 real estate license to perform these tasks.

10   Apartment properties and other commercial property are not affected by this law.
11 The law applies only to managers of residential homeowners' associations. Licenses are
12 issued to individuals, not to companies or corporations. To obtain a community associ-
13 ation manager's license, an individual must apply to DBPR's Division of Florida Land
14 Sales, Condominiums and Mobile Homes, pay appropriate fees, be of good moral char-
15 acter, and pass an examination. The Division provides a study guide designed to pre-
16 pare an applicant for the state exam. Prelicensing courses are not required.

Homeowners' Association Disclosure (Chapter 689, F.S.)

18 Some home buyers in Florida have been surprised shortly after the purchase when they
19 discovered that they must pay dues to a homeowners' association, or that there are
20 restrictive covenants that affect the use and occupancy of the property. Developers or
21 owners of the parcel must provide a Homeowners' Association/Community Disclosure
22 form before the buyer signs a purchase contract. If the disclosure is not given and if the
23 contract does not contain the following statement, the contract can be voided at the
24 buyer's option anytime until closing

25 **NEW LANGUAGE REQUIRED FOR CONTRACTS FOR SALES AND PURCHASE**

26 IF THE DISCLOSURE SUMMARY REQUIRED BY SECTION 689.26, FLORIDA STATUTES,
27 HAS NOT BEEN PROVIDED TO THE PROSPECTIVE PURCHASER BEFORE EXECUTING
28 THIS CONTRACT FOR SALE, THIS CONTRACT IS VOIDABLE BY BUYER BY DELIVERING
29 TO SELLER OR SELLER'S AGENT WRITTEN NOTICE OF THE BUYER'S INTENTION TO
30 CANCEL WITHIN 3 DAYS AFTER RECEIPT OF THE DISCLOSURE SUMMARY OR PRIOR TO
31 CLOSING, WHICHEVER OCCURS FIRST. ANY PURPORTED WAIVER OF THIS
32 VOIDABILITY RIGHT HAS NO EFFECT. BUYER'S RIGHT TO VOID THIS CONTRACT
33 SHALL TERMINATE AT CLOSING.

Residential Swimming Pool Safety Act (Chapter 515, F.S.)

35 Drowning is the leading cause of death of young children in Florida and is also a signif-
36 icant cause of death for medically frail elderly persons. This new law requires that all

new residential swimming pools, spas, and hot tubs be equipped with at least one pool safety feature, as listed below. It makes the Department of Health responsible for distributing a publication that provides the public with information on drowning prevention and the responsibilities of pool ownership. The Department must also provide a drowning prevention education program.

Requirements.   To pass final inspection and receive a certificate of completion, a residential swimming pool must meet *at least one of the following requirements* relating to pool safety features:

- The pool must be isolated from access to a home by an enclosure that meets the pool barrier requirements (see below).
- The pool must be equipped with an approved safety pool cover.
- All doors and windows providing direct access from the home to the pool must be equipped with an exit alarm that has a minimum sound pressure rating of 85 decibels at 10 feet.
- All doors providing direct access from the home to the pool must be equipped with a self-closing, self-latching device with a release mechanism placed no lower than 54 inches above the floor.

Residential swimming pool barrier requirements.   A residential swimming pool barrier must have all of the following characteristics:

- The barrier must be at least four feet high on the outside.
- The barrier may not have any gaps, openings, indentations, protrusions, or structural components that could allow a young child to crawl under, squeeze through, or climb over the barrier.
- The barrier must be placed around the perimeter of the pool and must be separate from any fence, wall, or other enclosure surrounding the yard unless the fence, wall, or other enclosure or portion thereof is situated on the perimeter of the pool, is being used as part of the barrier, and meets the barrier requirements of this section.
- The barrier must be placed sufficiently away from the water's edge to prevent a young child or medically frail elderly person who may have managed to penetrate the barrier from immediately falling into the water.

Gates that provide access to swimming pools must open outward away from the pool and be self-closing and equipped with a self-latching locking device, the release mechanism of which must be located on the pool side of the gate and so placed that it cannot be reached by a young child over the top or through any opening or gap.

Information required to be furnished to buyers.   A licensed pool contractor, on entering into an agreement with a buyer to build a residential swimming pool, or a licensed home builder or developer, on entering into an agreement with a buyer to build a house that includes a residential swimming pool, must give the buyer a document containing the requirements of this chapter and a copy of the publication produced by the department under Section 515.31 that provides information on drowning prevention and the responsibilities of pool ownership.

Penalties for violation.   A person who fails to equip a new residential swimming pool with at least one pool safety feature commits a misdemeanor of the second degree. However, no penalty shall be imposed if the person, within 45 days after arrest or issuance of a summons or a notice to appear, has equipped the pool with at least one safety feature and has attended a drowning prevention education program.

Unlicensed Activity and Building Code Violations

Hiring a "handyperson."   Before a real estate licensee recommends a "handyperson" who does not have a contractor's license to a customer, the licensee should be familiar with the legal requirements governing the activities of such workers.

There is a general exemption in the contractor's law that allows unlicensed persons to perform any work of a minor nature in which the total contract price for labor, materials, and all other items is less than $1,000. The exemption does not apply if the construction or repairs are part of a larger operation with several bills from the same or a different person for the purposes of evading this limitation. While the person who hires the unlicensed person doing work in excess of $1,000 has not violated the law, the person performing the work has.

Real estate licensees should also be aware that such unlicensed persons generally do not carry liability insurance or worker's compensation insurance. This could expose the seller or buyer to substantial liability in case of accident. [489.103(9), F.S.]

Real estate licensee's exemption from the contractor's law.   A provision in the state contractor's license law offers an exemption to real estate licensees. When a licensee, as agent for an owner, contracts for repairs, maintenance, remodeling, or improvements that total more than $5,000, the licensee must either have a contractor's license or employ a contractor. Dividing the work will not avoid this requirement. If the amount is $5,000 or less, however, the licensee is exempt from the contractor's license requirement. When hiring persons to do repairs or remodeling, and the work requires a licensed contractor to do it (such as running electrical lines), the licensee must hire licensed persons. [489.013(17), F.S.]

Disclosure of building code violations.   Sellers who have been cited for a building code violation, or have a citation pending, must disclose the fact in writing to buyers prior to closing a sale. The disclosure must:

- state the existence and nature of the violation and proceedings;
- provide a copy of the pleadings, notices and other materials received by the seller; and
- state the seller's agreement to be liable for correcting the code violation.

Within five days after transfer of the property, the seller must give notice to the code enforcement agency of the name and address of the new owner and give copies of the disclosure notices given to the buyer.

A seller who violates this provision is guilty of fraud. Real estate licensees should be certain that sellers are aware of this disclosure requirement. [125.69(2)(d)]

SUMMARY

Florida regulation of real estate practices has been strengthened considerably by passage of many consumer protection laws. Licensees who fail to maintain their professional education risk violation of new laws. In some cases, the violation occurs because licensees were unaware that the law existed.

In real estate transactions, licensees must be careful to disclose fully any material facts that affect the property's value. A licensee must avoid making statements that could result in a claim of misrepresentation. The licensee must take steps, such as using a property condition disclosure statement and inspecting the property, to ensure the buyer has full knowledge of defects.

Real estate licensees must observe fair housing laws and avoid situations that could be interpreted as steering or blockbusting. Advertising should not contain language that might be considered discriminatory. Other federal laws that should be understood include income tax provisions on real estate, the Truth-in-Lending Act, RESPA requirements, and lead-based paint disclosures.

Important Florida laws and disclosure requirements that licensees must observe include coastal zone laws, comprehensive plans and concurrency, condominium and time-share act requirements, the energy-efficiency disclosure, federal and state disability requirements, radon gas disclosures, and license requirements for community association managers.

The laws are numerous, and the professional real estate practitioner should maintain a checklist of required disclosures for every type of property. By observing the law and disclosing the required information, licensees enhance their reputation for fair and honest dealing, and the consumer is informed and protected.

Figure 2.8 shows the numerous disclosures required from licensees. It is a quick reference guide intended to help licensees understand when they are dealing with property or situations that have strict regulatory guidelines. The chart should not be considered all-inclusive, as more disclosure requirements are added periodically.

DEFINE THESE KEY TERMS

antitrust	material fact
blockbusting	misrepresentation
Coastal Construction Control Line (CCCL)	planned unit development
community association	property condition disclosure
concurrency	radon gas
Fair Housing Act	redlining
false or misleading statements	Regulation Z
infrastructure	RESPA
innocent purchaser status	steering
land-use contingency clause	Truth-In-Lending Act

FIGURE 2.8   FLORIDA REAL ESTATE DISCLOSURE CHART

Subject	Disclosure Trigger	To	Disclosure Requirement
Brokerage relationship disclosures			See Chapter 1
Property condition disclosure	When listing property At time of showing property	Seller Buyer	Any material defects that affect the property's value
Radon gas	Contracts for purchase or lease	Buyer or tenant	Statement as to the nature of the gas and how to get more information
Lead-based paint	Contracts for purchase or lease	Buyer or tenant	Lead hazard information pamphlet; disclosure of any known hazards; ten-day inspection and cancellation privilege
Federal Reserve's Regulation Z	When advertising financial terms on real property, a trigger item is included in ad	Readers of advertising	Full disclosure of all material factors in financing, including price, down payment, monthly payment, finance costs, and annual percentage rate of interest
Wood-destroying organisms report	Closing of a real estate transaction that includes commercial or residential buildings	Buyer	Wood-destroying organisms report signed by a licensed pest inspector, made within 30 days before closing date
Roof inspection ordinance— some jurisdictions	Closing of a real estate transaction	Buyer	Disclosure of condition of roof covering, decking, and framing, usually made within 30 days before closing
Land use disclaimer— some jurisdictions, but not statewide	Contract for purchase	Buyer	Restrictive covenants for the neighborhood; buyer's responsibility to investigate whether the anticipated land use conforms to comprehensive plan, zoning, building codes, etc.; public or private street and drainage maintenance
Landlord and Tenant Act	Within 30 days of signing lease	Tenant	Where deposit is being held; whether it is in an interest-bearing account and the interest rate, if any
Condominium Act–recreation lease	Contract to purchase	Buyer	Whether a recreational lease exists; when membership in a recreation facilities club is required; description of the facilities and the charges

FIGURE 2.8   FLORIDA REAL ESTATE DISCLOSURE CHART (Continued)

Subject	Disclosure Trigger	To	Disclosure Requirement
Condominium Act—purchase cancellation	Contract to purchase	Buyer	15-day cancellation privilege when buying from a developer; 3-day cancellation privilege when buying a resale unit
Time-share Act—purchase cancellation	Contract to purchase	Buyer	All material aspects of the property; rights and obligations of buyer and seller; ten-day cancellation privilege; notification that purchase is a leisure time activity, not an appreciating investment.
Time-share Act—unit assessments	Contract to purchase	Buyer	Annual assessment for common expenses
Florida Building Energy-Efficiency Act	Contract to purchase	Buyer	Energy-efficiency rating system description and how to get the building rated
Florida Uniform Land Sales Practices Act	Contract to purchase a property in subdivided lands with 50 or more lots	Buyer	Seven-day cancellation privilege; notification of financial exposure if purchased with a contract for deed
Florida Mobile Home Act	Lease agreements for mobile home lots with at least ten sites	Tenant	A prospectus detailing features of the park and certain expenses

CHAPTER 2 PRACTICE EXAM

1. Broker Sherrill is working with Loretta, who wishes to purchase a vacant site in Orange Park. Loretta is told that concurrency requirements may delay her building plans, and she asks Sherrill about the meaning of the word. Sherrill's response should be:

   a. "It is a requirement that you get a building permit and an environmental audit at the same time."
   b. "You must provide a development of regional impact statement before building."
   c. "You must disclose whether the building plans cover any recreational leases."
   d. "There could be a lack of infrastructure in place that would put a moratorium on construction until the situation is remedied."

2. In 1998, Henry has a capital gain of $197,000 on the sale of his home, which he owned for three years. The sales price was $425,000. Sales costs were $7,000, qualified fix-up costs were $1,000, and moving costs were $2,000. How much must Henry pay in capital gains taxes on this sale if his normal tax rate is 25 percent?

   a. $197,000
   b. $98,500
   c. $39,400
   d. $0

3. New concern about the presence of radon gas is the result of the increase in:

   a. radon levels at large factories.
   b. the number of energy efficient buildings.
   c. the depletion of the ozone layer.
   d. Freon in air-conditioning systems.

4. Broker Sandra Rodriguez was in the process of listing the Sitteson home when Mr. Sitteson stated that the foundation was cracked. He said there was no need to mention that to the buyer because there had never been a problem with it. In this situation:

   a. Sandra's agency is with the Sittesons, and she may follow the directive.
   b. the Sittesons could be sued for failure to disclose; Sandra could not.
   c. Sandra should tell the Sittesons that she could not withhold the information and that failure to disclose could result in civil damages to the Sittesons and to her.
   d. no requirement forces disclosure unless the cracked foundation results in further damage to the property.

5. Traci lived in Oxbottom Plantation Estates, which had more than 200 homes. She was offered a salaried position with the association as manager and helped prepare billing statements for the required annual dues. In this case:

   a. Traci can be a manager without a real estate license or a community association manager's license.
   b. Traci can be a manager if she has a real estate license but does not have a community association manager's license.
   c. Traci can be a manager without a real estate license, provided she has a community association manager's license.
   d. the association does not meet the requirements of a community association.

6. Stephen Sleper, a real estate sales associate, is asked by his client, Arthur Cody, whether the school zone for a prospective residence is Astoria Park Elementary School. Stephen sold a property in the neighborhood in May of last year, and the same question was asked. Based on his research then, Stephen told Arthur that the prospective home was in the Astoria Park school zone. Stephen did not know the zone had been changed in August and honestly believed that he had told the facts as best he knew them. Stephen is:

   a. guilty of fraud and is liable for civil damages.
   b. guilty of negligent misrepresentation and may be liable for civil damages.
   c. guilty of concealment and will be disciplined by FREC.
   d. not guilty because he was unaware of the school zone change.

7. Justine Bates, a sales associate for Greatview Realty, Inc., wrote an ad for property which stated, in part, ". . . monthly payments of $967 PITI." What is the significance of this statement to Justine?

   a. It subjects her to FREC disciplinary action because she knows the payment figure exactly.
   b. It violates antitrust statutes.
   c. It violates RESPA's settlement costs section.
   d. It triggers required disclosures under Federal Reserve Regulation Z.

8. What homeowner's expenses are deductible for federal income taxes?

   I. Repairs and maintenance
   II. Interest
   III. Property taxes
   IV. Insurance
   a. I and II only
   b. II and III only
   c. I, II, and III only
   d. I, II, III, and IV

9. Broker Sandra shows a beautiful condominium to Sean O'Brien. The property is owned and occupied by Mr. and Mrs. Saddler. Sean gives Sandra a $5,000 deposit. She writes a contract that Mr. and Mrs. Saddler accept and provides the required disclosure documents to Sean on the same day. Seven days later, Sean's attorney calls and states that after his review of the documents, he deems them unsatisfactory. He requests a return of the $5,000 deposit. Sean:

   a. is entitled to the deposit because his attorney found the documents to be unsatisfactory and the buyer has a ten-day cancellation period.
   b. is not entitled to the deposit because no cancellation period exists for resale condominiums.
   c. is not entitled to the deposit because a three-day cancellation period exists for resale condominiums, and his attorney waited too long.
   d. has the right to rescind within 15 days.

10. There is special significance for licensees who sell homes built before 1978. That has to do with:

   a. coastal management zones.
   b. lead-based paint disclosures.
   c. Americans with Disabilities Act properties.
   d. the end of freely assumable FHA loans.

11. The Fair Housing Act, as amended, extends protection to:

    a. persons of Asian heritage.
    b. pregnant women.
    c. clinically obese persons.
    d. all of the above.

12. The Florida Radon Gas Protection Act:

    a. applies only to sales, not to leases.
    b. applies to sales and leases of less than 45 days.
    c. requires that a radon gas inspection be completed and the results be disclosed to the purchaser.
    d. requires a disclosure on all sales and lease contracts for more than 45 days

13. Felix Hasco, a time-share sales associate with Horizon Towers, sold several time-share units this month before he realized that his real estate license expired the previous month. He immediately completed the required continuing education, paid a late renewal fee, and reinstated his license to active status. If this comes to the attention of the FREC:

    a. his license will be suspended for 90 days.
    b. the mandatory penalty is suspension and fine.
    c. under FREC guidelines, the penalty would be revocation.
    d. because Felix works for the developer, the expiration of his license is a nonissue, even if he is paid by commission.

14. The major hazard(s) of lead-based paint is/are:

    a. severe disfigurement.
    b. skin lesions.
    c. neurological damage.
    d. blindness.

15. When listing a time-share unit, sales associates must disclose that:

    a. the association disclaims liability for any toxic substances found on the property.
    b. a buyer has 15 days after receiving all documents to cancel the contract.
    c. a rating system exists for energy efficiency.
    d. a seller has no guarantee that the time-share can be sold at any particular price or within any particular time period.

16. Sara Wilson makes an offer to purchase a home for sale by private owner Jack Babitt. Jack declines her offer, stating that the neighbors would be angry if he sold to a single African American woman. If Sara wanted to bring an action against Jack, she should proceed under:

    a. the Fair Housing Act of 1968.
    b. the Civil Rights Act of 1964.
    c. the Civil Rights Act of 1866.
    d. none; private owners are exempt.

17. Which step can a licensee take to avoid later claims of property defects?

    a. Recommend that the buyer order a home inspection report
    b. Obtain a property condition disclosure statement
    c. Inspect the property thoroughly
    d. All of the above

18. Which word does HUD consider (a) discriminatory catchword(s)?

    a. *Exclusive*
    b. *Integrated neighborhood*
    c. *Traditional neighborhood*
    d. All of the above

19. Jim and Bob are competing brokers in West Palm Beach. They meet at an educational seminar in Orlando and have lunch. While talking, they discuss the inroads that Discount Brokerage, Inc., is making on their market share. Each agrees to persuade the sales associates of his agency not to show any listings of that company in an effort to hurt the discount brokerage's business. The agreement:

    a. violates the Consumer Credit Protection Act.
    b. violates the Fair Practices in Business Act of 1986.
    c. violates antitrust laws.
    d. is a perfectly legal competitive action.

20. To claim innocent purchaser status under the hazardous substance statutes, a purchaser should:

    a. refuse to purchase former gas stations.
    b. pay for and obtain an extensive environmental audit.
    c. show that the seller did not reveal any problems.
    d. ask the real estate agent about any problems and blame him if one turns up later.

ACTION LIST

APPLY WHAT YOU'VE LEARNED!

The authors suggest the following actions to reinforce the material in *Section I–Legal Issues in Real Estate Practice:*

- Write a concise description of each brokerage relationship disclosure form that you could use to explain the form to customers.
- List the customer contacts you have had in the previous two weeks. If you acted as a transaction broker, did you tend to favor one party over another?
- Write a short list of each of the fiduciary responsibilities required of a single agent. Analyze each carefully, then select the responsibility you believe is most likely to be violated in the real world. Explain why.
- Write a script that you could use with a seller for introducing and explaining the property condition disclosure statement.
- If you own a home, estimate the tax savings from deductions for interest and taxes that your home ownership makes possible. Because you could have taken the standard deduction, subtract that amount from your total deductions to find the net savings.
- Select a federal law in this section. Go to the Internet and find a site that includes the statutes. Print the statutes, then read the law, highlighting the important parts. Does your interpretation of the law agree with the authors' explanation? Use the feedback at the back of the book for suggestions.

SECTION II

PROFESSIONALISM IN REAL ESTATE

This section of the text emphasizes that a sales associate's basic business philosophy of ethical behavior and professionalism is more important than learning the steps of listing or selling property. Because ethical conduct attempts to achieve an even higher standard than the law, ethics is discussed in detail.

After honesty and fair dealing, information is the most important attribute of a successful licensee. Knowledge and expertise are the stock in trade of brokers and sales associates, and those who know how to find and communicate that information will bring credit to the profession. Licensees need to learn about the new technology if they wish to play a part in this information explosion.

SECTION II

CHAPTER 3—REAL ESTATE ETHICS, EDUCATION, AND PLANNING

LEARNING OBJECTIVES

Upon completion of this chapter, *you should be able to:*

1. explain why a real estate sales associate needs additional knowledge and experience to become even more professional;
2. distinguish between the terms *ethical* and *legal;*
3. list three types of communication skills that the professional real estate sales associate must master;
4. list two methods of acquiring each of the three types of communication skills;
5. list the three types of knowledge a real estate sales associate needs and distinguish the differences between each type;
6. name at least five real estate courses of study that allow a licensee to acquire greater professional knowledge in specialized areas;
7. list the five requirements for effective goal setting;
8. convert long-term goals into more manageable short-term objectives;
9. understand the need to make a daily time schedule and to-do list;
10. calculate the hourly value of a sales associate's time;
11. cite the benefits and the pitfalls of employing a personal assistant; and
12. list at least ten functions that an unlicensed personal assistant can perform.

CHAPTER 3

REAL ESTATE ETHICS, EDUCATION, AND PLANNING

1 ## ACHIEVING PROFESSIONALISM

2 Customers of real estate licensees expect them to be knowledgeable, organized, and
3 effective in their duties. Because of this, the Florida Real Estate Commission (FREC) has
4 established minimum standards of professional education. The prelicense course for
5 sales associates provides basic information to familiarize licensees with the legal require-
6 ments of real estate practice. This course, Post-Licensing Education for Real Estate Sales
7 Associates, became a legal requirement in 1989. It was designed to help new sales asso-
8 ciates become proficient in the day-to-day practice of real estate and to provide neces-
9 sary training and guidance that is not uniformly available from all brokerage firms.
10 After satisfying the post-license requirement for the first license renewal, a licensee
11 must complete the required 14-hour continuing education before subsequent renewals.
12 The purpose of the continuing education requirement is to keep licensees aware of new
13 laws and changes in the real estate industry, and to give them the resources to do their
14 jobs well.

15 FREC-mandated course requirements have increased licensees' competence and
16 enhanced consumer protection. The goal of professionalism, however, is not easily
17 achieved. Professional knowledge and behavior come from additional study and hard
18 work beyond minimum legal requirements. Those licensees who do not act profession-
19 ally and competently may experience complaints about ethics and law violations, a
20 higher incidence of dissatisfied customers, more problems in closing sales, reduced
21 career satisfaction, and lower income.

22 Many of today's most successful real estate practitioners believe that the former reli-
23 ance on sales techniques to make the sale has given way to a much higher professional
24 standard. They have found that the professional who provides honesty, service, dili-
25 gence, and knowledge is far more successful than the stereotypical "hard sell" sales asso-
26 ciate who "closes" with manipulative techniques. This chapter deals with qualities that
27 better serve clients and customers:

28 • Professional ethics
29 • Communication skills
30 • Professional education
31 • Goal setting
32 • Time management

PROFESSIONAL ETHICS

A distinct difference exists between what is *ethical* and what is *legal.* License laws set a minimum standard of professional behavior, while codes of ethics set the higher standard of what is honest and fair to all parties involved in a real estate transaction.

Even the appearance of impropriety may cause customers to avoid doing business with a sales associate and his or her brokerage firm. The expression "perception is reality" holds true; such shortcomings are very damaging to a real estate career.

The National Association of REALTORS® (NAR) has standardized a code of **professional ethics,** so that all members are aware of and follow their professional responsibilities. NAR's Code of Ethics is extremely influential, not only to REALTORS® but to other licensees, because ethical codes often later become license laws. The code may be the best available guideline for ethical behavior whether or not a licensee is a member of NAR.

A Company Philosophy

Many brokerage firms include the NAR Code of Ethics in their own statements of business philosophy. An additional written company philosophy covering ethics, competence, and accountability communicates the expectation that all personnel must be committed to these principles. The new licensee should help his or her broker establish a written statement if one does not exist. Posting the business philosophy keeps the priorities visible to all personnel and customers. A sample company philosophy is shown in Figure 3.1.

COMMUNICATION SKILLS

Communication is at the heart of the real estate brokerage business. A licensee may be knowledgeable, competent, and ethical, yet because of a lack of communication skills, be unable to help customers successfully. The three types of communication skills necessary are:

1. verbal communication skills,
2. written communication skills, and
3. nonverbal communication skills.

Verbal Communication Skills

Talking to buyers, sellers, appraisers, surveyors, and other licensees enables the professional to share information, ask questions, and better understand the needs of others. The professional must be able to express information completely, honestly, and clearly. The individual who fails to master **verbal communication skills** may be misinterpreted, creating an appearance of incompetence or even dishonesty.

How does a person gain verbal communication skills? Community colleges and universities offer communication and public speaking classes to the public. Dale Carnegie courses have been recommended by communicators for years. One inexpensive way to learn to speak effectively is by joining a Toastmasters Club, a nonprofit service organization devoted to enhancing verbal communication skills. Many professional real estate licensees point to their years in Toastmasters as a key factor in their success.

Web Link

http://www.toastmasters.com
ToastMasters International

FIGURE 3.1 A SAMPLE OF ONE COMPANY'S PHILOSOPHY STATEMENT

OUR COMPANY PHILOSOPHY

We believe that for this firm to be successful, we must set out our philosophy of doing business as clearly as possible. These things, above all else, are important to us:

INTEGRITY

No other single attribute of a person or a business can have such an impact on success or failure. We believe that every action must be taken with truth and honesty, and if we must ask ourselves whether it is all right to do something, it probably is not. There must be honesty in every action, truth in every word. We expect honesty from our employees and our sales staff.

SERVICE

Our clients and customers have a right to expect outstanding service. We are paid not for our time, but for our service. If we expect to be well paid, we must provide the highest level of service available. We expect our employees and our sales staff to provide excellent service.

HARD WORK

No organization can grow and prosper unless each member of the team puts forth the maximum effort. Often, we feel a tendency to "let down" and to do less than our best. We expect hard work from our employees and our sales staff.

PROFESSIONAL COMPETENCE

We never should undertake an assignment for a client or customer unless we have the training and experience to do the job. We believe in continuing education, for only by learning better ways to provide service can we enhance our reputation. We expect our employees and sales staff to continue learning.

COOPERATION

An organization can be great when all members work together for a common purpose. It can be only mediocre when some row in different directions. Once the firm's goals are set, all members of the firm should work together to achieve those goals. Helping one another when possible, going out of our way to cooperate with each other, will bring harmony and wealth. We expect cooperation from our employees and sales staff.

ACCOUNTABILITY

Sometimes even the most competent professionals make mistakes. We understand this fact. Our clients and customers must be happy with their transactions, or we shall not get repeat business. If we make a mistake, we must be willing to stand accountable and to make it right with the customer. We expect our sales staff to be accountable for mistakes if a client is damaged.

PROFESSIONAL ETHICS

The Code of Ethics of the National Association of REALTORS® is a guide for our daily business operations. The laws of this state are clear as to our obligations to our clients and customers. Our employees and sales staff must observe the law and abide by the Code of Ethics.

This is our business philosophy. These things, above all else, are important to us. We shall not vary from these principles under any circumstances. We expect that of you.

1   When licensees prepare for oral presentations, they should know exactly what they
2 are going to say. They must organize the presentations so listeners can follow the
3 thought processes easily and gain greater understanding.

4   Choice of words is extremely important. For instance, the statement "We can finish
5 the deal by the end of the month" would be better stated as "We should be able to close
6 the transaction by the end of the month." The use of jargon is another common
7 problem. **Jargon** is a word or an expression related to a specialized vocation that a lay-
8 person may not understand. For instance, *floor duty* is a term describing the period
9 during which a sales associate is entitled to take all customer calls. It is a well-known
10 expression in real estate circles but is not familiar to consumers. If a customer calls the
11 office for information on a listed property and is told "Just a minute, I'll let you talk to
12 the associate on the floor," he may wonder whether there has been an accident or just
13 a lack of chairs. By avoiding jargon, a real estate professional helps clients and cus-
14 tomers better understand the information he is trying to relate.

15 Written Communication Skills

16 Letters and other forms of written communication are often the first impression
17 licensees make on members of the public. A letter containing bad grammar and
18 misspellings makes a poor impression. Written communications are extremely impor-
19 tant when writing a contract provision. Ambiguous clauses in a contract may result in
20 lost sales, lawsuits, and disciplinary action by the FREC.

DISCUSSION EXERCISE 3.1

Les shows a town home to a married couple who are interested in purchasing it
despite the fact that the property has been poorly maintained. The seller has told
Les that he would be willing to make reasonable repairs if the buyers include them
in the sales contract. So Les writes the following special clause in the contract:

"Seller agrees to remodel the town home and put everything into first-class condition."

Based on this clause, what will the buyer expect?

What will the seller want to do?

Is there a possibility for miscommunication here?

---

21   **Written communication skills** may be enhanced by taking courses at community
22 colleges, by reading books to improve writing skills, or by purchasing a book of ready-
23 made real estate letters, such as *Power Real Estate Letters,* by William H. Pivar. A dictio-
24 nary, a spell-checker on a software's word-processing program, and a thesaurus are
25 minimum requirements for achieving better written communication.

26 Nonverbal Communication Skills

27 **Nonverbal communication,** often called **body language,** can be very important in sales.
28 The real estate sales associate who understands body language will be better able to read
29 the attitudes of customers and develop body language that can make a client com-
30 fortable and establish rapport. Often, nonverbal communication can be far more
31 revealing than what a person says. Some obvious body language styles include those
32 described in the following chart.

Body Language	Probably means...	Comments
Pyramiding fingertips—the classic "banker" look	I'm superior to you and I'm making some judgments about you	Don't do this when talking to a customer
Pyramiding, leaning back in the chair with hands joined behind the head—the "boss"	I'm superior to you. You have less status here	Don't do this when talking to a customer
Arms folded across the chest	Closed, defensive	Bad sign; you'll get nowhere in this presentation until you get the listener loosened up
Legs crossed at the knee away from the listener with body facing to the side	Closed, defensive	Bad sign. You'll get nowhere in this presentation until you get the listener loosened up
Customer looking away (no eye contact) during a sales presentation	Closed, often unfriendly	Bad sign, unlikely to buy until you can establish rapport
Palms toward the person just before speaking	Stop talking. I have more important things to say	Don't do this when talking to a customer
Stroking the chin (mostly males); fingertips to the neck (mostly females)	Sign of seriously considering the proposal	Get ready to write the offer
Scratching the head	Thinking; may be about to make a decision	Ask to help with any questions the customer may have
Staring at the ceiling	Thinking; trying to remember a fact	Ask to help with any questions the customer may have
Leaning forward into sales presentation	Interested, attentive	Good sign; you're doing something right
Customer frowning during sales presentation	May indicate the customer disagrees, or does not understand some point	Trouble; try to ask a question to find out what's happening here
Hands hiding mouth while person is talking	Sometimes a habit of persons who are not speaking honestly	Probably OK, but some information may be incorrect
Hands on hips, head bowed, staring at you	Aggressive stance; challenge	This could mean trouble

1 A real estate sales associate who wants to be more effective might consider using
2 some of the following body language:

3 • Your handshake should not be too hard, but not too soft, either.
4 • Usually, direct eye contact when you are talking or listening is good. Staring without
5   blinking or looking away occasionally may be disconcerting. In some areas of the
6   world, constant direct eye contact may be disrespectful.
7 • Cross nothing. Arms and legs should be open and relaxed.
8 • Lean forward into the conversation to display your interest. If you lean backward, it
9   may be a sign of superiority or aloofness.

10 **Web Link**

11 http://members.aol.com/nonverbal2/index.htm
12 Center for Nonverbal Studies. This is a site rich in observations of nonverbal commu-
13 nication.

DISCUSSION EXERCISE 3.2

Larry is making a listing presentation to Jack, a for-sale-by-owner. He notices Jack has faced to the side, folded his arms over his chest, and looked in another direction.

What feedback is Jack giving Larry about his presentations?

PROFESSIONAL EDUCATION

Licensees enhance their professionalism through continuing education. The law requires some basic continuing education before renewal of a license, but a great deal of the professional education available is not required by law. National organizations award professional designations to graduates of their educational programs. The designations make consumers aware of those persons who have exceeded the legally required continuing education. Figure 3.2 shows some of the many educational opportunities available for a real estate professional.

Other types of education, when combined with formal instruction, also enhance a licensee's competence. In *Real Estate Brokerage: A Success Guide,* by Cyr, Sobeck, and McAdams, the authors describe three types of knowledge sales associates need:

1. Technical knowledge
2. Marketing knowledge
3. Product knowledge

Technical Knowledge

Technical knowledge provides the tools of the business, such as completing contracts properly, knowing sellers' and buyers' costs, and understanding the comparative market analysis process. It includes the subject matter required in the prelicense course, such as legal descriptions, financing, deeds, property rights, and the laws and rules regulating the practice of real estate in Florida. Sales associates should not work in the field without the appropriate technical knowledge. For example, sales associates will feel quite incompetent if they cannot fill out the Cost Disclosure Statement or contract form. One of the purposes of this course is to provide the new licensee with the technical knowledge to become competent and confident with consumers. Technical knowledge also includes knowledge about state and federal laws, such as fair-housing and antitrust laws.

Marketing Knowledge

Learning how to sell real estate comes from **marketing knowledge.** It encompasses the knowledge of psychology and the ability to assess a consumer's specific housing needs. Marketing knowledge includes prospecting for listings, pricing the listings fairly, advertising, qualifying buyers, showing properties and closing transactions. Many sales training books and tapes are available commercially. Institutes and societies of the National Association of REALTORS® as well as local Boards of REALTORS® offer sales training classes. Many brokerage firms and franchise companies hold regular sales training courses for sales personnel. Marketing knowledge is an important tool of the trade, and it is a major part of the service consumers expect when buying and selling real estate.

FIGURE 3.2   EDUCATIONAL OPPORTUNITIES FOR REAL ESTATE PROFESSIONALS

SPECIALTY	DESIGNATION	ORGANIZATION
Agricultural	Accredited Land Consultant (ALC)	REALTORS® Land Institute
Appraising	Member, Appraisal Institute (MAI)	Appraisal Institute
	Senior Residential Appraiser (SRA)	Appraisal Institute
	Independent Fee Appraiser (IFA)	National Association of Independent Fee Appraisers
	Certified Business Appraiser (CBA)	Institute of Business Appraisers
Commercial investment	Certified Commercial Investment Member (CCIM)	Commercial Investment Real Estate Institute
Industrial	Professional Real Estate Executive (PRE)	Society of Industrial and Office REALTORS®
Property management	Certified Property Manager (CPM)	Institute of Real Estate Management
Residential	Graduate, REALTORS® Institute (GRI)	Florida Association of REALTORS®
	Certified Residential Specialist (CRS)	Residential Sales Council
	Certified Residential Broker (CRB)	Real Estate Brokerage Managers Council
Securities	Certified Real Estate Securities Member (CRESM)	Real Estate Securities and Syndication Institute

---

DISCUSSION EXERCISE 3.3

Traci has been in the real estate business for about a month and is working with her first buyer customers, referred to her from a close friend. She shows them a home listed by another sales associate in her office. The buyers immediately start to talk about where to place their furniture. "We think this is the one," they tell Traci.

It is Saturday afternoon, and Traci is unable to contact the broker to answer some questions about how to complete the required forms. Nervously, she tells the buyers, "You know, I hate to see you rush into anything. There are some other houses out there you might like better. I can show them to you tomorrow, if you like. That'll give you time to think about it all, too!"

What is Traci's main objective at this moment?

How could Traci have been better prepared for this situation?

Product Knowledge

Being in the marketplace is the best way for licensees to acquire **product knowledge** and to know what property is available. Customers expect their real estate sales associates to know the market. They want the benefits of that product knowledge in marketing a property or finding the right property for purchase. A new practitioner should work hard to get that knowledge as quickly as possible to best serve the consumer.

How does one gain product knowledge? By seeing property. Outstanding trainers say that the most important step a new licensee can take is to become familiar with the marketplace, which means looking at properties. Some firms recommend that their new sales associates take at least two weeks to see as many listings as possible. They suggest maintaining that product knowledge by regularly scheduling time to look at property.

Licensees gain knowledge from experience, formal classroom work and on-the-job training by brokers. The education from formal classroom sessions and continuing education is essential. There is an old saying that "experience is the best teacher." Most brokers and sales associates would disagree, however. Gaining experience without education and training is a risky, expensive, and difficult method of learning.

Most experts advise that, while they can use the experience of others, new licensees can learn more effectively from continuing education programs, formal broker training programs, professional seminars, and Board of REALTORS® programs. The professional sales associate starts from a higher level by learning from the classroom, books, and videos what others have learned from experience. Newton, who defined our laws of gravity, perhaps said it best: "If I saw farther, it was because I stood on the shoulders of giants."

Another benefit of professional training is the advantage it provides in saving wasted effort and time.

SETTING GOALS, PLANNING, AND TIME MANAGEMENT

To be successful in any venture, an individual must set **goals.** Goal setting is probably even more important in real estate sales. Real estate sales associates are usually independent contractors; they receive little supervision. This situation is very different from being an employee. Without goals, the practitioner may experience a lack of focus and direction. The goals should be written, measurable, attainable, and flexible and should contain deadlines. Once goals have been set, a **plan** should show how to achieve the goals. Time management is an important part of that plan.

A distinction can be made between goals, plans, and time management. For example, an automobile trip from Orlando to St. Louis requires all three:

1. The goal is St. Louis.
2. The plan is the road map on which is drawn the route and mileage.
3. Time management consists of the daily objectives: When do we leave, when do we stop for food, and how far should we go today?

Goal setting should begin with a long-term view: What accomplishments does a person want to achieve in his lifetime? Once this long-term view is established, the next step is to work back to the present, using smaller increments of time. By working from the long term to the short term, it becomes clear what a licensee must do this year, and this week, and today to achieve the long-term goal.

A new licensee who wishes to achieve high levels of professional competence and financial security must set goals. When setting these goals, the professional should always include personal and family objectives. An example of professional goal setting follows:

1   A licensee's five-year goals are:

2   • having a broker's license;
3   • owning and managing a brokerage firm with at least 15 associates;
4   • earning professional education designations to include the GRI, CRS, and CRB; and
5   • acquiring $40,000 in cash and securities.

6   To achieve the five-year goal, the licensee decides she must accomplish the following
7   within two years:

8   • Take and pass the Florida Broker Examination
9   • Earn the GRI professional designation and meet some of the CRS qualifications
10   • Acquire cash and securities of $16,000 (two-fifths of $40,000).

11   It is easy to convert the two-year goal into a one-year goal:

12   • Sales post-license course completed, broker course applied for
13   • Two of the required GRI courses completed
14   • Cash and securities of $8,000 acquired

15   Once the licensee establishes her one-year goal, she converts it into monthly and
16   weekly goals—short-term tasks.

17   Use the worksheet shown in Figure 3.3 to see what you must do today to achieve a
18   $48,000 income objective. If the assumptions shown are appropriate for your market
19   area, it is simple to project how you can accomplish the goal. This example focuses on
20   income goals, but the same exercise could be completed for other goals.

21   When the licensee is aware of what she must do today to achieve her long-term goals,
22   she writes out the goals in contract form. It can be a private contract or a "public" doc-
23   ument, with copies delivered to the broker and a mentor. Giving a copy to another
24   person usually strengthens a commitment to succeed in the goals. A sample goals con-
25   tract might look like the one in Figure 3.4.

26   The licensee then posts the goals where they are visible to her. "Out of sight, out of
27   mind" is true where goals are concerned.

Forms   28   A blank worksheet for your personal goals is included in the Forms-To-Go Section.

Daily Goals and Time Management

30   **Time management** goes hand in hand with goal setting. Goals can never work without
31   a schedule. Besides being measurable and attainable, a deadline must be set for
32   achieving the goals. For example, the goal of "making as many calls as possible to pro-
33   spective sellers" is attainable, but immeasurable because no time deadline has been
34   established. The statement "I will make five calls to prospective sellers by 6 P.M. today"
35   is clear and measurable and results in accomplishing the goal.

36   The licensee should make a **"to-do" list** before each workday starts. She should keep
37   the list nearby and check off each item as it is completed. This ensures that all items are
38   covered and provides a sense of accomplishment and motivation to continue. Some
39   helpful points to remember about the list:

40   • Transfer unfinished tasks from the previous day.
41   • Include those daily tasks from the goals worksheet that are necessary to achieve long-
42   term goals.
43   • **Prioritize** items on the list.
44   • Put the least pleasant items at the beginning of the list ("Eat the frog first"). Complet-
45   ing the tough tasks results in the ability to get on with achieving important goals.
46   • Establish times for completing each task. Even if they need to be adjusted later, you
47   have established a basic guideline to follow.
48   • Make notes for items to include on tomorrow's list.

FIGURE 3.3

GOALS WORKSHEET

1. During the next 12 months, I want to earn	$48,000
2. That works out to be monthly earnings of (Line 1 ÷ 12)	$ 4,000
3. Probably 60% of my earnings should come from listings sold (Line 2 × .60)	$ 2,400
4. Probably 40% of my earnings should come from sales made (Line 2 × .40)	$ 1,600

Achieving my listing income:

5. In my market area, the average listing commission amount is (Get this amount from your broker.)	$ 1,200
6. So I must have the following number of listings sold (Line 3 ÷ Line 5)	2
7. If only 75% of my listings sell, I have to get this many listings (Line 6 ÷ .75)	2.67
8. It may take this many listing appointments to get a listing (Get this number from your broker.)	5
9. So I need to go on this many listing appointments (Line 7 × Line 8)	13.3
10. It may take this many calls to get an appointment (Get this number from your broker.)	10
11. So I have to make this many calls per month (Line 9 × Line 10)	133
12. Which means I must make this many calls per week (Line 11 ÷ 4.3 weeks per month)	31

Achieving my sales income:

13. In my market area, the average sales commission is (Get this amount from your broker.)	$ 1,200
14. So I've got to make this many sales per month (Line 4 ÷ Line 13)	1.3
15. It takes about this many showings to make a sale (Get this number from your broker.)	20
16. So I must show this many properties per month (Line 14 × Line 15)	26

Time Management Hints

A licensee can do many things that help him manage his time more effectively:

- Schedule time for family, recreation, exercise, and relaxation. Failing to plan for these items can result in guilt feelings, discontent, poor health, or burnout.
- Make a time log of all activities (in 15-minute segments) for about two weeks. This should show where time is wasted and may give clues for being a more effective time manager.
- Review from the log the percentage of time actually spent with clients and customers.

Doubling your income may not require working twice as many total hours, just increasing the time you spend with qualified buyers and sellers. Use the following hints to help you achieve that goal:

- Qualify sellers and buyers based on their financial ability to complete a transaction, as well as on their motivation. Working with unqualified buyers and sellers is both a disservice to the consumers and a nonproductive use of time.

FIGURE 3.4

GOALS CONTRACT

I, _____, have determined my career and financial goals voluntarily, independently and without coercion. I now formally commit to the following:

During the next 12 months, I will earn (from Line 1)	$48,000
I will obtain at least this number of listings per month (from Line 7)	2.67
I will go on this number of listing appointments weekly (Line 9 ÷ 4.3)	3
I will make this many listing calls weekly (from Line 12)	31
I will make this many sales each month (from Line 14)	1.3
I will show this many properties each week (Line 16 ÷ 4.3)	6

If I begin to fall behind, I request that my broker remind me of this commitment and prod me to stay on schedule so that I can achieve my goals.

_____   _____
Date   My signature

_____   _____
Date   My broker's signature

_____   _____
Date   My mentor's signature

- Be on time for appointments. Being late is a quick way to lose the confidence of customers. Plan for contingencies such as rush-hour traffic, last-minute phone calls, and weather-related inconveniences.
- Understand how much each hour of your day is worth. For example, if you earn $48,000 per year and work 290 days per year, nine hours per day, you work 2,610 hours, and the hourly rate is approximately $18.40.
- Make cost-effective decisions. Hiring a personal assistant at $7 per hour, for instance, may be more cost effective than doing your own mailouts and clerical work for $18.40 per hour. Going home to wash the car Monday afternoon may cost you $18.40 versus $5.95 at a car wash.
- Utilize technology to increase productivity.
- Avoid those activities that waste time. Examples include idle conversation, poor organization and planning, and uncontrolled interruptions. Therefore, if your time is worth $18.40 per hour, it is easy to calculate that idle conversation for four hours each week with associates in the office costs you nearly $75!

Time Management and the Use of a Personal Assistant

Licensed Personal Assistants. Licensed personal assistants are very valuable and can provide a full range of real estate services for the customers of the employing licensee, including showing and listing properties, calling prospects, and providing access

DISCUSSION EXERCISE 3.4

Do a role-playing session, assigning parts to Sharon, John, and the broker.

Sharon: (*Excited*) I did it! I got that FSBO over on Killearney Way!
Now I have another showing appointment. I *love* this business.
Gotta go! See you later!

John: (Dejected, shaking head) How does she keep doing it? She seems to get
one appointment after another. I'm still slogging along trying to finish
up my daily plan. I've got eight more things to do!

Broker: (*Sympathetically*) Tell me what you have done today, John.

John: Well, I had to make copies of the plat book pages for my farm area,
make up a list of all the people on Scenic Drive, take my clothes to the
cleaners, shop for a financial calculator, go to the title insurance company to get a rate card, and get my car washed. I did all that.

Broker: What is still on the list to do?

John: I still need to find some listings for the guy who called on my floor duty
yesterday and tell him about some property. I've got to get back in touch
with the buyer I showed property to last week to set up another appointment.

Oh! And I need to get a market report back to my wife's friends who said
they're interested in selling their house. I also got a response to the
notice of sale cards I mailed last week. I need to call those people back.
They said they might consider selling. And the tenants on Jackson Bluff
Road think they may be ready to buy. I need to call them and set up a
time.

There's just not enough time in the day!

Can you help John evaluate his time management skills so he can be as productive
as Sharon?

to a listed property. A licensed personal assistant must be registered under the employing broker and may be paid for brokerage activities only by the broker. A sales associate
may pay the licensed personal assistant for nonselling activities, but may not compensate a personal assistant for performance of brokerage activities that require a license.

Unlicensed Personal Assistants. Many licensees now employ unlicensed assistants
to help complete routine office activities, such as mass mailings, writing ads, and preparing comparative market analyses. Sales associates who employ such assistants, and
their brokers, must ensure that the assistant does not perform any activities that violate
the law. A list of activities that may be performed by unlicensed personal assistants is
shown in Figure 3.5.

An unlicensed individual may *not* negotiate or agree to any commission split or referral fee on behalf of a licensee.

FIGURE 3.5   UNLICENSED PERSONAL ASSISTANT ACTIVITIES

1. Answer and forward telephone calls.
2. Fill out and submit listings and changes to any multiple-listing service.
3. Follow up on loan commitments after a contract has been negotiated and generally secure status reports on the loan application.
4. Assemble documents for closing.
5. Secure public information documents from courthouse, utility district, etc.
6. Make keys for company listings.
7. Write ads for approval of licensee and supervising broker, place advertising in newspapers, etc.
8. Receive, record, and deposit earnest money, security deposits, and advance rents.
9. Type contract forms for approval by licensee and supervising broker.
10. Monitor licenses and personnel files.
11. Compute commission checks.
12. Place signs on property.
13. Order items of repair as directed by the licensee.
14. Prepare flyers and promotional information for approval by licensee and supervising broker.
15. Act as a courier service to deliver documents, pick up keys.
16. Place routine telephone calls on late rent payments.
17. Schedule appointments for licensees to show *listed* property.
18. Be at an open house for
    a. security purposes.
    b. to hand out materials (brochures).
    c. to respond to questions that may be answered with objective information from preprinted information.
19. Answer verbal questions concerning a listing if the answer to the question may be obtained from preprinted information, is objective in nature, and no subjective comments are made.
20. Gather information for a comparative market analysis (CMA).
21. Gather information for an appraisal.
22. Hand out objective, written information on a listing or rental.
23. Drive a customer or client to a listing or rental.
24. Give a key to a prospect at the licensee's office and nowhere else.

Unlicensed personal assistants, since they are paid by salary and may not be paid commissions, are under the control of their licensee employers. They may not be classified as independent contractors. The employers must withhold and pay FICA and income taxes and file withholding tax reports on a timely basis. Penalties for noncompliance can be substantial. Licensed personal assistants may be paid by commission, but commissions may be paid only by the broker. If the licensed assistant is paid a salary, or assigned specific working hours or told how to do the work, she would be an employee rather than an independent contractor.

A licensee also should be aware of the liability of having employees. An accident on the job could make the licensee employer liable, as could an employee who injures another person while running errands for the licensee.

SUMMARY

Licensees who meet only the minimum education requirements of the license law cannot be called professionals in the true sense of the word. To be classified as a professional, a real estate sales associate will:

- display an ethical and moral code of conduct so that their business practices bring credit to the themselves, the brokerage firm and the industry;
- acquire and use verbal, written, and nonverbal communication skills to share information in a clear, easily understood manner in order to reduce the chance of misunderstandings and misrepresentation;
- acquire greater real estate knowledge through education programs and specialization (The three types of knowledge required are technical knowledge, marketing knowledge, and product knowledge.);
- set goals that are written, measurable, attainable, flexible, and that establish deadlines (Setting goals allows new licensees to achieve those business and personal objectives that provide the ability to grow professionally and provide better customer service. Time management allows sales associates to meet commitments and maximize their efforts to provide good service.); and
- be evaluated constantly by prospective customers (The fine tapestry of professionalism is woven by using all the threads of ethics, communication skills, education, time management, and available tools such as computers.).

This book is designed to give licensees knowledge and practical applications that will assist them in becoming more professional. Higher levels of professionalism result in an enhanced reputation for the real estate industry in Florida.

DEFINE THESE KEY TERMS

body language	prioritize
ethical	product knowledge
goal	professional ethics
jargon	technical knowledge
legal	time management
marketing knowledge	"to-do" list
nonverbal communication	verbal communication skills
plan	written communication skills

CHAPTER 3 PRACTICE EXAM

1. Jacqueline is a new agent with Seashore Realty. She hires an unlicensed personal assistant for $7 per hour. The unlicensed assistant can NOT:

   a. write ads for approval by the licensee and her supervising broker and place classified advertising.
   b. place signs on properties.
   c. show a buyer several listed properties (inside and out), provide complete information, and help the buyer write the offer.
   d. gather information for a CMA.

2. A licensee working as a property manager who wants to become more professional in that field probably wants to become a(n):

   a. MAI.
   b. GRI.
   c. CCIM.
   d. CPM.

3. Within five years, Cindy wants to have $50,000 in cash in the bank. She is just starting out in real estate and has just enough cash available for her living expenses. Without considering interest on the funds, how much cash should Cindy have by the end of year three if she is to make her goal?

   a. $35,000
   b. $32,000
   c. $30,000
   d. $24,000

4. The best available formal guideline for licensee behavior that is not a legal requirement is:

   a. FREC rules.
   b. Chapter 475. F.S.
   c. the Florida Administrative Code.
   d. the NAR Code of Ethics.

5. You can improve your written communication skills by:

   a. attending a community college course on writing.
   b. joining Toastmasters.
   c. reading books on the subject.
   d. doing both a and c.

6. Jonathon calls Jones Realty to speak with Arthur about a property he wants to see. Arthur's secretary tells him, "Arthur is on the caravan." Puzzled, Jonathon hangs up with thoughts of the desert. This is an example of:

   a. Jonathon's lack of communication skills.
   b. jargon.
   c. nonverbal communication.
   d. a common term that buyers and sellers of real estate should understand.

7. Jan is in the office when she gets a call from a property owner who wants to list her home. Jan is uncertain about how to do a CMA and how to complete the necessary forms. Based on this information, Jan lacks:

   a. technical knowledge.
   b. product knowledge.
   c. marketing knowledge.
   d. communication skills.

8. What is true about an unlicensed personal assistant?

   a. The employing licensee may be financially liable for accidents involving the personal assistant.
   b. The employing licensee may be responsible for violations of the license law or FREC rules.
   c. The licensee's employing broker may be financially responsible for acts of the personal assistant, as well as for violations of the license law or FREC rules.
   d. All of the above are true.

9. Setting and meeting goals involves:

   a. starting with short-range increments.
   b. starting with long-term goals, then breaking them down into short-term objectives.
   c. writing them down.
   d. doing both b and c.

10. Tim's goal is to make $58,000 in gross collected commissions next year. He feels that his listings should contribute about 50 percent of the required income. The average commission per transaction in his office is $1,200, and about two-thirds of his listings are expected to sell. He gets about three listings in five listing presentations. Approximately how many presentations must he make monthly to stay on target?

   a. Two
   b. Three
   c. Five
   d. Ten

11. Larry's goal is "to make as much money as I can next year." What is true about his goal?

   a. As long as he works toward the goal, it is effective.
   b. It is not measurable.
   c. It is not attainable.
   d. It should be combined with a time management plan that says "I'll work until I get tired most days."

12. An effective method of finding out where time is wasted in a daily schedule is to:

   a. keep good goal sheets.
   b. make a time log of activities.
   c. ask your spouse.
   d. measure the distance from appointment to appointment.

SECTION II

CHAPTER 4—INFORMATION AND TECHNOLOGY

LEARNING OBJECTIVES

Upon completion of this chapter, *you should be able to:*

1. list at least six ways that computers can help a licensee become more professional;
2. list at least five pieces of peripheral computer equipment that enhance a computer's performance;
3. describe the functions performed by at least five of the general-purpose software categories;
4. list seven types of software specifically designed to help real estate practitioners serve their customers and principals more effectively;
5. explain the two major benefits to a licensee who uses the Internet;
6. define the term *hypertext* and understand its use;
7. explain the two primary methods of searching for information on the Internet;
8. explain the FREC rules relating to marketing on the internet;
9. list four major objectives in Web site design;
10. describe the advantages in designing and publishing your own Web site;
11. describe the components of a Web site that require more time for it to load;
12. describe the benefits of using e-mail in real estate practice; and
13. explain the purpose and effect of the Federal E-sign legislation.

CHAPTER 4

INFORMATION AND TECHNOLOGY

1 Real estate is an information business, and technology is changing the way real estate
2 professionals gather and distribute information. Powerful computers and software are
3 now distributed in huge quantities, and prices have come down to a level that makes it
4 possible for even more people to enjoy the benefits.

5 The Internet, which may be as significant as Gutenberg's printing press in its ability
6 to deliver information, provides licensees with more resources to give customers the
7 highest level of service.

8 This chapter will cover some of the following areas:

9 • Computer hardware
10 • Software
11 • The Internet
12 • Internet conferences
13 • E-mail

COMPUTERS

15 Computers are the most important productivity tools available to real estate licensees,
16 giving them:

17 • easy access to multiple-listing service (MLS) listing data and other online informa-
18   tion, such as property tax information;
19 • print quality with laser and inkjet printers nearly equal to professional typesetting;
20 • ease of writing and editing with computer word processors, which provide better
21   products in less time than do electric typewriters (Many offices no longer even *have*
22   typewriters!);
23 • the ability to include computer graphics in brochures and flyers, giving attractive pre-
24   sentations more marketing impact;
25 • accounting packages that provide immediate financial statements (The programs
26   have options for analysis that would be too time-consuming with manual bookkeep-
27   ing methods.);
28 • quick monthly property management statements; and
29 • spreadsheet analyses that give commercial brokers the ability to immediately see the
30   financial effect on an investor if basic assumptions about the property are changed.

1   A licensee who wants to purchase a computer should first talk to several brokers and
2   sales associates who currently use computers in their businesses. Before making a deci-
3   sion to buy, the licensee should get answers to some of the following questions:

4   • What tasks does the broker or sales associate use the computer to accomplish?
5   • If the broker or sales associate were buying new equipment today, which computer
6   would she purchase?
7   • Which printer best fulfills a licensee's needs?
8   • What peripheral equipment should the licensee purchase?
9   • Which software does the broker or sales associate recommend?

10   The licensee also can gain valuable information by reading recent issues of computer
11   magazines like *PC Magazine, Windows Magazine,* and *PC World.* Both *REALTOR*®
12   *Magazine,* published by the National Association of REALTORS® (NAR), and *Florida*
13   *REALTOR*® magazine feature regular columns about real estate computer applications.

14   Two important decisions for the licensee are which equipment (hardware) and which
15   programs (software) to purchase.

16 COMPUTER HARDWARE

17   Today's computers are far more powerful, but much cheaper. In 1992, computing
18   power cost $120 for each *million instructions per second (MIPS).* By 2003, the cost had
19   declined to about 72 cents per MIPS. Entry-level computer system prices have dropped
20   enough so that almost everyone can afford one. Some of the considerations include
21   whether it should be a laptop or desktop, and what features are necessary.

22 Laptop or Desktop?

23   Should the new licensee buy a **laptop** or a **desktop** computer? Most sales associates'
24   work areas are where they are at the moment. That may be in the car, at home, at the
25   office, or in a customer's home. Laptops are portable and are probably the best choice.
26   By regularly downloading the MLS data, the information is online and available imme-
27   diately. Without a laptop, the sales associate would need one computer at home and one
28   computer at the office, so even though laptop computers cost more, it can be consid-
29   ered a saving. The screen displays on laptop computers now rival those of a conven-
30   tional monitor.

31 Get a Big Color Monitor

32   The minimum size monitor for comfort today is 17 inches. While it costs somewhat
33   more than a 15-inch monitor, the user can display much more data and reduce eye-
34   strain. Flat screen monitors are becoming the standard.

35 Get a Fast Computer with Lots of Memory

36   The processor power speed should be 2 gigahertz or higher. Slower computers will do
37   many tasks, but for graphics, the faster the better. A fast processor is wasted, however,
38   if the computer does not have enough memory. **Random access memory (RAM)** is the
39   "live" memory used while the computer is on. Generally, a person should buy as much
40   memory as they can afford. Because of the size of today's software programs,
41   128 megabytes of RAM is the minimum to consider on a new machine, with at least
42   512 megabytes recommended. More memory makes the computer work faster. It also
43   allows the user to have many software applications open at once. Inadequate memory
44   can cause a system **"crash."** A system crash results in loss of any unsaved data.

Get a Big Hard Drive

All information in RAM is lost when the computer is turned off, so programs and data should be saved permanently on a "hard drive." Because software programs are becoming much larger with each new version, choose a drive with at least 40 but preferably 100 gigabytes of memory or more.

Get a Rewritable CD Drive

A **compact disc (CD) drive** allows the user to access large collections of data or graphics without having to store all of the data on the hard drive. Many CD collections have thousands of photos and clip art graphics. Most software programs are sold on CDs. The CD drive should be fast, at least 24 times the basic speed ("24X") for satisfactory performance, especially when sound and videos are used.

It is preferable to spend more to get a **rewritable CD drive (CD-RW)** that will write data to a compact disc. The CD-RW is an excellent device for backing up large quantities of data, graphics, or sound files. It is worth the extra cost to eliminate the need to buy a backup tape drive. This CD backup will protect against data loss in case of a hard disk crash. Almost every user has had that experience, and those who haven't are about to. All data should be backed up at least weekly.

Protect the Power Supply

Protecting the computer against temporary power loss is essential. An uninterruptible power supply (UPS) is a surge protector that instantly switches to battery backup if electric power is cut off. The user then has time to save the work in progress, close each program, and shut down the computer correctly, with no data loss.

Get a Fast Modem

A **modem** lets the computer talk with other computers by phone, send and receive faxes, and act as an answering machine, with many voice-mail stations. The modem should be the fastest available. Using the Internet with a slow modem is frustrating and time-consuming. The time saved in transferring files will justify the small additional cost of a fast modem.

DSL Lines and Cable Modems Move Data Much Faster

Fiber-optic cable lines with cable modems allow transfer rates many times faster than standard voice telephone lines. DSL lines allow the user to use only one phone line for voice and simultaneous computer use. The DSL technology greatly speeds data transmission. Competition will probably bring prices even lower.

Scanners Put Pictures or Text into Your Computer

A **scanner** allows the user to copy pictures or text into the computer. The photos can be cropped, edited, and resized. Text can be stored or edited, resulting in a substantial time saving over retyping. Licensees can also use the scanner to archive important documents.

A Good Printer Makes a Better Impression

Laser printers are available today that print text and graphics with outstanding quality. Color ink-jet printers provide full color printing approaching photo quality. While the printers are inexpensive, color printing is quite costly. A page of black-and-white text costs eight cents to print on an **inkjet printer,** vs. three cents on a laser printer. Photo printing on glossy paper can cost up to $1 per page.

Digital Cameras Save Time and Money

Digital cameras offer significant savings to real estate licensees and appraisers. One busy appraiser reported annual savings on film and processing alone was three or four times the cost of the camera. Licensees may take photos, and put them directly into the computer, where they can be cropped and enhanced. A good camera costs around $600 and produces high quality photos.

Handheld Computers Bring Your Office on the Road

Handheld computers, also called *personal digital assistants* (PDAs) give licensees an entirely new way to send e-mails while on the road and to keep appointment schedules, address books, and task lists. The PDAs are fast replacing the daily planners in book form. Most PDAs have Web browsers, word processors, and spreadsheets, and are able to convert handwriting into text. Some include built-in microphone, speaker, stereo headphone jack, and the ability to record and play back voice notes. Handhelds can be set up to synchronize files with a desktop computer system.

Real estate professionals most often select PDAs that run the Palm operating system because they provide better service and easier uploads when used with contact managers such as Top Producer or ACT. They can be very useful for downloading all or part of the MLS database for use in the field. Entering text or numbers, however, can be cumbersome unless the user attaches a small optional keyboard. Most users enter text and numbers into their desktop or laptop computers, then download into the PDA.

Web Links

www.

http://www.zdnet.com/products/
>   ZDNet has reviews of nearly every type of computer hardware and peripherals, as well as price comparisons.

http://www.cnet.com/
>   CNET has many hardware and software reviews, price comparisons, and downloads of free software and shareware.

COMPUTER PROGRAMS (SOFTWARE)

Computer **hardware** is an assortment of chips and transistors that cannot do much without computer programs. The **software** does the tasks we want accomplished. Most users want several general purpose programs, available at computer stores, by mail order, or through the Internet. Real estate software is designed specifically for real estate practitioners.

General Purpose Software

Some basic software is necessary for general office tasks, such as word processing, spreadsheet calculations, accounting, lists, and presentations:

Word Processing Programs.   This software simplifies the production of documents and brochures. In fact, once the licensee is familiar with the product, the typewriter becomes obsolete. The ability to cut and paste makes editing much simpler, and graphics and charts are included easily for greater impact. Spell checking, a thesaurus, and grammar checking are included in most programs. Outstanding word processing software includes *WordPerfect* and *MS Word*.

Spreadsheet Programs.   **Spreadsheet** software accomplishes tasks such as preparation of financial data, amortization schedules, and charts. The spreadsheet has impres-

1 sive power because of the user's ability to make a template with formulas. Adjustments
2 to one amount change all other data based on the formulas entered. Many templates
3 and samples are available for a wide range of financial calculations, giving the user a
4 head start. *Excel* and *Lotus 1-2-3* are outstanding spreadsheet programs.

5 **Database Programs.**   Database software allows the user to enter lists of people, prop-
6 erties, or organizations and sort records by many characteristics. Licensees can import
7 information from the MLS or from the tax rolls and convert the data into mailing lists
8 or prospect files.

DISCUSSION EXERCISE 4.1

Most people who use a computer regularly have a favorite program they recommend to others. What is your principal word processor? Do you have a favorite spreadsheet? What other programs do you recommend?

---

9 **Bookkeeping Programs.**   Bookkeeping software lets the licensee manage business
10 and personal finances, print checks, and prepare tax returns at year end. Financial state-
11 ments are quick and easy to display, with many formats. Budget preparation is simple,
12 and bookkeeping programs compare actual income and expenses with the current
13 budget and with prior periods. *Quicken* is the market leader; other software includes
14 *Managing Your Money* and *Money*. *Quickbooks* and *Peachtree Accounting* are more powerful
15 accounting programs for small businesses.

16 **Presentation Programs.**   These programs help licensees give listing and sales presen-
17 tations and training sessions. Color graphics, moving charts and sound bring excite-
18 ment to the presentations. Many licensees use *Powerpoint* and *Freelance*.

19 **Clip Art Collections.**   Such collections are offered on CD format, and many have hun-
20 dreds of thousands of graphics, including photos, clip art and borders. These programs
21 give licensees the resources to design presentation flyers or publish an interesting and
22 attractive Web site.

23 **Mapping Programs.**   Using mapping software, licensees can produce colorful loca-
24 tion maps of properties for sale with captions for roads, buildings, and other landmarks.
25 These maps can help market a client's listing.

26 **Real Estate Software.**   While general purpose software is important because of its
27 versatility, real estate agents often need software designed for specific real estate spe-
28 cialties, as discussed below.

29 **Ad-Writing Programs.**   Advertising software composes imaginative real estate ads
30 based on property information a licensee enters. Most programs are designed to comply
31 with fair housing laws and truth-in-lending laws, although the licensee remains ultimately
32 responsible for ensuring that all advertising complies with the laws. Some programs
33 also keep track of advertising costs and number of calls generated for each property.

34 **Comparative Market Analysis (CMA) Programs.**   CMA software generates profes-
35 sional reports on which licensees base their opinions of value for single-family homes or
36 small income properties. Most programs allow downloads of comparable information
37 from a local MLS or from another source, such as the local tax appraiser. CMA prepa-
38 ration is discussed more fully in Chapter 5.

DISCUSSION EXERCISE 4.2

What is the most commonly used method of preparing CMAs in your market area? Is raw data printed directly from the MLS? Have you worked with a CMA software program? Are you looking into the purchase of a CMA program?

---

1 **Multipurpose Programs.**   Some real estate software, such as *Top Producer, Prep,* and
2 *The On-Line Agent,* include several modules that help licensees with client follow-up,
3 CMA preparation, listing presentations, flyer templates, ad writing, letter libraries, con-
4 tract tracking and more. Licensees who use these programs can offer very professional
5 material to consumers.

6 **Web Link**

www. 7 http://www.topproducer.com/
↖ 8   Top Producer software home page

9 **Commercial and Investment Programs.**   Some software packages feature database
10 programs for tracking apartments, offices, retail buildings, industrial properties and
11 vacant land. They also have modules that help licensees in investment analysis on
12 income properties.

13 **Computer-Assisted Design Programs.**   Some residential and commercial brokers
14 use computer-assisted design (CAD) software to prepare simple floor plan representa-
15 tions of properties for sale for flyers and advertising.

16 **Deed-Mapping Programs.**   These programs are different from most mapping
17 programs. The licensee enters a property's metes-and-bounds legal description and
18 immediately sees a plot plan. He also can generate the number of square feet or acreage
19 in the parcel easily. Deed-mapping programs are particularly useful for brokers who
20 specialize in agricultural and development property.

21 **Property Management Programs.**   Such software is essential for brokerage firms
22 that manage more than five units. Entering rent receipts and expenses keyed to each
23 property makes reports immediately available. Also, lists of delinquent tenants help in
24 collections, lease expirations sorted by date help in generating renewals, owner state-
25 ments are available monthly, and brokers will appreciate the reconciliation features to
26 keep the escrow accounting balanced and documented.

27 **Office Management Programs.**   Office management software is one of the most
28 important tools in operating a brokerage firm. Sales management reports provide infor-
29 mation about production for each associate, comparing his or her current goal with
30 prior years. The accounting functions give cash flow projections for future closings as
31 well as escrow accounting and commission payments.

32 **Education and Training Programs.**   Educational software can be one of the most
33 effective methods of learning. Training programs allow brokers, real estate schools, and
34 trainers to prepare lesson plans for students. Using text, graphics, and question-and-
35 answer sections, students can move ahead at their own speed, repeating any areas as
36 needed.

37 **Contact Management Programs.**   Contact management programs allow the li-
38 censee to organize all customer contacts, maintain address books, set up daily task lists,

1 schedule appointments, write letters, and keep a history of activities. This type of pro-
2 gram is indispensable to an active professional. Probably the most well-known is *Act*.

3 ## THE INTERNET

4 Many people believe that the most exciting revolution in the history of information is
5 happening in our lifetime. The **Internet** is a global network of computers connected by
6 phone lines. The **World Wide Web** (the **Web**) is the collection of documents on those
7 computers. The Web is estimated to have nearly 30 million pages of information and is
8 growing dramatically. At the rate of 200 pages viewed per day, a person could spend
9 more than 400 years just looking at the current information. Commercial Web sites
10 have grown from a relatively small number in 1990 to millions of sites today.

11 To gain access to the Net, a user needs an **Internet Service Provider (ISP).** Once con-
12 nected, the user may view Web sites anywhere in the world without paying long-distance
13 telephone charges. A typical ISP may charge $20 per month for unlimited hours.

THE DIVISION OF REAL ESTATE ON THE INTERNET

The Division of Real Estate's Web site is very useful to licensees. It is a great
resource for finding information and taking care of licensing requirements. The
site has:

- the Florida Real Estate Commission Handbook online, so users can print
  Chapter 475, F.S., and the Rules of the FREC. It includes other statutes relating to administration of the license law.
- a full range of forms, such as 400.5, that licensees can fill out and submit online.
- the availability of license renewal by credit card.
- minutes of Florida Real Estate Commission meetings, and agendas for future
  meetings.
- information for applicants on Florida's license requirements.
- The Real Estate Education Newsletter.

---

14 **Web Links**

www.
15 http://www.myflorida.com
16 http://www.myflorida.com/dbpr/myflorida/business/learn/realestate/comm/
17 frec.html

18 **Note:** The Florida Real Estate Commission Web site has a very long address. It is easier
19 to start at MyFlorida.com. Click on "Business and Industry," go to the "Learn" section
20 and click on "Real Estate." On the next page, click on "Florida Real Estate Commission."

21 www.state.fl.us/dbpr/
22 Department of Business and Professional Regulation

23 www.state.fl.us/dbpr/re/index.shtml
24 Division of Real Estate

25 So much information is available online that users are often frustrated trying to sift
26 through it all to find exactly what they seek. One observer noted that asking for infor-
27 mation on the Internet is like trying to take a drink of water from a fire hose. Users also
28 must be cautious because they have no guarantee that the information is accurate.

Web Browsers

Programs have been designed to make browsing (**"surfing"**) the Web easier. The leading **browsers** are from Netscape and Microsoft. The programs have many features that allow users to see videos, hear sounds, print pages as needed, and send and receive e-mail. The browsers also provide access to **Usenet,** a collection of discussion pages on thousands of topics.

Hypertext

A compelling feature of the Internet is a user's ability to jump to another related "link" by clicking the mouse on a **hyperlink**—that is, words or graphics underlined or highlighted. When the user clicks on underlined words, called **hypertext,** he is transported to the section, page, or Web site he wants. The user can see related information, go deeper into a document, or visit another Web site. For instance, a real estate school's Web site might have a link to the DBPR for its license status page, another to the Florida Legislature for online text of Chapter 475, and another to a local real estate brokerage firm.

If this book were on the Internet, for example, a reader could click on the table of contents. When that page appears, clicking on hypertext reading "Information and Technology" would bring up this chapter. Clicking on another link named "The Internet" would display this section of the chapter.

However wonderful, hypertext can trap the adventurous. Beginning a search for specific information and ending up far afield is easy when the user follows a series of interesting links. Compare this with starting on a car trip from Miami to Jacksonville, taking a detour to visit an interesting location described on a sign, then continuing to take other intriguing forks in the road. The day may pass with the traveler having driven 500 miles, but no closer to her final destination and hopelessly lost. Browsers retain a "history" of sites visited which, when viewed, helps the traveler get back on the main road.

Each page in the Web has a specific address, called a **Uniform Resource Locator (URL).** This unique address may be as simple as http://www.yahoo.com or may be much longer. The user simply types in the address on the entry line for immediate access to the site. The prefix **http** stands for "hypertext transport protocol." The prefix **https** means that the site is secure for use with banking transactions, securities trading and other confidential activities.

Finding Information on the Internet

One of the two major benefits a licensee derives from using the Internet is easy accessibility and abundant information. (The other—marketing—is discussed in the following section.) The Internet offers many ways to find information. The most popular is to use a **search engine** such as *Yahoo* or *Google.* If the user knows exactly what she is searching for, simply typing in the key words *real estate* is like looking in a book's index, except that she finds many more references. For instance, a recent search using the key words *real estate* brought up 3,070,000 page references. Obviously, the search needs to be refined. Entering *Florida real estate* filters out much of the material. Entering *Lake County commercial real estate* zeroes in on even more specific information.

Another search can be done by clicking on one of the search engine's general categories, similar to a table of contents. Clicking on a general category such as "business" brings up another page with more detailed information. Working deeper into each menu allows the user to go from general to specialized information.

Internet Real Estate Marketing

Internet marketing is creating significant changes in the brokerage business. It is a low-cost delivery system, much more efficient than print media. Multibillion-dollar companies are actively marketing travel, personal finance, and real estate on the Internet. It clearly shows how important the Internet is to marketing.

Many brokers and sales associates advertise their listings and professional qualifications on the Web. Many have one or more pages under an umbrella service provider such as a Board of REALTORS® or the NAR. A sample Web page address for Reginald Jones, broker, might be "www.rednet.com/jonesr.htm." Or, Mr. Jones could obtain a "domain name" by paying a fee and by reserving the name of his choice, if available. For instance, Mr. Jones might select "www.jonesrealty.com." The personalized domain name provides greater recognition, easier access for customers, and a higher position on search engine results.

Internet Legal Issues for Brokers and Sales Associates

While most brokers carefully review printed advertising to ensure there are no law violations, not as many have developed a company Internet policy. This is a mistake. Because the broker is responsible for advertising, he or she must be certain that all Internet advertising is legal. This is difficult when each sales associate may have his own Web site. At a minimum, the broker should require all sales associates to provide the URL for any Web sites on which they advertise. The broker should bookmark these sites and inspect them at least once every month.

Licensees with a Web site are subject to the same advertising prohibitions associated with print advertising, including discrimination, misrepresentation, blind ads, and truth-in-lending. Sometimes, a sales associate may put a listing in her Web site, and fail to refresh the page on a regular basis. Two licensees in Ohio were recently suspended because expired and sold listings had been left on their Internet advertising pages too long. This may be considered "bait and switch" advertising, which is illegal.

FREC ADVERTISING RULES

61J2-10.025 Advertising

(1) All advertising must be in a manner in which reasonable persons would know they are dealing with a real estate licensee. All real estate advertisements must include the licensed name of the brokerage firm. No real estate advertisement placed or caused to be placed by a licensee shall be fraudulent, false, deceptive or misleading.

(2) When the licensee's personal name appears in the advertisement, at the very least the licensee's last name must be used in the manner in which it is registered with the Commission.

(3)(a) When advertising on a site on the Internet, the brokerage firm name as required in paragraph (1) above shall be placed adjacent to or immediately above or below the point of contact information. "Point of contact information" refers to any means by which to contact the brokerage firm or individual licensee including mailing address(es), physical street address(es), e-mail address(es), telephone number(s) or facsimile telephone number(s).

(b) The remaining requirements of paragraphs (1) and (2) apply to advertising on a site on the Internet.

Once a broker or sales associate has decided to publish his own Web page, the next step is to find an Internet service provider to act as the site's host. This is often the same firm contracted for using the Internet. Prices vary widely for Web site hosting, and careful shopping can result in significant monthly savings. The firm should have the fastest equipment available and a reputation for uninterrupted service and good technical help.

Hiring a Web Site Designer

Writing and designing a site that will achieve the desired result is challenging; therefore, licensees usually employ Web site designers. The selection of a designer is very important. A talented designer can construct pages that are informative and esthetically pleasing, achieve the licensee's objectives, and load quickly. It is no different from hiring an advertising agency. The licensee must have an idea of what the material is to accomplish and be prepared to be part of the design team.

One of the best ways to find a good designer is to browse sites for other real estate companies and sales associates. The best sites often have the designers' names (and perhaps other links) in the credits sections. Designers often provide complete price lists of their services.

By carefully inspecting pages of similar businesses, the licensee can develop some effective ideas. The licensee should print out the best pages to give the designer a better idea of the type of site the licensee wants. Remember, copying another site's design, text, or graphics can violate copyright laws, but the licensee can use design ideas to get a general sense of the site design the licensee finds most attractive.

Do-It-Yourself Web Design

Licensees who are comfortable with computers and familiar with the Web may decide to design and publish their own sites. Programs like *MS FrontPage* make it possible for nonprogrammers to develop attractive business pages on the Web. The advantages of a licensee's designing his own site include control over every facet of the site, easy changes to the pages, the ability to keep the site current, and reduced costs. New listings can be added immediately and sold listings removed. Price changes can be reflected on the same day they go into effect and new brokerage services featured. If the sales associate must wait for the Web designer to get to the changes, the pages are quickly out of date. Daily changes also can result in substantial designer fees.

Brokers know that the office phone should not ring more than four times or the caller may hang up. Likewise, a Web page that loads too slowly may result in an impatient customer pushing the stop button. With this in mind, a designer should avoid large pictures and fancy gizmos that move around on the screen—they take lots of time to load. When a licensee wants to advertise listings with photos, using smaller photos next to the descriptions (**"thumbnails"**) is usually best. If a customer wishes to see a larger photo for a property, clicking on the thumbnail brings it up. Loading time for the page is faster.

Those people who have new computers with large monitors often wonder why they see so much white space on the right side of the screen in most Web sites. Web designers know that many consumers have slow modems, slow connections, old browsers, and old, small monitors. A wider page will not be completely visible on a small monitor. This causes the frustrated viewer to have to scroll across each line.

Another important factor in designing a Web site is to be certain that the reader will benefit by visiting. Licensees should fill their sites with market facts, qualifying information or other information besides the licensee's qualifications. The first page of a Web site must load quickly and is the best page to make the viewer want to see more.

MLS Broker Reciprocity

The National Association of REALTORS® has mandated, effective January 2002, that brokers who are members of an MLS® may download the entire MLS database for inclusion in their firm's Web pages. This would allow even small firms to advertise "No brokerage firm has more listings to show you!" or some such slogan. Individual brokers can refuse reciprocity and block their listings from being used on other brokers' Web pages, but those who "opt out" will be unable to download the database into their pages.

The size, design, and maintenance requirements of the new system may be difficult for some smaller firms to implement on their own. Software companies and/or broker organizations are expected to provide platforms so a broker would need only a home page, with a link to the database. The link would be invisible to users.

Other Technology

Electronic Mail (E-mail). One of the most important benefits of the Internet is the ability to send and receive **e-mail** (electronic mail). Those who use e-mail wonder how they ever operated without it. Many real estate managers insist that all closing information be handled by e-mail with lenders, title agents, surveyors, pest control firms and insurance agents. This eliminates telephone tag and leaves a paper trail for messages, which can be printed and filed.

The ability to transfer files as an attachment with the e-mail allows almost instantaneous receipt of large documents. Also, overnight shipping fees are avoided and the document is less likely to be late or lost. Licensees who do not use e-mail are missing out on one of the truly great ways to communicate.

Facsimile Machines. Ten years ago, an office with a fax machine was at the forefront of technology. While that is no longer true, faxes are still extremely important communication devices. Contracts, surveys, closing statements, and other documents that may not be stored in a computer are transmitted easily by fax. Many manufacturers are producing combination fax/scanner/copier machines at very reasonable prices. Licensees should be aware of the prohibitions in the law about sending unsolicited faxes advertising property for sale. Such advertisements inflict the cost of the advertising on the unwilling recipients and tie up important communication technology.

A new wrinkle on the old fax machine is electronic faxes. By enrolling with companies like E-Fax, all incoming faxes can be directed to the computer as e-mail. This helps save paper by screening junk-mail faxes before printing and prevents machine jams and out-of-paper problems when an important fax is being received. After enrolling for the service, the user will receive a permanent fax phone number to give to persons who want to send an e-mail fax. The fax is sent normally to the service, and the fax is converted to an e-mail. The e-mail can be read by an optical character reader (OCR) so that the text can be placed into a word processor for editing.

Sending faxes by e-mail is often more convenient because:

- there is no need to have a computer file printed before faxing, as would be necessary using a conventional fax machine;
- large files can be sent from the computer more easily because many sheets of paper in a fax machine often jam; and
- electronic signature files may be affixed to the fax.

Web Link

http://www.efax.com

E-mail fax service. The incoming fax service is free. To send e-mail faxes, there is a small monthly fixed charge.

Internet Conference Calls. *MS NetMeeting, Netscape Conference,* and other similar programs allow people connected to the Net to chat with others who are also online. A "virtual telephone" rings on the screen, and the parties can type out messages to each other online. If the parties have audio and video capability, they can converse with each other face to face. The participants in this conference call can sketch on a whiteboard and collaborate on different programs in real time. Large corporations use this new technology to reduce travel budgets because their employees can see and hear each other as if they were together.

Mobile Telephones. Mobile phones have changed the way brokers and sales associates do business. The licensee never misses a call, even when the office is closed. Appointments may be made, postponed, or rescheduled quickly and easily.

Property Information Answering Machines. Brokerage firms can provide information to callers 24 hours per day by way of machines that record up to 500 different property messages. By entering listing code numbers from property advertising and signs, callers may listen to information about the property or have a fax sent automatically. By using different codes on the same property, depending on the advertising medium, a firm can track which ads pull in the most calls. Caller ID is usually part of such a system, allowing the agent to contact the caller to offer further information. The newer answering machines can place calls to pagers or e-mail agents automatically.

The Talking House. This machine, placed in a listed property, transmits a continuous radio broadcast about the property. Prospective buyers within range can tune to the correct frequency, featured on a property sign, and hear the property's features.

Satellite Training Programs. Many large real estate franchises and other training organizations offer training by satellite communications. This allows some very expensive talent to reach many licensees in their real estate offices every day with training programs on every imaginable real estate subject. Many organizations offer up to 60 hours of weekly satellite training.

ELECTRONIC SIGNATURES IN THE GLOBAL AND NATIONAL COMMERCE ACT

Eliminating Legal Barriers to Electronic Commerce

The "E-Sign" law became effective in October 2000. In the past, many laws required some contracts to be written on paper and signed with pen-and-ink signatures. Individuals and companies had been deterred from doing business electronically because of doubt that online contracts would be legally enforceable. Because of this, parties had to send "hard" copies back and forth for signature, slowing down the pace of business. Real estate licensees are familiar with the delays experienced with "mail-away" closing packages.

This new law is a start to overcome these barriers by:

- **preempting paper requirements:** The act provides that no contract, signature, or record shall be denied legal effect solely because it is in electronic form. Some items such as wills and codicils are excluded.
- **establishing technology neutrality:** The act does not favor one type of technology over another.
- **ensuring accuracy of electronic records:** Most electronic contracts and records will be legally enforceable only if they are in a form that can be retained and accurately reproduced for later reference by the appropriate parties.

Electronically endorsed contracts are now legally enforceable. The law defines an electronic signature as "an electronic sound, symbol, or process, attached to or logically associated with a contract." The law simply eliminates requirements that certain contracts and other records be written and signed on paper. Of course, the parties are still free to decide whether to enter a contract electronically.

The transfer and financing of real estate is an important factor in the legislation, and many technical problems remain. The legislation does not require encryption and/or authentication of digital signatures. That could create a problem establishing the consent and the identity of the customer. If a vendor had to sue to enforce the terms of an electronically signed contract, the vendor would still have to prove that the customer actually agreed to its terms.

The Electronic Financial Services Council, with members including Microsoft, Fannie Mae, and Countrywide Home Loans, is working to establish standards for electronic loan documentation. Fannie Mae issued industry guidelines in October 2000 for the electronic delivery of mortgages, but the day when such transactions are commonplace may be some years away.

SETTING PRIORITIES IN TECHNOLOGY

This section is designed to help new licensees evaluate the different ways technology can be used to increase their business and give customers the best service possible. A selection of equipment and software is shown below. On the left side of the page there is a blank before each of the items. You should enter a number from 1 to 3, based on the priority you feel it should have in a new licensee's budget.

1. must have right away; necessary to do the most basic tasks.
2. can come a little later, and will increase my efficiency and make more money.
3. way off in the future, but it would be nice.

Don't pick more than eight items of each priority, to simulate a new licensee's budget. This list is quite subjective and the priority of items will depend on the expertise of the user and the type of work to be done. There are no right or wrong answers, just what's right for you.

Your ranking

____ Desktop computer no more than two years old, with memory of at least 32 megabytes of RAM, and a large hard drive

____ 64 to 128 megabytes of RAM

____ 56k modem with internet connection and a fast CD-ROM

____ Digital camera

____ Cable modem or DSL line for broadband (fast) Internet connection

____ CD-RW drive for making CD backups and property presentations

____ Laser printer in addition to the inkjet

____ Efficient method for storing data backups

____ Printer (color inkjet)

____ Word processing software

____ Desktop publishing software

____ Bookkeeping software

____ Mobile phone

____ Fax machine

____ Scanner

____ Real estate-specific software, such as *Top Producer* or *PREP*

____ Clip art collection

(continued)

1   ____   Photo-editing software
2   ____   Spreadsheet software
3   ____   Presentation software
4   ____   Personal digital assistant (PDA)
5   ____   Laptop computer no more than two years old with standard package of
6   features
7   ____   Digital camera with video capability
8   ____   Video editing software
9
     Other items you believe should be on the list:
10   ____   _____
11   ____   _____
12   ____   _____
13   ____   _____

SUMMARY

Computers are one of the most important productivity tools available to real estate licensees. Using the computer to access information from the MLS, prepare detailed property management reports, design effective listing brochures, and perform spreadsheet analyses for better investment counseling are just some benefits of the technology. Therefore, a licensee should decide which tasks she wants her computer to accomplish before making a purchase decision. Laptop computers are ideal for licensees who use computers in many locations. CD drives, modems, laser and inkjet printers, and digital cameras also are becoming essential equipment for licensees.

Software programs make computers do useful things. Some necessary software includes word processing, spreadsheet, database, and bookkeeping programs. Software written specifically for real estate licensees includes CMA, client follow-up, and ad-writing programs. Property management software is essential for licensees working in that field, and educators find that interactive training software is extremely effective.

The Internet connects computers worldwide. The Web is the information stored on those computers. Surfing the Net is made easier by hyperlinks, which allow movement from one site to another. Finding specific information on the Net is easy using search engines, which maintain an index on millions of pages.

Many licensees advertise on the Web under umbrella pages, but many also have their own Web site addresses (URLs). Most who want to publish Web sites hire designers, but many licensees use programs that allow the licensees to do it themselves. A Web site should be informative and attractive and should load quickly. It must meet the FREC legal requirements.

E-mail is one of the Net's greatest benefits. It is cheaper and faster than the postal service or overnight couriers and allows the transmission of large documents.

Other technology improvements helping Florida real estate licensees provide their best service ever include mobile telephones, satellite training programs, and facsimile machines.

DEFINE THESE KEY TERMS

browser
compact disc (CD) drive
computer-assisted design (CAD)
crash
database
desktop
digital camera
e-mail
hardware
http
https
hyperlink
hypertext
inkjet printer
Internet
Internet service provider (ISP)

laptop
laser printer
modem
random access memory (RAM)
rewritable CD drive (CD-RW)
scanner
search engine
software
spreadsheet
surfing
thumbnail
Uniform Resource Locator (URL)
Usenet
Web
World Wide Web

CHAPTER 4 PRACTICE EXAM

1. The two major benefits to a licensee who uses the Internet are accessibility of information and the ability to:

    a. download music.
    b. get stock quotes.
    c. make travel arrangements.
    d. market property listings.

2. One principal cause of a computer "crash" is:

    a. a slow modem.
    b. a tape drive that is inadequately sized.
    c. a CD that is less than 12X speed.
    d. insufficient memory.

3. The most efficient method of backing up a hard drive is to use:

    a. a modem.
    b. a rewritable CD drive (CD-RW).
    c. 3½-inch diskettes.
    d. a scanner.

4. John, a commercial investment broker, wants to use his computer to do an investment analysis with a five-year cash flow projection for Sanders Properties, Inc. He would like to be able to use the template again for other properties. Which program should John get?

    a. Database
    b. Spreadsheet
    c. Presentation
    d. Project management

5. John faxes all real estate offices in his city whenever he gets a new listing. He believes faxing is better than the MLS system and quicker than mailing a flyer. He:

    a. could do better by using a combination of all three methods.
    b. may be alienating brokers from the other offices.
    c. is violating the law that prohibits transmission of unsolicited advertising.
    d. Both b and c are correct.

6. Howard Skau has just finished publishing his Web site and wants to advertise an address that will be remembered easily. He settles on http://www.skau.com. Once he purchases the rights to this address, it is now called his:

    a. hypertext transport protocol.
    b. domain name.
    c. search engine.
    d. hyperlink.

7. Broker Sandra Rodriguez likes to print a brochure with photos for each of her listings. What equipment will help Sandra in this process?

    I. Tape drive
    II. Scanner
    III. Digital camera
    a. I only
    b. I and II
    c. II and/or III
    d. I, II, and III

8. Ms. Connell, who sells agricultural property, often is given legal descriptions without surveys. She knows she can market a seller's property better with a boundary sketch. What program would be helpful?

    a. Computer-assisted design
    b. Street-mapping
    c. Deed-mapping
    d. Database

9. Clicking on certain underlined words in a Web site transports the viewer quickly to another location on the Web. These words are called:

    a. search engines.
    b. hypertext.
    c. hotbots.
    d. URLs.

10. Once a person has decided to publish his own Web site, he must find a hosting company, more commonly called a(n):

    a. URL.
    b. http.
    c. ISP.
    d. net host.

ACTION LIST

APPLY WHAT YOU'VE LEARNED!

The authors suggest the following actions to reinforce the material in *Section II–Professionalism in Real Estate:*

- List your personal characteristics that you believe will be of most value to you in your real estate career, then refine the list by showing which activities will best use those strengths.
- List your personal characteristics that you believe need improvement to enhance your career. Make one action plan focusing on ways to achieve those improvements and another focusing on ways to reduce the impact of those personal characteristics that are hard to change.
- At the next meeting of your Board of REALTORS®, don't hesitate to give an opinion on the subject under discussion or to market your listing during the marketing time.
- Prepare a to-do list for tomorrow, arranged by priority.
- Set a goal of getting one new listing within the next seven days, and write out an action plan to achieve the goal.
- Prepare a short-term goal that includes the number of customer contacts you intend to make each day for the next ten days.
- If you are unfamiliar with the Internet, find a knowledgeable person who will help you understand how to use it. Ask your friend/mentor whether she will let you spend some time browsing.
- Log onto the Internet, and go to a search engine like *www.google.com*. Search the following subjects, and record the number of sites for each:

Subject material	No. of sites
1. Real estate law	_____
2. Real estate financing	_____
3. Newspapers online	_____
4. Real estate companies in your city	_____
5. Weather	_____

- Spend a day learning a software program by using the manual or taking the tutorial, if one is included.

SECTION III

VALUATION AND LISTING

Most real estate professionals know that the key to success is the ability to find and maintain good, salable listings. Sales associates must understand that sellers may or may not be aware of the market values of their properties and need professional assistance when setting realistic prices.

Real estate licensees must be knowledgeable about the pricing of property and will be held accountable under the standards of care, skill, and diligence. Licensees must understand the principles of real estate valuation and know how to prepare a comparative market analysis correctly.

When a seller decides to list her property, the sales associate should provide an estimate of the cash proceeds the seller can expect after paying off the mortgage and other expenses. Additionally, the sales associate should understand completely and be able to explain the listing agreement to the seller.

SECTION III

CHAPTER 5—VALUING RESIDENTIAL PROPERTY

LEARNING OBJECTIVES

Upon completion of this chapter, *you should be able to:*

1. explain the types of appraisals a real estate licensee may provide for a fee;
2. explain the difference between an appraisal and an opinion of value;
3. list at least four basic principles of value;
4. list the three appraisal methods;
5. list the four conditions of the comparable sales approach that must be met when selecting a comparable property;
6. list the three categories of properties shown in a CMA;
7. list at least three sources of information used in compiling a CMA;
8. list at least six elements of comparison used in a CMA;
9. list three important factors to consider when evaluating kitchens;
10. explain the adjustment process and direction of the adjustment;
11. explain why giving a range of values to the seller may be more helpful than stating a single value;
12. explain the advantage of computer-generated CMAs;
13. describe the sequence for making the CMA presentation to the customer;
14. list two visual aids that may be helpful to the CMA presentation; and
15. explain the advantages and disadvantages in making adjustments to the comparable properties in a CMA.

CHAPTER 5

VALUING RESIDENTIAL PROPERTY

1 A duty owed to customers by single agents and transaction brokers is the duty of skill,
2 care, and diligence. Assisting a seller in setting a realistic listing price or helping a buyer
3 understand the market and assisting in setting a realistic offering price are two of the
4 most important services a sales associate can offer.

5   All real estate activity is related to value. A valid estimate of property value has a sig-
6 nificant effect on many aspects of a real estate transaction, whether the transaction
7 involves a sale, an insurance policy, a mortgage loan, or a real estate tax levy.

8   While many value terms and measures of value are used in real estate, one term—
9 *market value*—is the most important to real estate transactions. The market value of real
10 estate is the most probable price a property should bring in an arm's-length transaction
11 occurring in a competitive and open market.

12   When a person is selling, buying, leasing, exchanging, developing, financing,
13 insuring, or assessing real property, valuation of that property is at the heart of the
14 activity. The process of estimating the value of a parcel of real property is called
15 **appraising.** Real estate licensees use the appraisal process to produce opinions of value,
16 *comparative market analyses (CMAs),* and non-federally related appraisals.

17   Licensees must be familiar with the valuation of real property. While most licensees
18 do not prepare formal real estate appraisals, they will go through the appraisal process
19 to some degree during the listing of properties. Licensees must have a good working
20 knowledge of the market in which they operate to be able to use evaluation methods
21 competently.

OPINION OF VALUE VERSUS CERTIFIED APPRAISAL

23 Real estate licensees may not refer to themselves as appraisers unless they are licensed
24 or are certified appraisers. An appraiser must be a licensed or a certified appraiser to
25 prepare an appraisal in a **federally related transaction.** However, the lack of state
26 certification as an appraiser does not prevent a real estate licensee from appraising a
27 property for compensation in a non-federally related transaction. Chapter 475 requires
28 that appraisals made by real estate licensees be done in conformance with the **Uniform**
29 **Standards of Professional Appraisal Practice (USPAP).** All active licensees are entitled
30 to be paid for providing appraisals or appraisal services as long as they do not represent
31 themselves or their reports as being certified. An appraisal must be professionally and
32 competently completed. Failure to do so leaves the licensee open to civil liability and

1 disciplinary action. A licensee involved in the listing or sale of a property should not pre-
2 pare an appraisal for that property. The report may be called an **opinion of value.**

3   Any active licensee may give an opinion of value when making a prospective sale or
4 taking a listing. This opinion of value may not, however, be referred to as an *appraisal*
5 or a *certified appraisal* because the licensee has a personal interest in the transaction.
6 Licensees interested in the formal appraisal process should consider taking the Florida
7 Real Estate Appraisal Board's 75-hour course leading to registration as an appraiser.
8 This chapter focuses primarily on preparing "opinions of value."

Basic Principles of Value

10 Many economic principles influence the value of real property. They are interrelated,
11 and their relative importance varies, depending on local conditions. The following prin-
12 ciples are important to licensees attempting to estimate market value:

13 • Substitution
14 • Highest and best use
15 • Law of supply and demand
16 • Conformity
17 • Contribution
18 • Law of increasing and diminishing returns
19 • Competition
20 • Change
21 • Anticipation

22 **Substitution.**   This is probably the most important factor in pricing residential
23 property in a neighborhood with an active market. The value of a given parcel of
24 real property is determined by using the principle of substitution. The maximum
25 worth of the real estate is influenced by the cost of acquiring a substitute or compa-
26 rable property.

DISCUSSION EXERCISE 5.1

You have prepared a CMA for Savannah Cooley. Your opinion of value, based on
sales of comparable homes, falls in a range between $92,000 and $95,000. Similar
properties in the neighborhood are listed at $92,000 to $97,000. Cooley needs
$105,000 from the sale of her home to pay a number of obligations and requests
that you list it at that price. Give four persuasive arguments for listing her property
at market value.

---

27 **Highest and Best Use.**   Of all the factors that influence market value, the primary
28 consideration is the highest and best use of the real estate. A property's highest and best
29 use is its most profitable legally and physically permitted use—that is, the use that pro-
30 vides the highest present value.

31 **Law of Supply and Demand.**   As it does with any marketable commodity, the law
32 of supply and demand affects real estate. Property values rise as demand increases or
33 supply decreases. For example, the last building lot in a desirable residential develop-
34 ment probably is worth much more than the first lot sold in the development.

35 **Conformity.**   In neighborhoods of single-family houses, buildings normally should
36 follow the principle of conformity; that is, they should be similar in design, construc-

1   tion, and age to other buildings in the neighborhood to realize their maximum value.
2   An elaborate mansion on a large lot with a spacious lawn is worth more in a neighbor-
3   hood of similar homes than it would be in a neighborhood of more modest homes on
4   smaller lots. Subdivision restrictive covenants are designed to promote the principle of
5   conformity to maintain and enhance values.

6   **Contribution.**   Any improvement to a property, whether to vacant land or a building,
7   is worth only what it adds to the property's market value. An improvement's contribu-
8   tion to the value of the entire property may be greater or smaller than its cost. A
9   licensee's opinion should be governed by a feature's contribution to value, not its
10 reported cost.

DISCUSSION EXERCISE 5.2

You have prepared a CMA for Phyllis, who lives in Scenic Heights, an area of $75,000 homes. Phyllis reviews the recent sales and sees that her house has a large swimming pool, a feature that is not present in the homes in the report. She produces the invoices for the cost of her pool, which total $15,000, and suggests a $90,000 list price. You believe that pools in the neighborhood add about $4,000 to the properties' list prices.

   Do a role-playing exercise, with another person taking Phyllis' part, and discuss the principles involved.

---

11 **Law of Increasing and Diminishing Returns.**   Improvements to land and struc-
12 tures reach a point at which they have no positive effect on property values. As long as
13 money spent on such improvements produces a proportionate increase in income or
14 value, the law of increasing returns is in effect. When additional improvements bring
15 no corresponding increase in income or value, one can observe the law of diminishing
16 returns.

17   Smaller homes in a neighborhood of larger homes may experience increasing returns
18 by improvement. Homes that are the same size or larger than surrounding homes
19 should not be improved significantly until the owners have considered the economics
20 of their decisions.

DISCUSSION EXERCISE 5.3

Sandy Brantly purchased a two-bedroom home in Betton Hills for $200,000. She builds an extra bedroom and bath and finds that the value has increased by much more than the cost of the improvements. She continues improving the property by adding two more bedrooms and a large family room with a fireplace. Sandy decides to sell, and she calls you to list the property. Your CMA shows that the value increase was much less than the construction cost. Sandy disagrees with your findings.

   Do a role-playing exercise, with another person playing the part of Sandy, while you explain to her why the value may not have increased as much as the cost of improvements.

1 **Competition.** All residential properties are susceptible to competition, some more
2 than others. The only house for sale in a nice, well-maintained neighborhood has a
3 better chance of selling at or near market value than if several houses on the same street
4 were for sale.

5 **Change.** All property is influenced by the principle of change. No physical or
6 economic condition remains constant. Licensees must be aware of market forces when
7 preparing opinions of value.

DISCUSSION EXERCISE 5.4

Tom Simple was called to list a vacant four-unit apartment building on Coral Way
in Miami, shortly after a hurricane hit. The building was not damaged, but the
owner felt that she didn't want the responsibilities of property management any
longer, and the hurricane sealed her decision. Tom quickly found some prestorm
comparable sales and listed the property based on those prices. The property sold
almost immediately with a contingency of new financing. When the appraisal was
made, Tom was stunned. The market value was 25 percent higher, based primarily
on the increase in rental prices since the storm. The seller wanted to void the contract based on that information, but the buyer demanded that the contract be
closed.

Should Tom have taken the changed market conditions into consideration
when pricing the property? Discuss the situation and possible consequences.

---

8 **Anticipation.** Most buyers purchase real estate with the expectation that its value will
9 increase—and they have been rewarded when the anticipation proves correct. In infla-
10 tionary times, the anticipation of higher prices creates a multitude of buyers, driving
11 prices higher than can be supported for long periods. When the market begins to top
12 out, the anticipation of a price recession often causes investors to dump property on the
13 market, forcing prices lower. Anticipation also is important to prices of property in times
14 of decreasing interest rates, when builders rush to fill the expected demand. Licensees
15 must be aware of the importance of anticipation when valuing property for sale.

---

16 ## THREE APPRAISAL METHODS

17 Three basic approaches are used to do a complete appraisal: the cost-depreciation,
18 income capitalization, and comparable sales methods. The value of residential real
19 estate is estimated primarily by the comparable sales approach. Real estate licensees use
20 that approach to prepare a CMA.

21 ### Cost-Depreciation Approach

22 The **cost-depreciation approach,** also called the *cost approach,* is based on the premise
23 that a property's value can be estimated by the total investment required to reproduce
24 the building, less the accumulated depreciation and obsolescence, plus the value of the
25 site (land plus utilities) and the value of any site improvements. Building value, site
26 value, and site improvements value are obtained separately, then added to get market
27 value. The six basic steps in the cost-depreciation approach to estimating value follow:

28 1. Estimate the current cost to reproduce the building new.
29 2. Estimate the total accrued depreciation and obsolescence of the building.

3. Subtract total accrued depreciation and obsolescence from the current cost to reproduce the building new.
4. Estimate the value of the site as if it were vacant.
5. Estimate the value of any site improvements.
6. Add site value and site improvements value to depreciated reproduction cost to obtain estimated market value.

While this approach is important to appraisers, real estate licensees normally do not prepare cost evaluations. For that reason, the technique is not discussed in detail in this text.

Income Capitalization Approach

The object of the **income capitalization approach,** also called the *income approach,* is to measure the present value of a flow of income projected into the future. It is not concerned with the cost of a lot or with the reproduction cost of a building. Using the income capitalization approach, an estimated market value is developed based on the present worth of future income from the property. It is the primary approach for appraising income-producing property and for comparing potential investments.

A licensee must know the net income a property produces. He may have access to the accounts or have the information provided. In some cases, the licensee may project the net income from available information and experience. He then divides net income by a capitalization rate to obtain present market value. This approach is very important in establishing value for commercial and investment properties. Most real estate licensees normally do not prepare income property valuations. For that reason, the technique is not discussed in detail in this text.

Comparable Sales Approach

The comparable sales approach is based on the principle of substitution. It is a method of valuation that compares the actual sales of properties similar to the **subject property.** The process involves making adjustments to the sales prices of **comparable properties** so they assume all of the relevant characteristics of the subject property. The adjusted prices of the comparables imply the subject property's most probable sales price. Although the comparable sales approach is the most widely used method for valuing residential property, it should be used only when comparables exist in a reasonably active market where sufficient, reliable market sales information is available.

A comparable property should meet four conditions before it is used in a CMA:

1. It should be substantially similar to the subject property.
2. It should have sold recently—within the past year.
3. It should be located in the same market area as the subject property.
4. It should have changed owners as a result of an arm's-length transaction.

Comparables should be similar to the subject in size, age, design, construction, amenities, and other features. They also should be located in the same neighborhood as the subject property. Some **property characteristics** to be considered are shown in Figure 5.1.

COMPARATIVE MARKET ANALYSIS

While the three techniques for estimating market value described above are important, licensees rarely prepare appraisals using the three approaches. Most licensees use a *comparative market analysis* for arriving at an opinion of value. A CMA is a process of gathering and analyzing information on homes currently for sale, homes recently sold, and homes listed that did not sell. It may range in form from a simple list of recent sales with

FIGURE 5.1   SAMPLE PROPERTY CHARACTERISTICS*

Physical Characteristics

Style
Design
Age
Quality of construction
General condition
Number of bedrooms
Number of bathrooms
Size of building
Size and shape of lot
Landscaping

Locational Characteristics

Neighborhood (trend)
Schools (access)
Recreation areas (access)
Public services (quality)
Zoning (protection)
Retail areas (access)
Employment area (time)
Churches, synagogues (access)
Utilities
Visual appeal

*These are selected examples only; more or fewer characteristics may be applicable.

no adjustments to a detailed adjustment grid. Whether she takes a simple or a complex approach, a licensee needs to ensure that she has met all of the conditions for selecting comparables.

Gathering CMA Data

First, the sales associate must have knowledge of the subject property. If it is a standard floor plan subdivision home, it may be possible to complete a market analysis without a property inspection. However, if the seller has made many improvements or if the home has other amenities not typical of the market, it may be difficult to make adjustments during the CMA's presentation phase. The truly professional approach is to inspect the property before completing the CMA.

Once the property inspection has been completed, the licensee should select the best properties for comparison. Three categories of comparison help sellers and buyers better understand the market:

1. Properties that have sold
2. Properties that are now on the market
3. Property listings that have expired

Reviewing actual sales prices of comparable properties helps buyers and sellers see what buyers actually pay in the marketplace. Comparable sales data are important when new financing is necessary because an appraiser relies on these data to estimate market value. Many sales are contingent on financing the purchase price, so it is of no value to overprice a property, only to lose the sale when the lender and buyer receive the appraisal report.

Reviewing the prices of comparable properties now on the market shows the seller what owners of properties with similar characteristics are asking. These are the properties that will compete with the seller's. The principle of substitution means that a buyer will select the property with the best price, all other things being equal. A seller who wishes to position her property in the most effective price window values it just above recent sales and just below competing properties. A properly priced listing should experience a reasonably quick sale at the optimum price.

The listing prices of properties that do not sell tell a great deal about the resistance level of buyers to overpriced listings. In almost every case, the expired listing has been priced too high for the amenities offered.

DISCUSSION EXERCISE 5.5

Silas Dean is trying to set a price for a 1,500-square-foot home in Green Hills. He finds the following comparable sales:

Price	Square Feet	Price per Square Foot
$49,500	980	$50.51
51,000	1,025	49.76
50,000	1,000	50.00
61,500	1,500	41.00

The average price per square foot for these properties is $47.81. Sam Williamson, who owns the home, asks, "What is it worth?" Dean replies, "Houses sell for $47.81 per square foot in this neighborhood. Based on that, your property should sell for about $71,700." Williamson agrees and lists at $71,500.

Do you agree with Dean's analysis? If not, why not?

1   The best sources for gathering CMA information include:

2   • multiple-listing service (MLS) records,
3   • company files,
4   • public records,
5   • other agents, and
6   • data service companies,

7   MLS records are the most convenient and comprehensive method of getting listings
8 and sales information. MLS computer records can be searched by address and subdivi-
9 sion for ease in finding comparable sales. The information can be retrieved for sold,
10 current, or expired property listings.

11   Company files are limited in scope, but may be more complete as to property descrip-
12 tions and financing used in purchases.

13   The public records include information recorded in the clerk's office and informa-
14 tion on file with the tax appraiser. Except for verification of sales data and identities of
15 the parties, the information from the clerk's office is not as important as the informa-
16 tion available at the tax appraiser's office. While the information from the property
17 appraiser's records is sometimes outdated, the records are still a useful source of data.
18 The "sold" section of the CMA should include for-sale-by-owner properties, and the
19 appraiser's office is often the best information source for such sales.

20   Licensees often know of properties that have just closed. The information given
21 should be verified and added to the report to include current sales.

22   Data service companies compile property sales data and sell the information to inter-
23 ested parties. This information does not give complete property descriptions and is best
24 used as a checklist to ensure that all sales have been considered.

25 ## Selecting Comparable Properties

26 When a licensee prepares a CMA, she has two choices when selecting properties to com-
27 pare. The first is to report every sale and every listing in the neighborhood, together

1   with features and prices. The other is to analyze only the properties that are compa-
2   rable.

3   Reporting all properties gives the seller an overview of the entire neighborhood
4   market. Some sellers believe a list is incomplete if they know of a neighbor's home that
5   sold recently but is not on the list; therefore, a complete list may make sellers more
6   comfortable. However, problems sometimes arise with this all-inclusive list. Properties
7   that are not comparable may mislead a seller concerning values.

8   Listing only three or four comparable properties makes a clearer presentation for a
9   seller and reduces the chance for confusion about values. This is the approach
10 appraisers use.

11   Perhaps the best approach for the licensee is to prepare a comprehensive list of all
12 properties that have sold, are listed currently, or have expired, then select the most
13 comparable properties from that list for analysis. This method satisfies the needs of
14 completeness and clarity. The characteristics for comparison are described below.

15 Common Elements of Comparison

16 Clearly, the accuracy of the comparable sales approach relies on the elements of com-
17 parison selected for adjustment. The elements listed on the CMA chart in Figure 5.2 are
18 some of the most common and significant factors that affect value in standard residen-
19 tial appraisals. In any given analysis, it may be necessary to include other adjustments.
20 The easiest way to fill out the CMA is to list all of the details of the subject property,
21 then evaluate each comparable with the data that have been gathered.

22 **Location.**   What are the three most important determinants of property value? The
23 old expression "location, location, location" is the best answer. Location is so important
24 that only in very unusual circumstances would a licensee use a property outside the
25 subject's neighborhood as a comparable sale. In such a case, the comparable should
26 come from a similar neighborhood. Even within the same neighborhood, locations can
27 result in significant variances. A property across the street from a park is more valuable
28 than one across the street from a commercial area.

DISCUSSION EXERCISE 5.6

Sara Bilina wants a for-sale-by-owner to list with her, but the FSBO says that the commission added to his price would make the property overpriced. Sara really wants the listing, so she finds several homes the same size as the FSBO's property and prepares a CMA. However, the comparables she uses are located in another, more upscale neighborhood. The owner looks at the CMA and lists with Sara.

Has Sara prepared an acceptable CMA? Why or why not?

Has Sara violated any ethical or legal code? Why or why not?

---

29 **Size and Shape of Lot.**   Irregularities can make portions of a site unusable for
30 building, impair privacy, or restrict on-site parking, which could require major adjust-
31 ments. Street frontage and total square footage are other important considerations.

32 **Landscaping.**   Trees, plantings, and other types of landscaping should be evaluated
33 as to maturity, quantity, and quality.

1 **Construction Quality.**   If construction quality of a comparable is not equivalent to
2 that of the subject property, a major adjustment must be made. It is possible that the
3 difference in quality might disqualify the property as a comparable.

4 **Style.**   Generally, the style of a house follows the rule of conformity (a house should
5 not be the only one of its type in the neighborhood). An important aspect of style is the
6 number of floors of the residence. A one-story ranch house probably could be com-
7 pared to a split-level, with some adjustment made. A three-story house is not compa-
8 rable to a one-story ranch house, however.

9 **Design.**   Design must be viewed from both functional and aesthetic standpoints. Func-
10 tional aspects include the existing traffic patterns in a house, placement of doors and
11 windows, room-to-room relationships, and the usefulness of rooms. Aesthetic aspects
12 focus on how pleasant and attractive an interior appears to an observer.

13 **Age.**   Because most subdivisions are built within a relatively short period of time,
14 there may not be significant age differences among comparables. A brand-new home is
15 likely valued by the builder according to actual costs, overhead, and profit. While overall
16 upkeep is important, the home's age may alert the licensee to outmoded design and
17 fixtures or to needed repairs.

18 **Square Feet of Gross Living Area.**   This is one of the most common areas for
19 making adjustments, since size differences among homes can be calculated easily. If li-
20 censees make adjustments for square footage, they also must be careful when adjusting
21 for number of rooms or bedrooms because this could lead to double counting. Adjust-
22 ments for gross living area can be misleading if all properties are not comparable. For
23 instance, a small house normally sells for more per square foot than a large house in
24 the same area. A one-story house has a higher cost per square foot than a two-story
25 house. Be sure that all properties used are comparable to the subject property.
26 Appraisers normally do not count any floor area that is below grade as gross living area,
27 so do not use such properties unless the subject also has below-grade area.

28 **Measuring Practice.**   Measurement of a house is extremely important. An error
29 could cause problems in pricing the property if the home's square footage is given to
30 buyers. Calculate the square footage of gross living area of the house shown below:

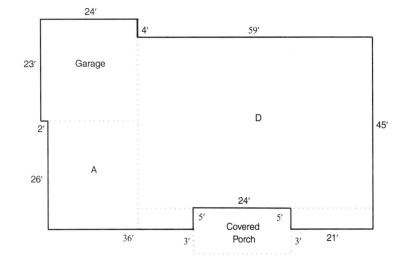

DISCUSSION EXERCISE 5.7

You have done a market report for the Meadows at Woodrun subdivision. Your analysis of property value, based on several 1,200-square-foot homes, indicates that homes sell at prices averaging $50 per square foot. When talking by phone with a prospective seller, you quote that figure after setting the listing appointment. When you arrive at the property with your listing information in hand, the seller proudly shows you the 500-square-foot two-car garage that has been converted into a heated and cooled family room. He indicates that the price at which you should list the home is $85,000, based on 1,700 square feet times your $50-per-square foot figure. Role-play this situation, and explain why it may be difficult to market this home at $85,000. Also discuss some methods of arriving at a more realistic price.

Number of Rooms.   The total number of rooms in a house does not include the foyer or bathrooms and generally does not include basement rooms. Don't double count when adjusting for square feet and number of bedrooms.

Number of Bedrooms.   A major adjustment is needed if the subject property has two bedrooms and the comparables have at least three, or vice versa. Don't double count when adjusting for square feet.

Number of Baths.   Full baths (lavatory, toilet, and tub, with or without shower), three-quarter baths (lavatory, toilet, and shower), and half baths (lavatory and toilet) compose this category. Modern plumbing is assumed, so an adjustment must be made for out-of-date fixtures, if different from the subject property.

Kitchen.   Licensees should focus on certain key factors:

- Location
- Counter space and storage
- Service triangle
- Appliances.

The location of the kitchen is an important factor, based on its convenience to dining areas and accessibility for unloading groceries. The market will not accept a kitchen with inadequate counter and storage space. The service triangle is calculated by drawing straight lines connecting refrigerator, range, and sink. Most consumer polls show that the total length of the three lines should be greater than 12 feet, but should not exceed 22 feet. Appliances represent a sizable portion of the home's cost, and their age and condition are important.

Other Space.   Unfinished attic, porch, utility room, Florida room, or any other room not part of the primary house area is included in this category.

Condition of Exterior.   An adjustment should be made for any needed repair work.

Condition of Interior.   An adjustment should be made for needed repairs. Luxurious finishing, such as real wood paneling, adds to a home's value.

Garage.   If the subject does not have one, any garage on a comparable property requires an adjustment. Garages on the subject and comparable properties must be compared for type of construction and size.

Other Improvements. An adjustment should be made for differences between the subject property and the comparable.

Adjusting for Differences

Ideally, the licensee wants to find comparable sales that are identical in characteristics to the subject property. In the real world, this doesn't always happen. While the CMA is not meant to be an appraisal, it is necessary to make **adjustments** for some of the differences discussed above. A major difference between the subject property and comparable property, such as a pool, could make an opinion of value very misleading if no adjustment is made for the pool. Many licensees recognize the difficulty in doing a CMA because when they look at a sold property, they see it as it is *today,* not how it looked when it went under contract. The important consideration in adjusting the comparable sale is how it looked at the time of sale.

Example: Whitney Cooley, a licensed sales associate, is preparing a CMA for Brian Edward's three-bedroom two-bath home in Eastgate. One of the comparable properties with the same floor plan sold recently for $73,000. The only difference between the properties is that the comparable property has a swimming pool. Whitney has done CMAs in Eastgate before and estimates that a pool contributes about $4,000 to value. The subject property doesn't have a pool, so Whitney makes a minus adjustment of $4,000 to the comparable's sales price. This indicates a value of $69,000 for the subject.

How did Whitney determine that a pool contributes $4,000 to value in that neighborhood? The matched pair technique helped her make the estimate. She examined two recent sales in which the only difference was the fact that one property had a pool. The property with the pool sold for $4,000 more than the home without the pool. Since the pool was the only difference, the $4,000 must be attributable to that amenity. It would be better to make the comparison with several matched pairs to support the conclusion, but the technique is valid. The cost to build the pool is not added, just the value buyers and sellers place on the pool.

Adjustments are always made to the comparable property, never to the subject. Adjustments are subtracted from the comparable property if the comparable is bigger or better. Adjustments are added if the comparable is smaller or less desirable. An easy way to remember is "CIA, CBS":

- If the Comparable is Inferior, Add.
- If the Comparable is Better, Subtract.

Adjustments should be made for sold properties, listed properties, and expired properties; then each category should be reconciled.

Reconciliation

Reconciliation is the resolution of several adjusted values on CMAs into a single estimate of value. While an appraiser is expected to report a single-market value amount, a licensee making an opinion of value may prefer to report a range of values, from lowest to highest adjusted value of the comparables. Presenting a range rather than a single estimate of value allows a seller to price the property somewhat higher than the sold properties would indicate. The seller should understand that the home will likely sell at some price other than the list price and should consider all offers within the range of values.

Reconciliation enables the licensee to set the range differently. The first step is to estimate the value for each section of the report (sold properties, listed properties, and expired listings). Reconciliation is not simply the averaging of these values. The process requires the licensee to examine carefully the similarity of each comparable property to

1 the subject property. If one comparable is nearly identical to the subject, including all
2 relevant **transactional characteristics,** the sales price of that comparable might approx-
3 imate 100 percent of the subject's estimated market value. When the comparables vary
4 in their degree of similarity to the subject, the comparable property judged most similar
5 is assigned the greatest weight (percentage) in the reconciliation process.

6   The estimates for each section should be rounded. The range would then be from
7 the reconciled value of sold properties and the reconciled value of properties listed
8 currently.

9   Another method for setting a range of values is to reconcile the sold properties to a
10 value estimate, then check to see what properties sell for as a percentage of list price, then
11 divide the value estimate by that amount. The two values compose the range high and low.

DISCUSSION EXERCISE 5.8

You have just completed a CMA for Luke Gast's home at 1112 Bristol Court. The
reconciled market value of his home is $127,500. MLS statistics indicate that
homes sell at approximately 95 percent of list price.

   What is the range of value you quote to Luke?

---

12 ## A Visual Aid to the CMA

13 "A picture is worth a thousand words" is a timeworn expression because it is true. Sellers
14 who review CMAs with licensees often have difficulty visualizing the comparable proper-
15 ties. The licensee who provides visual data can make a clearer presentation, which may
16 result in more realistic pricing. Owners who are motivated to sell do not set out to over-
17 price their properties. Overpricing is usually the result of an inadequate understanding of
18 the market, and that responsibility belongs to the listing sales associate.

19   Valuable visual aids include plat maps of the subdivision and pictures of the compa-
20 rable properties. The plat map should be color-coded to show which properties were
21 sold, which properties are now for sale, and which listings have expired (see Figure 5.3).
22 Photos can be clipped from an MLS book, printed from the MLS computer system, or
23 taken with a digital camera. The licensee who wants the listing should not fail to include
24 a photo of the seller's home, also. The seller will appreciate your personal touch and the
25 extra photo for her scrapbook. Leaving a family home of some years can be a sentimental
26 experience, and the seller will remember a licensee who is sensitive to those feelings.

CASE STUDY

Comparative Market Analysis

Getting information from the owner. You have just received a request from John Halliburton to discuss listing his family's home. Mr. Halliburton gives you some basic information:

- The full name of all persons on the deed
  John Halliburton and Susan C. Halliburton, HW
- The property address
  4316 Landtowne Drive, Orlando

CASE STUDY (Continued)

Comparative Market Analysis

- The owner's home and office phone number
  (407) 555-3557; (407) 555-3917
- The number of bedrooms and baths in the home
  Four bedrooms, two baths
- A description of extras in the home
  1,920 square feet of gross living area, two-car garage
- A convenient time for an appointment. This is the time to decide whether to do a pre-presentation inspection of the property (two appointments required: one to inspect the property, one to present the CMA).

You decide to have one appointment at 6:20 this evening, and will inspect the property at that time.

Gathering information from the online tax rolls through the MLS system. The tax rolls for Orange County show the following information for the property:

Legal description:	Lot 14, Block H, Landover Hills, Unit 2 - Orange County
Property tax appraisal:	$149,300
Annual taxes (including the homestead exemption):	$2,986.45
Year built:	1989
Base area:	1,920 square feet (later verified by physical measurement)
Total area:	2,420 square feet (includes 2-car garage)
Last sale:	1996
Last sale price:	$128,000
Mortgage:	Sun Title Bank

A search of the tax records shows seven sales in the subdivision within the previous year, ranging from $168,000 to $174,800. Six of the seven sales were reported in the MLS. The sales are shown in the first section of the CMA in Figure 5.2.

There are four properties currently for sale in the MLS, shown in the second section of the CMA, and three listings have expired within the last 12 months, shown in the third section.

Analysis of amounts contributed by amenities. Over a period of time, in reviewing data on sold properties, we can estimate what a pool, a garage, an extra bedroom, or a fireplace contributes to value. The matched pair technique would compare similar houses with and without a particular feature. The difference in price would tend to show what the feature contributes in value.

For purposes of this CMA, we shall assume that sold properties in the neighborhood have shown the following value contributions over time:

- The contribution of a pool is $7,000.
- The contribution of a fireplace is $1,800.
- The contribution of an extra garage stall (2 cars, rather than 1) is $2,800.
- The contribution of extra square footage differences is $50/sq. ft.
- The contribution of a screened porch is $2,000.

The CMA has been filled in with the exception of the adjustments shown above. Please compare the subject property with the comparable properties and make adjustments to the comparable properties. Then complete the analysis and estimate the marketing range for the property.

FIGURE 5.2   COMPARATIVE MARKET ANALYSIS

Comparative Market Analysis

Prepared by: _____

Date: _____

Prepared for: _____
Property Address: _____
Features: _____

Properties sold within the previous 12 months

Property Address	Sales Price	List Price	Days on Mkt.	Living Area	Features	Estimated Adjustment	Adjusted Sales Price	Comments
1816 Hibiscus	172,800	180,000	120	1,820	Pool, FP, Screen Porch			
2412 Nasturtium	169,900	177,900	71	1,920	FP			
1763 Camellia	173,500	182,000	45	1,900	Pool			
1421 Azalea	168,900	175,000	52	2,000	Screen Porch			
1640 Clover	171,200	179,500	61	2,000	1 Car Garage			
2210 Hibiscus	168,000	175,900	32	1,900				
1240 Camelia	174,800	182,500	70	1,920	Screen Porch, FP			

Percent sales price/list price _____ %

Properties currently on the market

Property Address	List Price	Days on Mkt.	Living Area	Features	Estimated Adjustment	As Adjusted	Comments
1818 Azalea	191,000	75	2,100	Pool			
1740 Hibiscus	178,800	120	1,900	FP			
2210 Clover	185,000	38	1,820	Screen Porch, Pool			
1604 Magnolia	177,000	45	1,920	Screen Porch			

Properties which were listed but failed to sell during the previous 12 months

Property Address	List Price	Days on Mkt.	Living Area	Features	Estimated Adjustment	As Adjusted	Comments
2212 Camelia	192,800	180	1,900	Pool, FP, Screen Porch			
1812 Hibiscus	185,500	240	2,000	Screen Porch			
2211 Azalae	186,600	140	1,800	FP			

Median $ _____

The suggested marketing range is $ _____ to $ _____

This information is believed to be accurate, but is not warranted.
This is an opinion of value and should not be considered an appraisal.

FIGURE 5.3   PLAT MAP OF NEIGHBORHOOD

Real Estate Activity in Your Neighborhood
Prepared by Sandra Rodriguez
Action Realty, Inc.

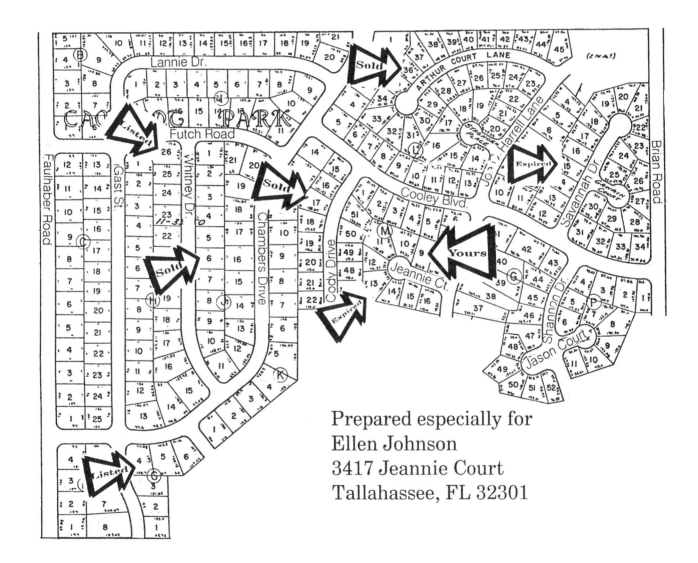

Prepared especially for
Ellen Johnson
3417 Jeannie Court
Tallahassee, FL 32301

CMAs Using Comparable Sales and Listings (No Adjustments)

Licensees commonly use this method in pricing property. It involves listing properties for sale now, properties sold in the previous year, and expired listings, without adjustments. Its simplicity is appealing to licensees and sellers alike because it provides an overview of the market. However, if properties on the chart are not comparable and the subject property is priced from an average of sales prices or square-foot calculations, the pricing method can be misleading.

DISCUSSION EXERCISE 5.9

In this role-playing session, assume the CMA has been explained, but the seller is attempting to set an unreasonably high listing price. Come up with as many persuasive points as possible to encourage the seller to price the property in the range suggested.

Computer-Generated CMAs

As computers have become more important in every phase of the real estate business, software programs have been written that make impressive presentations to buyers and sellers. Many of these programs are formatted to print out an entire listing presentation to the seller, tailored to his specific needs. In many cases, the time required is less than that of handwriting the old CMA grids. Most of the programs are designed to interface directly with the MLS system program and download the necessary data. This saves the licensee time because she does not have to type the information. Most programs provide raw sales data without adjustment, although the sales associate, by selecting only comparable properties, can come quite close to market value. Sample portions of a CMA from a software program are shown in Figure 5.4.

Presenting the CMA to the Seller

Many licensees spend a great deal of time preparing professional CMAs, then lose the benefit of their work by making poor presentations to the sellers. A licensee's presentation should provide information the seller needs to fully understand the listing process. Agents who state their opinions of value without going over the CMAs may lose the opportunity for realistic pricing if the sellers are surprised and offended at the amounts. A proper presentation should proceed in the following sequence:

1. Explain the importance of pricing the property within the selling range.
2. Inform the seller that the purpose of the CMA is to determine the best list price for the property.
3. Explain how each section of the CMA is important in the decision-making process by giving the seller an overview of the following:

   - Sold listings prove what selling prices have been and what bank appraisals might show.
   - Homes now for sale illustrate the importance of competitive pricing.
   - Expired listings demonstrate the futility of pricing property at an unrealistically high price.

4. Review individual properties on the report while referring to visual aids such as a subdivision map and photos.
5. Ask the seller for questions or comments.
6. Give the seller time to arrive at a range of values independently.

1   7. If the seller wants to price the property too high, discuss the reasons why that
2   approach is unproductive.
3   8. When a realistic listing price has been agreed upon, complete the seller's net pro-
4   ceeds statement (see Chapter 6).

DISCUSSION EXERCISE 5.10

Using the CMA report in Figure 5.2, role-play the complete presentation of a
CMA. The instructor might assign several persons to present the different sections
of the material. Assign a classmate to represent a "reasonably motivated" seller
who is kind to the agent.

SUMMARY

A real estate licensee may prepare an appraisal in a transaction that is not federally
related. F.S. 475 requires that the appraisal be done in conformity with the Uniform
Standards of Professional Appraisal Practice. Normally, when listing or selling property,
licensees prepare a comparative market analysis, and give their *opinion of value.* Many
important principles of value exist, including highest and best use, substitution, supply
and demand, contribution, and conformity.

The comparable sales approach to estimating value is the most appropriate method
appraisers use to value homes and vacant sites. The comparative market analysis is
the method most licensees use to prepare an opinion of value. The three sections of a
CMA are properties that have sold recently, properties for sale now, and properties that
did not sell during the listing periods. Data for the CMA are gathered primarily from
the MLS and county property appraiser's records. Only comparable properties should
be used in the analysis. A range of values is provided to the seller because it is more
meaningful than a single value.

DEFINE THESE KEY TERMS

adjustments
appraising
comparable property
comparable sales approach
comparative market analysis (CMA)
cost-depreciation approach
federally related transaction

income capitalization approach
opinion of value
property characteristics
reconciliation
subject property
transactional characteristics

FIGURE 5.4 EXAMPLE OF COMPUTER-GENERATED CMA

402 Warren

Area	Gig Harbor
Beds	3
Baths	2
Age	12
Sqft	2,750
Price	$256,000
Pr\Sqft	$93.09

Features: Stone Construction, Composition Roof, One Story, Central Heat, Ceiling Fan, Central Air Conditioning, Fireplace, Formal Dining Room, Breakfast Area, Wall to Wall Carpeting, Wood Floors, Dishwasher, Disposal, Double Oven, Trash Compactor, Three or more Car Garage, Auto Garage Door Opener, Spa, Lot Size: .42 Acres, Eanes Grade School

Days On Market: 23

436 Marks Lane

Area	Gig Harbor
Beds	3
Baths	3
Age	11
Sqft	3,000
Price	$267,000
Pr\Sqft	$89.00

Features: Frame Construction, Metal Roof, Two Story, Central Heat, Central Air Conditioning, Fireplace, Breakfast Area, Tile Floors, Wall to Wall Carpeting, Two Car Garage, Community Pool, Spa, View, Lot Size: .32 Acres, Cedar Co. Grade School, Hill Co. Middle School, Westlake High School

Days On Market: 36

311 Peaceful

Area	Gig Harbor
Beds	4
Baths	2+
Age	6
Sqft	2,990
Price	$272,000
Pr\Sqft	$90.97

Features: Composition Roof, Two Story, Central Heat, Heat Pump, Ceiling Fan, Central Air Conditioning, Fireplace, Formal Dining Room, Breakfast Area, Tile Floors, Wall to Wall Carpeting, JennAir Type Range, Microwave, Trash Compactor, Two Car Garage, Auto Garage Door Opener, Patio, City Lights View, Lot Size: .33 Acres, Eanes Grade School

Days On Market: 45

Total Listings: 3

Lowest Price	Highest Price	Avg List Price	Avg Price/Sqft
$256,000	$272,000	$265,000	$91.02

CHAPTER 5 PRACTICE EXAM

1. An appraisal of real property is a(n):

   a. accurate determination of its value.
   b. process of arriving at its value.
   c. estimate of its value.
   d. reconciled statement of just value.

2. Of all the factors that influence market value, the primary consideration is the:

   a. principle of substitution.
   b. highest and best use.
   c. law of increasing and diminishing returns.
   d. principle of conformity.

3. An appraisal is NOT used to make decisions about:

   a. a realistic listing price.
   b. how much money should be loaned.
   c. the value of the property as an investment for an individual.
   d. the best time of year to sell.

4. The most profitable legally and physically permitted use of real property is called its:

   a. market value.
   b. appraised value.
   c. location.
   d. highest and best use.

5. The comparable sales approach is *least* effective as a value indicator for:

   a. residential properties.
   b. duplexes.
   c. public school properties.
   d. vacant properties.

6. Which is designed to promote the principle of conformity to maintain and enhance value in a subdivision?

   a. Restrictive covenants
   b. Zoning codes
   c. Comprehensive plans
   d. Land use codes

7. When Mr. Wilson added a family room to his house, which was already too large for the area, what principle was demonstrated?

   a. Highest and best use of the land
   b. Increase in value at least equal to the cost of construction
   c. Law of increasing returns
   d. Law of diminishing returns

8. When listing a property in the ordinary course of business, any active real estate licensee in Florida is authorized to prepare an:

    a. opinion of value.
    b. appraisal report.
    c. appraisal assignment report.
    d. analysis assignment report.

9. A mansion in a neighborhood of smaller, more average homes would violate the principle of:

    a. change.
    b. conformity.
    c. competition.
    d. contribution.

10. In a neighborhood of three-bedroom, two-bath homes, an owner added a second bathroom at a cost of $1,600. An appraiser adjusted the value of the home upward by $2,000 due to the improvement. This is an example of the principle of:

    a. change.
    b. conformity.
    c. competition.
    d. contribution.

11. Traci is preparing a CMA for property located in Arbor Hills. She finds three homes that sold recently: a four-bedroom home with a pool that sold for $90,000; a three-bedroom home with no pool that sold for $81,000; and a three-bedroom home with a pool that sold for $85,000. Based solely on the above information, what does a swimming pool contribute to value in Arbor Hills?

    a. $9,000
    b. $5,000
    c. $4,000
    d. $0

12. The income capitalization approach to value is based on the capitalization of:

    a. potential gross income.
    b. effective gross income.
    c. net operating income.
    d. net taxable income.

13. The ideal kitchen service triangle should be from:

    a. 9 to 25 feet.
    b. 12 to 22 feet.
    c. 120 square feet.
    d. 12 by 24 feet.

14. The comparable sales approach to value is based primarily on what principle of valuation?

   a. Conformity
   b. Substitution
   c. Supply and demand
   d. Highest and best use

15. Which one of the following is not important in comparing properties using the comparable sales approach?

   a. Date of sale
   b. Size of house
   c. Original cost of improvements
   d. General condition and appearance

16. You are preparing a CMA and want to be certain that it reflects comparable sales of properties sold directly by owners. The best place to find the information is in:

   a. either the clerk's office or the tax appraiser's office.
   b. city hall.
   c. the MLS records.
   d. the tax collector's office.

17. When the term *recently* is used to describe a comparable sale, it is generally understood to mean that the property sold within the past how many months?

   a. 12
   b. 8–15
   c. 12–18
   d. 18

18. Which one of the following is *not* a condition that a licensee must meet when selecting comparable properties using the comparable sales approach to value?

   a. Similar
   b. Sold recently
   c. Same market area
   d. Same floor plan

19. When preparing a CMA, John evaluated three sales in the neighborhood, as shown below. Based solely on the figures shown, on which comparable sale should John place the most reliance?

	Sale A	Sale B	Sale C
Sale price	$167,000	$168,000	$157,000
Adjustments	– 14,000	– 14,000	– 2,000
As adjusted	$153,000	$154,000	$155,000

   a. Sale A
   b. Sale B
   c. Sale C
   d. All comparables should be treated equally and averaged.

20. You are estimating the value of a vacant lot zoned for single-family residence use. One year ago, a comparable lot sold for $25,000. Your analysis of market conditions and property characteristics produced the following needed adjustments: subject lot, $2,000 inferior; subject site location, $3,000 superior. These adjustments result in an estimated market value for the subject lot of:

   a. $26,000.
   b. $23,000.
   c. $24,000.
   d. $27,000.

CHAPTER 6—LISTING REAL PROPERTY

LEARNING OBJECTIVES

Upon completion of this chapter, *you should be able to:*

1. describe the optimum times and situations for disclosing brokerage relationships;
2. explain the basic layout of the Seller's Net Proceeds form;
3. list at least eight costs that a seller may be expected to pay at closing;
4. explain why insurance and escrow amounts usually are not included in the Seller's Net Proceeds form;
5. explain the reasons for rounding all figures used in the Seller's Net Proceeds form;
6. prepare a Seller's Net Proceeds form;
7. explain the wording that could be used to protect both seller and broker from commission disputes caused by a buyer who improperly tries to leave the broker out of the transaction in an open listing;
8. state the legally required elements in a listing contract and their required treatment;
9. explain the distinguishing characteristics of each of the following types of listings: open, exclusive agency, and exclusive-right-of-sale;
10. discuss the purpose of an owner's warranty in a listing contract;
11. discuss the purpose of the latent defects disclosure in the process of listing real property for sale;
12. describe the Florida no-solicitation telephone laws that affect licensees who make cold calls;
13. explain the steps required to complete a residential profile sheet;
14. complete the residential profile sheet;
15. complete a listing contract;
16. explain each paragraph of the listing agreement that applies to your market area; and
17. design a listing servicing program for your personal listings.

CHAPTER 6

LISTING REAL PROPERTY

SOURCES OF LISTINGS

Listings are the lifeblood of the real estate business; sales associates must know how to find sellers in need of their professional services. The methods used in prospecting for listings are beyond the FREC-mandated scope of this course. The sales associate who wishes to acquire a good inventory of listings should take sales training classes, attend GRI (Graduate REALTORS® Institute) or CRS (Certified Residential Specialist) classes, and check out books and videotapes on the subject. These sources describe how listing prospects can be found through:

- centers of influence,
- personal contact,
- for sale by owners,
- for rent by owners,
- expired listings,
- farming,
- canvassing,
- notices of listings and sales to neighbors and out-of-town owners.

No matter which method a sales associate uses to locate prospective listings, he must prepare for the listing appointments carefully. The CMA, discussed in the previous chapter, is necessary to help price the listing. The sales associate also must understand what costs the seller can be expected to pay, how to complete and explain the listing agreement, and how to market and service the listing.

ESTIMATING THE SELLER'S PROCEEDS

A seller generally is reluctant to enter into a listing agreement until she understands what expenses she must pay at closing. The **net proceeds** after paying off the mortgage and expenses of a sale are of primary interest to the seller and are often a factor in setting a list price. It is extremely important that a licensee use skill, care, and diligence in estimating the seller's proceeds from the sale. A discussion of the **seller's net proceeds form** (see Figure 6.1) follows.

FIGURE 6.1   SELLER'S NET PROCEEDS FORM

Seller's Name: _____

Property Address: _____

Selling Price	$	$
Less: 1st Mortgage 2nd Mortgage Other		
Seller's Equity	$	$
Less: Expenses		
Doc Stamps on Deed		
Termite Inspection and Treatment		
Title Insurance		
Homeowner's Warranty		
Buyer's Closing Costs Buyer's Origination Fee Buyer's Discount Points		
Repairs and Replacements		
Seller's Attorney Fee		
Brokerage Fee		
Other Miscellaneous Costs		
Other		
Total Expenses	$	$
Less: Prorations		
Property Taxes		
Interest		
Homeowner's Dues		
Rents and Deposits		
Total Prorations	$	$
Net Proceeds to Seller	$	$

These figures are estimates and intended only as a guide. They will vary at closing because of prorations, the mortgage balance, and unforeseen costs. An exact itemization will be provided to you at closing. Please read this and all other documents relating to this sale carefully. If you require further explanation, please consult an attorney.

Date: _____   Prepared by: _____

Seller: _____   Seller: _____

Seller's Net Proceeds Form

A section for the seller's name and the property address should be completed. The left side of the form itemizes income and expenses related to the sale. Two columns are provided for calculations:

- *When listing the property.* The licensee might use column 1 when calculating an estimate based on a recommended price; the agent would use column 2 if the seller wanted to know how much a different list price would net.
- *When giving the seller a range of values.* The sales associate could provide for the seller a high-end list price and a low-end list price.
- *At the time of listing.* Column 1 could be used for showing the net proceeds if customary seller's expenses were paid; column 2 could be used if the seller were asked to pay the buyer's loan closing costs. This is much like a best-case, worst-case scenario.
- *For estimates given at the time of listing.* Column 1 is for listing proceeds; column 2 could be used when an offer is submitted.
- *At the time an offer is submitted.* Column 1 shows the seller's net if the contract were accepted; column 2 shows the seller's net if a counteroffer were accepted.

Seller's Equity Section. The seller's **equity** section consists of the sales price, less mortgage balances and other encumbrances. Special assessment liens and construction liens would be shown in the space provided for other encumbrances. All items should be rounded because this is an estimate. An exact mortgage balance is unnecessary because of the closing date's uncertainty. Uneven dollars and cents amounts should not be included. Exact amounts imply an accuracy that does not exist in the estimate.

Expenses Section. Any expenses that the seller might be required to pay should be listed. It is better to overestimate than to underestimate the expenses. A seller will not be unhappy if he receives more at the time of closing than he had expected, but likely will be upset if expenses have been underestimated. Even though the bottom of the form provides a disclaimer, the licensee must be careful to avoid errors. Some expenses that should be discussed follow:

- Documentary stamps on deed are $.70 per $100 or fraction thereof of the sales price. The seller normally pays the cost of these stamps.
- Termite inspection (treatment and repairs) could be a substantial expense to the seller, but is not known at the time of listing or contract. A conservative approach would be to show the cost of both in this section. A licensee should stay current on the costs of inspection and treatment in her market area. In many areas, the inspection is the buyer's expense.
- When making the seller's statement, the licensee would include the typical charge a seller might be expected to pay for title insurance and related costs based on local practice.
- Homeowner's warranty costs often are associated with the seller's need to assure the buyer that the home is in good condition and will be warranted against many defects by an independent home warranty company. Depending on the company, these costs may range from $300 to $500.
- Buyer's closing costs, the origination fee, and discount points can be very substantial expenses to the seller if the seller elects to pay them. When taking a listing, a sales associate should include these items if the custom in the market area dictates. When preparing this estimate at the time of contract, the sales associate should take extra care if the seller will pay the buyer's costs. The licensee should use the lender's good-faith estimate, with a maximum amount agreed to in the contract. Leaving this open-ended in a contract can be disastrous if the discount points or other costs increase between the time of acceptance and the time of closing.

1 • Repairs and replacements usually are those that a lender might require. They also
2 could be the result of wood-destroying organisms or nonfunctioning appliances. The
3 licensee should use a cushion for such contingencies.
4 • The seller's attorney fee is an expense left to the seller to decide. The licensee should
5 list the normal closing review fee for the seller in his market area.
6 • The brokerage fee is the commission the brokerage firm charges.
7 • Other miscellaneous costs include items like express mail fees for mortgage payoffs
8 and recording mortgage satisfactions. The licensee should include a cushion here,
9 which allows for contingencies. A seller on a tight budget cannot afford unpleas-
10 ant surprises. This line also could be used to round uneven expense amounts into
11 even amounts. For example, if the expenses were $8,945.60, the miscellaneous costs
12 could be estimated at $54.40, resulting in total estimated expenses of $9,000.

13 **Prorations Section.**   This section, if not carefully estimated, could result in an
14 unpleasant surprise for the seller, because most prorations are debits (charges) to the
15 seller. Because the closing date is not certain, it is not necessary to do exact prorations;
16 approximations are satisfactory if amounts are rounded higher. The statement offers
17 no provision for insurance prorations or proceeds from a lender's escrow account.
18 Insurance should *not* be prorated; the buyer should purchase her own policy, and the
19 seller should get a cancellation refund. Because the insurance refund and escrow refund
20 from loans paid off are not received at closing, the net proceeds statement does not
21 include the items (If the mortgage is to be assumed, the prorations could be offset by
22 the amounts held in escrow, as the buyer will be expected to reimburse the seller for
23 those amounts.):

24 • Property taxes should be estimated for the year if tax information is not available.
25 An assumed closing date is used to estimate prorations. If the closing were antici-
26 pated for June 28, for example, the licensee would show a charge to the seller for half
27 the year's taxes.
28 • Interest prorations can be difficult to calculate. The amount depends on the time of
29 month for the closing. Most interest is paid in arrears, but not all loans have that
30 feature. The safest policy (if the loan is current) is to show a charge for a full month's
31 interest.
32 • Homeowner's dues can be substantial in some areas, particularly with condomini-
33 ums and other properties having substantial common maintenance areas. The dues
34 may be paid in advance, but often are paid in arrears. The homeowner should be
35 questioned about the status of the dues.
36 • Rents and deposits can be major charges to the seller of an income property. If the
37 seller has collected rent in advance, the buyer is entitled to the rent for the part of
38 the month after the closing. The buyer also should be paid the security deposits.

39 **Net Proceeds to Seller.**   The net proceeds equal the seller's equity less total expenses
40 and total prorations. The amount of the seller's proceeds should be rounded to the next
41 lowest $100.

42 Exercise: Estimating Net Proceeds to Seller

43 Estimating the seller's net proceeds properly is extremely important. This exercise
44 should be completed carefully using the seller's net proceeds form shown in Figure 6.1.
45 Round up on expenses, prorations, and mortgages, and do not use cents. The final esti-
46 mate should be rounded to the lowest hundred, using the following information:

47 Seller's name   Cindy Lewis
48 Property address   1947 Oldfield Circle
49 Prepared by   Janice Brown
50 Estimated closing date   August 26
51 Sales price $93,800.00

1	Existing first mortgage (8.5%)	47,425.67
2	Home equity loan (11%)	14,659.42
3	Brokerage fee	7%
4	Termite inspection and treatment	400.00
5	Buyer's title insurance	650.00
6	Repairs and replacements	450.00
7	Seller's attorney fee	350.00
8	Homeowner's warranty	375.00
9	Discount points	2,100.00
10	Annual taxes	1,325.00
11	Interest	?
11	Annual homeowner's dues	150.00

DISCUSSION EXERCISE 6.1

Using the seller's net proceeds form prepared in the above exercise, role-play the presentation of the form to the seller. The instructor might assign several persons to present the different sections of the material. Assign a reasonably motivated seller who is kind to the agent. The licensee should ask a closing question when showing the net proceeds from the sale.

LISTING CONTRACTS

A listing contract is an agreement between a real estate broker and a member of the public, most often a property owner. The listing contract specifies the duties of both the broker and the owner in the sale of the owner's real property. Without listing contracts, there would be little or no inventory to sell, exchange, lease, rent, or auction.

In Florida, a listing contract may be written, oral, or implied by the knowledge and consent of either party or both parties. Every written listing agreement must include a definite expiration date, a description of the property, the price and terms, the fee or commission, and the principal's signature. A legible, signed, true, and correct copy of the listing agreement must be given to the principal(s) within 24 hours of obtaining the written listing agreement. Also, a written listing contract may not contain a self-renewing or an automatic renewal provision. If it contains such a provision, the agreement is void. It is important to understand that a listing agreement is a personal services (employment) contract that requires the licensee (broker) to perform one or more professional services to fulfill the agreement. The broker may seek assistance from other licensees, but the primary responsibility remains with the listing broker. The listing contract is a broker's employment contract, and all listings should be in writing. If litigation should result from some misunderstanding, default, or breach, it is much easier to resolve by showing the terms of a written contract than by obtaining testimony to prove the terms or conditions of an oral listing. Because listing contracts are not covered by the statute of frauds, oral listing contracts are enforceable with the proper amount of evidence and testimony.

Types of Listing Contracts

In this chapter, three types of listing contracts are identified. The exclusive-right-of-sale listing contract is emphasized because of its predominance in residential property transactions.

Open Listing.   An **open listing** is a contract in which an owner reserves the right to employ any number of brokers. Brokers may work simultaneously, but the first broker who produces a ready, willing, and able buyer at the price and terms of the listing is the only one who earns a commission. If the owner himself sells the property without the aid of any of the brokers, he is not obligated to pay any commission; but if a broker can prove she was the procuring cause of the transaction, she may be entitled to a commission. While most residential brokers will not accept open listings, commercial and agricultural property brokers sometimes work with sellers with this type of listing.

Any listing contract normally creates an open listing unless the contract is worded in a manner that specifically provides for a different type of listing. While open listings may be either oral or implied, a contract does not exist until terms are negotiated. For example, a for-sale-by-owner sign that indicates brokers protected or in some way invites offers from brokers does not create a listing contract.

Either or all parties may terminate an open listing at will, and in the absence of formal notification, an open listing may terminate after a reasonable time. The owner principal is not obligated to notify any of the brokers that the property has been sold.

Exclusive-Agency Listing (Exclusive Listing).   The **exclusive-agency listing** is the preferred listing agreement of an owner who has selected one particular broker as his or her exclusive agent, for a specified period of time, to sell real property according to the owner's stated terms. In an exclusive-agency listing, the owner appoints the broker but reserves the right to sell the property without paying a commission to the broker if the broker has not introduced or identified the buyer. If the broker performs by selling the property before the owner can do so, the broker is entitled to a commission. Exclusive-agency residential listings are less common than exclusive-right-of-sale listings.

A common problem with exclusive-agency and open listings is the exposure to lawsuits for procuring cause between the broker and the seller.

DISCUSSION EXERCISE 6.2

Arthur Cody lists Donald Wilson's home under an exclusive-agency listing agreement. Arthur shows the property to William Farkas. William notices that the seller has a sign on the property saying For Sale By Owner—555-1145. Arthur drops William off and writes a letter to Donald, registering William as a prospect. Immediately after Arthur drops him off, William calls Donald directly. Donald does not know that Arthur has shown the property and agrees to a reduced price since no commission is involved. Donald and William enter into a contract for sale. It is only after the contract is signed that Donald gets Arthur's prospect registration letter. When the sale closes, Arthur brings suit for commission as the procuring cause of the sale.

Role-play the court argument: Arthur, arguing for a commission on the sale, and Donald, explaining why no commission is due.

In the discussion exercise above, Donald, who we assume to be an honest person, was sued because of the buyer's actions, not his own. How can a broker prevent this type of misunderstanding? Registration is not enough, because the notification may come after the parties have entered into a contract. A better method to help the seller receive fair disclosure is for the sales associate to recommend that the seller require the following words in all contracts the seller believes to be the procuring cause of the sale:

> This property is listed with a broker under an agreement that the broker will be paid a commission for procuring a buyer for the property. Buyer warrants to seller that he or she was not shown or made aware of this property by any real estate broker or sales associate. Buyer agrees that if information to the contrary is proven by a broker claiming a commission, buyer will reimburse seller for commissions due to said real estate broker as well as legal fees.

A buyer who has seen the property with a broker will refuse to sign such a statement, putting the seller on notice that the buyer is trying to save the commission by excluding the broker.

Two other problems can arise from an exclusive-agency agreement. First, a broker is reluctant to show property to a buyer if the owner's phone number is displayed prominently on a sign in front of the property. The sign invites the buyer to exclude the broker to get a better price. If the broker takes the listing under an exclusive agency, the broker should get the owner's agreement to remove the sign.

Another problem the broker faces is the possibility of the owner's advertising a lower price (broker's price less commission). The broker likely will lose the buyer if the buyer sees the owner's ad. The broker and the owner should quote the same price.

Exclusive-Right-of-Sale Listing.   The **exclusive-right-of-sale listing** is the most advantageous listing from the broker's viewpoint and the most common type of listing. The listing is given to a selected broker, who then becomes the exclusive broker for the sale of the property. The broker is due a commission regardless of who sells the property. That is, if the owner sells the property during the contract period, the broker still earns a commission. Also, if the owner sells the property within a designated time period after the listing contract has expired to a buyer originally introduced to the property by the broker, the owner usually is liable for a sales commission to the broker.

To be enforceable, this type of listing contract should be in writing and include valuable consideration. Only exclusive-right-of-sale and exclusive-agency listings may be entered into the MLS by the listing brokers.

Warranties by the Owner.   If the listing broker is a single agent for the seller, both the broker and the seller have obligations under the listing agreement. The principal has legal obligations to the broker, including performance of all promises made in the contract, as well as the obligation to engage in honest, straightforward dealing. The actions and misrepresentations of a seller can become a liability to the agent. For example, if a seller tells a sales associate that the plumbing pipes are copper and the sales associate passes along that information to a buyer without qualification, both the seller and the brokerage firm may be liable for damages if the buyer later discovers the plumbing pipes are polybutylene. Litigation may result in damages assessed against both the owner principal and the broker agent.

Latent Defects Disclosure.   To reduce the liability, most listing contracts in Florida contain a **warranty of owner** clause. The clause has a promise that the seller will warrant the accuracy of information set forth herein and on the data sheets, exhibits, and addenda attached hereto and to indemnify and hold harmless the licensee in the transaction or anyone relying on the owner's representations. The changing attitude of the courts today can be seen in the relatively new practice of attaching **latent defects addenda** to listing contracts. The owner and the broker are liable for failing to disclose known defects that materially affect the value of residential property. The disclosure is simply an attempt to create a degree of protection for the broker against potential liability resulting from oversight or the owner's dishonesty. It is closely related to the property condition disclosure described earlier.

Telephone Cold-Calling Restraints.   The Florida Department of Agriculture maintains a no-solicitation list. If you call a person on the list and try to sell him something, you could be subject to a $10,000 fine. However, telephone solicitation calls made by real estate licensees to actual or prospective sellers or lessors of real property are permitted when such calls are made in response to yard signs (FSBOs) or other forms of advertisement placed by the sellers or lessors, whether or not the sellers or lessors are on the list. As before, licensees also may contact clients with whom they have had previous business relationships, even if the clients are on the no-solicitation list (F.S. 501.059).

Effective October 1, 2003, a national "Do Not Call" list created a telemarketing law that supersedes all state laws that are less strict. It removes the provisions of Florida's law that allows licensees to call FSBOs. If a business relationship has been established, a person may call the customer for up to 18 months. Florida licensees must now refer to both the Florida and the national lists before making prospecting calls.

Web Link

www.donotcall.gov
National Do Not Call Registry

Preparation of the Residential Profile Sheet

While different areas of the state use different listing forms, **profile sheets** and exclusive-right-of-sale listing contracts, they all require the same basic information. The listing form used in your area should be substituted for the one in this chapter. (See Figure 6.2.) If none is available, complete the sample residential profile sheet and listing contract in this text to develop the skill needed to gather important information. Use the following case study to fill out the residential profile sheet.

On December 13, 20AA, John K. and Elizabeth J. Scott conclude a contractual agreement with you, a licensed real estate sales associate. You have a six-month exclusive right to sell their home, which has been granted homestead tax exemption and is owned as an estate by the entireties. The house is an all-electric, three-bedroom, two-bath, single-story structure, with an efficient traffic pattern. The master bath has an oversized, Roman-style bath. The house is brick veneer over concrete block with a Spanish tile roof. Insulation used in the attic space has an R-23 rating. The house is five years old, but a new heat-pump-type air-conditioner and heater was installed in November 20AA.

The entire neighborhood is zoned R-1A and consists of quality homes on quiet, tree-lined streets, with city and county utilities and telephone and power lines underground. City bus service is two blocks away, and elementary, junior high, and high schools are all within six blocks of the property.

The Scotts have decided that $71,500 is a fair selling price. The 110' × 150' lot has been assessed by the county at $15,000, and the dwelling has been assessed at $55,600. The Scotts briefly considered an offer of a year's lease at $600 per month, but decided to sell instead. The property, located at 1234 Sunny Circle, Sunshine City, is legally described as Lot 21, Block C, Cool Canal Subdivision, Sunshine City, as recorded in Plat Book 39, Page 543, Lottery County, Florida.

The lot is completely landscaped and well-maintained. The house consists of a 14' × 24' great room, 14' × 18' master bedroom, 10' × 14' den, 14' × 14' second bedroom, and 12' × 14' third bedroom. The dining area between the 10' × 10' kitchen and the great room is 12' × 12'. A utility room, a foyer, a pantry, a hall, two baths, and four large closets bring the total air-conditioned and heated living area to 1,776 square feet. An unusually large garage of 720 square feet brings the total square footage under roof to 2,496.

FIGURE 6.2   RESIDENTIAL PROFILE SHEET

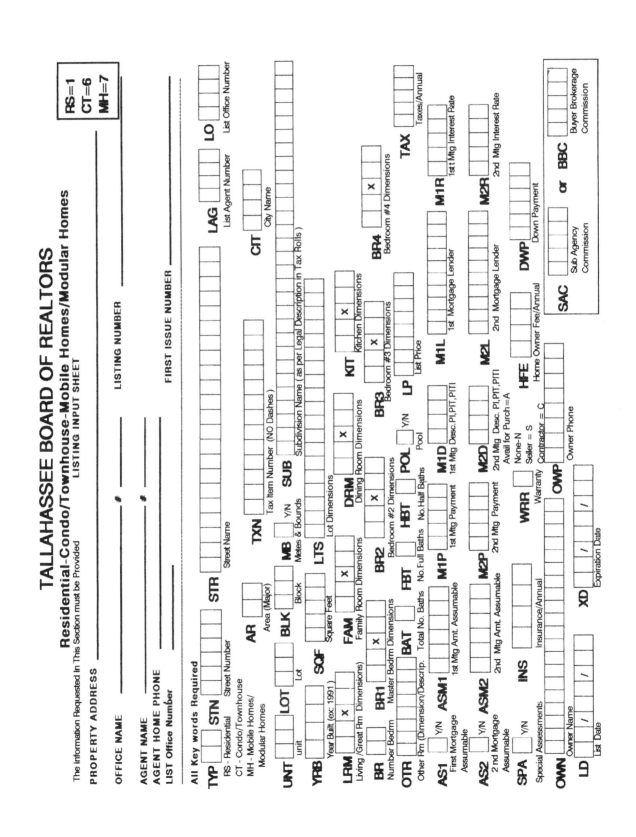

FIGURE 6.2 RESIDENTIAL PROFILE SHEET (Continued)

WHEN SOLD, CHANGE REMARKS TO REFLECT TERMS AND OTHER SALES INFORMATION

RE1 — Remarks Line 1
RE2 — Remarks Line 2
RE3 — Remarks Line 3
RE4 — Remarks Line 4
DIR — Directions

All Coded Info. is Searchable & MUST be entered in Alpha Order
* Denotes Required Fields

*BKD - Book Desc.
A - New Construction — NEW CONST
B - ReSale — RESALE

*CAT - Category
A - Single Family — SNGL FAM
B - Single Family & Acreage — SNGL FAM+ACR
C - Coastal Property — COASTAL PROP
D - Office - Residential — OFFICE-RES

*CON - Construction
A - Brick/Brick Veneer 2 Sides or Less — BRK-2
B - Brick/Brick Veneer 3 Sides — BRK-3
C - Brick/Brick Veneer 4 Sides — BRK-4
D - Frame — FRA
E - Redwood/Cedar/Cypress — RW/CED
F - Stucco — STUC
G - Concrete Block — CONC
H - Manuf. Siding — M.SID
I - Vinyl Siding — V.SID
J - Aluminum Siding — A.SID
K - Masonite — MASON
L - Asbestos Siding — ASB
M - Log — LOG
N - Stone — STONE
O - Other — OTH

*COO - Cooling
A - Central — CENT
B - Heat Pump — HPMP
C - Electric — ELEC
D - Natural Gas — GAS
E - Window/Wall — WW
F - Solar — SOL
G - Ceiling Fans — C-FAN
H - Attic Fans — A-FAN
I - None — NONE

*LAD - Living Area Description
A - Eat-in-Kitchen — EAT-IN-K
B - Separate Kitchen — SEP-KIT
C - Separate Dining Rm — SEP-DIN
D - Kit/Din Rm/Liv Rm — KT/DR/LR
e - Kit/Family Rm — KT/FR
F - Living Rm/Dining Rm — LR/DR
G - Family Rm/Dining Rm — FR/DR
H - Great Room — GRT RM
I - Family Room — FAM RM
J - Galley Kitchen — GALLEY
K - Kitchen w/Bar — KT W/BAR

EQP - Equipment
A - Range — RNG
B - Refrig/Icemaker — REF-I
C - Refrigerator — REF
D - Dishwasher — DSHW
E - Disposal — DISP
F - Microwave — MICRO
G - Garage Door Opener — GAR-O
H - Security System — SECSYS
I - Smoke Detector — SM-D
J - Deadbolt — BOLT
K - Trash Compactor — TR-COMP
L - Washer — WASH
M - Dryer — DRY
N - Intercom — INTERCOM
O - Central Vacuum — C-VAC
P - TV Antenna — TV-A
Q - Satellite Dish — S-DISH
R - Gas Grill — GAS GRL
S - Sprinkler Sys-Lawn — SPR SYS
T - None — NONE

LT - Listing Type
A - Exclusive Right of Sale — ERS
B - Exclusive Right of Sale w/Named Exemption — ERS-E
C - Exclusive Agency — EA

*FEE - Fee Includes
A - Road Maint. — RD MAINT
B - Common Area — COM AREA
C - Water/Sewer — WTR/SWR
D - Exterior Maint. — EXT MAINT
E - Insurance — INS
F - Trash/Garbage — TRSH/GRBG
G - Pool — POOL
H - Street Lights — ST LITE
I - Cable TV — CABLE-TV
J - Tennis Membership — TENNIS
K - Other — OTH
L - None — NONE

*FLO - Flooring
A - Slab — SLAB
B - Off Grade — OF-GD
C - Hardwood — HARDWD
D - Parquet — PARQ
E - Carpet — CARPET
F - Some Carpet — S-CRPT
G - Ceramic/Clay — C-TILE
H - Vinyl Tile — V-TILE
I - Vinyl — VINYL
J - Terrazo — TRZO

FIGURE 6.2   RESIDENTIAL PROFILE SHEET (Continued)

1/6/7

Coded Information
All Coded Information is Searchable
Must Enter in Alpha Order

* Denotes Required Fields

*FMF - Existing First Mortgage Financing
A - Non-Assumable — NO-ASM
B - Assumable-Non Qualify — ASM-NQ
C - Assumable-Qualify — ASM-Q
D - Conventional — CONV
E - FHA — FHA
F - VA — VA
G - Wrap — WRAP
H - Private — PRIV
I - GPM — GPM
J - ARM — ARM
K - Assume Current Rate — ASM CUR
L - Assume Escalating — ASM ESC
M - None — NONE
N - Other — OTH

FRT - Frontage
A - Golf Course — GOLF
B - Pond — POND
C - Canal — CANAL
D - Gulf — GULF
E - Bay — BAY
F - River — RIVER
G - Stream/Creek — STRM/C
H - Spring — SPRING
I - Government Forest — GOV-F
J - Lake — LAKE
K - Greenbelt — GREENB
L - Park — PARK

GAR - Garage
A - 1 Car Carport — 1-CPT
B - 2 Car Carport — 2-CPT
C - 3+ Car Carport — 3+CPT
D - 1 Car Garage — 1-GAR
E - 2 Car Garage — 2-GAR
F - 3+ Car Garage — 3+GAR
G - Driveway Only — DRV

HEA - Heating
A - Central — CENT
B - Heat Pump — HPMP
C - Electric — ELEC
D - Natural Gas — GAS
E - Propane Gas — PROP
F - Oil — OIL
G - Solar — SOL

PTY - Pool Type
A - Inground Pool — IG POOL
B - Above Ground Pool — AG POOL
C - Concrete — CONC
D - Vinyl Liner — VINYL LNR
E - Screened Pool — SC POOL
F - Pool Equipment — POOL EQPT

*ROA - Road Frontage Type
A - Gov. Maint. — GOV MNT
B - Other Maint. — OTH MNT
C - Paved — PAVD
D - Unpaved — UNPVD
E - Curb & Gutters — CB&GT
F - Street Lights — ST LITE
G - Sidewalks — SD WLKS
H - Other Access — OTH-ACC

DRV - Driveway
A - Concrete — CONC
B - Gravel/Dirt — GRVL
C - Asphalt — ASPLT
D - Exposed Aggregate — EXPAGG
E - Circle Drive — CRC DRV
F - Unpaved Maint — UNPVD
G - Assoc. Maint — ASSN MNT
H - Other — OTH

*SHO - Showing Instructions
A - Vacant — VAC
B - Owner Occupied — OC-OW
C - Tenant Occupied — OC-TN
D - Lock Box — LB
E - Appointment Only — AP
F - Call Occupant — OO
G - Call Manager — CM
H - Call Listing Office — CL
I - Key in Listing Office — KL
J - Caution!! Guard Dog — G-DOG
K - Caution!! Pets — PETS
L - Leave Card — LC
M - Day Sleeper — DAY SLPR
N - Under Construction Renovation — UN CONST
O - Proposed Construction — PROPOSE

STY - Style
A - Traditional — TRAD
B - Ranch — RNCH
C - Contemporary — CONTEMP
D - Colonial — COLONIAL
E - Spanish — SPAN
F - 2 Story — 2STY
G - Split Level — SPLIT
H - Raised Ranch — RAISE
I - Split Foyer — SPLIT F
J - Victorian — VICT
K - Cape Cod — CAPE
L - 1 Story — 1STY
M - 2 Story Br Down — 2STY BR D
N - 2 Story Br Up — ALL BR-UP

*TRM - Terms (Potential Financing)
A - Owner — OWN
B - Wraparound — WRAP
C - Second — 2ND
D - FHA — FHA
E - VA — VA
F - Conventional — CONV
G - Contract for Deed — DEED
H - Lease/Purchase — LEA/PUR
I - Exchange — EXCH
J - Private — PRIV
K - Subordination — SUBOR
L - ARM — ARM
M - GPM — GPM
N - FHMA — FHMA
O - Federal Land Bank — FLB
P - Cash — CASH
Q - Assumable-N/Q — ASM-NQ
R - Assumable -Qualify — ASM-Q
S - Call LAG for Terms — C-LAG
T - Other — OTH

*WHT - Water Heater
A - Gas — GAS
B - Electric — ELEC
C - Solar — SOLAR
D - 2+ Heaters — 2+HTR
E - 40 or Less Gallons — -40 GAL
F - 40 or More Gallons — +40 GAL
G - Other — OTH

FIGURE 6.2   RESIDENTIAL PROFILE SHEET (Continued)

H - Wood Burning Stove ... WOOD
I - Space/Wall ... SP/WA
J - None ... NONE

MSC - Miscellaneous Items Included

A - Some Items Excluded ... EXCLUD
B - Wood Burning Fireplace ... W-FRPL
C - Other Fireplace ... O-FRPL
D - Deck ... DECK
E - Patio ... PATIO
F - Fenced ... FENCE
G - Privacy Fence ... PRIV FEN
H - Cathedral Ceiling ... CATH CEL
I - Window Treatments ... WND TRT
J - Some wind Treatments ... S-WIND T
K - Hot Tub ... H-TUB
L - Whirlpool ... WHRLPL
M - Garden Tub ... GDN TUB
N - Shower Stall ... SHW STALL
O - Sauna ... SAUNA
P - Cable TV ... CABLE
Q - Wallpaper ... WALLPAP
R - Wet Bar ... WETBAR
S - Storage Shed ... SHED
T - Gazebo ... GAZBO
U - Barbeque Pit ... BBQ
V - Stables ... STBL
W - Tennis Court ... TENNIS
X - 1-5 Acres ... 1-5 AC
Y - 5+ Acres ... 5+ AC

ORM - Other Rooms

A - Family Room ... FAM RM
B - Utility Room Inside ... UT RM IN
C - Utility Room Outside ... UT RM OT
D - Garage Enclosed ... GAR-ENC
E - Master Br-Apart ... M BR-AP
F - Master Br-Suite ... M BR-SU
G - Bedroom-Down ... BR-DWN
H - Walk-in Closet ... W/CLOS
I - Study/Office ... ST/OFC
J - Breakfast Room ... BRKFST
K - Pantry ... PTRY
L - Recreation Room ... REC RM
M - Foyer ... FOYR
N - Guest Apartment ... G-APT
O - Screened Porch ... S-PORCH
P - Workshop ... WRKSHP
Q - Greenhouse ... GREENHS
R - Atrium/Solarium ... ATRM/SLRM

SMF - Existing Second Mortgage Financing

A - Non-Assumable ... NO-ASM
B - Assumable-Non-Qualify ... ASM-NQ
C - Assumable-Qualify ... ASM-Q
D - Assm Current Rate ... ASM CUR
E - Assumable Escalating ... ASM-ESC
F - Private ... PRIV
G - Conventional ... CONV
H - Wraparound ... WRAP
I - ARM ... ARM
J - Other ... OTH

SPE - Special Exemption

A - No Homestead ... NOH
B - Homestead ... HOM
C - Other Exemptions ... OTH
D - Tax on Lot Only ... TXLT
E - Partial Homestead ... PART

DFC - Distance from Capitol

A - Less than 3 Miles ... LESS 3 MI
B - 3-5 Miles ... 3-5 MI
C - 6 - 10 Miles ... 6-10 MI
D - 11 - 15 Miles ... 11-15 MI
E - 16 - 20 Miles ... 16-20 MI
F - 21 - 25 Miles ... 21-25 MI
G - 25 + Miles ... 25+ MI

WND - Windows

A - Single Hung ... SNGL HUNG
B - Double Hung ... DBL HUNG
C - Insulated ... INSUL
D - Sliding Glass ... SLID GLAS
E - Wood Sash ... WOOD SASH
F - Jalousie ... JALS
G - Casement ... CASE
H - Bay Window ... BAY WNDW
I - Skylight ... SKYLITE
J - Storm Window ... STRM WNDW
K - Stained Glass ... STAINED
L - Garden Window ... GDN WNDW
M - Aluminum Awning ... ALUM AWN
N - Vinyl Clad ... VINYL CLD
O - Picture Window ... PICT WNDW
P - Clerestory ... CLERE
Q - Other ... OTH

WTR - Water

A - City ... CITY
B - Talquin ... TALQ
C - Well Installed ... WELL-I
D - Private System ... PRIV
E - Community ... COMM
F - Other ... OTH

PHO - Photo

A - Photo Needed ... TAKE PHO
B - Photo Submitted ... PHO SUB
C - Sketch Submitted ... SKT SUB
D - No Photo Required ... NO PHO
E - Out of Area ... OUT
F - Photo Taken ... PHO TAKN
G - Photo Retake ... PHO RETK
H - Addn'l Photo/Call Agt ... ADL PHO

FLP - Floor Plan

A - One Story ... 1-STRY
B - Two Story ... 2-STRY
C - Ground Floor Unit ... GRD FLR
D - Upstairs Unit ... UP UNT
E - End Unit ... END UNT
F - Interior Unit ... INT UNT

MAJOR AREA

1 Northeast Quadrant
2 Northwest Quadrant
3 Southeast Quadrant
4 Southwest Quadrant
5 Jefferson County
6 Franklin County
7 Gadsden County
8 Wakulla County
20 Other Areas

APD

Additional Photo Description
(Only if Choice H is Selected from PHO)

The Scotts have paid the property taxes for 20AA. Because John must report to his new job in another state by April 1, 20BB, at the latest, he will pay the new owner the 20BB taxes, which will be prorated at the closing. The city, county and school board tax rate for the subdivision was 29 mills for 20AA, including all bond and tax levies.

The Scotts have just refinanced and now hold a 10.5 percent, 30-year conventional mortgage in the amount of $55,000 with the Secured Profit Savings Association. Their monthly payment for principal and interest is $503.11. A comprehensive homeowner's hazard and liability policy with a face value of $56,500, purchased at a cost of $264 for one year, is due to expire at midnight, October 18, 20BB.

All floors except the kitchen and bathrooms have custom carpets, and every window is equipped with custom-made draperies. The Scotts are willing to leave all carpets and draperies. The kitchen is all-electric, and the electric water heater is a 60-gallon, quick-recovery unit. The kitchen appliances include a large, beverage-center-type refrigerator, a built-in food processor; a microwave oven; an electric oven over range; a disposal; a dishwasher; and a trash compactor. The Scotts have decided to leave all of the appliances except the refrigerator.

The Scotts have stipulated that their home is to be shown by appointment only and have provided you with their telephone number (654-3210). They have indicated a willingness to take back a second mortgage or a contract for deed, but they will not agree to any financing that results in a cost to them. Your employer, Super Real Estate, Inc. (987-6543), and the Scotts have agreed on a 7½ percent sales commission on the gross sales price. They will allow you to split with buyers' brokers or transaction brokers. The Scotts have agreed to give possession no later than the actual date of closing. If the Scotts withdraw the listing, the fee will be 1 percent. You agree to put the listing into the MLS within three working days. In case the Scotts want to lease the property, your fee is 10 percent. The Scotts authorize you to put a **lockbox** on the home.

Preparation of an Exclusive-Right-of-Sale Listing Contract

Once she has gathered and entered the property information on the profile sheet, the licensee should prepare the listing agreement. The sales associate should complete as much of the paperwork as possible before the listing appointment. Because the task can be done in a controlled environment without distractions, it is more likely to be correct. The advance preparation also results in a more efficient process once the sales associate is with the seller.

A listing contract is shown in Figure 6.3. Fill in the information on this form or on one used in your area, as appropriate.

The real estate licensee is expected to be knowledgeable about the listing contract and able to explain the provisions clearly and completely. Sellers lose confidence in a sales associate who stumbles through an explanation of the agreement or who doesn't know the meaning of a clause.

The sample shown is distributed by the Florida Association of REALTORS®. If you use a different form, the clauses in your listing agreement probably are very similar. The numbered paragraphs below correspond to the 11 paragraphs in the agreement.

Parties. The parties are the owner(s) of the property and the brokerage firm, not the sales associate. All persons owning an interest in the property should be included here. The licensee should check the sellers' deed to ensure that all persons on the deed sign the listing. Corporations, partnerships, trusts, and estates require special treatment. See the broker or an attorney for advice:

1. *Authority to Sell Property.* This paragraph gives the broker an exclusive right to sell the property. The listing term also is shown here. Many brokerage firms have policies for the listing term, depending on the type of property. A typical residential period is six months. The licensee should examine that policy carefully,

FIGURE 6.3   EXCLUSIVE RIGHT OF SALE CONTRACT

Exclusive Right of Sale Listing Agreement
FLORIDA ASSOCIATION OF REALTORS®

This Exclusive Right of Sale Listing Agreement ("Agreement") is between

_____ ("**Seller**") and

_____ ("**Broker**").

1. AUTHORITY TO SELL PROPERTY: Seller gives **Broker** the EXCLUSIVE RIGHT TO SELL the real and personal property (collectively "Property") described below, at the price and terms described below, beginning the _____ day of _____, _____ and terminating at 11:59 p.m. the _____ day of _____, _____ ("Termination Date"). Upon full execution of a contract for sale and purchase of the Property, all rights and obligations of this Agreement will automatically extend through the date of the actual closing of the sales contract. **Seller** and **Broker** acknowledge that this Agreement does not guarantee a sale. This Property will be offered to any person without regard to race, color, religion, sex, handicap, familial status, national origin or any other factor protected by federal, state or local law. **Seller** certifies and represents that he/she/it is legally entitled to convey the Property and all improvements.

2. DESCRIPTION OF PROPERTY:
  (a) Real Property Street Address: _____

  Legal Description:_____
  _____ ❏ See Attachment _____
  (b) Personal Property, including appliances:_____
  _____
  _____ ❏ See Attachment _____
  (c) Occupancy: Property ❏ is ❏ is not currently occupied by a tenant. If occupied, the lease term expires _____.

3. PRICE AND TERMS: The property is offered for sale on the following terms, or on other terms acceptable to **Seller**:
  (a) Price: $_____
  (b) Financing Terms: ❏ Cash ❏ Conventional ❏ VA ❏ FHA ❏ Other _____
  ❏ **Seller** Financing: **Seller** will hold a purchase money mortgage in the amount of $_____ with the following terms: _____
  ❏ Assumption of Existing Mortgage: **Buyer** may assume existing mortgage for $_____ plus an assumption fee of $_____. The mortgage is for a term of _____ years beginning in _____, at an interest rate of _____% ❏ fixed ❏ variable (describe) _____
  Lender approval of assumption ❏ is required ❏ is not required ❏ unknown. Notice to **Seller**: You may remain liable for an assumed mortgage for a number of years after the Property is sold. Check with your lender to determine the extent of your liability. **Seller** will ensure that all mortgage payments and required escrow deposits are current at the time of closing and will convey the escrow deposit to the buyer at closing.
  (c) Seller Expenses: Seller will pay mortgage discount or other closing costs not to exceed _____% of the purchase price; and any other expenses **Seller** agrees to pay in connection with a transaction.

4. BROKER OBLIGATIONS AND AUTHORITY: Broker agrees to make diligent and continued efforts to sell the Property until a sales contract is pending on the Property. **Seller** authorizes **Broker** to:
  (a) Advertise the Property as **Broker** deems advisable in newspapers, publications, computer networks including the Internet and other media; place appropriate transaction signs on the Property, including "For Sale" signs and "Sold" signs (once **Seller** signs a sales contract); and use **Seller's** name in connection with marketing or advertising the Property;
  (b) Obtain information relating to the present mortgage(s) on the Property.
  (c) Place the property in a multiple listing service(s) (MLS). **Seller** authorizes **Broker** to report to the MLS/Association of Realtors® this listing information and price, terms and financing information on any resulting sale. **Seller** authorizes **Broker**, the MLS and/or Association of Realtors® to use, license or sell the active listing and sold data.
  (d) Provide objective comparative market analysis information to potential buyers; and
  (e) (Check if applicable) ❏ Use a lock box system to show and access the Property. A lock box does not ensure the Property's security; **Seller** is advised to secure or remove valuables. **Seller** agrees that the lock box is for **Seller's** benefit and releases **Broker**, persons working through **Broker** and **Broker's** local Realtor Board / Association from all liability and responsibility in connection with any loss that occurs. ❏ Withhold verbal offers. ❏ Withhold all offers once **Seller** accepts a sales contract for the Property.
  (f) Act as a single agent of **Seller** with consent to transition to transaction broker.

5. SELLER OBLIGATIONS: In consideration of **Broker's** obligations, **Seller** agrees to:
  (a) Cooperate with **Broker** in carrying out the purpose of this Agreement, including referring immediately to **Broker** all inquiries regarding the Property's transfer, whether by purchase or any other means of transfer.
  (b) Provide **Broker** with keys to the Property and make the Property available for **Broker** to show during reasonable times.
  (c) Inform **Broker** prior to leasing, mortgaging or otherwise encumbering the Property.
  (d) Indemnify **Broker** and hold **Broker** harmless from losses, damages, costs and expenses of any nature, including attorney's

ERS-10tn   Rev. 7/03   © 2003   Florida Association of REALTORS®   All Rights Reserved   Page 1 of 5

FIGURE 6.3   EXCLUSIVE RIGHT OF SALE CONTRACT (Continued)

fees, and from liability to any person, that **Broker** incurs because of (1) **Seller's** negligence, representations, misrepresentations, actions or inactions, (2) the use of a lock box, (3) the existence of undisclosed material facts about the Property, or (4) a court or arbitration decision that a broker who was not compensated in connection with a transaction is entitled to compensation from **Broker**. This clause will survive **Broker's** performance and the transfer of title.

(e) To perform any act reasonably necessary to comply with FIRPTA (Internal Revenue Code Section 1445).

(f) Make all legally required disclosures, including all facts that materially affect the Property's value and are not readily observable or known by the buyer. **Seller** represents there are no material facts (building code violations, pending code citations, unobservable defects, etc.) other than the following:_____

_____

Seller will immediately inform **Broker** of any material facts that arise after signing this Agreement.

(g) Consult appropriate professionals for related legal, tax, property condition, environmental, foreign reporting requirements and other specialized advice.

6. COMPENSATION: Seller will compensate **Broker** as specified below for procuring a buyer who is ready, willing and able to purchase the Property or any interest in the Property on the terms of this Agreement or on any other terms acceptable to **Seller**. **Seller** will pay **Broker** as follows (plus applicable sales tax):

(a) _____% of the total purchase price OR $_____, no later than the date of closing specified in the sales contract. However, closing is not a prerequisite for **Broker's** fee being earned.

(b) _____ ($ or %) of the consideration paid for an option, at the time an option is created. If the option is exercised, **Seller** will pay **Broker** the paragraph 6(a) fee, less the amount **Broker** received under this subparagraph.

(c) _____ ($ or %) of gross lease value as a leasing fee, on the date **Seller** enters into a lease or agreement to lease, whichever is soonest. This fee is not due if the Property is or becomes the subject of a contract granting an exclusive right to lease the Property.

(d) Broker's fee is due in the following circumstances: (1) If any interest in the Property is transferred, whether by sale, lease, exchange, governmental action, bankruptcy or any other means of transfer, regardless of whether the buyer is secured by **Broker**, **Seller** or any other person. (2) If **Seller** refuses or fails to sign an offer at the price and terms stated in this Agreement, defaults on an executed sales contract or agrees with a buyer to cancel an executed sales contract. (3) If, within _____ days after Termination Date ("Protection Period"), **Seller** transfers or contracts to transfer the Property or any interest in the Property to any prospects with whom **Seller**, **Broker** or any real estate licensee communicated regarding the Property prior to Termination Date. However, no fee will be due **Broker** if the Property is relisted after Termination Date and sold through another broker.

(e) Retained Deposits: As consideration for **Broker's** services, **Broker** is entitled to receive _____% of all deposits that **Seller** retains as liquidated damages for a buyer's default in a transaction, not to exceed the paragraph 6(a) fee.

7. COOPERATION AND COMPENSATION WITH OTHER BROKERS: Broker's office policy is to cooperate with all other brokers except when not in **Seller's** best interest: ❑ and to offer compensation in the amount of _____% of the purchase price or $_____ to **Buyer's** agents, who represent the interest of the buyers, and not the interest of **Seller** in a transaction; ❑ and to offer compensation in the amount of _____% of the purchase price or $_____ to a broker who has no brokerage relationship with the **Buyer** or **Seller**; ❑ and to offer compensation in the amount of _____% of the purchase price or $_____ to Transaction brokers for the **Buyer**; ❑ None of the above (if this is checked, the Property cannot be placed in the MLS.)

8. BROKERAGE RELATIONSHIP:

IMPORTANT NOTICE

FLORIDA LAW REQUIRES THAT REAL ESTATE LICENSEES PROVIDE THIS NOTICE TO POTENTIAL SELLERS AND BUYERS OF REAL ESTATE.

You should not assume that any real estate broker or salesperson represents you unless you agree to engage a real estate licensee in an authorized brokerage relationship, either as a single agent or as a transaction broker. You are advised not to disclose any information you want to be held in confidence until you make a decision on representation.

SINGLE AGENT NOTICE

FLORIDA LAW REQUIRES THAT REAL ESTATE LICENSEES OPERATING AS SINGLE AGENTS DISCLOSE TO BUYERS AND SELLERS THEIR DUTIES.

As a single agent, _____ and its associates owe to you the following duties:

 1. Dealing honestly and fairly;

 2. Loyalty;

 3. Confidentiality;

FIGURE 6.3   EXCLUSIVE RIGHT OF SALE CONTRACT (Continued)

4. Obedience;
5. Full disclosure;
6. Accounting for all funds;
7. Skill, care, and diligence in the transaction;
8. Presenting all offers and counteroffers in a timely manner, unless a party has previously directed the licensee otherwise in writing; and
9. Disclosing all known facts that materially affect the value of residential real property and are not readily observable.

_____   _____
Date   Signature

CONSENT TO TRANSITION TO TRANSACTION BROKER

FLORIDA LAW ALLOWS REAL ESTATE LICENSEES WHO REPRESENT A BUYER OR SELLER AS A SINGLE AGENT TO CHANGE FROM A SINGLE AGENT RELATIONSHIP TO A TRANSACTION BROKERAGE RELATIONSHIP IN ORDER FOR THE LICENSEE TO ASSIST BOTH PARTIES IN A REAL ESTATE TRANSACTION BY PROVIDING A LIMITED FORM OF REPRESENTATION TO BOTH THE BUYER AND THE SELLER. THIS CHANGE IN RELATIONSHIP CANNOT OCCUR WITHOUT YOUR PRIOR WRITTEN CONSENT.

As a transaction broker, _____ and its
associates, provides to you a limited form of representation that includes the following duties:
1. Dealing honestly and fairly;
2. Accounting for all funds;
3. Using skill, care, and diligence in the transaction;
4. Disclosing all known facts that materially affect the value of residential real property and are not readily observable to the buyer;
5. Presenting all offers and counteroffers in a timely manner, unless a party has previously directed the licensee otherwise in writing;
6. Limited confidentiality, unless waived in writing by a party. This limited confidentiality will prevent disclosure that the seller will accept a price less than the asking or listed price, that the buyer will pay a price greater than the price submitted in a written offer, of the motivation of any party for selling or buying property, that a seller or buyer will agree to financing terms other than those offered, or of any other information requested by a party to remain confidential; and
7. Any additional duties that are entered into by this or by separate written agreement.
Limited representation means that a buyer or seller is not responsible for the acts of the licensee. Additionally, parties are giving up their rights to the undivided loyalty of the licensee. This aspect of limited representation allows a licensee to facilitate a real estate transaction by assisting both the buyer and the seller, but a licensee will not work to represent one party to the detriment of the other party when acting as a transaction broker to both parties.

_____I agree that my agent may assume the role and duties of a transaction broker. (must be initialed or signed)

_____   _____   _____
Date   Signature   Signature

IMPORTANT NOTICE

FLORIDA LAW REQUIRES THAT REAL ESTATE LICENSEES PROVIDE THIS NOTICE TO POTENTIAL SELLERS AND BUYERS OF REAL ESTATE.

You should not assume that any real estate broker or salesperson represents you unless you agree to engage a real estate licensee in an authorized brokerage relationship, either as a single agent or as a transaction broker. You are advised not to disclose any information you want to be held in confidence until you make a decision on representation.

TRANSACTION BROKER NOTICE

FLORIDA LAW REQUIRES THAT REAL ESTATE LICENSEES OPERATING AS TRANSACTION BROKERS DISCLOSE TO BUYERS AND SELLERS THEIR ROLE AND DUTIES IN PROVIDING A LIMITED FORM OF REPRESENTATION.
As a transaction broker, _____ and its
associates, provides to you a limited form of representation that includes the following duties:
1. Dealing honestly and fairly;
2. Accounting for all funds;
3. Using skill, care, and diligence in the transaction;
4. Disclosing all known facts that materially affect the value of residential real property and are not readily observable to the buyer;

FIGURE 6.3 EXCLUSIVE RIGHT OF SALE CONTRACT (Continued)

5. Presenting all offers and counteroffers in a timely manner, unless a party has previously directed the licensee otherwise in writing;

6. Limited confidentiality, unless waived in writing by a party. This limited confidentiality will prevent disclosure that the seller will accept a price less than the asking or listed price, that the buyer will pay a price greater than the price submitted in a written offer, of the motivation of any party for selling or buying property, that a seller or buyer will agree to financing terms other than those offered, or of any other information requested by a party to remain confidential; and

7. Any additional duties that are entered into by this or by separate written agreement.

Limited representation means that a buyer or seller is not responsible for the acts of the licensee. Additionally, parties are giving up their rights to the undivided loyalty of the licensee. This aspect of limited representation allows a licensee to facilitate a real estate transaction by assisting both the buyer and the seller, but a licensee will not work to represent one party to the detriment of the other party when acting as a transaction broker to both parties.

| _____ | _____ | _____ |
| Date | Signature | Signature |

9. **CONDITIONAL TERMINATION:** At **Seller's** request, **Broker** may agree to conditionally terminate this Agreement. If **Broker** agrees to conditional termination, **Seller** must sign a withdrawal agreement, reimburse **Broker** for all direct expenses incurred in marketing the Property and pay a cancellation fee of $_____ plus applicable sales tax. **Broker** may void the conditional termination and **Seller** will pay the fee stated in paragraph 6(a) less the cancellation fee if **Seller** transfers or contracts to transfer the Property or any interest in the Property during the time period from the date of conditional termination to Termination Date and Protection Period, if applicable.

10. **DISPUTE RESOLUTION:** This Agreement will be construed under Florida law. All controversies, claims and other matters in question between the parties arising out of or relating to this Agreement or the breach thereof will be settled by first attempting mediation under the rules of the American Arbitration Association or other mediator agreed upon by the parties. If litigation arises out of this Agreement, the prevailing party will be entitled to recover reasonable attorney's fees and costs, unless the parties agree that disputes will be settled by arbitration as follows: **Arbitration:** By initialing in the space provided, **Seller** (_____) (_____), Listing Associate (_____) and Listing Broker (_____) agree that disputes not resolved by mediation will be settled by neutral binding arbitration in the county in which the Property is located in accordance with the rules of the American Arbitration Association or other arbitrator agreed upon by the parties. Each party to any arbitration or litigation (including appeals and interpleaders) will pay its own fees, costs and expenses, including attorney's fees, and will equally split the arbitrators' fees and administrative fees of arbitration.

11. **MISCELLANEOUS:** This Agreement is binding on **Broker's** and **Seller's** heirs, personal representatives, administrators, successors and assigns. **Broker** may assign this Agreement to another listing office. Signatures, initials and modifications communicated by facsimile will be considered as originals. The term "buyer" as used in this Agreement includes buyers, tenants, exchangors, optionees and other categories of potential or actual transferees.

12. **ADDITIONAL TERMS:** _____

FIGURE 6.3   EXCLUSIVE RIGHT OF SALE CONTRACT (Continued)

Date: _____   **Seller:** _____   Tax ID No: _____

Telephone #'s: Home_____   Work_____   Cell_____   Fax:_____

Address: _____E-mail: _____

Date: _____   **Seller:** _____   Tax ID No: _____

Telephone #'s: Home_____   Work_____   Cell_____   Fax:_____

Address: _____E-mail: _____

Date: _____   **Authorized Listing Associate or Broker:** _____

Brokerage Firm Name: _____ Telephone: _____

Address: _____

The copyright laws of the United States (17 U.S. Code) forbid the unauthorized reproduction of this form by any means including facsimile or computerized forms.

Copy returned to **Seller** on the _____ day of _____, _____ by: ❏ personal delivery ❏ mail ❏ facsimile.

however, in light of the best marketing period. For instance, in many areas of Florida, the best sales period is from May through August. If that is the case, a six-month listing taken on January 2 expires July 2, with two months remaining in the best selling period. A far better approach is a minimum of six months, provided all listings remain active at least through August 31. A contract written during the listing period extends the listing until the closing. The seller agrees to offer the property without unlawful discrimination. The seller warrants that he can convey the property legally.

2. (a) ***Description of Property.*** The property address is entered here. The legal description should be taken from the public records or from the owner's deed, if available. If it is a metes-and-bounds description, it should be attached. A description taken from the tax records or from former listing information is not satisfactory, as these sources are not always reliable.

(b) ***Personal Property.*** Fixtures as well as other personal property must be listed here. Often a seller agrees to leave a refrigerator, drapes, or a washer/dryer; however, the licensee should discuss with the seller the possibility of holding back the offer of these items, using them as negotiating tools when an offer is made. (For example, "The seller says that if you can increase your offer by $1,000, she will give you her washer-dryer.")

Not included as part of the agreement. The licensee should ask the seller an important question: "Is any item attached to the property which you *do not want to be included with the sale?*" The agreement does not provide a section for this exclusion, but the licensee should be certain to include any such items on an addendum. If possible, the fixture should be removed before the home is shown.

(c) ***Occupancy.*** This section covers the seller's representation about occupancy rights by another party. If a third party is in possession of the property, the buyer's rights are subject to those of the tenant.

3. (a) ***Price.*** Here the licensee records the price at which the property will be offered.

(b) ***Financing Terms.*** The terms are important to the seller and the listing broker, particularly in the way the property is marketed. If the seller agrees to seller financing, the terms of such financing are stated here. If there is an existing mortgage on the property, the seller is asked whether it can be assumed with or without lender approval. The seller is warned about liability in case of an assumption. The seller also agrees that the loan is current in case of assumption.

(c) ***Seller Expenses.*** This section limits the amount the seller agrees to pay for discount points and other closing costs as a percentage of the sales price. The licensee should take care to ensure that the amount shown here is enough to pay typical costs of sale, including a commission. Of course, the seller could agree to pay more when signing a contract for sale. The licensee should disclose anticipated seller's costs on the Seller's Net Proceeds statement before presenting the listing agreement and each time an offer is presented to the seller.

4. ***Broker Obligations and Authority.*** The broker makes promises in this section (the consideration that makes this a bilateral contract) that include working diligently to sell the property. The seller authorizes the broker to take the following steps (however, the broker does not *promise* to do so):

(a) Advertise the property as the broker deems advisable, place an appropriate sign on the property, and use the seller's name in marketing the property.

(b) Obtain information about the mortgage (usually a signed request from the seller for a status letter).

(c) Place the property in the MLS. Some brokers hold a listing out for an extended period of time, during which the broker attempts to sell the property himself. If the licensee is a single agent, this could be considered as subordinating the principal's interests to the broker's personal interests, a clear violation of fiduciary duties.

1   (d) Place a lockbox on the property if the seller specifically authorizes it. The seller
2   is asked to relieve the broker, staff, and Board of REALTORS® from liability due to
3   loss. The seller may request that the broker withhold verbal offers and *all* offers
4   once the seller accepts a contract.

5   5. *Seller Obligations.* The seller agrees to:
6   (a) cooperate with the broker to obtain a sale and refer all inquiries to the broker;
7   (b) give keys to the broker and make property available for showing during reason-
8   able times;
9   (c) inform the broker before leasing or mortgaging the property;
10 (d) hold the broker harmless because of (1) the seller's negligence or misrepre-
11 sentations, (2) losses from the use of a lockbox, (3) the existence of undisclosed
12 facts about the property, or (4) arbitration or lawsuits against the broker by
13 another broker (This serves as a warranty that the seller's statements to the broker
14 are true and that indemnifies the broker against representations made by the seller
15 that the broker passes on to a buyer. The warranty against seller misrepresenta-
16 tions is commonly called the *warranty of owner clause.*);
17 (e) comply with the Foreign Investment in Real Property Tax Act (FIRPTA)
18 requirements in case the seller is a foreign national (This could require that the
19 buyer withhold 10 percent of the sales proceeds and forward the funds to the IRS.);
20 (f) make legally required disclosures affecting the property's value (This section
21 requires due diligence by the licensee, who must question the seller on all aspects
22 of the property. Obviously, comments the seller makes in this section should be
23 disclosed to prospective buyers.); and
24 (g) consult with qualified professionals for legal, tax, and other matters, the intent
25 of which is to reduce the licensee's liability.

26 6. *Compensation.* This is an agreement to find a purchaser who is ready, willing, and
27 able to buy, either at the list price or any other price agreeable to the seller. It is
28 not dependent on a closing (as in a listing "to effect a sale").
29 (a) This paragraph sets the commission as a percentage of the price or as a dollar
30 amount. The commission is due no later than closing, but may be due whether or
31 not a closing occurs.
32 (b) In case the seller and a buyer agree to an option contract, this paragraph
33 sets the commission as a percentage of the option amount or as a dollar
34 amount. The commission is due at the time the option is created. The total
35 commission, less the commission received from the option, is due when the
36 option is exercised.
37 (c) In case a lease agreement is created, this paragraph sets the commission as a
38 percentage of the price or as a dollar amount. The commission is due when the
39 seller enters into an agreement to lease. An exception occurs if the seller employs
40 another broker under an exclusive-right-to-lease agreement.
41 (d) Broker's Fee. This paragraph describes when the broker's fee is due.
42 (1) if any interest in the property is transferred, whether by sale, lease, exchange,
43 governmental action (e.g., eminent domain), or bankruptcy, no matter who finds
44 the buyer;
45 (2) if the seller refuses to sign an offer at full price and terms, defaults on a con-
46 tract, or agrees with a buyer to cancel an executed sales contract; or
47 (3) if, after the listing's expiration, a prospect who learned about the property
48 through a broker buys the property within the protection period. An exception
49 occurs if the property has been subsequently listed by another broker.
50 (e) Retained Deposits. This paragraph entitles the broker to a specified percent-
51 age of all deposits that the seller retains as liquidated damages for a buyer's
52 default. The amount cannot exceed the total commission as shown in para-
53 graph 6(a).

7. *Cooperation with Other Brokers.* This section states that the broker's policy is to cooperate with all other brokers except when it would not be in the seller's best interests. It authorizes the listing broker to offer commission splits with other brokers. The seller checks her approval for splits with (1) buyers' agents, (2) nonrepresentatives, (3) transaction brokers, (4) subagents (if the listing broker is a single agent), or (5) none of the above. If the seller checks "none of the above," the listing broker may not put the listing into the MLS, because the MLS requires an offer of compensation to a cooperating broker.

8. *Brokerage Relationship.* As described in Chapter 1, brokers may work with buyers or sellers as nonrepresentatives, single agents or transaction brokers. The listing contract includes the disclosure forms for single agent or transaction broker. The seller should sign the forms, or, if the seller declines to do so, the licensee should so indicate on the listing contract form. If the broker is starting as a single agent and may become a transaction broker, the transition notice *must* be signed.

9. *Conditional Termination.* If the seller decides not to sell the property, the broker may agree to terminate the contract. The seller must sign a withdrawal agreement, then pay the broker's direct expenses and a specified cancellation fee. If the seller contracts to transfer the property during the protection period, the broker may cancel the termination and collect the balance of the commission due.

10. *Dispute Resolution.* This paragraph requires that conflicts be submitted to a mediator agreed to by the parties. If the mediation is not successful, and unless the parties agree in advance to arbitration, either party may sue. The prevailing party is entitled to recover attorney's fees and costs.

11. *Arbitration.* This section allows the parties (seller, listing associate, and listing broker) to agree to settle disputes by binding arbitration in the county where the property is located. The parties agree to split the costs equally. The inclusion of the listing associate in the contract is curious, since the listing agreement is between the seller and the broker, and only the broker is authorized to take action for a commission. If the intent was to protect the broker from the sales associate's later claims for a commission if arbitration was unsuccessful, that might be better handled in the employment agreement. The agreement suggests that the costs will be split among the three parties.

12. *Miscellaneous.* The agreement may be assigned to another listing office, which is a departure from the former practice. Fax communications are enforceable.

13. *Information and Signature section.* This section provides personal information, including tax ID numbers as well as signature lines. Note that the listing sales associate may be authorized to sign the listing for the broker. This facilitates giving the seller a copy of the agreement immediately, satisfying the 24-hour requirement. The box at the bottom of the contract indicates when the seller's copy was legally delivered.

Explaining the Agreement to the Seller. The presentation of the listing agreement to the seller needs to be thorough to ensure that the seller fully understands. Sales associates sometimes take a casual approach to explaining the listing agreement or offer no explanation at all to the seller. A sales associate may say, "Don't worry, it's the standard agreement. Sign here." Or the sales associate might try an explanation even though he doesn't understand the agreement himself. This misleads the seller and is not acceptable. The licensee's job is to give the seller an understanding of the important provisions the agreement contains.

New sales associates should understand the agreement totally and explain each paragraph clearly. If a seller asks, "What happens during the listing period if I decide I want to lease the property to a tenant?" the sales associate should answer, "If you'll look at paragraph 6(c), you'll see that the property can be leased. You agree to pay my company a fee of _____ percent, but the fee does not include management."

1   The professional sales associate explains the listing agreement in language which the
2 seller understands easily. Role-playing is an excellent method of learning this skill.
3 When the role-playing results in wording that sounds appropriate, the sales associate
4 should write it down so she can then refer to the written explanation during the list-
5 ing appointment.

6   The following scenario might result from a licensee's role-playing exercise:

7   "Mr. Jones, this is the standard agreement all brokers use for homes listed in the MLS
8 system. Let's go over it together, paragraph by paragraph."

9   1. "This section shows your name as the seller and _____ Realty as the broker.
10   Do I have your names spelled correctly?"
11   2. "The next section shows that you give my company the authority to sell your
12   property starting today and ending on _____. You understand that I can't
13   *guarantee* a sale of the property. I must offer property without violating any fair
14   housing laws. And you agree that you can legally sell the property."
15   3. The address of the property is _____. And the legal description of the prop-
16   erty taken from your deed is shown here."

17   The sales associate continues to explain paragraphs 4 through 11 of the listing con-
18 tract in a similar manner. She refers to the checklist in Figure 6.4 to be certain she has
19 completed all the necessary documents and taken all the necessary actions in regard to
20 the listing.

DISCUSSION EXERCISE 6.3

Using the listing agreement for your market area, paraphrase the legal words in
everyday language that will help a seller understand the agreement better. In a
group situation, each person should be assigned a paragraph. The person then
explains the paragraph to the group in lay language, and the group provides constructive criticism. Because each person would explain each paragraph differently,
every sales associate should prepare his own written text for use in presentations.

---

21 ## Marketing the Listing

22 The seller employs the listing broker to market the property. Many sellers believe that
23 the licensee has not done her job unless the listing broker actually sells the listing. The
24 licensee should discuss this misconception with the seller during the listing presenta-
25 tion. The seller should understand that if the licensee does her job properly, the house
26 will sell through the licensee's marketing efforts—both to potential buyers and to other
27 licensees, who will show the property to their buyers.

28   The broker has been hired to get the best price in the shortest time and with the least
29 inconvenience to the seller. This requires the licensee to market the property in ways
30 other than just showing it herself. Some of these activities include:

31 • disseminating the property information to all agents in the company;
32 • putting the sign on the property;
33 • putting an MLS lockbox on the property (if approved by the seller and available in
34   the market area);
35 • arranging for all company sales associates to inspect the listing on caravan day;
36 • getting the information into the MLS service as soon as possible (It is unethical and
37   self-serving to withhold the information from other brokers and sales associates while
38   the agent attempts to sell the property herself.);

FIGURE 6.4   LISTING PROCEDURE CHECKLIST

Complete Brokerage Relationship Disclosures in accordance with Chapter 475, F.S.

This form should accompany all listings.

Property Address: _____

Listing Associate: _____

Listing Packet Contents (bold print indicates seller's signature is required):

_____	Competitive Market Analysis
_____	Brokerage Relationship Disclosures
_____	**EXCLUSIVE-RIGHT-OF-SALE AGREEMENT**
_____	MLS Profile Sheet
_____	**MORTGAGE STATUS REQUEST**
_____	**PROPERTY CONDITION DISCLOSURE STATEMENT**
_____	**HOME WARRANTY AGREEMENT**
_____	**SELLER'S NET SHEET**
_____	Survey, if available
_____	Copy of mortgage and note
_____	Copy of deed restrictions
_____	Title Insurance Policy
_____	Key to property
_____	Floor plan, if available
_____	Copy of seller or buyer referral sent out
_____	Three ads
_____	Sign installation form
_____	Lockbox installation form
_____	Client contact sheet
_____	Copy of computer printout

Office Action:

_____	Get office manager's approval on listing forms.
_____	Enter listing data into computer.
_____	Put copy of printout into Floor Duty Book.
_____	Distribute copies of printout to all sales associates.
_____	Turn in listing packet to secretary.

Follow-up Action:

_____	Return all original documents to seller.
_____	Send seller copy of the MLS listing book photo and information.
_____	Contact seller weekly.
_____	Send seller copy of mortgage status letter when received.
_____	Send copies of all ads to seller.

---

1 ● announcing the listing at company sales meetings and at Board of REALTORS® mar-
2   keting meetings;
3 ● preparing a brochure to place in the home for prospective buyers and cooperating
4   licensees;
5 ● scheduling an open house, if appropriate for the listing;
6 ● writing at least three good ads to generate potential buyers;
7 ● putting listing on Web sites (personal page, company page, and other advertiser's
8   pages);
9 ● using e-mail auto responders to get immediate feedback for customers who ask for
10   information from a Web site;

1   • preparing mailouts to send to potential buyers;

2   • preparing a property brochure for potential buyers and other sales associates;

3   • telling 20 neighbors about the listing by mail;

4   • calling the neighbors to ask for help in finding buyers;

5   • holding a REALTORS® luncheon at the property to increase activity; and

6   • reviewing sales and listing activity in the neighborhood. Update the CMA at least

7   once a month.

8   A detailed marketing program such as this could be the basis for a "Satisfaction Guar-

9 antee" or "Steps to a Successful Sale" listing presentation.

DISCUSSION EXERCISE 6.4

In small groups, prepare a 30-point marketing plan for a brochure you use in your listing presentation. Brainstorm to come up with different marketing ideas.

---

10 ## Servicing the Listing

11 **Servicing the listing** often is more important than acquiring it. "I never hear from him!"

12 is probably the complaint sellers make most often about their sales associates. If a seller

13 does not hear from his listing sales associate, the seller believes, often correctly, that she

14 is not doing the job proficiently.

DISCUSSION EXERCISE 6.5

You are a real estate sales associate who is quite busy and disorganized. You have had a listing for six months that is about to expire, and you wish to renew it. Despite your best intentions, you have failed to contact your clients, Harold and Deidra, for more than two months. As the time progressed, it became even harder for you to make the call. You set an appointment to visit the home at 7:30 P.M. Because you are caught in traffic, you are 20 minutes late when you walk up to the house. You are surprised to see that a competitor has listed the property next door. Even worse, it has a "contract pending" sign attached. The door is answered by an un-smiling Harold, who nods his head and says, "Well, stranger. Long time no see!"

Role-play this situation. Try your best to reestablish the trust and rapport you had at the beginning of the listing period. It may be instructive enough that you will never allow this situation to happen in your career.

---

15   Those professional licensees who are successful consistently do not accomplish this

16 on the strength of salesmanship alone. The licensees are successful because they pro-

17 vide service to their clients and customers. Often, a family's home is the largest asset it

18 will ever have, so a sales associate never must take the marketing of the home lightly.

19 Failure to maintain regular contact with a seller is a detriment to a sales associate's

20 future success.

Several methods ensure that a sales associate will contact each seller at least once a week:

- The sales associate selects one evening each week, such as Thursday night, to service listings.
- The sales associate contacts every seller, in person, by phone, or if personal contact is not successful, by mail. If she calls and the seller does not answer, the sales associate writes a card immediately to let them know the seller was called.
- The sales associate clips every ad from every paper and homes magazine, then pastes it on a note card and mails it with a note that says, "Thought you'd like to see a recent ad on your home. Regards, Sally."
- The sales associate asks every seller to call her immediately if another licensee shows the property. The licensee then follows up to help achieve a sale.
- The sales associate calls every seller after talking to a cooperating broker and gives feedback about a visit to the home.

Often sales associates lose touch with sellers because they don't know what to talk about and feel that they sound like broken records because they say the same things over and over. Each sales associate should prepare a Listing Servicing Schedule, which provides a basic format for the servicing of every listing. A sample form is shown in Figure 6.5.

SUMMARY

A seller usually is more interested in the net proceeds from the sale of his property than the home's actual sales price. The Seller's Net Proceeds Form—the financial disclosure to the seller—consists of three major sections. The seller's equity section provides the sales price less mortgage balances, with the difference being the seller's equity. The expenses section shows expenses the seller must pay at closing. The prorations section includes taxes, interest, rents and homeowner's dues.

Three major types of listing agreements are open listings, exclusive-agency listings and exclusive-right-of-sale listings. An owner's warranty in a listing indemnifies the broker from false statements the owner makes to the broker. A latent defects addendum to a contract holds the owner accountable for existing defects to the property that are known or should have been known.

Licensees should observe the no-solicitation law and may not call any person on the state list, except for-sale-by-owners and past customers. A licensee must furnish roof or termite reports to buyers upon written request.

Licensees should review carefully and understand thoroughly the listing contracts they use. A licensee should be able to explain clearly to a seller the important provisions of a listing agreement.

A licensee must market property with skill, care, and diligence. A major part of the licensee's professional duties, in addition to listing and selling, is servicing listings and keeping in touch with sellers on a regular basis.

DEFINE THESE KEY TERMS

equity	open listing
exclusive-agency listing	profile sheet
exclusive-right-of-sale listing	seller's net proceeds form
latent defects addenda	servicing the listing
lockbox	warranty of owner
net proceeds	

FIGURE 6.5 LISTING SERVICING SCHEDULE

Property Address_____ HPhone: _____ WPhone: _____

Sellers' Names _____ Children: _____

First Day:

_____ Verify tax information and legal description.

_____ Send out mortgage status request.

_____ Write three ads.

_____ Place listing on Web page.

_____ Send thank you card to seller.

_____ Enter listing information in computer.

_____ Put copies of listing information in floor book.

_____ Distribute copies of listing information to all sales associates.

_____ Put sign and lockbox on property.

Second Day:

_____ Mail out notice of listing cards to at least 20 neighbors.

_____ Call or e-mail seller to tell of above steps.

End of First Week:

_____ Send letter to seller signed by broker.

Day after Caravan:

_____ Collect caravan comment sheets.

_____ Visit with seller to evaluate results of caravan and comments.

Second Week:

_____ Clip ads of property. Send to seller in postcard format.

_____ Check MLS information on computer, verify information, then e-mail to seller.

_____ Call seller to tell of progress. Ask seller to call when house is shown.

Third Week:

_____ Clip ads of property. Send to seller in postcard format.

_____ Run MLS computer check for new listings and listings under contract, then e-mail information to seller.

_____ Call or e-mail seller to find out who has seen home.

_____ Check with sales associates who have shown home; give feedback to seller.

Fourth Week:

_____ Clip ads of property. Send to seller in postcard format.

_____ Run MLS computer check for new listings and listings under contract, then e-mail information to seller.

_____ Call or e-mail seller to find out about who has seen home.

_____ Check with sales associates who have shown home; give feedback to seller.

Fifth Week:

_____ Clip ads of property. Send to seller in postcard format.

_____ Run MLS computer check for new listings and listings under contract, then e-mail information to seller.

_____ Visit seller in the home, and go over CMA. Get price reduction if appropriate.

_____ Walk through property again. Point out areas needing attention.

FIGURE 6.5   LISTING SERVICING SCHEDULE (Continued)

Sixth Week:

_____   Clip ads of property. Send to seller in postcard format.

_____   Run MLS computer check for new listings and listings under contract, then e-mail information to seller.

_____   Call or e-mail seller to find out who has seen home.

_____   Check with sales associates who have shown home; give feedback to seller.

_____   Schedule open house for the property, if appropriate.

_____   Send notice of open house to at least 20 neighbors.

Seventh Week:

_____   Run open house, and leave a note for seller on results. Call later.

_____   Clip ads of property. Send to seller in postcard format.

_____   Run MLS computer check for new listings and listings under contract, then e-mail information to seller.

_____   Call or e-mail seller to find out who has seen home.

_____   Check with sales associates who have shown home; give feedback to seller.

_____   Send out notice of listing to additional 20 homes in neighborhood.

Eighth Week:

_____   Clip ads of property. Send to seller in postcard format.

_____   Run MLS computer check for new listings and listings under contract, then e-mail information to seller.

_____   Call or e-mail seller to find out who has seen home.

_____   Check with sales associates who have shown home; give feedback to seller.

Ninth Week:

_____   Clip ads of property. Send to seller in postcard format.

_____   Run MLS computer check for new listings and listings under contract; then e-mail information to seller.

_____   Call or e-mail seller to find out who has seen home.

_____   Check with sales associates who have shown home; give feedback to seller.

_____   Do another CMA. Visit with seller, and get price reduction and extension.

_____   Schedule luncheon for sales agents.

Tenth Week:

_____   Clip ads of property. Send to seller in postcard format.

_____   Run MLS computer check for new listings and listings under contract, then e-mail information to seller.

_____   Call or e-mail seller to find out who has seen home.

_____   Check with sales associates who have shown home; give feedback to seller.

Continue this pattern until listing has been sold.

CHAPTER 6 PRACTICE EXAM

1. The reason for eliminating cents and rounding to the nearest $100 on the seller's net proceeds statement is to:

   a. avoid giving the impression that the figures will be exactly as shown at closing.
   b. make the statement easier to understand.
   c. provide a cushion in the estimate.
   d. All of the above

2. The components of the seller's equity section of the Seller's Net Proceeds Statement include:

   a. seller's equity, expenses, and seller's net proceeds.
   b. sales price, prorations, and expenses.
   c. seller's equity, prorations, and seller's net proceeds.
   d. sales price, mortgages, and seller's equity.

3. Broker Jim just listed a house for six months. The listing will automatically renew for an additional three months unless canceled in writing by either party. This type of agreement:

   a. is advantageous to the seller and is endorsed by the National Association of REALTORS®.
   b. is a violation of the license law.
   c. is permissible provided full disclosure is made to the seller of its self-renewing provision.
   d. may be used only by single agents and is not available to transaction brokers.

4. The portion of the listing contract that contains a promise by the owner certifying that all of the information related to the property is true and accurate is called the _____ clause.

   a. property owner's
   b. property condition
   c. warranty of owner
   d. owner's certification

5. The addition to a listing contract in Florida that states that the owner has a duty to disclose any facts materially affecting the property's value is called the _____ addendum.

   a. caveat emptor
   b. latent defects
   c. special clauses
   d. hold harmless

6. The type of listing favored by an owner who selects one brokerage firm to sell his property, but reserves the right to sell the property personally and not pay a commission, is the _____ listing.

   a. exclusive-right-of-sale
   b. exclusive-agency
   c. open
   d. option contract

7. A seller refuses to allow the listing broker to split commissions with buyers' brokers, transaction brokers, or nonrepresentation brokers. "Let the buyer pay them!" the seller exclaims. Based on this information, which of the following statements is correct?

    a. The seller's viewpoints are perfectly acceptable and understandable; the broker may take the listing and enter it in the MLS.
    b. The broker may not take the listing under these circumstances.
    c. The broker may take the listing, but may not enter it in the MLS.
    d. The listing may be placed into MLS only if it is an exclusive right of sale.

8. Diane, the seller, explains to Todd, the sales associate, that she intends to take the ceiling fan when she moves, so he should be sure the listing information shows that it is not part of the sale. In this case, Todd should do which of the following?

    a. Tell Diane that the ceiling fan is a fixture and must stay with the property.
    b. Tell Diane, "Let's wait and see if it's mentioned in the purchase contract; if it is not specifically itemized, you can take it."
    c. Strongly urge Diane to leave the fan.
    d. Tell Diane to remove the fan before the property is shown.

Use the following information to answer questions 9 through 12.

Broker Sharon is compiling a seller's net proceeds statement for Ellen Johnson. The figures she gathers are as follows:

Brokerage fee	7%
Title insurance	$ 780.00
Termite inspection and treatment	300.00
Sales price	127,500.00
Existing first mortgage @ 10%	98,601.60
Documentary stamps-deed	?
Property taxes for the year	1,745.60
Interest proration (paid in arrears)	?
Closing date	June 30

9. What is the seller's equity, rounded to the nearest $100?

    a. $29,000
    b. $28,900
    c. $20,000
    d. $16,300

10. What are the total expenses, rounded to the next highest $100?

    a. $10,100
    b. $10,800
    c. $10,900
    d. $11,800

11. What are the total prorations, rounded to the nearest $100? Will the prorations be added or subtracted from the equity?

    a. $2,600 added
    b. $900 subtracted
    c. $1,300 subtracted
    d. $1,700 subtracted

12. What are the seller's net proceeds, rounded to the nearest $100?

    a. $14,500
    b. $15,400
    c. $16,300
    d. $17,100

13. Broker John lists a large townhome in Pebble Creek. How long does John have to give the seller a signed copy of the agreement?

    a. It must be done before John leaves the seller's presence.
    b. Within 48 hours
    c. Within 7 days
    d. Within 24 hours

14. Broker Carol Chambers is talking with Wesley about listing his home. If Wesley says that he is ready to list, but has two people he wants to exclude from the listing for three weeks, what should Carol do?

    a. Wait three weeks, then come and get the listing.
    b. Have Wesley sign an open listing.
    c. Have Wesley sign an exclusive-right-of-sale listing.
    d. Have Wesley sign an exclusive-agency listing that automatically turns into an exclusive-right-of-sale listing later.

15. The two biggest problems faced by a licensee who has taken an exclusive-agency listing are:

    a. a dishonest seller and a dishonest broker.
    b. other brokers and other sales associates.
    c. an owner's sign on the property and the owner advertising a different price.
    d. a buyer going to another broker and the other broker failing to disclose his brokerage relationship.

16. The maximum period between a listing sales associate's calls to the seller should be how many days?

    a. 1
    b. 7
    c. 10
    d. 14

17. Jennifer is a real estate sales associate who wants to increase her business activity. She makes 60 canvassing phone calls to a neighborhood, straight from the crisscross directory, with no reference to other material. In this case, which of the following statements is correct?

    a. Using this method is best for a new sales associate.
    b. If she called a party on the state no-solicitation list, Jennifer could face a $1,000 fine.
    c. If she called a party on the state no-solicitation list, Jennifer could face a $10,000 fine.
    d. If she called a FSBO whose name was on the state no-solicitation list, Jennifer could face a $10,000 fine.

18. On June 18, Broker Susan listed the Smith's house for six months. On August 16, the Smiths terminated the listing, paying Susan a cancellation fee of $250. In September, the Smiths listed their house with Cobble Realty. They accepted a contract in October, which closed on November 28. Based on the conditional termination clause of the FAR listing agreement, the Smiths:

   a. are liable to Broker Susan for the full commission.
   b. have acted in violation of state law.
   c. have terminated the original listing and need pay only Cobble Realty.
   d. may owe Broker Susan up to one percent of the sales price of the home.

19. The parties to a listing agreement are the:

   a. seller and buyer.
   b. seller and sales associate.
   c. sales associate and broker.
   d. seller and broker.

20. Susan lists property with Jack Smith, a multimillion-dollar producer. Jack's agreement calls for him to enter the listing into the MLS within three working days. On the second day, Jack shows the property to Sally Shuler, who loves it. She is leaving town the next day, she tells him, but will be back in one week to purchase it if it is still on the market. Jack wants to double his commission by selling his own listing, so he withholds the information from the MLS for ten days. Based on this information, which of the following statements is correct?

   a. Jack is following a legal, time-honored tradition in real estate by working to sell his own listing.
   b. Jack is liable to the seller for violating fiduciary duties required by the listing agreement.
   c. Jack could be disciplined by the Florida Real Estate Commission.
   d. Both b and c are correct.

ACTION LIST

APPLY WHAT YOU'VE LEARNED!

The authors suggest the following actions to reinforce the material in *Section III–Valuation and Listing:*

- If you own a home, estimate its current value, then prepare a CMA. If you do not own your home, do this exercise for a friend. Does the CMA support the value you guessed?
- Based on the CMA you did on your or your friend's house, prepare a Seller's Net Proceeds Statement.
- Complete a listing agreement for your home, along with other forms required by your broker. Ask your broker to review them.
- Prepare an MLS computer input form describing the features of your house. Be certain it is complete.
- Write three practice ads to market your home.
- Pick a neighborhood in your city with homes priced from $100,000 to $150,000. Find as many sales as possible for the previous 12 months. Using the matched pair technique, identify the dollar contribution from
  - a swimming pool,
  - an extra bedroom,
  - an enclosed garage, and
  - a corner lot.
- Using the same analysis, calculate the percentage difference between listing price and selling price.
- Using MLS data, divide the number of houses on the market by the number of house sales last week to find how many weeks' supply of homes are on the market. Do this at least once a month. It's an excellent indicator of market activity.
- Write a script for the explanation of a CMA to a prospective seller. Record your presentation on audiotape to hear how it sounds. Edit as necessary until it sounds just right.
- Record your explanation of the listing agreement used in your office. Edit your remarks until you are satisfied.

SECTION IV

SELLING REAL PROPERTY

A sales associate must understand the buyer's needs and financial abilities. Licensees should understand how to find buyers and to live up to the buyers' expectations. Buyers expect licensees to have broad knowledge about properties on the market and market values. They also want to know how much they can afford to pay for a house based on their income.

The sales associate must understand how to estimate the buyer's costs so that the buyer who contracts for a property is aware of the cash requirements expected at closing.

Knowledge of contracts is extremely important to sales associates. Not only do licensees need to know how to prepare purchase agreements, they must be able to explain the basic terms of the agreements so that buyers and sellers are aware of their rights and responsibilities.

This section will prepare the licensee to help buyers locate and purchase the right properties.

SECTION IV

CHAPTER 7—WORKING WITH BUYERS

LEARNING OBJECTIVES

Upon completion of this chapter, *you should be able to:*

1. explain four different ways to enhance a sales associate's product knowledge;
2. list at least five sources of buyers;
3. give at least three methods to show a buyer why an appointment with you will benefit the buyer;
4. list the two important reasons for qualifying a buyer;
5. explain how prioritizing buyers benefits both the buyers and the sales associate;
6. list the three primary methods of qualifying a buyer financially;
7. qualify a buyer using the Fannie Mae/Freddie Mac housing expense ratio and the total obligations ratio;
8. calculate the total monthly payment (PITI) on a mortgage loan;
9. qualify a buyer using the do-it-yourself prequalification form;
10. list two benefits in having a buyer prequalify at a mortgage lender's office;
11. list the steps between setting up an initial appointment with a buyer and writing a contract for purchase; and
12. explain why you would show only a limited number of homes to a potential buyer in one day.

CHAPTER 7

WORKING WITH BUYERS

1 Working with buyers is an important function of the professional real estate sales asso-
2 ciate. Buyers are interested in working with knowledgeable, caring sales associates and
3 generally are reluctant to make appointments without evaluating the sales associate's
4 skills. A sales associate must be adept at handling telephone inquiries, must know the
5 inventory, and must stay current with available financing plans. Above all, the sales asso-
6 ciate must understand and observe the laws with respect to required disclosures and fair
7 housing.

8 BUYER BROKERAGE AGREEMENT

9 While licensees nearly always require a written agreement from sellers, they often work
10 with buyers on an "open listing" basis. A licensee may give the customer valuable infor-
11 mation on the market and other ideas on purchasing a home, but may end up working
12 for nothing. Many successful licensees are requesting that buyers also enter into a
13 written **buyer brokerage agreement** for representation by the licensee, either as a single
14 agent or as a **transaction broker.**

15 Some prospective buyers will be reluctant to sign such an agreement because they
16 may be required to pay a commission. They may not be aware that the agreement calls
17 for the broker to offset the commission from monies received from a seller if the prop-
18 erty is listed with a cooperating broker. A buyer who understands the benefits will be
19 more likely to sign the agreement. When the buyer agrees to pay a commission, the
20 broker can show the buyer unlisted property (FSBOs, properties being foreclosed, real
21 estate owned by banks, etc.). Buyers would not see such properties without a commis-
22 sion agreement.

23 The real estate licensee should understand the Exclusive Buyer Brokerage Agree-
24 ment (Figure 7.1) and be able to explain its provisions clearly and concisely. The num-
25 bered paragraphs below correspond with the 14 sections of the agreement.

26 1. **Parties:** The parties are the buyer and the broker. This paragraph also defines the
27 terms of "acquisition" to be purchase, option, exchange, lease, or other acquisition
28 or ownership or equity interest in real property.
29 2. **Term:** This paragraph sets forth the dates the agreement will be effective. Notice
30 that if there is a contract pending on the expiration date of the agreement, the
31 agreement is extended until the contract is closed or terminated.
32 3. **Property:** This section shows the
33 a. *Type of Property,* for example, residential, agricultural, office, etc.

b. *Location* would normally be used to describe a city or county, or another geographic area.

c. *Price range* would set the minimum and maximum limits the broker should use in selecting properties to show. This section also discloses that the buyer may have already been pre-approved for a mortgage.

d. *Preferred terms and conditions:* sets out the buyers preferences, such as owner financing, small down payment, lease-purchase, etc.

4. **Broker's Obligations:**

a. *Broker assistance:* The broker agrees to cooperate with seller's brokers to effect a transaction. It also states that even if the broker is paid a commission split from the seller's broker, the broker's duties to the buyer are not reduced.

b. *Other buyers:* This section discloses to the buyer that the broker may work with another buyer interested in the same property but must maintain confidentiality as to the terms of any offers.

c. *Fair housing:* Broker states he or she will not participate in unlawful discrimination.

d. *Service providers:* Broker shall not be responsible for acts of a third party recommended by the broker, such as a home inspector or title insurance company.

5. **Buyer's Obligations:**

In this section, the buyer agrees to tell sellers or other brokers he is working under contract with a broker, to conduct all negotiations through the broker, to give the broker personal financial information and allow the broker to run a credit check, to hold the broker harmless for any damages, and to consult an appropriate professional for tax, legal, and other services.

6. **Retainer:** Many licensees ask prospective buyers for a nonrefundable retainer at the time this contract is signed. It has an option for the retainer to be credited to the total compensation.

7. **Compensation:** This obligates the buyer to pay a commission to the broker, offset by any commissions the broker may receive from a seller or a broker working with the seller. The broker is entitled to his or her commission if the customer purchases, leases, or options the property. The commission may be stated as a percentage of the sale, lease, or option, or it can be a fixed fee. The broker is also entitled to a commission if the buyer defaults on any contract.

8. **Protection Period:** If the broker has shown property to the buyer and the buyer purchases the property within the agreement period, the buyer will owe the commission unless the buyer has entered into a buyer brokerage agreement with another broker after the termination date.

9. **Early Termination:** The buyer may terminate the agreement, but if the buyer buys property the buyer learned about during the contract term, the buyer owes the commission. The broker may terminate the agreement at any time by giving written notice.

10. **Dispute Resolution:** Disputes must be mediated first. If mediation is not successful, the parties must agree to submit the dispute to binding arbitration.

11. **Assignment:** The broker is allowed to assign the agreement to another broker.

12. **Brokerage Relationship:** This section has several checkboxes for the parties to indicate what type of broker relationship they will have. Note: The fact that a box is checked does not discharge the broker from giving the buyer the prescribed brokerage relationship notice before showing a property or entering into this agreement.

13. **Special Clauses:** This gives the parties additional space to add other provisions to the agreement.

Signatures: There are spaces for signature of the buyer(s), sales associate, and broker.

FIGURE 7.1   EXCLUSIVE BUYER BROKERAGE AGREEMENT

Exclusive Buyer Brokerage Agreement
FLORIDA ASSOCIATION OF REALTORS®

1. **PARTIES:** _____ ("**Buyer**") grants

_____ ("**Broker**")
Real Estate Broker   /   Office

the exclusive right to work with and assist **Buyer** in locating and negotiating the acquisition of suitable real property as described below. The term "acquire" or "acquisition" includes any purchase, option, exchange, lease or other acquisition of an ownership or equity interest in real property.

2. **TERM:** This Agreement will begin on the _____ day of _____, _____ and will terminate at 11:59 p.m. on the _____ day of _____, _____ ("Termination Date"). However, if **Buyer** enters into an agreement to acquire property that is pending on the Termination Date, this Agreement will continue in effect until that transaction has closed or otherwise terminated.

3. **PROPERTY: Buyer** is interested in acquiring real property as follows or as otherwise acceptable to **Buyer** ("Property"):

   (a) **Type of property:** _____

   (b) **Location:** _____

   (c) **Price range:** $_____ to $_____.

   ❑ **Buyer** has been ❑ pre-qualified ❑ pre-approved by _____

   for (amount and terms, if any) _____

   (d) **Preferred terms and conditions:** _____

   _____

   _____

   _____

4. **BROKER'S OBLIGATIONS:**
   (a) **Broker Assistance. Broker** will
       * use **Broker's** professional knowledge and skills;
       * assist **Buyer** in determining **Buyer's** financial capability and financing options;
       * discuss property requirements and assist **Buyer** in locating and viewing suitable properties;
       * assist **Buyer** to contract for property, monitor deadlines and close any resulting transaction;
       * cooperate with real estate licensees working with the seller, if any, to effect a transaction. **Buyer** understands that even if **Broker** is compensated by a seller or a real estate licensee who is working with a seller, such compensation does not compromise **Broker's** duties to **Buyer**.
   (b) **Other Buyers. Buyer** understands that **Broker** may work with other prospective buyers who want to acquire the same property as **Buyer**. If **Broker** submits offers by competing buyers, **Broker** will notify **Buyer** that a competing offer has been made, but will not disclose any of the offer's material terms or conditions. **Buyer** agrees that **Broker** may make competing buyers aware of the existence of any offer **Buyer** makes, so long as **Broker** does not reveal any material terms or conditions of the offer without **Buyer's** prior written consent.
   (c) **Fair Housing. Broker** adheres to the principles expressed in the Fair Housing Act and will not participate in any act that unlawfully discriminates on the basis of race, color, religion, sex, handicap, familial status, country of national origin or any other category protected under federal, state or local law.
   (d) **Service Providers. Broker** does not warrant or guarantee products or services provided by any third party whom **Broker**, at **Buyer's** request, refers or recommends to **Buyer** in connection with property acquisition.

FIGURE 7.1   EXCLUSIVE BUYER BROKERAGE AGREEMENT (Continued)

5. **BUYER'S OBLIGATIONS: Buyer** agrees to cooperate with **Broker** in accomplishing the objectives of this Agreement, including:
(a) Conducting all negotiations and efforts to locate suitable property only through **Broker** and referring to **Broker** all inquiries of any kind from real estate licensees, property owners or any other source. If **Buyer** contacts or is contacted by a seller or a real estate licensee who is working with a seller or views a property unaccompanied by **Broker**, **Buyer** will, at first opportunity, advise the seller or real estate licensee that **Buyer** is working with and represented exclusively by **Broker**.
(b) Providing **Broker** with accurate personal and financial information requested by **Broker** in connection with ensuring **Buyer's** ability to acquire property. **Buyer** authorizes **Broker** to run a credit check to verify **Buyer's** credit information.
(c) Being available to meet with **Broker** at reasonable times for consultations and to view properties.
(d) Indemnifying and holding **Broker** harmless from and against all losses, damages, costs and expenses of any kind, including attorney's fees, and from liability to any person, that **Broker** incurs because of acting on **Buyer's** behalf.
(e) Not asking or expecting to restrict the acquisition of a property according to race, color, religion, sex, handicap, familial status, country of national origin or any other category protected under federal, state or local law.
(f) Consulting an appropriate professional for legal, tax, environmental, engineering, foreign reporting requirements and other specialized advice.

6. RETAINER: Upon final execution of this Agreement, **Buyer** will pay to **Broker** a non-refundable retainer fee of $_____ for **Broker's** services ("Retainer"). This fee is not refundable and ❏ will ❏ will not be credited to **Buyer** if compensation is earned by **Broker** as specified in this Agreement.

7. COMPENSATION: Broker's compensation is earned when, during the term of this Agreement or any renewal or extension, **Buyer** or any person acting for or on behalf of **Buyer** contracts to acquire real property as specified in this Agreement. **Buyer** will be responsible for paying **Broker** the amount specified below plus any applicable taxes but will be credited with any amount which **Broker** receives from a seller or a real estate licensee who is working with a seller.
(a) Purchase or exchange: $_____ or _____% (select only one) of the total purchase price or other consideration for the acquired property, to be paid at closing.
(b) Lease: $_____ or _____% (select only one) of the gross lease value, to be paid when **Buyer** enters into the lease. If **Buyer** enters into a lease-purchase agreement, the amount of the leasing fee which **Broker** receives will be credited toward the amount due **Broker** for the purchase.
(c) Option: Broker will be paid $_____ or _____% of the option amount (select only one), to be paid when **Buyer** enters into the option agreement. If **Buyer** enters into a lease with option to purchase, **Broker** will be compensated for both the lease and the option. If **Buyer** subsequently exercises the option, the amounts received by **Broker** for the lease and option will be credited toward the amount due **Broker** for the purchase.
(d) Other: Broker will be compensated for all other types of acquisitions as if such acquisition were a purchase or exchange.
(e) Buyer Default: Buyer will pay **Broker's** compensation immediately upon **Buyer's** default on any contract to acquire property.

8. PROTECTION PERIOD: Buyer will pay **Broker's** compensation if, within _____ days after Termination Date, **Buyer** contracts to acquire any property which was called to **Buyer's** attention by **Broker** or any other person or found by **Buyer** during the term of this Agreement. **Buyer's** obligation to pay **Broker's** fee ceases upon **Buyer** entering into a good faith exclusive buyer brokerage agreement with another broker after Termination Date.

9. EARLY TERMINATION: Buyer may terminate this Agreement at any time by written notice to **Broker** but will remain responsible for paying **Broker's** compensation if, from the early termination date to Termination Date plus Protection Period, if applicable, **Buyer** contracts to acquire any property which, prior to the early termination date, was found by **Buyer** or called to **Buyer's** attention by **Broker** or any other person. **Broker** may terminate this Agreement at any time by written notice to **Buyer**, in which event **Buyer** will be released from all further obligations under this Agreement.

10. DISPUTE RESOLUTION: Any unresolveable dispute between **Buyer** and **Broker** will be mediated. If a settlement is not reached in mediation, the matter will be submitted to binding arbitration in accordance with the rules of the American Arbitration Association or other mutually agreeable arbitrator.

11. ASSIGNMENT; PERSONS BOUND: Broker may assign this Agreement to another broker. This Agreement will bind and inure to **Broker's** and **Buyer's** heirs, personal representatives, successors and assigns.

EBBA-4   Rev. 10/98   ©1998 Florida Association of REALTORS®   All Rights Reserved

FIGURE 7.1   EXCLUSIVE BUYER BROKERAGE AGREEMENT (Continued)

12. BROKERAGE RELATIONSHIP: Buyer authorizes **Broker** to operate as (check which is applicable):

❑ single agent of **Buyer.**
❑ transaction broker.
❑ single agent of **Buyer** with consent to transition into a transaction broker.
❑ nonrepresentative of **Buyer.**

13. SPECIAL CLAUSES: _____

_____

_____

_____

_____

_____

14. ACKNOWLEDGMENT; MODIFICATIONS: Buyer has read this Agreement and understands its contents. This Agreement cannot be changed except by written agreement signed by both parties.

Date: _____   **Buyer:** _____   Tax ID No: _ _ _ - _ _ - _ _ _ _

                        Address: _____

                        Zip: _____   Telephone: _____   Facsimile: _____

Date: _____   **Buyer:** _____   Tax ID No: _ _ _ - _ _ - _ _ _ _

                        Address: _____

                        Zip: _____   Telephone: _____   Facsimile: _____

Date: _____   **Real Estate Associate:** _____

Date: _____   **Real Estate Broker:** _____

EBBA-4   Rev. 10/98   ©1998 Florida Association of REALTORS® All Rights Reserved   **Page 2 of 2**

FIGURE 7.2   BEST BUYS

BEST BUYS ON THE MARKET				
				Date:
Price Range	**Address**	**Price**	**MLS #**	**Comments**
$170,000–$180,000	116 Belmont Rd.	$171,900	15432	Great deck, vaulted ceiling
	1272 Scenic Rd.	$174,500	16523	Brick, large oak in front
	784 Wilson Ave.	$175,000	16132	Wood frame colonial
	1216 Kara Dr.	$175,000	15478	Huge back yard with hot tub
	8754 Skate Dr.	$178,500	15843	Heavily wooded, secluded
	124 E. Call St.	$179,900	16021	Downtown, arched doorways

PRODUCT KNOWLEDGE

A buyer usually benefits from working with a licensee, regardless of the brokerage relationship, because of the licensee's product knowledge. It is hard work to acquire the extensive product knowledge that buyers expect. To become proficient, the sales associate should accomplish the following goals:

- Spend a majority of the first few weeks in real estate looking at property.
- See at least 30 new properties each week.
- Keep a record of listings she has viewed by using one of the client follow-up programs mentioned in Chapter 4 or even by using index cards grouped by price range and outstanding features. The sales associate may use the cards like flash cards to remember five good listings in each price range or five with pools or five fixer-uppers. With practice, the sales associate can remember more listings than five.
- Constantly practice matching neighborhoods with price ranges or school zones.
- Prepare a best-buys-on-the-market sheet for each price range (for instance, $70,000 to $80,000), such as the one shown in Figure 7.2.

If a buyer calls to ask for an address of one of the sales associate's listings, the sales associate should provide the information to the caller and, if needed, use "my five favorite homes on the market in your price range" to get an appointment with the buyer. See a sample "best buys" listing in Figure 7.2.

DISCUSSION EXERCISE 7.1

If you actively sell residential properties, try to name from memory the location for at least three single-story, four-bedroom listings. Try to name the location for four listed homes with swimming pools.

FINDING BUYERS

Some good sources of buyers include:

- calls resulting from advertising,
- calls resulting from signs,
- past customers and clients,
- friends and family,
- open house visitors,
- canvassing prospects, and
- buyer seminar attendees.

DISCUSSION EXERCISE 7.2

Carol is on floor duty when she receives a call from a buyer who says, "I'm looking for a four-bedroom home with a pool, northeast, but it's got to have a large workshop. Do you have anything like that listed in the $150,000 range?"

"No, I don't have any listings like that," she says, "but I can show you another company's listing which may be just right for you. I saw it last week. It's very spacious, in an elegant setting with a great view. I believe it's priced at $148,500. I'm available to show it to you this afternoon at 4:30, or I have another time available at 6:15. Which is better for you?"

Is Carol likely to get an appointment to show the property? Why or why not? Is there something she said that you would say differently?

Calls Resulting from Advertising

Advertisement calls are an extremely important source of buyers. A buyer calls for more information to determine whether a house is right for him. A buyer seldom calls to make an appointment with a sales associate. The sales associate's objective is *always to get the appointment with the buyer.* The sales associate must remember two important points when answering buyer advertisement calls:

1. It is difficult for the sales associate to talk intelligently about properties that she has not seen. For this reason, the sales associate *should see every company listing* before answering calls on ads or signs.
2. The sales associate should review all company advertising in newspapers and homes magazines. The licensee should clip each ad and paste it on a separate piece of notebook paper or index card. A **fall-back list,** sometimes called a *switch list,* or *pivot list* should be prepared for each ad. A fall-back list comprises three to five properties that are similar to the property being advertised. The list can consist of the sales associate's personal listings, the brokerage firm's listings or other brokers' listings. If a caller isn't satisfied after learning more about the property in question, the sales associate can refer to the fall-back list of other properties that might be suitable. The fall-back list becomes invaluable in getting the appointment and helping the buyer find the right property. A sample fall-back list is shown in Figure 7.3.

Often, a caller wants a property's address but is unwilling to give her name or phone number. "I just want to ride by to see whether I like it," the caller says. The sales associate will not get the appointment unless the caller feels she will benefit by meeting with the sales associate. The best-buys sheet and the fall-back list may come in handy to get

FIGURE 7.3 "FALL-BACK LIST"

"FALL-BACK LIST" FOR 3415 MONITOR LANE			
Address	**MLS #**	**Price**	**Comments**
1546 Merrimac Dr.	16546	$89,500	Large workshop, lots of trees, 2 streets over
1247 Thresher Ln.	16478	$94,500	20′ × 30′ deck, screened pool area, spotless
1687 Woodgate Way	16521	$95,000	2 stories, 4 bedrooms, close to town
1856 Hoffman Dr.	16493	$85,000	Huge oak in front, lots of azaleas, big kitchen
1260 Dunston Ct.	16470	$92,500	Quiet street off Meridian, very clean, bright

the appointment. Most buyers would feel that the sales associate had market information that would make it worthwhile to make an appointment.

Another way to suggest to the caller that meeting with the sales associate would benefit the caller is to explain that many listings are not advertised. A lot of the best properties are sold almost immediately by sales associates who watch carefully for new listings for their clients or customers. Many buyers want to know that someone constantly watches the market for the right properties for them. "Would you like to have first opportunity to see these prime properties?" is the question that can get the appointment.

When a caller is adamant about wanting an address but will not make an appointment, some sales associates do not give the address because they will lose the call. It is not worthwhile, however, to generate ill will with the consumer. Perhaps a better approach is to be helpful in every way. Ask how many property ads the caller has circled in the newspaper or homes magazine. Tell the caller you will give him an address and information on each listing advertisement, even though other real estate companies hold the listings. You should have a copy of the classified ad section and a homes magazine handy. Follow along with the caller, mark each ad, and set a time that you can get together. Prepare a list with addresses, prices, square footage, and other property features. The attraction to the buyer? One call gets it all because the consumer sees a benefit to meeting with the licensee. The attraction to the sales associate? The buyer places no calls to the competition, and an appointment has been set.

Once an appointment is made, it is time to evaluate the buyer's needs and financial capabilities. This is called **qualifying** the buyer.

DISCUSSION EXERCISE 7.3

Do a role-playing exercise, with a class member calling on an ad for 3415 Monitor Lane. Try to get an appointment using one of the methods discussed.

Often the first visit with the buyer is strictly a get-acquainted visit, meant for making required disclosures and for qualifying. After this is completed, a second appointment is set to show properties.

Calls Resulting from Signs

Another source of buyers is calls on property signs. Callers on real estate ads generally want the properties' addresses. Callers on signs generally want the prices because they already know the locations. A sales associate should handle a sign call like an ad call, with the exception of the information provided.

Past Customers and Clients

One of the best sources of buyers is past customers and clients because they already have enjoyed the benefits of the sales associate's services. Agency representation may be a problem, however. If the sales associate listed a client's property in a prior relationship, the person may feel that the same agency relationship exists in the purchase of a new home. The sales associate must give the buyer the appropriate brokerage relationship disclosures.

Friends and Family

Among the sales associate's first sources of buyers when he starts in real estate are friends and family. The agent should write to everyone he knows and stay in contact for news of potential customers. When working with a friend or family member, the sales associate must evaluate the loyalty issue to decide whether being a single agent for the buyer is more appropriate than being a transaction broker.

Open House Visitors

Holding open houses is a good way to find prospective buyers. The primary objective of an open house is *not* to make the seller happy (a sale makes the seller happy) but to get buyer prospects. If the buyer purchases the home on display, so much the better. The sales associate should prepare a brochure for the home with the sales associate's name and picture prominently placed.

Usually, open house visitors are just looking. The sales associate should tell them that they are welcome to walk through the home, but that she wants to point out a few features that are not readily apparent. If this home is not right for the visitors, the licensee should have ready her list of the five best homes in the price range as well as a fallback list, then set an appointment to talk.

Canvassing Prospects

Canvassing by phone is an excellent method of finding buyers. The sales associate must remember to refer to the appropriate no-solicitation list. The same canvassing call works to generate buyers or sellers. The sales associate might ask, "Do you know someone who may be getting ready to buy or sell real estate?" Often the answer is yes, and the sales associate can set an appointment.

Web Links

http://doacs.state.fl.us/consumer/index.html
Florida Department of Agriculture and Consumer Services.

www.donotcall.gov
Federal Do Not Call List.

Buyer Seminar Attendees

Many sales associates and brokers consider buyer seminars to be outstanding prospecting tools and offer them to the public to attract large numbers of buyers at one time. Some real estate companies have impressive materials and workbooks for attendees of the classes, which run over two or three evenings. Often attendees pay a nominal fee to cover the cost of books. Most seminars entitle an attendee to schedule a one-hour consultation with the seminar leader about a specific real estate problem or need. This can benefit both the consumer and the licensee if a business relationship results. Remember that the appropriate brokerage relationship disclosures must be made.

Qualifying the Buyer

Before a sales associate shows property to a buyer, the sales associate must give the buyer the appropriate brokerage relationship notice as discussed in Chapter 1. The sales associate must know the answers to two important questions. What house does the buyer want, and what can the buyer afford to pay?

What Are the Buyer's Housing Objectives?

The sales associate should ask the buyer what features the home *must have* and what features would be *nice to have*. The *must have* could be features like a particular area of town, four bedrooms, and a two-car garage. The *nice to have* might be features like high ceilings, heat pump, or a wood deck.

The sales associate also needs to know the buyer's urgency level. Each buyer should be classified based on urgency and motivation to purchase. A person needing to move within the next 30 days, for example, is a Priority 1 buyer, needing immediate attention. A person who doesn't have an immediate need, but who should not be ignored, is classified as Priority 2. A buyer who either will not or cannot purchase immediately is Priority 3 and should be contacted regularly for showings. If a buyer relocating to the city is in town just for the weekend to purchase a home, the sales associate knows this is a Priority 1 buyer. After financial qualifying shows the buyer to be capable of making a purchase, the sales associate might say, "It sounds like your situation needs my full attention. If you approve, I'll clear my calendar so we can find the right home for you." A buyer whose present lease expires in six months has less urgency to purchase now and is classified as Priority 3.

Another important piece of information for the sales associate is whether someone else will be involved in making the final purchasing decision. If the buyer's uncle will evaluate the final choice, the sales associate should try to get the uncle to see each property along with the buyer. Why? The uncle will have a better grasp of the market and of property values and may help the buyer reach a decision sooner.

At the first meeting with the buyer, the sales associate should provide, in addition to the agency disclosure form, a clear picture of the entire process, from the time of this first meeting right up until the day the buyer moves into his new home. The buyer who understands the process is less likely to become uneasy or reluctant to purchase when he finds the right property. The buyer should be given a copy of the purchase agreement, and the sales associate should explain important provisions in the agreement. A buyer's cost disclosure should be prepared for the home the buyer desires. This also helps in the financial qualifying process.

What Are the Buyer's Financial Capabilities?

Financial qualification is crucial to a successful sale. If the buyer contracts for a home and applies for a loan that is later denied, seller, buyer, and sales associate have wasted time and effort. In addition, loan application fees ranging from $250 to $500, depending on the lender, could be at risk. Licensees should explain both issues to their customers to help them understand the importance of financial qualifying.

DISCUSSION EXERCISE 7.4

Write out the important steps involved when a buyer purchases and closes on a new home. When this has been completed, do a role-play situation (with a sales associate and two buyers), and explain the process in a manner that is informative and designed to make the buyers feel comfortable. The buyers might ask questions during the session, but should be cooperative. The sales associate needs to know what the buyers *must* have in their new home, as well as the amenities the buyers would *like* to have. Careful questioning is necessary because the sales associate often is surprised when the buyers choose a home quite different from the home described at the first meeting.

Financial qualification is designed to determine how much money the buyer can borrow for the purchase of property. The sales associate has three common ways to qualify the buyers financially:

1. Compare the buyer's financial information with the national secondary mortgage market guidelines.
2. Use a Do-It-Yourself Prequalification form.
3. Arrange for a mortgage loan officer at a financial institution to qualify the buyer.

National Secondary Mortgage Market Guidelines. The sales associate could use the national secondary mortgage market guidelines to get a close estimate of the loan amount for which the buyer would qualify. Table 7.1 provides an estimate of the maximum conventional mortgage loans for which borrowers might qualify if they have good credit ratings, acceptable amounts of outstanding debt, and the ability to make 10 percent down payments. The table assumes each buyer has typical monthly obligations. If the buyer's obligations are more or less than average, the

---

TABLE 7.1   PREQUALIFICATION LOAN ESTIMATES

	CONVENTIONAL LOAN MAXIMUM LOAN AMOUNT WITH A 10% DOWN PAYMENT				
Annual Gross Income	**Mortgage Interest Rate**				
	5%	**6%**	**7%**	**8%**	**9%**
$40,000	$127,000	$120,000	$112,000	$105,000	$97,000
50,000	159,000	150,000	140,000	131,000	121,000
60,000	191,000	180,000	168,000	157,000	145,000
70,000	223,000	210,000	196,000	183,000	169,000
80,000	255,000	240,000	224,000	209,000	193,000
90,000	288,000	270,000	252,000	235,000	217,000
100,000	322,000	302,000	282,000	262,000	242,000

loan amount will vary. When the buyer qualifies for a loan using this approach, the sales associate can go immediately to method number two.

Do-It-Yourself Prequalification Form. The advantage of the **prequalification** form (see example, Figure 7.4) is that it provides an opportunity for the licensee to explain each entry on the form and thereby dispel some of the uneasiness that the potential borrower typically feels. Although lenders do not have to adhere to the Fannie Mae/Freddie Mac standards in reviewing loan applicants, those agencies recommend the maximum housing expense ratio of 28 percent and the maximum total obligations ratio of 36 percent for qualifying potential buyers for first mortgage (conforming) loans. If it is not anticipated that the loans will be sold in the secondary market (nonconforming), lenders may establish more flexible ratios (25 percent to 33 percent for the housing expense ratio and 33 percent to 40 percent for the total obligations ratio) based on the purpose and loan-to-value ratio of a request. The Federal Housing Administration's (FHA's) maximum housing expense ratio is 29 percent, and the maximum total obligations ratio is 41 percent.

After qualifying the buyer with the do-it-yourself prequalification form, the sales associate can begin to work immediately with the buyer in showing properties.

Lender Prequalifying. Having a lender prequalify or preapprove the buyer is the safest approach and should be used before the buyer actually contracts for property.

**FIGURE 7.4   DO-IT-YOURSELF PREQUALIFICATION FORM
(for CONVENTIONAL MORTGAGE LOANS)**

Purchase price	$115,000.00 (A)
Desired mortgage amount	$92,000.00 (B)
Term of mortgage	30 years
Mortgage rate	7.0%
Loan-to-value ratio: (B) ÷ (A) =	80.0% (C)
GROSS MONTHLY INCOME	$ 3,000.00 (D)
Mortgage principal and interest payment: (Payment factor: 6.6530) × (B) ÷ 1,000 =	$ 612.08
Annual real estate taxes ÷ 12 =	+ 110.21
Homeowner's insurance premium ÷ 12 =	+ 50.00
MONTHLY HOUSING EXPENSE	$ 772.29 (E)
Car payments	+ 250.00
Alimony or child support payments	+ 225.00
Credit card or charge account payments	+ 50.00
Other loan payments	+
FIXED MONTHLY OBLIGATIONS	$ 1,297.29 (F)
HOUSING RATIO (E) ÷ (D) = 25.7%	
DEBT RATIO (F) ÷ (D) = 43.2%	

Source: Thomas C. Steinmetz, *The Mortgage Kit,* 4th ed., (Chicago: Dearborn Financial Publishing, Inc.®, 1998), 33.

1 This allows the sales associate to feel confident when writing the contract and to be able
2 to tell the seller or the seller's agent that the buyer has been prequalified.

DISCUSSION EXERCISE 7.5

As a sales associate for Prestige Properties, you are meeting with Morgan and
Hunter Futch, who wish to look at a home priced at $170,000. They have $40,000
cash, of which $30,000 will be a down payment. The Futches wonder whether they
can afford the home and ask how much they need in gross income. Interest rates
currently are at 7 percent.

Using Table 7.1, do a role-playing situation, with members of the group playing
Morgan and Hunter. Change the purchase price of the home to qualify again
with different members of the group. Change the interest rate to 7.5 percent, and
role-play the scenario again.

DISCUSSION EXERCISE 7.6

Sally and Will Cleare make $41,400 in gross annual income. They wish to purchase
a $150,000 home, with $30,000 as a down payment. Fixed-rate 30-year mortgages
are at 7 percent. The monthly principal and interest payment is $798.36. Taxes
for a home in this price range are approximately $1,440 per year. Insurance is
approximately $540.00 per year. No private mortgage insurance is necessary if the
loan-to-value ratio does not exceed 80 percent.

The Cleares have installment loan payments totaling $70 a month and a car
payment of $320.

Using the Do-it-Yourself Prequalification Form in Figure 7.5, determine
whether the Cleares qualify for this loan.

DISCUSSION EXERCISE 7.7

The following role-playing skit, designed to highlight mistakes some sales associates make in their first meetings with prospective buyers, allows both spectators
and participants to learn from the process. Three actors are needed—a sales associate and two buyers. The persons in the skit should be enthusiastic and as realistic
as possible. During the presentation, if the sales associate says something that may
violate the law or ethics, group members should hit their buzzers, zapping to signify their disapproval. At the end of the skit, group members should be able to
itemize the sales associate's errors and recommend responses to the buyers' questions.

FIGURE 7.5   DO-IT-YOURSELF PREQUALIFICATION FORM
(for CONVENTIONAL MORTGAGE LOANS)

Purchase price	_____ (A)
Desired mortgage amount	_____ (B)
Term of mortgage	_____
Mortgage rate	_____
Loan-to-value ratio: (B) ÷ (A)	_____ (C)
GROSS MONTHLY INCOME	_____ (D)
Mortgage principal and interest payment: (Payment factor for a ____%, ____-year loan: _____) × (B) ÷ 1,000	_____
Annual Real Estate Taxes ÷ 12	_____
Homeowner's insurance premium ÷ 12	_____
Mortgage insurance: (B) × .00025 (if (C) is more than .80)	_____
MONTHLY HOUSING EXPENSE	_____ (E)
Car payments	_____
Alimony and child support payments	_____
Credit card and charge account payments	_____
Other loan payments	_____
FIXED MONTHLY OBLIGATIONS	_____ (F)
HOUSING RATIO (E) ÷ (D) = %	_____
DEBT RATIO (F) ÷ (D) = %	_____

Source: Thomas C. Steinmetz, *The Mortgage Kit,* 4th ed., (Chicago: Dearborn Financial Publishing, Inc.®, 1998), 33.

SKIT

Buyers' First Meeting with a Licensee

Buyers walk in, are greeted by sales associate.

Licensee:	Hello, may I help you?
Husband:	Yes, we are here to see Lee Wilson.
Licensee:	I'm Lee. You must be Mr. and Mrs. Camp?
Wife:	Yes, we are. Very nice to meet you.
Licensee:	Great. Please sit down. (*Pause while they sit*.)
Husband:	Our mutual friends, the Joneses, recommended we get in touch with you.
Licensee:	Yeah, the Joneses send me lots of people. By the way, if you send me anyone who buys a house, I'll give you $50.
Wife:	That's what they told us. I hope you can f ind us a good deal, too.
Licensee:	I love working with buyers, Mrs. Camp, and because I'm a transaction broker, I can work harder on your behalf.
Wife:	Well, do you have any distress sales of houses in the $100,000 range that we could take advantage of?

1	Licensee:	As a matter of fact, my company just listed one. The listing sales associate
2		suggested that I look at it. Confidentially, the owners' business is in
3		trouble, and they need to sell quickly. The listing sales associate says they
4		are desperate and probably would come off the price as much as $6,000,
5		but we should start even lower to get the best counteroffer.
6	Husband:	Tell us about it.
7	Licensee:	Well, it's in Bent Tree Estates, close to Lake Jackson. It's got three bed-
8		rooms, two baths, a large lot, and a two-car garage. It's in absolutely
9		perfect condition.
10	Wife:	The newspaper ran an article last week suggesting that buyers get a home
11		inspection. Is that a good idea?
12	Licensee:	It is if you want to spend $300 for nothing. I've looked over the house,
13		and it's just perfect. No problems whatsoever.
14	Husband:	I need to tell you that we may have a problem qualifying for a new loan.
15		I had some credit problems last year, and we got turned down on
16		another house we tried to buy. We really need to get an assumable loan
17		with no qualifying.
18	Licensee:	Well, we're in luck again. If you like this house, you can buy it with less than
19		$8,000 down. We'll have to structure a wraparound loan to beat the due-
20		on-sale clause, but I do that all the time. Can you work with $8,000 down?
21	Husband:	I think we can come up with that much, if we can get the price right. Can
22		we put some kind of contingency in the contract in case I can't get the
23		money?
24	Licensee:	Hey! I can write up a contract with contingencies that will let you out at
25		any time with no risk. Don't worry about that. But let's go see it.
26	Husband:	Should we have an attorney?
27	Licensee:	You know what's wrong with five attorneys up to their necks in sand?
28	Husband:	(*Smiles*) No, what?
29	Licensee:	Not enough sand. (*He laughs.*) Seriously, folks, you don't need an attor-
30		ney. I can help you with anything an attorney can.
31	Wife:	Can we ask you some more questions first?
32	Licensee:	Sure. Go ahead.
33	Wife:	Is it a good neighborhood?
34	Licensee:	Oh, yeah, there are hardly any minorities living there!
35	Wife:	Well, I didn't mean that. I meant is it pleasant and well maintained?
36	Licensee:	Uh-oh, sorry. Yes it's really nice.
37	Husband:	Do you need us to sign any disclosure forms now?
38	Licensee:	No, not really. Not until we write a contract for a house.
39	Husband:	Well, let's go looking. I hope it works out.
40	Licensee:	I'll do everything I can for you. (*Leaves*)
41		(*To an associate in the office*) Hey, Jim! I'll be back in a while. I've got some
42		flakes with no money again, but I'm going to show a house!

43 Is it possible to learn from mistakes? The mistakes made in this skit may seem ridic-
44 ulous, but these statements are actually made—although probably not all in a single
45 transaction. Sales associates must be alert in their presentations and when answering
46 questions to avoid these mistakes.

SHOWING THE PROPERTY

Once the buyer has been qualified, it is time to show properties that meet the buyer's needs. The sales associate should adhere to the following sequence in the showing and contracting process:

1. Setting the appointment.
2. Previewing the properties.
3. Planning the route.
4. Entering and showing the properties.
5. Evaluating the buyer's level of interest.
6. Estimating the buyer's costs and making required disclosures.
7. Writing the contract.

Steps 1 through 6 are discussed in the following section. Step 7, writing the contract, is the subject of Chapter 8.

Setting the Appointment

This step is important not only for the obvious reason (nothing can happen until a meeting occurs) but also from a timing standpoint. Does the sales associate set the appointment before he has previewed prospective homes or after? Many times a sales associate will not set an appointment until he has previewed homes and is confident that good choices are available to show. The advantage of this method is that the sales associate can describe properties he thinks the buyer will like and that meet the buyer's needs. Two disadvantages in this approach follow:

1. The sales associate might spend a lot of time looking at properties only to find that the buyer is working with another licensee.
2. If the sales associate can't find anything just right and puts the buyer off, he might force the buyer to work with another licensee.

Other sales associates say, "If you set the appointment, you'll find the properties." The premises here are that (1) showing homes helps the buyer focus on likes and dislikes and (2) showing homes that are not quite right is better than not showing homes at all. The sales associate must decide which works best in each situation.

It is important to keep in contact with the buyer regularly, based on priority status. At least weekly, the sales associate should match the buyer's profile with new listings, then call the buyer for an appointment. If the sales associate wants a Saturday showing appointment, she should make the appointment far enough in advance that the buyer can arrange his schedule. Saturday morning is too late to make the call. Early in the week is the best time to call for weekend showing appointments.

The best way to keep up with the buyer and match him with property is to use one of the client follow-up programs mentioned in Chapter 4. A separate card may be printed for each property. Match-ups between buyers and properties also are possible using some of the MLS system software. If the sales associate does not have access to a computer, it is simple to enter the buyer information on prospect cards. Spread out the cards on a tabletop and group them by price range when reviewing new listings. Listings should be matched to the buyer, and the sales associate should call the buyer about the properties. The more frequently the sales associate makes the buyer aware that the sales associate continually searches for the right property for the buyer, the more likely it is that the buyer will call on properties he has seen.

Previewing the Properties

The sales associate should preview properties before actually showing them to the buyer. The sales associate would be surprised and embarrassed if she brought the buyer to a property in terrible condition when the sales associate has told the buyer, "I think you'll like this next one!"

Each time the sales associate sees a new property, whether on a showing appointment, a preview day, or an office caravan of new listings, the sales associate should match that property with one of her buyers. She should take careful notes so that she can contact the appropriate buyer about a new property on the market.

Planning the Route

Normally, the sales associate should show no more than five properties in one tour. However, if a Priority 1 buyer is in town for the weekend for the purpose of buying a home, the sales associate must continue to show homes or risk losing the buyer.

When setting the appointment to show properties, the sales associate must consider in which order the homes will be shown. Buyers go through a continual evaluation process during the inspection tour, and the sales associate should help that process. Many sales associates like to schedule the home they consider just the right property as the last on the tour. While there are good arguments for this procedure, there are also disadvantages. The biggest problem is that if the houses get better between numbers one and five, and five is the best, the buyer wants to see house number six. Most brokers recommend showing the best house early in the tour. This sets a standard against which all other homes are measured. It usually makes the tour faster because the buyer can decide quickly that the home shown earlier was more to his liking.

Once the route has been decided, the sales associates should make appointments for the showings with the property owners. The time scheduled for each showing should not be fixed, but should fall in a range, because it is often difficult for the sales associate to judge how long the buyer will stay in each home on the tour. The seller should be asked to prepare the home for showing by opening the drapes and turning on all the lights so that the house will be bright and pleasant. The sales associate should ask the seller to vacate the property during the showing so that the buyer can have emotional possession of the property. If the sales associate has a cell phone, she should call the seller when leaving the previous house on the tour. If the seller owns a dog, the sales associate should ask that the seller make arrangements to contain the pet. If the sales associate will be later than scheduled or must cancel, common courtesy as a professional dictates that the sales associate should call the seller to explain the circumstances. Nothing is more disappointing to a seller than to needlessly prepare the home for a showing.

The route taken on the way to each property also is important. A trip past a beautiful park nearby makes the homesite more interesting to the buyer, as does a trip past the shopping areas and schools closest to the home. While the initial route might avoid unsightly areas, they should be shown on the way out. Failure to show such surroundings is misrepresentation.

The licensee should discuss negative features she knows about a home on the way to the property—for example, "When I previewed the home yesterday, the housekeeping was not up to its usual standard because the kids are out of school this week. I hope that's OK." This reduces the shock the buyer might feel when entering. Often, the buyer defends the property: "Considering everything, the house is surprisingly clean!"

The sales associate should avoid exaggerating a home's positive aspects to the buyer. This exaggeration may create an expectation that the house does not meet. It is better that the buyer be pleasantly surprised when discovering the features.

Entering and Showing the Properties

This process depends on a property's general appearance. If the home's exterior is outstanding, the presentation should give the buyer time to appreciate this feature. Many sales associates park across the street so that a buyer's walk to a house is as pleasant as possible.

1   When highlighting a property's features, the sales associate must remember the most
2   important words in any sales presentation:

3   • Fact
4   • Bridge
5   • Benefit and
6   • Picture

7   The sales associate often points out facts that she believes to be important to the
8   buyer and expects the buyer to be able to translate each fact into a benefit. "This house
9   is on a cul-de-sac" might be a typical comment when driving up to the property. The
10 sales associate believes this is important information to the buyer. The buyer might be
11 thinking, "Yes, that's quite obvious. So what?" The full presentation should include fact,
12 bridge, benefit, and picture.

13 The *fact* is that the property is on the cul-de-sac. The *bridge* might be "What that means
14 to you, Mr. and Mrs. Jones . . . " The *benefit* is the rest of the sentence: "is that because
15 there is no through-traffic, automobiles travel very slowly, resulting in greater safety
16 to your children." The *picture* is a word picture: "Imagine being out here on the street
17 while your children roller-skate safely."

DISCUSSION EXERCISE 7.8

Picture a house that you have been in recently. Try to think of as many features of
the house as you can, then express those features to represent fact, bridge, benefit, and picture statements.

Set up a group contest to see who can come up with the most fact-bridge-
benefit-picture statements about a house that is familiar to all of you.

---

18 The sales associate should practice this technique whenever she can: when driving in
19 the car alone, when **previewing properties,** or when on the office caravan of listings.
20 Once it becomes a habit, buyers will find the sales associate's statements clearer and
21 more interesting, and the sales associate will make more sales.

22 Many times, the listing office gives out the key to the back door, or the back door key
23 may be the only key provided in the lockbox, or **keysafe,** at the house. Although the
24 sales associate must go in through the door to which she has a key, the buyer always
25 should enter through the front door.

26 Finally, the sales associate should not "overshow" a property. The buyer should be
27 allowed to discover some of the best features on his own. The classic example of over-
28 showing is walking through a property making statements like "This is the dining room."

29 ## Evaluating the Buyer's Level of Interest

30 The buyer usually knows immediately when he is not interested in a house. If the seller
31 is at home, the sales associate should explain tactfully that the house does not satisfy the
32 buyer's needs. The sales associate should stop showing the property and proceed to the
33 next. If the buyer does not express interest in a property and states several objections,
34 the sales associate should not attempt to answer the objections. Doing so would be
35 pointless and of no benefit to the buyer or the sales associate. However, objections are
36 useful sales tools to a sales associate. They reflect a buyer's level of interest in a property
37 or his need for more information.

If the buyer expresses interest as well as objections, the sales associate should be certain that she understands an objection; then she must isolate it and respond to it. Understanding the objection is extremely important. If the buyer says "This house costs too much money!" the sales associate might respond quickly, "No, it doesn't. I did a CMA, and it's priced right!" The buyer might well have been stating that he doesn't feel he can afford the house. The sales associate must ask clarifying questions to be sure what the buyer is saying.

Before answering an objection, the sales associate should determine whether the buyer has other objections. If he has many, the property probably is not suitable for the buyer. Isolating the objection is a means of finding out whether there are other objections. The sales associate might ask, for example, "If it were not for the lack of a pool, would you be ready to purchase the home?" A no answer indicates that the buyer has other objections. A yes answer tells the sales associate, "Satisfy me regarding this problem, and I'll buy."

Many objections can be turned into immediate selling points. "The house needs paint" could provoke an argument from an unprofessional sales associate. The empathetic sales associate simply asks, "Would you paint it yourself, or would you hire someone to paint it for you?" With a positive response from the buyer, both parties are happy.

Estimating the Buyer's Costs and Making Required Disclosures

When the buyer finds the right property, the licensee should be prepared to provide a cost-disclosure statement such as the one shown in Figure 7.6. If the purchase will require the buyer to obtain new institutional financing, the licensee should call the mortgage lender and have a good-faith estimate faxed. Ideally, the sales associate would have done this even before showing a particular property so that when the buyer says "okay," the sales associate can prepare the estimate.

Using the blank form in Figure 7.6, calculate the buyer's closing costs and monthly payments based on the information given below:

Purchaser	Kyle and Kari Buyers
Property address	1460 Lime Drive
Date of contract	March 20, 2001
Mortgage lender	Security First
Prepared by	(Your name)
Sales price	$200,000
First mortgage:	$160,000
Closing Costs:	
Title insurance	$1,250
Origination fee	1%
Discount points	½
Recording fees	$60
Credit report	50
Appraisal fee	300
Survey	180
Underwriting fee	125
Express mail fee	20
Attorney's fee	300
Escrow/Prepaid Items:	
Taxes—3 months	600
Hazard insurance (1 year)	900
Hazard insurance (2 months)	150
Monthly mortgage insurance premium (2 months)	44
Prepaid interest (1 month)	935

Mr. and Mrs. Buyers will give a deposit of $4,000. The principal and interest on the 7 percent, 30-year, fixed-rate loan amount is $1,064.48.

FIGURE 7.6   REAL PROPERTY SALES DISCLOSURE
Buyer's Estimated Costs

PURCHASER: _____   PROPERTY ADDRESS: _____

Date of Contract: _____	**Sales Price** $ _____		$_____
Mortgage Lender: _____	**1st Mortgage** $ _____	+ _____ FHA MIP OR FUNDNG	$_____ TOTAL LOAN AMOUNT
Prepared by: _____	**2nd Mortgage** $ _____		$_____
		Estimated Down Payment (1)	$_____

Estimated closing costs:
1. Title Insurance: ❑ owner's ❑ mortgagee's . . . .   _____
2. Title Insurance Endorsements . . . .   _____
3. Origination fee ____% . . . .   _____
4. Discount points estimated _____% . . . .   _____
5. Intangible Tax ($.002/$1) on new mortgage . . .   _____
6. Documentary Stamps ($.35/$100) on all notes .   _____
7. Recording Fees . . . .   _____
8. Credit Report . . . .   _____
9. Appraisal Fee. . . . .   _____
10. Survey . . . .   _____
11. Document Preparation Fee. . . . .   _____
12. Tax Service Fee . . . .   _____
13. Underwriting Fee . . . .   _____
14. Express Mail Fee(s) . . . .   _____
15. VA Funding Fee at _____% . . . .   _____
16. Assumption Fee on Existing Mortgage. . . . .   _____
17. Purchase of Escrow Account. . . . .   _____
18. Home Inspection Fee . . . .   _____
19. Homeowner's Warranty . . . . _____   _____
20. Attorney's Fee (if any).   _____
21. _____ . . . .   _____
22. _____ . . . .   _____

Total Estimated Closing Costs (2)	$_____

Estimated escrow/prepaid items:
1. Taxes _____ months . . . .   _____
2. Hazard Insurance, 1 year . . . .   _____
3. Hazard Insurance, 2 months. . . . .   _____
4. First year Mortgage Insurance . . . .   _____
5. Mortgage Insurance, 2 months. . . . .   _____
6. Flood Insurance, 14 months. . . . .   _____
7. Prepaid Interest. . . . .   _____
8. Homeowner's Assn. Dues . . . .   _____

Total Estimated escrow/prepaid items (3)	$_____
Total Lines 1, 2 and 3	$_____
Less: Deposit money	$_____

ESTIMATED MONTHLY PAYMENTS	
❑ Fixed ❑ ARM ___% Interest Rate ___Years	
Principal & Interest	$_____
Property Taxes	_____
Hazard Insurance	_____
Mortgage Insurance	_____
Other _____	_____
TOTAL. . . . . $	_____
Other Association fees may be due monthly	

Estimated Total due at Closing	$_____
(Must be tendered in cash or certified funds)	

DISCUSSION EXERCISE 7.9

After the disclosure has been completed, do a role-playing session in class, with two students playing Mr. and Mrs. Buyers and one student playing the sales associate. The sales associate should present the completed form to the buyers, who should ask some simple questions in a positive way.

SUMMARY

When working with buyers, a sales associate must be certain that he makes required agency disclosures on a timely basis. A buyer benefits most when a licensee represents the buyer and no one else. Extensive product knowledge is necessary if a sales associate is to provide the best service to a consumer. The sales associate has many ways to acquire product knowledge, but all consist of looking at properties. Index cards help the licensee remember properties, and a best-buys-on-the-market list helps the sales associate better exhibit her product knowledge.

Sales associates draw buyers from a number of sources: calls on ads or signs, past customers or clients, friends and family, open house visitors, canvassing, and buyer seminars. When handling an ad or a sign call, a licensee's primary objective is to get an appointment. Sales associates should prepare carefully for ad calls, know the properties advertised and have fall-back lists.

A sales associate should qualify a buyer's housing objectives and have the buyers preapproved for a loan, as well as prioritize buyers based on the immediacy of their needs. When showing properties, the sales associate should describe benefits and be careful not to overshow the properties.

When a buyer is ready to purchase a property, the sales associate should be able to show the buyer the total costs of the transaction and the cash requirements. The sales associate also should calculate the loan payment for the buyer.

DEFINE THESE KEY TERMS

buyer brokerage agreement
canvassing
fall-back list
keysafe

prequalification
previewing properties
qualifying
transaction broker

CHAPTER 7 PRACTICE EXAM

1. Most brokers recommend showing the best house:

   a. last.
   b. early in the tour.
   c. second to last.
   d. whenever—it doesn't matter.

2. Before showing properties to a buyer, a sales associate should:

   a. qualify the buyer's financial abilities and housing needs.
   b. preview the homes to be shown.
   c. make the required brokerage relationship disclosures.
   d. do all of the above.

3. A Priority 1 buyer is one who:

   a. has an immediate need to buy.
   b. is important, but not as important as Priority 3.
   c. will not buy right away, but should be contacted regularly.
   d. is not highly motivated.

4. Normally, the prospective buyer calling about a property with a "For Sale" sign wants information from the sales associate about the property's:

   a. location.
   b. lot size.
   c. price.
   d. address.

Use the following information and Fannie Mae/Freddie Mac guidelines to answer questions 5 through 8.

William is a new sales associate. On Saturday afternoon, the Sharpes visit his office and want to look at homes. They give William the following information:

Gross income	$60,000
House price	140,000
Monthly payment (PITI)	1,350
Other monthly obligations	600

5. What is the Sharpes' housing expense ratio?

   a. 12 percent
   b. 27 percent
   c. 39 percent
   d. 44.4 percent

6. What is the Sharpes' total obligations ratio?

   a. 12 percent
   b. 27 percent
   c. 39 percent
   d. 44.4 percent

7. Will the Sharpes qualify for the loan?

   a. Yes, provided they escrow for taxes and insurance.
   b. No, the housing expense ratio is too high.
   c. No, the total obligations ratio is too high.
   d. No, both ratios are out of line.

8. How high a monthly payment can the Sharpes qualify for?

   a. $1,200
   b. $1,350
   c. $1,800
   d. $2,000

9. How does a buyer benefit by agreeing to pay a brokerage commission to her broker?

   a. The commission will be lower than if the seller has to pay a commission.
   b. The broker will automatically be the buyer's single agent.
   c. The broker will be able to work harder on the buyer's financing alternatives.
   d. The broker can show the buyer unlisted properties like FSBOs and fore-closures.

10. For a buyer to decide to work with a licensee, the most important factor probably is the licensee's:

    a. low fee.
    b. product knowledge.
    c. dress code.
    d. automobile make and model.

11. When making an appointment with a seller to show her property, a sales associate should do which of the following?

    a. Set the time as a range rather than a specific time.
    b. Tell the seller to turn on the lights.
    c. Tell the seller to leave the home during the showing.
    d. All of the above

12. A sales associate's primary objective when answering a sign call or an ad call is to:

    a. give out the information requested.
    b. make a friend.
    c. make an appointment.
    d. get a name.

13. A fall-back list consists of:

    a. past customers.
    b. answers to objections.
    c. places to find part-time employment.
    d. properties similar to those advertised.

14. If a property is particularly attractive from the front, the best way to show the property is by:

    a. parking in the garage.
    b. parking at the street.
    c. sending a photo to the buyer.
    d. driving up and down the street first.

15. Before a buyer begins seeing properties, the sales associate should have a good grasp of the buyer's:

    a. checkbook.
    b. housing objectives.
    c. financial capabilities.
    d. Both b and c

16. The reason a sales associate asks a seller to vacate the property while it is being shown is:

    a. so the seller can't hear what the sales associate is saying about the property.
    b. to allow the buyer to take emotional possession of the property during the showing.
    c. to allow the buyer's children to use the bathroom, if necessary.
    d. so the buyer can inspect the structure for defects.

17. Generally, the only features a sales associate should discuss with a buyer on the way to viewing a property are the:

    a. home's most outstanding attributes.
    b. negative features.
    c. beautiful Jacuzzi and huge master suite.
    d. features previously discussed.

18. One method of finding large numbers of buyers at one time is:

    a. calling friends.
    b. calling past customers.
    c. canvassing.
    d. conducting buyer seminars.

19. A sales associate's statement that "the house is built of brick" should be followed immediately by the:

    a. fact.
    b. bridge.
    c. benefit.
    d. picture.

20. The safest way for a sales associate to prequalify a buyer is to:

    a. let a lender do it.
    b. use national mortgage market guidelines.
    c. use Fannie Mae/Freddie Mac underwriting guidelines.
    d. use any of the above methods.

SECTION IV

CHAPTER 8—SALES AND OPTION CONTRACTS

LEARNING OBJECTIVES

Upon completion of this section, *you should be able to:*

1. discuss the unique features of a real estate contract versus a normal business contract;
2. define what is meant by a valid contract;
3. distinguish between an implied contract and a quasi-contract;
4. distinguish between a voidable contract and a void contract;
5. define what is meant by an unconscionable contract;
6. distinguish the difference between the statute of frauds and the statute of limitations;
7. explain the exceptions to the statute of frauds that are recognized as valid real estate transactions;
8. list at least three transactions that are *not* suitable for using the FAR/BAR contract;
9. describe the legal test for the sufficiency of a legal description;
10. name and explain at least ten important sections or provisions in a real estate sales contract;
11. complete a sales contract; and
12. list the requirements for completing an option contract.

CHAPTER 8

SALES AND OPTION CONTRACTS

1 Contracts are part of our everyday lives. When a person orders telephone service, buys
2 a refrigerator, or pays for an airline ticket, a contract has been formed.

3   Licensees regularly work with many different kinds of contracts. The broker's
4 employment agreement, listing contracts, buyer brokerage agreements, leases, options,
5 and sales contracts are just a few. Understanding the information in a contract and
6 being able to correctly explain it to sellers and buyers is an important function of a sales
7 associate. Licensees may legally prepare listing contracts, sales contracts, and option
8 contracts. Preparing notes, mortgages, or deeds is unauthorized practice of law.

ANALYSIS OF REAL ESTATE CONTRACTS

10 A **contract** is a promise or set of promises that must be performed. Once the promise
11 is given, the law recognizes performance of that promise as a duty. If the promise is
12 broken or breached, the law provides a legal remedy for the injured party. However,
13 one promise, standing alone, does not constitute a contract. Some specific act by the
14 party to whom the promise is made, or a mutual promise from that party, is required to
15 conclude a contract. For example, if you promise to fix your neighbor's roof and the
16 neighbor thanks you, no contract exists since you asked for nothing in return for your
17 promise. If your neighbor promises to give you $1,000 to fix her roof and you promise
18 to do it, mutual promises have been exchanged, and a contract has been made.

Types and Legal Standings of Contracts

20 A number of contract types and classifications exist, each having certain legal effects.
21 Newly licensed sales associates will remember having been exposed to certain classifica-
22 tions of contracts and to the fact that a contract can change from one classification to
23 another as **performance** progresses.

24   A **bilateral contract,** the most common type, is a mutual agreement by both sides to
25 perform. A real estate sales contract is an example of a bilateral contract because the
26 seller promises to sell a parcel of real property and to deliver title, and the buyer prom-
27 ises to pay a certain sum of money for the property. A **unilateral contract,** on the other
28 hand, is a one-sided promise. One party makes an obligation to perform without
29 receiving a promise to perform from the other party. In effect, it is an offer that can be
30 accepted only by performance on the terms offered. An example of a unilateral contract
31 is the ordinary option, in which the person granting the option (optionor) is obligated
32 not to sell to anyone but the person asking for the option (optionee) during the life of
33 the option. The optionee is not required to buy.

Two additional examples of a unilateral contract are:

1. an open listing agreement, where the seller agrees to pay a commission if the broker performs, but the broker makes no promises to market the property and
2. a broker's promise to pay a $5,000 bonus to the sales associate who sells the most homes in a subdivision.

An **express contract** is a mutual agreement between parties stated in words, either oral or written. An **implied contract** is an unwritten agreement inferred from the actions or conduct of the parties that shows intent to be bound by the agreement. For example, if a broker buys property in his name on behalf of his principal, the law implies a promise on the broker's part to deliver the property to the principal. A second example of an implied contract is a situation in which a broker tells a seller that she has a buyer willing and able to pay for the seller's property, and the seller accepts the buyer's offer. The law usually requires the seller to pay the broker a typical rate of commission because of the parties' acts.

An **executory contract** is an agreement in which some future act remains to be done by one or both parties. For example, a real estate sales contract, between signing and title closing, is an executory contract. An **executed contract,** on the other hand, is an agreement in which the parties have fulfilled their promises and thus performed the contract. For example, a sales contract becomes an executed agreement after title closing and after all parties have fully performed. (**Note:** Do not confuse the term *executed contract* with the use of the word *execute,* which refers to the signing of a legal document such as a contract.)

A **valid contract** is an agreement that contains all of the essential elements—**c**ontractual capacity, **o**ffer and acceptance, **l**awful purpose, **i**n writing and signed, and **c**onsideration (COLIC)—and is binding and enforceable on both parties in a court of law.

A **quasi-contract** is an obligation imposed by law in the absence of a contract to prevent unjust enrichment. Thus, it is not a contract at all because it does not depend on the parties' intentions; it was "invented" to allow the courts to preserve justice and fair dealing. For example, if a person comes into the possession of money that belongs to another, the law deduces the existence of a promise to pay the money to the person entitled to it.

A **voidable contract** is an agreement that appears to be valid and enforceable, but may be rescinded by one of the parties. For example, an agreement entered into with a minor usually is voidable by the minor. The competent parties element of a valid contract is absent. For another example, a contract may contain a clause (provision) related to time of performance by both parties. If either party fails to perform on or before a specified date, the other party has the right to void or nullify the contract. Thus, a voidable contract may be seen as midway between a valid contract and a void contract: it remains valid until the party with the power to void the agreement chooses to do so. A **void contract** is an agreement that is unenforceable under the law. It has no legal force because it does not contain the essential elements of a contract. For example, a listing contract in which a broker agrees to illegal discrimination based on race, sex, color, religion, national origin, family status, or handicap probably voids the document.

An **unconscionable contract** is an agreement that, if the contract were enforced, would be too harsh on or oppressive to one of the parties. The word *unconscionable* means unreasonable or excessive. The Uniform Commercial Code (UCC) provides that a court may refuse to enforce an unconscionable contract, may strike out an unconscionable clause, or simply may tailor enforcement of a contract prevent an unconscionable result. This interpretation of the UCC by the courts is an example of the rapidly growing judicial trend toward preventing informed and knowledgeable parties from taking advantage of uninformed parties. It is not necessary that fraud be an element in a dispute for the provisions of the law to be applied. Any agreement or clause in a contract related to consumer credit,

1 a consumer lease, or a consumer loan is void if the agreement or clause is unconscion-
2 able. For example, a seller may insist on an "as is" provision in the sales contract. A
3 buyer compelled to sign the contract with the clause "Buyer represents that he or she has
4 examined the entire property and declares that he or she has not relied on any represen-
5 tation made by the Seller" seemingly is being prevented from raising a defense of fraud
6 or misrepresentation should its existence be revealed later. Any contract that appears to
7 create a one-sided bargain is in danger of being declared unconscionable.

DISCUSSION EXERCISE 8.1

You are a sales associate who has listed John Wilson's home in Foxcroft. Mr. Wilson would rather not repair several property defects (such as a cracked foundation). He suggests the use of an "as is" clause in the contract so that a buyer can do any inspection desired. "Based on this clause," Wilson tells you, "we have no need to disclose."

Does the use of an "as is" clause in a sales contract excuse a broker from disclosing material facts regarding a property? Explain.

---

8 ## Statute of Frauds

9 Before the enactment of the **statute of frauds,** it was not uncommon for a person to pay
10 "witnesses" to falsify testimony to support a nonexistent oral contract for the sale of real
11 property. The law commonly called the *statute of frauds* requires that certain types of
12 contracts, in order to be enforceable, be in writing and be signed by the party against
13 whom enforcement is sought. Contracts that must be in writing and signed are of two
14 general types: those that will not be performed fully within a short period of time and
15 those that deal with specific subjects.

16 In Florida, an agreement or a promise that cannot be performed by both parties
17 within one year after the contract date must be evidenced by a written document. Also,
18 an agreement to sell or the actual sale of any interest in real property is subject to the
19 statute of frauds and must be in writing and signed by all parties bound by the contract
20 to be enforceable. Witnesses are not required.

21 Two common exceptions to the statute of frauds are recognized:

22 1. **Executed contracts.** Performance of the promise made proves the contract
23 existed; therefore, the function of the statute of frauds has been accomplished, and
24 a written form is not required.
25 2. **Partial performance.** Usually, the statute of frauds does not apply to partially per-
26 formed contracts as long as two conditions have been met: (1) partial or full payment
27 has been made and (2) the buyer has either taken physical possession of or made
28 improvements to the subject property. For example, if a buyer has evidence of a
29 $500 payment toward the purchase of a parcel of land, then moves onto the property
30 and plants a crop of tomatoes, the statute's function has been accomplished. The pay-
31 ment and possession are regarded as evidence that a valid contract exists.

32 ## SALES CONTRACTS

33 A **sales contract,** also referred to as a *purchase and sale contract* or a *contract for sale and*
34 *purchase,* is a written agreement setting forth the terms for the transfer of real property
35 from seller to buyer, with both signing the document. The standard contract for sale
36 and purchase developed cooperatively by the Florida Association of REALTORS® and the

Florida Bar (the FAR/BAR contract) is the most widely used preprinted sales contract form in the state (see Figure 8.1). This section of the chapter presents specific in-struc-tions for the correct preparation of the FAR/BAR Contract For Sale and Purchase, pro-viding licensees with hands-on practice in preparing contracts to increase their professional skills. If licensees in your area use a different sales contract form, substitute that form for the FAR/BAR contract. The discussion that follows applies to your con-tract form as well.

Whether To Use a Printed Form

No two real estate transactions are exactly alike. Even two nearly identical houses lo-cated adjacent to one another may require different contractual handling. The earnest money deposits, mortgage sources, and prices, as well as many other items, must be con-sidered. Even the tried-and-proven clauses in a standard form may need to be adapted to the requirements of a particular transaction. Therefore, licensees should use printed form contracts cautiously.

The **FAR/BAR Contract for Sale and Purchase** is intended for use in routine transac-tions involving the sale of single-family dwellings or unimproved real property. If a licen-see is involved in any one of the following types of transactions, the FAR/BAR contract is *not* suitable:

- Business purchase or sale
- Construction or improvements contract
- Contract for deed (installment contract, agreement for deed)
- Exchange agreement (contract for exchange of real property)
- Lease with option to buy
- Option contract (to be described later in this chapter)
- Unique or complex transactions

If vacant land (other than a single-family vacant lot) is involved in a transaction, spe-cial provisions should be included in the contract concerning the **concurrency** status of the property for development purposes, as well as suitability for its intended use relative to the area's comprehensive plan.

Responsibility for Preparation.   The FAR/BAR contract, intended to function as a bilateral contract, is constructed to express the complete intent of the parties to a trans-action. The sales contract is the most important instrument for closing a real estate trans-action. It is the culmination of all the offers and negotiations that have taken place, and it must be prepared with care and diligence. Any time a licensee is not certain whether an attorney is required in preparing any special clause or type of contract, the best course of action is to advise the buyer and seller to consult an experienced real estate attorney.

The licensee who prepares the contract and, normally, the licensee's employer are responsible for any mistakes in the agreement. If any errors, omissions or ambiguities exist regarding material terms, the courts will not go outside the contents of the con-tract to determine intent. The licensee who prepared the contract will not be allowed to explain later an intent not indicated in the contract contents. If the contract is vague and unenforceable, the result could be no transaction at all, loss of commission and a possible civil lawsuit against the licensee.

Stated Performance Dates.   While licensees are expected to be familiar with all of the provisions of the FAR/BAR contract, some of the contract contents that are espe-cially critical are the stipulated dates and deadlines that govern times allowed for per-formance:

- Paragraph III   Time for acceptance, effective date, facsimile;
- Paragraph IV   Financing: time for buyer to obtain a written commitment, time for

1   buyer to make application for financing, time for seller to furnish
2   statements from all mortgagees;
3 • Paragraph V   Title evidence: time for seller to deliver either an abstract of title or
4   a title insurance commitment;
5 • Paragraph VI   Closing date; and
6 • Standards A, C, D, F, I, and N.

7 **"Time Is of the Essence" Provision.** This single-sentence provision included in
8 Standard I, that **time is of the essence,** has enormous legal effect. Failure of any party
9 to perform the duties or promises made within the exact time limits established in the
10 contract constitutes an automatic default by the nonperforming party. This default then
11 creates a right of cancellation on the part of the other party (voidable contract). All of
12 this emphasizes how important it is to pay special attention in all instances involving
13 dates and times, being certain to:

14 • use realistic time periods;
15 • check that the time periods complement and are consistent with times in other blank
16   spaces; and
17 • set up calendar deadlines in the file to monitor performance by the parties to the
18   sales contract once it has been signed.

19 **Gathering Contract Data.** Collecting the information required to complete all of
20 the entry blanks in the FAR/BAR contract is a sizable task. Information should become
21 available or should be obtained as the real estate licensee helps negotiate the contract.
22 Once the licensee gathers all of the information, she must verify it for accuracy and cur-
23 rency. Including obsolete information in a contract may be more harmful to a successful
24 conclusion than having insufficient information to complete the contract. The licensee
25 should pay particular attention to and be sure to verify the following two categories of
26 data:

27 1. *The owner/seller's name and address and the property's legal description.* MLS data, prop-
28   erty appraiser information, and even listing agreements have been in error on
29   occasion. Place more reliance on an existing or a prior title insurance policy, a
30   deed, or a survey for the information.
31 2. *Financial information.* Financial data tend to change frequently and require last-
32   minute updating. Check with local lenders to make certain that times allowed for
33   obtaining financial commitments are realistic and that the rates and terms contem-
34   plated actually are available. If assumption of an existing mortgage is required,
35   read the mortgage instrument to determine whether the loan is assumable. Even
36   when lending institutions claim that a loan is not assumable, the actual instrument
37   may prove it to be so. When reasonable doubt exists, seek legal advice.

38 ## Preparing Sales Contracts

39 While the following guidelines are provided as an aid in understanding and preparing
40 each element in the FAR/BAR Contract for Sale and Purchase, these instructions are
41 generic in description and therefore apply to *all* sales contracts. Each specific provision
42 of the form, both preprinted and fill-in, is described separately to help licensees
43 examine the contract thoroughly. The 23 Standards for Real Estate Transactions on the
44 back of the FAR/BAR contract form govern the rights and obligations of the buyer and
45 the seller just as forcefully as do other provisions in the contract. They represent cus-
46 toms relating to the sale and purchase of real property developed over the years. Stan-
47 dardizing customs helps to simplify transactions and gives the parties the comfort of
48 knowing that they will not be subjected to unfamiliar provisions and unexpected
49 charges. While elaboration of the standards is beyond the scope of this chapter, close
50 examination by all licensees is warranted to achieve a working knowledge of each
51 standard.

Contract for Sale and Purchase

Parties
Seller:

In General: Seller's name(s) should be shown in the manner in which title is held, reciting the marital status of each seller. Obtain this information from the prior title insurance policy or a copy of the recorded deed.

Residence: If a house is located on the property and the property is owned individually by a married person, obtain the signature of the spouse to avoid possible future litigation.

Joint Ownership: If the property is jointly owned, obtain the signatures of all joint owners. If a residence is located on the property, obtain the signatures of joint owners and their spouses.

Corporations, Partnerships, Estates, Trusts, and Use of Powers of Attorney: Each requires special attention and instructions. Seek broker or legal counsel, as appropriate.

Buyer:

In General: Buyer's name(s) should be shown in the same manner as the buyer wishes title to be taken at closing. In this regard:

1. Each buyer shown on the contract must execute the contract.
2. If the buyer later desires to take title in some other manner and this is permitted by the contract, an appropriate assignment or amendment to the contract should be obtained at closing.
3. Buyers often seek advice as to the manner in which they should take title to property—for example, tenancy by the entireties, tenants in common, and so on. If the buyer asks how title should be taken, advise him to see his attorney. Under no circumstances express an opinion.

Non–U.S. Corporations, U.S. Corporations, Partnerships, Etc.: Seek broker or legal counsel, as appropriate.

Addresses and Telephone Numbers: Include complete information concerning these items to make handling the transaction easier for all involved.

Legal Description

Description of Real Property
Material Term: The legal description of the property to be sold is an essential provision of the contract. A defective legal description can render the contract unenforceable.

Sufficiency Test: The classic test of the sufficiency of a legal description is whether a surveyor can locate the property by reference to the description used.

Reliable Information: Do not rely on tax roll descriptions. The tax rolls are filled with errors and abbreviated descriptions that could be regarded as legally insufficient. Also, do not rely on descriptions contained in MLS listing sheets because they may only repeat errors others have made. Instead, rely on copies of prior deeds, prior title insurance policies, or prior surveys.

Description Not Known at Time of Contract: If any question remains as to the property's exact location, size, or description, and if the question cannot be resolved before the execution of the contract, agreement must be reached as to the survey of the property and as to who will bear the expense of the survey. Furthermore, agreement must reflect that the legal description will be amended to conform to the contract. The buyer also should have the right to terminate the contract if the property location and size are not substantially as represented.

Easements, Other Interests: The legal description should include any interest in the property being conveyed—for example, private right-of-way or common elements. This information usually is found on the deed or title insurance policy.

Quantity: From the seller's point of view, references to exact acreage in the legal description should be avoided. This could give rise to a right on the part of the buyer either to cancel the contract or to reduce the purchase price should the actual acreage prove to be materially different.

Minimum Description Requirements—Platted Subdivision:
- County in which property is located
- Lot and block numbers
- Name of subdivision (include phase or unit, if applicable)
- Plat book and page number of recorded plat

Minimum Description Requirements—Condominium:
- County in which property is located
- Condominium unit or parcel number
- Name of condominium complex
- Identification of common elements—for example, parking spaces and storage spaces, if applicable
- Recording information (official record book and page number) of original declaration of condominium and any amendments
- Reference to ground lease or recreational lease and recording information, if applicable

Minimum Description Requirements—Unplatted Property:
- County in which property is located
- Legal description provided by survey or prior deed(s)
- Reference to section, township, and range

Street Address: If the street address, city, and ZIP code are available, insert them. This may render an otherwise insufficient legal description legally sufficient.

Personal Property

Inventory: Prepare an accurate description and inventory of all personal property to be included in the sale. The preprinted portion of the contract includes range, refrigerator, dishwasher, ceiling fans, light fixtures, and window treatments, unless specifically excluded in the following paragraph. Personal property being purchased by the buyer (even though it represents a minor portion of the purchase price) may be regarded as a material term of the contract; thus, inaccurate, incomplete, or insufficient descriptions of the personal property to be transferred can render the entire contract voidable or unenforceable. Most lenders are more comfortable with wording such as "the attached inventory of personal property is being left as a convenience to the seller." This reduces appraisal problems and potential sales tax liability.

What To Include: In the normal residential transaction, a detailed inventory of all personal property (with defects disclosed, if applicable) should be prepared and attached to the contract. The list should include all kitchen equipment and appliances, whether built in or not, plus other equipment and appliances, such as outside television antennas and satellite dishes, pool equipment, lawn furniture, and other easily removable "fixtures." Quantify items where applicable. Failure to provide an accurate and complete inventory of all property included in the sale can lead to closing day problems, and the broker may have to make up any difference to close the transaction.

Florida Sales Tax on Personal Property: The Florida Department of Revenue has made several rulings on the tax liability of personal property included in the sale of real property. If itemized in the sales contract, with a separately stated value for each item, sales tax must be paid. No sales tax is due if the contract simply lists the property, such as a "refrigerator, range, microwave, and washer/dryer combination."

1 **Purchase Price and Method of Payment**
2   *Fixed Purchase Price:* The format of the preprinted contract calls for a fixed purchase
3 price to be expressed in monetary terms.

4   *Variable Price:* If the full purchase price cannot be expressed in monetary terms, the
5 manner in which it might be determined accurately should be stated in the contract in
6 an addendum. For example, if acreage is involved, and the parties agree on a price per
7 acre, that price per acre should be set forth in an addendum (under "Special Clauses,"
8 check "Addendum is attached") together with a provision for an accurate survey deter-
9 mination. Whenever an addendum is used, it should have the date of the original con-
10 tract, the complete names of the parties, and a complete legal description. It also must
11 be dated and signed by the parties.

12   *Method of Payment:* The subparagraphs set forth the manner in which the purchase
13 price is to be paid. The sum total of the monetary amounts set forth in these subpara-
14 graphs should equal the purchase price.

DISCUSSION EXERCISE 8.2

You are writing a contract for the purchase of a tract of land that is to be subdivided. The parties mark on the actual property lines where the division is to be
made, but can only estimate the size of the property at about 24 acres. Both parties
agree on a price of $12,500 per acre.

Write a special clause that will set forth the parties' agreement and be legally
binding.

---

15   *Deposit To Be Held in Trust By:* Complete paragraph II(a) by identifying the escrow
16 agent and inserting the amount of the deposit made by the buyer at the time the contract
17 is executed by the buyer. Paragraph II(b) should be used when the payment of the deposit
18 is split between the initial deposit and an additional deposit. Typically, the second deposit
19 is much larger than the initial deposit. The better practice is to avoid installment payments
20 of deposits. The amount of the additional deposit and the number of days within which it
21 must be made should be inserted. The contract allows the seller to recover not only the
22 initial deposit but also any unpaid deposit. If the buyer defaults by failing to make the addi-
23 tional deposit, the seller is faced with having to initiate litigation to recover the balance.
24 While the seller has an alternate remedy of specific performance, the seller's best remedy
25 in the event of buyer default is a forfeiture of the deposit.

26   *Existing Mortgages–Assumption:* Describe any existing mortgage that the buyer is
27 assuming. The contract goes into further detail as to the terms of the existing mortgage,
28 requirements for assumption, and so on. Both paragraphs must be completed if a mort-
29 gage is being assumed. In connection with any transaction involving the assumption of
30 an existing mortgage, the following should be considered:
31   1. *Obtain Copies of Mortgage(s) in Advance:* Have a copy of any existing mortgage avail-
32   able for review by the buyer or the buyer's attorney.
33   2. *Obtain Accurate Information:* Before the full execution of the Contract, make certain
34   that the stated balance of the mortgage to be assumed is accurate. In this connec-
35   tion, do not rely on "guesstimates" by the seller (which may have found their way
36   onto the MLS listing sheet). Contact the lender. If the lender will not furnish such
37   information, have the seller contact the lender. The lender must furnish state-
38   ments to the borrower. While the contract form might allow minor variations
39   between the actual balance of the existing mortgage and the amount stated, any
40   material differences could create a right of cancellation on the part of the buyer.

New Mortgage Financing with a Lender: Insert the amount of any new institutional loan.

Purchase-Money Mortgage: State that portion of the purchase price that will be deferred and secured by a purchase-money mortgage. Also:

1. The mortgage or note amount is to be inserted. The interest rate and terms should be put on a separate addendum.
2. Identify in this section only financing furnished by the seller.
3. Refer to Standard B, which defines in some additional detail the terms and provisions that the purchase-money mortgage will contain. Any terms and provisions agreed on by the parties that are not covered in these two sections or that are in conflict must be covered in a provision inserted in an addendum.
4. Where the parties have agreed to a purchase-money mortgage that contains an unusual provision—for example, a wraparound mortgage, partial release clause, or subordination clause—attach the mortgage form to the contract as an exhibit. Otherwise, the parties may be negotiating the mortgage terms on the day of closing. Where the purchase-money mortgage is beyond the scope of the description of paragraph II(c) and Standard B, seek the assistance of an attorney for the purpose of drafting the mortgage clauses or the mortgage form. Ambiguous descriptions of what the parties intend should be avoided; for example, avoid statements like "Seller shall take back a purchase-money wraparound mortgage."
5. A **cross-defaulting clause** should be included in the special clauses so that a default on the first mortgage automatically triggers a default on the second mortgage. This requires that the title closing agent place such a clause in the purchase-money mortgage.

Other: Describe in paragraph II(e) any form of payment of the purchase price other than those specified earlier. For example, if two mortgages are being assumed, reference to the assumption of an additional mortgage could be made in this section. This section is not intended to describe any third-party financing.

Cash: State the balance of the cash to be paid after adjustment of the purchase price or assumed mortgages, purchase-money mortgages, cash deposits, and any other setoffs against the purchase price.

Balance To Close: Note that prorations and adjustments are offset against cash due at closing. This refers to property taxes and other prorations and expenses chargeable to the buyer. The contract requires either cash or a locally drawn certified or cashier's check, not a personal check, in order to speed up disbursement of funds at closing.

Time for Acceptance of Offer, Effective Date, Facsimile

Fact of Execution Communicated: The contract requires that the **fact of execution** be communicated in writing or electronically to the other party before a specific date. It is, therefore, not enough that the seller actually accepts and signs the contract (lower portion of form). The contract must be delivered to the buyer, or the fact of execution must be communicated in writing to the buyer. With facsimile (fax) machines so prevalent, a buyer can sign the contract offer, then fax it to the seller. The seller then executes the faxed copy or a photocopy of the faxed copy and sends the fully executed contract back to the buyer via fax. All occurs within a few minutes. The faxed copy of the contract, when delivered, constitutes written communication of the fact of execution, and the faxed copy with all of its signatures is, for practical purposes, treated as an original.

Time: The date to be inserted should be taken into account:

1. *Requirements of the Buyer:* That is, how long will the buyer permit the seller to consider the offer?
2. *Transmitting the Contract:* The licensee should provide enough time to transmit the contract and obtain its acceptance and execution.

Counteroffers: This clause is not intended as a restriction on the time for acceptance of a **counteroffer** or, for that matter, subsequent counteroffers. If the seller is counter-

---

DISCUSSION EXERCISE 8.3

On Saturday, June 12, at noon, you are writing a contract for the sale of property at 1618 Buck Lake Road. The buyer is in town just for the weekend to find a property. The seller was home when you showed the property this morning. You have gotten to the "Time for Acceptance" portion of the agreement.

What date will you enter on this line? Why? Does it matter which party you represent?

---

1 offering and wishes to restrict the time the buyer has to accept the counteroffer, a spe-
2 cial clause (addendum) should be attached—for example, the FAR counteroffer
3 standard form). A counteroffer terminates the original offer.

4 *Effective Date:* It is important that the dates of execution by the seller and buyer be
5 completed so that the date of the contract (when the last party signs *and* communicates
6 it to the other in writing) can be determined for purposes of measuring other time
7 periods referred to in the contract.

8 **Financing**
9 *Financing:* There are four options that can be selected in this section:

10 1. A cash transaction with no financing contingency
11 2. Third-party financing
12 3. Assumption of an existing mortgage
13 4. Seller financing

14 **New Mortgages**
15 *Know the Mortgage Market:* All active licensees should have current information on
16 the local mortgage market, including data on available interest rates (fixed and adjust-
17 able), points, time for processing applications, and so on.

18 *Contingency Should Be Broad:* Whether the buyer or the seller is the principal, make
19 certain that the financing contingency clause describes a mortgage that is obtainable by
20 the Buyer.

21 *Time To Get Commitment:* The number of days the buyer has to obtain a loan com-
22 mitment is sometimes based on how much time the seller will give the buyer to find
23 financing. In any event, the broker or sales associate should know approximately how
24 long local institutions take to process loan applications. Then a reasonable period of
25 time should be inserted.

26 *Type of Mortgage:* A mortgage loan can be obtained on the basis of either a fixed rate
27 or an adjustable rate, and the appropriate box should be checked. If the buyer has not
28 decided, the third block should be checked, indicating that the buyer will seek a com-
29 mitment for either a fixed-rate or an adjustable-rate loan. If the buyer seeks a different
30 type of mortgage, address this in an addendum.

31 *Term of Mortgage:* Fill in the percentage rate and term of the mortgage that the buyer
32 must accept, having consulted with the buyer to determine the interest rate acceptable
33 and having made sure that the desired rate is obtainable.

34 *Principal Amount:* The principal amount of the third-party mortgage that the buyer
35 seeks is inserted. Licensees should have a working knowledge of what is available in the
36 local financial market.

37 *Prompt Application:* The number of days the buyer will have to make an application
38 is inserted. Except under unusual circumstances, it should be possible for the buyer to

make an application for the mortgage almost immediately. The broker or sales associate should ensure that the buyer proceeds diligently to make a loan application. Keep in mind that paragraph XIII of the contract makes time of the essence, and failure to make a timely application may constitute a default. In this case, the seller has a right to all remedies permitted in the contract, including cancellation.

Monitor the Buyer: It is in the licensee's interest to monitor the steps the buyer is taking to obtain a loan commitment pursuant to the contract terms. If the buyer fails to use reasonable diligence under this provision, the seller may declare a default and require the buyer to forfeit the deposit. If additional time is needed to obtain a loan commitment and the parties agree, amend the contract to extend the time.

DISCUSSION EXERCISE 8.4

You have sold your listing at 137 West Waters Avenue to Henry Woodward. You are acting as a transaction broker. Henry is having a serious problem getting the financing necessary to complete the sale; credit problems have shown up that were not disclosed earlier. You are aware that the seller is packing and preparing to vacate the property in ten days to prepare for the closing date. Henry tells you not to disclose the problem to the seller.

Discuss your response in a role-playing situation with Henry.

Relation to Closing Date: Standard P provides that if the lender imposes requirements relating to place, time of day, and procedures for closing and disbursing mortgage proceeds, those requirements control and supersede other contrary contract provisions. This does not mean that the title closing date may be extended by the lender's requirements. If delays occur as a result of loan application processing or loan closing, it may be necessary to amend the contract to extend the title closing date.

Assumption of Existing Mortgage

Terms of the Existing Mortgage: To complete this section, the licensee must have accurate information concerning the terms and provisions of the existing mortgage. Specifically, answers to the following are needed:

1. Is the interest rate adjustable or fixed? What is the present interest rate?
2. If it is a fixed interest rate, can the lender increase the interest rate as a condition to permitting assumption? If so, what increased interest rate is the buyer willing to pay?
3. What are the requirements for assumption, and what are the fees?

Policy of Institution: The answers to the question of whether a mortgage is assumable, and on what terms, depends on the mortgage provisions. If no provision relates to the sale of the property or the assumption of the existing mortgage, the mortgage is assumable, even without notifying the existing mortgagee. Mortgage forms generally contain a due-on-sale clause that gives the mortgagee control over an assumption.

Actions Required of Parties: This clause requires that the seller obtain a statement from the mortgagee concerning the principal balance, etc. The buyer must complete the application and documents necessary for assumption.

Assumption Fees: The contract provides a blank space for the amount of an assumption fee. Who pays this fee is negotiable, with the amount not to be exceeded inserted. If the parties have agreed, for example, that the buyer will pay the entire assumption fee, the agreed-on amount must be inserted. If the space is left blank, the parties share the expense equally, as indicated in the contract.

Excessive Demands of Lender: If the lender's conditions relating to assumption impose an unacceptable burden on the buyer (for example, an increase in an interest rate exceeding that stated or an assumption fee exceeding the amount stated), the seller or buyer may cancel the contract unless either party elects to pay the increase in the interest rate or the excess assumption charge (or other charges). For the seller to pay "any increase in the interest rate," computation of an amount that could be paid presently to the lender (or buyer) to cause an adjustment in the interest rate (a **paydown**) is required. This emphasizes the importance of inserting accurate information concerning the terms of the existing mortgage to be assumed. An error concerning an interest rate increase or an assumption charge could result in a canceled transaction.

Title Evidence

Seller's Obligation: Either the seller or the buyer may pay the cost of either a **title insurance** policy or an up-to-date **abstract** of title. Refer to and become familiar with Standard A on the back of the contract. The title insurance premium must be charged for the title insurance commitment or binder, whether or not a policy is issued. There is no charge for a policy issued pursuant to an issued commitment.

Time To Deliver: The time limit for delivery of title evidence may depend on several factors, such as the satisfaction of contingencies. Generally speaking, however, it is desirable to provide for delivery of title evidence as quickly as possible so that if any title problems are discovered, there will be as much time as possible to deal with them. Where the time period between the date of the contract and the closing date is prolonged, it is desirable to provide in the contract a provision that the title insurance binder will be updated by endorsement to reflect any intervening title matters that might have arisen.

Abstracts or Title Insurance: The contract offers a choice between delivery of abstracts of title or title insurance commitment. Abstracts are now rarely used in property transactions in Florida, since lenders require title insurance.

Time Limits: The buyer has 30 days (if an abstract) or five days (if a commitment) from time of receipt of same to examine it and find any defects. The buyer must notify the seller in writing of any defects within three days after the above applicable time period. Keep in mind that time is of the essence, and time for delivery of title evidence and examination could be critical. Avoid using a phrase such as "to be delivered at closing." The contract requires that the seller deliver the abstract or commitment so many days before the closing. The purpose is to make certain that the buyer has enough time to check for defects in the title. At least eight days should be entered if the transaction requires a title commitment, and 33 days should be noted if abstracts will be delivered.

Restrictions

Restrictions, Easements, Limitations: If any title matters exist other than those dealt with in the form, they should be listed in the first space in this paragraph. It is important to have reliable information concerning title to the property.

Comprehensive Land-Use Plans, Zoning, and Subdivision Restrictions: Many lenders require title insurance coverage ensuring that comprehensive land-use plans, zoning, and subdivision restrictions have not been violated. The buyer should be encouraged to obtain professional assistance with respect to land uses. Thus, the buyer also should be advised to obtain a survey to show whether zoning or subdivision codes have been violated.

Defects Shown by Survey: Standard C of the contract provides that if the survey shows an encroachment or a violation, the fact of such encroachment or violation will be regarded as a title defect, and the curing provisions of Standard A will apply. If, for example, zoning setback violations are found, these curing provisions would give the seller an opportunity to seek an appropriate variance from zoning authorities.

Title Exceptions: In completing this provision, it is important that some form of prior title evidence be available so that a determination can be made as to whether any matters other than those listed in the contract need to be itemized as exceptions to title.

Furthermore, if the property is in a subdivision, refer to a copy of the recorded plat to make certain that public utility easements are within the limitations referred to in this provision. If not, they must be referred to specifically as an acceptable title exception in a special provision.

Existing or Intended Use: Note that the clause further provides that none of the foregoing "prevents use of Real Property for purposes of [insert the existing use or the intended use]"; in either event, that use should be consistent with applicable subdivision restrictions and zoning laws. Even when all easements and other matters are set forth specifically in the contract, if any of them would prevent the intended use of the property, the buyer may properly object. For example, side lot-line easements existing between two lots being purchased would prevent the construction of a residence (using both lots as one site). For the transaction to close, the seller must seek and obtain a release of such easements.

If an unusual title matter affects the property that is not on the contract (for example, a special restriction not common to the subdivision, a private easement, a license to use a well on the property or a private mineral reservation), it must be identified specifically. Otherwise, the buyer may reject title.

The contract makes no provision for nonconforming uses or structures—that is, those that were legal under applicable zoning laws when begun or built but due to changes in zoning laws became nonconforming. Normally, such uses and structures are permitted to continue, subject to various restrictions relating to repair, reconstruction, and expansion. Consequently, the buyer cannot object under this provision. The licensee should determine in advance the property's zoning and whether any nonconforming uses or structures exist. If so, they should be disclosed through a special provision incorporated into an addendum to the contract.

Closing Date

Time Is of the Essence, Standard I: The failure of either party to close on the closing date, assuming the closing date is not extended, causes a default.

Conditions: The closing date should be set for a reasonable period of time after any conditions have been satisfied and the title evidence delivered. Because the parties may want to close as soon as possible, the words *on or before* may be used. However, this provision does not obligate either party to close before the specific date unless both agree in writing. The words *on or about* are ambiguous and should not be used.

DISCUSSION EXERCISE 8.5

You are writing a FAR/BAR contract for the sale of a 160-acre farm and home. All parties have agreed that the buyer should have 40 days from the contract date to produce a written commitment for financing the purchase.

What would be an optimum time for the contract closing date?

Extensions: Note the phrase "unless extended by other provisions of Contract." As previously stated, the contract sets forth many deadlines for performance. Where any of these provisions would require or allow performance to take place after the closing date, the closing date will be deemed extended.

Occupancy

Occupancy by Seller beyond the Closing Date: Rental terms must be stated as special provisions in the contract. This requires the drafting of a separate residential lease agreement.

1   *Early Occupancy by Buyer:* Despite the provisions concerning risk of loss and accep-
2   tance of the property "as is," it is recommended that, if at all possible, this kind of
3   arrangement be avoided. If, however, the parties intend otherwise, a separate lease must
4   be prepared, setting forth the nature and terms of the early occupancy by the buyer—
5   that is, date of occupancy, rent to be paid, and so on. Avoid the use of an early occu-
6   pancy agreement because Florida law does not allow for evictions when early occupancy
7   is allowed in a sales contract.

DISCUSSION EXERCISE 8.6

You are presenting a contract to your principal, the builder of a new home at 346
NW 125th Street. The buyer has requested to have immediate occupancy before
closing. Your principal, the builder, asks your opinion. You believe that the buyer
probably will not purchase unless the occupancy is granted.

In a role-play situation, discuss the pros and cons of the provision with your
principal.

---

8   *Occupancy by Existing Tenant:* Insert a special clause reciting the fact that tenants
9   occupy the property under written/oral leases. The tenants' identity should be set forth
10   in a special clause, along with a brief description of the rental terms. Standard F of the
11   contract requires that the seller furnish **estoppel letters** and copies of all written leases
12   to the buyer not less than 15 days before closing.

13   *Insurance:* If the parties intend that the buyer take early occupancy or if the seller will
14   remain in possession following closing, special care should be taken to make certain that
15   proper fire, casualty, and liability insurance is obtained. When the property is used for
16   rental purposes, the existing insurance may no longer afford appropriate coverage.

17   *Disclosures:* The following disclosures are made a part of the contract:

18   • The existence of special assessments and who is required to pay them.
19   • Radon gas.
20   • Building Energy-Efficiency brochure.
21   • Lead-based paint rider disclosure.
22   • Agreement that if the seller is a foreign person as described in the Foreign Invest-
23   ment in Real Property Tax Act (FIRPTA), the parties will comply with that act.
24   • Agreement that if the buyer is required to become a member of a homeowners' asso-
25   ciation, the buyer has received and read the homeowners' association disclosure.

26   *Maximum Repair Costs:* This section limits the seller's payments for treatment and
27   repair of wood-destroying organisms and for items warranted by the seller.

28   **Other Contract Provisions**
29   *Typewritten or Handwritten Provisions:* This paragraph is meant to protect the con-
30   tract should a licensee fail to delete an inconsistent provision covered in "Special
31   Clauses" or to protect any riders or addenda that are designed to show the parties' true
32   intent. To know whether it is necessary to revoke, amend, or replace a printed provi-
33   sion, a licensee must know the content of the printed provisions.

34   *Assignability:* This provision acknowledges the fact that unless a provision to the con-
35   trary is included, sales contracts are freely assignable (able to transfer property rights,
36   title, and interests). Generally speaking, it is not in the seller's best interest to allow the
37   contract to be assigned. The paragraph provides three check boxes:

38   1. The buyer may assign and thereby be released from any further liability under the
39   contract. This box would be checked, for example, when the buyer acts as an agent

1   for another. The licensee should pay close attention to this paragraph, however.
2   Most sellers contract with a buyer because they believe the buyer is qualified to pur-
3   chase the property. If a seller takes the property off the market for an extended
4   period, and the buyer later assigns the contract to a nonqualified buyer, the seller
5   could be harmed financially.

6 2. The buyer may assign, but not be released from, liability under the contract. This
7   is a more standard provision that better protects the seller from, for instance, an
8   assignee who fails to qualify for a financing contingency.

9 3. The buyer may not assign the contract.

10   ***Riders:*** Several **riders** (additions to a document) are listed in this provision. Various
11 laws and regulations require that some riders be attached to the contract and that other
12 riders expand and clarify contract terms. All of the riders listed are available as pre-
13 printed forms.

14   (a) *Homeowners' Association Disclosure:* The contract clause shown in Chapter 2 must
15 be included in every contract for sale and purchase for property with a homeowners'
16 association that has the power to place a lien on the property for homeowners' dues, or
17 is subject to restrictive covenants governing the property's use and occupancy. If the
18 clause is not included in the contract, the buyer may cancel the contract anytime before
19 the closing date.

20   (b) *Condominium Rider:* Because the contract's printed clauses do not contain any spe-
21 cific provisions relating to the sale and purchase of condominium units, this rider
22 should be attached to the contract form. The rider contains provisions for such matters
23 as approval of the buyer by the condominium association, payment of assessments and
24 special assessments, and delivery of condominium documents. An approved condo-
25 minium rider form should be available in every brokerage firm.

26   (c) *"As Is" Rider:* This rider shows the buyer's agreement to take the property with no
27 warranties about its condition. The rider does not relieve the licensees or the seller of
28 the duty to disclose material defects in the property that affect value.

29   (d) *FHA/VA Rider:* Because transactions involving Federal Housing Administration
30 (FHA) or Department of Veterans Affairs (VA) financing include numerous unique ele-
31 ments, the contract's standard provisions conflict in many ways with the lender require-
32 ments in an FHA or a VA transaction. The rider contains clauses, both preprinted and
33 fill-in, that amend the contract with specific seller and buyer understandings and obliga-
34 tions. Consequently, attachment of the rider is a necessity when FHA or VA financing is
35 involved.

36   (e) *Residential Lead-Based Paint Hazard Disclosure:* This disclosure is required for all
37 homes built before 1978.

38   (f) *Insulation Rider:* Because the Federal Trade Commission (FTC) requires the attach-
39 ment of this rider to a contract where the sale involves new residential improved real
40 property, the required information of insulation having been or to be installed in walls,
41 ceilings, and other areas must be obtained from the owner/builder.

42   (g) *Coastal Construction Control Line (CCCL) Rider:* Because a great deal of Florida's
43 real property is located in coastal areas (24 of 67 counties), a seller must provide a buyer,
44 at or before closing, an affidavit or a survey delineating the CCCL location. The buyer
45 may waive this requirement, and the waiver must be in writing.

46   (h) *Other:* Because no sales contract has been devised that covers all situations at all
47 times, a or rider can be attached to the contract to reflect the special situation involved.

48   ***Special Clauses:*** If more than one addendum to the contract are attached, indicate the
49 number of such attachments in the space to the right of Item XV. Be certain, in addi-
50 tion, that every attachment (addendum, rider, etc.) includes the date of the original con-
51 tract, the complete names of the parties, and a complete legal description. It also must
52 be dated and signed by the parties. Because Florida case law has suggested that the

---

DISCUSSION EXERCISE 8.7

You represent Jim Wells in a transaction in which he intends to purchase property and assume a nonqualifying FHA loan. In this case, the seller will remain responsible for the debt. You become aware, while writing the contract, that Jim intends to sell his contract and assign it to another person. While Jim could qualify easily, if necessary, the second person could not.

Do a role-playing discussion with Wells about the situation.

Do a role-playing discussion with the seller when asked about the seller's exposure to a default judgment.

---

1   "time is of the essence" clause in the printed form of the contract may not necessarily
2   apply to provisions contained in an addendum, consider inserting the following clause
3   in the addendum: "The Time Is of the Essence Clause set forth in paragraph XII of the
4   printed form portion of this Contract shall apply with respect to provisions contained
5   in this addendum."

6   Where the agreement of the parties is contrary to any of the provisions or standards
7   in a preprinted sales contract, it is best to line through the standard and insert one or
8   more special clauses.

9   ***Remainder of Contract Paragraphs, Blank Spaces, and Standards:*** Examine closely all
10 of the above elements and the responses required as well as the signature portion of the
11 contract. The current FAR/BAR contract is reproduced in its entirety on the following
12 pages as Figure 8.1.

13 ## Preparing the FAR/BAR Contract for Sale and Purchase
14 While the following guidelines follow the layout of the FAR/BAR Contract for Sale and
15 Purchase, most of the comments are applicable to other sales contracts as well. This
16 exercise is designed to help licensees understand all sections of the FAR/BAR contract.
17 Based on the following information, please fill in the blanks on the form:

	Section	**Specific information**
18		
19	I. Sale and Purchase	
20	Seller:	Wendall and Susan Topoleski, a married couple
21	Buyer:	Roberto and Esther Gonzalez, a married couple
22	County:	Lafayette
23	Legal Description:	Lot 27, Block D, Bluebird Subdivision, Unit 2
24	Address:	1125 North Bird Avenue, Sinclair, FL 33398
25	Personal Property:	Refrigerator
26	Fixtures Excluded:	
27	**II. Purchase Price**	
28	Purchase Price:	$178,000
29	Deposit Held by:	Sinclair Real Estate Company
30	Deposit Amount:	$5,000
31	New Mortgage:	$142,400
32	Balance to Close:	$ (Student to calculate)
33	**III. Time for Acceptance**	
34	Time for Acceptance:	Two days from today

1 **IV. Financing:**
2   The contract is contingent upon the buyer obtaining a new conventional loan.
3   Approval Within: 45 days
4   Type Loan: Fixed rate
5   Amount Financed: $142,400
6   Interest Rate: 7%
7   Points Maximum: 2%
8   Loan Term: 30 years

9 **VI. Restrictions**
10   Property Use: Residential

11 **VII. Closing Date**
12   Closing Date   45 days from today

13 **X. Assignability**
14   Contract may be assigned, but the buyer may not be released from liability.

15   The licensee must be certain that all pages have been initialed by buyers and sellers
16 and that buyers and sellers have dated and signed the agreement.

OPTION CONTRACTS

18 An **option contract** is a contract between a property owner (optionor) and another
19 (optionee) in which the optionee, for a consideration, has the right (not the obligation)
20 to purchase or lease the property at a specified price during a designated period. To be
21 enforceable in Florida, an option must contain all of the essential elements of a contract.

22   Strictly speaking, it is important to distinguish between an *option contract* and an
23 *option* (in actual practice, the terms are often used interchangeably). If you offer to sell
24 your house to a friend for $100,000 and your friend says she wants to think about the
25 offer for a day or so, your friend might have an option, but she does not have an option
26 contract. Therefore, you could revoke your offer to sell and no breach of contract would
27 occur because no contract exists when there is a lack of consideration (exchange of
28 promises). Had your friend paid you $1,000 in consideration of a 30-day or 60-day
29 period to decide about your offer and you agreed to those terms, an option contract
30 would have been concluded. The consideration given legally may be applied as part of
31 the purchase price in the event the option is **exercised.**

32   Chapter 475.43, F.S., states in part: "All contracts, options, or other devices not based
33 upon a substantial consideration, or that are otherwise employed to permit an unli-
34 censed person to sell, lease or let real estate, the beneficial title to which has not, in good
35 faith, passed to such party for a substantial consideration, are hereby declared void and
36 ineffective in all cases, suits, or proceedings. . . ." An assistant attorney general's inter-
37 pretation of this portion of 475.43 states: "Obviously, the state legislature recognized a
38 way by which an unlicensed person could use an option contract to act as a broker and
39 thereby get around the license law."

40   An option creates a contractual right; it does not create an estate in the optioned
41 property. When first written and executed, an option contract is unilateral. The owner/
42 optionor is obligated to sell if given proper notice by the buyer/optionee, but the
43 buyer/optionee is not obligated to purchase and may allow the option to expire.
44 Options frequently are used to give a developer or buyer time to resolve problems

1 related to financing, zoning, title, or feasibility before committing to purchase or lease.
2 Options also are useful instruments in the land assemblage process.

3   In addition to the required information in an option contract, other provisions
4 should or may be included. For example, a statement of the method of notice required
5 to exercise the option normally is provided. Also, some provision should be included
6 concerning the option money (the consideration) if the option is not exercised. Unless
7 expressly prohibited by the wording of the terms, an option normally is assignable.

8   Option contracts often are written with less care and attention than they deserve.
9 Keep in mind that an option contract is converted into a sales contract when the option
10 is exercised. However, if the option fails to include all the terms material to the transac-
11 tion and leaves some terms or decisions for future agreement, the option contract nor-
12 mally is not enforceable. For example, if the option calls for a purchase-money
13 mortgage as part of the method of payment and does not include the mortgage interest
14 rate or the duration, courts normally would refuse to enforce the contract. Generally, it
15 pays to have a competent real estate attorney construct an option agreement.

DISCUSSION EXERCISE 8.8

Oscar paid Silvio $2,000 for a 30-day option to buy Silvio's house for $160,000.
Two weeks later, Silvio sold his house to Benny for $175,000.

   Can Oscar enforce his option and require the property to be sold to him? Why
or why not?

---

16   The optionee may wish to record the option. This establishes the optionee's rights
17 back to the option date and gives priority over subsequent rights of third parties. Good
18 title practice requires that a release of option be recorded later in the event a recorded
19 option is not exercised. Otherwise, the expired option may create a cloud on the title.
20 Many times, an option is constructed to include a defeasance clause stating that the
21 recorded option will automatically cease to be a lien on the property upon expiration
22 of the exercise date.

23   An example of the general form of an exercise of option is shown in Figure 8.2.

SUMMARY

A contract is a legally enforceable agreement that can be classified in a number of ways,
such as bilateral, unilateral, express, implied, executory, executed, quasi, voidable, and
void. Each classification has specific legal effects in a court of law. The licensee is permitted to "prepare" three types of real estate contracts: listing, sales, and option contracts. A sales contract is an agreement for the sale and purchase of real property. The
various provisions and standards contained in a sales contract include information on
the parties to the agreement, a legal description of the property, the purchase price and
method of payment, deadline times and dates, information about financing, and riders
to the contract. An option contract is an agreement to keep open, for a set period, an
offer to sell or lease real property; it is converted into a sales contract if the option is
exercised.

FIGURE 8.1 CONTRACT FOR SALE AND PURCHASE

THIS FORM HAS BEEN APPROVED BY THE FLORIDA ASSOCIATION OF REALTORS® AND THE FLORIDA BAR

Contract For Sale And Purchase
FLORIDA ASSOCIATION OF REALTORS® AND THE FLORIDA BAR

1* **PARTIES:** _____ ("Seller"),
2* and _____ ("Buyer"),
3 hereby agree that Seller shall sell and Buyer shall buy the following described Real Property and Personal Property (collectively "Property")
4 pursuant to the terms and conditions of this Contract for Sale and Purchase and any riders and addenda ("Contract"):

5 **I. DESCRIPTION:**
6*   (a) Legal description of the Real Property located in _____ County, Florida: _____
7* _____
8* _____
9*   (b) Street address, city, zip, of the Property: _____
10   (c) Personal Property includes existing range, refrigerator, dishwasher, ceiling fans, light fixtures, and window treatments unless
11 specifically excluded below.
12* Other items included are: _____
13* _____
14* Items of Personal Property (and leased items, if any) excluded are: _____
15* _____

16* **II. PURCHASE PRICE** (U.S. currency): . . . . $ _____
17   **PAYMENT:**
18*   (a) Deposit held in escrow by _____ (Escrow Agent) in the amount of . . $ _____
19*   (b) Additional escrow deposit to be made to Escrow Agent within ____ days after Effective Date
20*   (see Paragraph III) in the amount of . . . . $ _____
21   (c) Assumption of existing mortgage in good standing (see Paragraph IV(c)) having an approximate
22* present principal balance of . . . . $ _____
23*   (d) New mortgage financing with a Lender (see Paragraph IV(b)) in the amount of . . . . $ _____
24*   (e) Purchase money mortgage and note to Seller (See Paragraph IV(d)) in the amount of . . . . $ _____
25*   (f) Other: _____ . . . . . . $ _____
26   (g) Balance to close by cash or LOCALLY DRAWN cashier's or official bank check(s), subject
27* to adjustments or prorations . . . . $ _____

28 **III. TIME FOR ACCEPTANCE OF OFFER AND COUNTEROFFERS; EFFECTIVE DATE:**
29   (a) If this offer is not executed by and delivered to all parties OR FACT OF EXECUTION communicated in writing between the parties on or
30* before _____, the deposit(s) will, at Buyer's option, be returned and this offer withdrawn. **UNLESS OTH-**
31 **ERWISE STATED, THE TIME FOR ACCEPTANCE OF ANY COUNTEROFFERS SHALL BE 2 DAYS FROM THE DATE THE COUN-**
32 **TEROFFER IS DELIVERED.**
33   (b) The date of Contract ("Effective Date") will be the date when the last one of the Buyer and Seller has signed or initialed this offer or the
34 final counteroffer. If such date is not otherwise set forth in this Contract, then the "Effective Date" shall be the date determined above for
35 acceptance of this offer or, if applicable, the final counteroffer.

36 **IV. FINANCING:**
37*   ❏ (a) This is a cash transaction with no contingencies for financing;
38*   ❏ (b) This Contract is contingent on Buyer obtaining approval of a loan ("Loan Approval") within ____ days after Effective Date for (CHECK
39* ONLY ONE): ❏ a fixed; ❏ an adjustable; or ❏ a fixed or adjustable rate loan, in the principal amount of $ _____, at an initial inter-
40* est rate not to exceed _____%, discount and origination fees not to exceed _____% of principal amount, and for a term of _____
41* years. Buyer will make application within _____ days (if blank, then 5 days) after Effective Date and use reasonable diligence to obtain Loan
42 Approval and, thereafter, to satisfy terms and conditions of the Loan Approval and close the loan. Buyer shall pay all loan expenses. If Buyer
43 fails to obtain a Loan Approval or fails to waive Buyer's rights under this subparagraph within the time for obtaining Loan Approval or, after
44 diligent, good faith effort, fails to meet the terms and conditions of the Loan Approval by Closing, then either party thereafter, by written notice
45 to the other, may cancel this Contract and Buyer shall be refunded the deposit(s);
46*   ❏ (c) Assumption of existing mortgage (see rider for terms); or
47*   ❏ (d) Seller financing (see Standard B and riders; addenda; or special clauses for terms).

48* **V. TITLE EVIDENCE:** At least ____ days (if blank, then 5 days) before Closing:
49*   ❏ (a) Title insurance commitment with legible copies of instruments listed as exceptions attached thereto ("Title Commitment") and, after
50* Closing, an owner's policy of title insurance (see Standard A for terms); or ❏ (b) Abstract of title or other evidence of title (see rider for terms),
51* shall be obtained by (CHECK ONLY ONE): ❏ (1) Seller, at Seller's expense and delivered to Buyer or Buyer's attorney; or
52*   ❏ (2) Buyer at Buyer's expense.

53* **VI. CLOSING DATE:** This transaction shall be closed and the closing documents delivered on _____ ("Closing"), unless
54 modified by other provisions of this Contract. If Buyer is unable to obtain Hazard, Wind, Flood, or Homeowners' insurance at a reasonable rate
55 due to extreme weather conditions, Buyer may delay Closing for up to 5 days after such coverage becomes available.

56 **VII. RESTRICTIONS; EASEMENTS; LIMITATIONS:** Seller shall convey marketable title subject to: comprehensive land use plans, zoning,
57 restrictions, prohibitions and other requirements imposed by governmental authority; restrictions and matters appearing on the plat or otherwise
58 common to the subdivision; outstanding oil, gas and mineral rights of record without right of entry; unplatted public utility easements of record
59 (located contiguous to real property lines and not more than 10 feet in width as to the rear or front lines and 7 1/2 feet in width as to the side

FAR/BAR-6S 10/01   Page 1 of 4

FIGURE 8.1   CONTRACT FOR SALE AND PURCHASE (Continued)

60 lines); taxes for year of Closing and subsequent years; and assumed mortgages and purchase money mortgages, if any (if additional items, see
61 addendum); provided, that there exists at Closing no violation of the foregoing and none prevent use of the Property for
62* _____ purpose(s).
63 **VIII. OCCUPANCY:** Seller shall deliver occupancy of Property to Buyer at time of Closing unless otherwise stated herein. If Property is intended
64 to be rented or occupied beyond Closing, the fact and terms thereof and the tenant(s) or occupants shall be disclosed pursuant to Standard F.
65 If occupancy is to be delivered before Closing, Buyer assumes all risks of loss to Property from date of occupancy, shall be responsible and liable
66 for maintenance from that date, and shall be deemed to have accepted Property in its existing condition as of time of taking occupancy.
67 **IX. TYPEWRITTEN OR HANDWRITTEN PROVISIONS:** Typewritten or handwritten provisions, riders and addenda shall control all printed pro-
68 visions of this Contract in conflict with them.
69* **X. ASSIGNABILITY:** (CHECK ONLY ONE): Buyer ❏ may assign and thereby be released from any further liability under this Contract; ❏ may
70* assign but not be released from liability under this Contract; or ❏ may not assign this Contract.
71 **XI. DISCLOSURES:**
72*   (a) ❏ CHECK HERE if the Property is subject to a special assessment lien imposed by a public body payable in installments which
73*   continue beyond Closing and, if so, specify who shall pay amounts due after Closing: ❏ Seller ❏ Buyer ❏ Other (see addendum).
74   (b) Radon is a naturally occurring radioactive gas that when accumulated in a building in sufficient quantities may present health risks to per-
75   sons who are exposed to it over time. Levels of radon that exceed federal and state guidelines have been found in buildings in Florida.
76   Additional information regarding radon or radon testing may be obtained from your County Public Health unit.
77   (c) Buyer acknowledges receipt of the Florida Building Energy-Efficiency Rating System Brochure.
78   (d) If the real property includes pre-1978 residential housing then a lead-based paint rider is mandatory.
79   (e) If Seller is a "foreign person" as defined by the Foreign Investment in Real Property Tax Act, the parties shall comply with that Act.
80   (f) If Buyer will be obligated to be a member of a homeowners' association, **BUYER SHOULD NOT EXECUTE THIS CONTRACT UNTIL**
81   **BUYER HAS RECEIVED AND READ THE HOMEOWNERS' ASSOCIATION DISCLOSURE.**
82 **XII. MAXIMUM REPAIR COSTS:** Seller shall not be responsible for payments in excess of:
83*   (a) $_____ for treatment and repair under Standard D (if blank, then 2% of the Purchase Price).
84*   (b) $_____ for repair and replacement under Standard N not caused by Wood Destroying Organisms (if blank, then 3% of
85   the Purchase Price).
86 **XIII. RIDERS; ADDENDA; SPECIAL CLAUSES:**
87   CHECK those riders which are applicable AND are attached to this Contract:
88* ❏ CONDOMINIUM   ❏ VA/FHA   ❏ HOMEOWNERS' ASSN.   ❏ LEAD-BASED PAINT
89* ❏ COASTAL CONSTRUCTION CONTROL LINE   ❏ INSULATION   ❏ "AS IS"   ❏ Other Comprehensive Rider Provisions
90* ❏ Addenda
91* Special Clauses(s): _____
92* _____
93* _____
94* _____
95* _____

96 **XIV. STANDARDS FOR REAL ESTATE TRANSACTIONS ("Standards"):** Buyer and Seller acknowledge receipt of a copy of Standards A
97 through W on the reverse side or attached, which are incorporated as part of this Contract.
98   **THIS IS INTENDED TO BE A LEGALLY BINDING CONTRACT. IF NOT FULLY UNDERSTOOD, SEEK THE ADVICE OF**
99   **AN ATTORNEY PRIOR TO SIGNING.**
100   THIS FORM HAS BEEN APPROVED BY THE FLORIDA ASSOCIATION OF REALTORS® AND THE FLORIDA BAR.
101   Approval does not constitute an opinion that any of the terms and conditions in this Contract should be accepted by the parties in a
102   particular transaction. Terms and conditions should be negotiated based upon the respective interests, objectives and bargaining
103   positions of all interested persons.
104   AN ASTERISK(*) FOLLOWING A LINE NUMBER IN THE THE MARGIN INDICATES THE LINE CONTAINS A BLANK TO BE COMPLETED.

105* _____   _____   _____   _____
106 (BUYER)   (DATE)   (SELLER)   (DATE)

107* _____   _____   _____   _____
108 (BUYER)   (DATE)   (SELLER)   (DATE)

109* Buyers' address for purposes of notice _____   Sellers' address for purposes of notice_____
110* _____   _____
111* _____ Phone   _____ Phone

112* Deposit under Paragraph II (a) received (Checks are subject to clearance.):_____(Escrow Agent)
113 **BROKERS:** The brokers named below, including listing and cooperating brokers, are the only brokers entitled to compensation in connection
114 with this Contract:

115* Name:_____
116   **Cooperating Brokers, if any**   **Listing Broker**

FIGURE 8.1 CONTRACT FOR SALE AND PURCHASE (Continued)

117   **STANDARDS FOR REAL ESTATE TRANSACTIONS**

118 **A. TITLE INSURANCE:** The Title Commitment shall be issued by a Florida licensed title insurer agreeing to issue Buyer, upon recording of the deed to Buyer,
119 an owner's policy of title insurance in the amount of the purchase price, insuring Buyer's marketable title to the Real Property, subject only to matters contained
120 in Paragraph VII and those to be discharged by Seller at or before Closing. Marketable title shall be determined according to applicable Title Standards adopt-
121 ed by authority of The Florida Bar and in accordance with law. Buyer shall have 5 days from date of receiving the Title Commitment to examine it, and if title is
122 found defective, notify Seller in writing specifying defect(s) which render title unmarketable. Seller shall have 30 days from receipt of notice to remove the
123 defects, failing which Buyer shall, within 5 days after expiration of the 30 day period, deliver written notice to Seller either: (1) extending the time for a reason-
124 able period not to exceed 120 days within which Seller shall use diligent effort to remove the defects; or (2) requesting a refund of deposit(s) paid which shall
125 be returned to Buyer. If Buyer fails to so notify Seller, Buyer shall be deemed to have accepted the title as it then is. Seller shall, if title is found unmarketable,
126 use diligent effort to correct defect(s) within the time provided. If Seller is unable to timely correct the defects, Buyer shall either waive the defects, or receive a
127 refund of deposit(s), thereby releasing Buyer and Seller from all further obligations under this Contract. If Seller is to provide the Title Commitment and it is deliv-
128 ered to Buyer less than 5 days prior to Closing, Buyer may extend Closing so that Buyer shall have up to 5 days from date of receipt to examine same in accor-
129 dance with this Standard.
130 **B. PURCHASE MONEY MORTGAGE; SECURITY AGREEMENT TO SELLER:** A purchase money mortgage and mortgage note to Seller shall provide for a
131 30 day grace period in the event of default if a first mortgage and a 15 day grace period if a second or lesser mortgage; shall provide for right of prepayment
132 in whole or in part without penalty; shall permit acceleration in event of transfer of the Real Property; shall require all prior liens and encumbrances to be kept
133 in good standing; shall forbid modifications of, or future advances under, prior mortgage(s); shall require Buyer to maintain policies of insurance containing a
134 standard mortgagee clause covering all improvements located on the Real Property against fire and all perils included within the term "extended coverage
135 endorsements" and such other risks and perils as Seller may reasonably require, in an amount equal to their highest insurable value; and the mortgage, note
136 and security agreement shall be otherwise in form and content required by Seller, but Seller may only require clauses and coverage customarily found in mort-
137 gages, mortgage notes and security agreements generally utilized by savings and loan institutions or state or national banks located in the county wherein the
138 Real Property is located. All Personal Property and leases being conveyed or assigned will, at Seller's option, be subject to the lien of a security agreement evi-
139 denced by recorded or filed financing statements or certificates of title. If a balloon mortgage, the final payment will exceed the periodic payments thereon.
140 **C. SURVEY:** Buyer, at Buyer's expense, within time allowed to deliver evidence of title and to examine same, may have the Real Property surveyed and certified
141 by a registered Florida surveyor. If the survey discloses encroachments on the Real Property or that improvements located thereon encroach on setback lines, ease-
142 ments, lands of others or violate any restrictions, Contract covenants or applicable governmental regulations, the same shall constitute a title defect.
143 **D. WOOD DESTROYING ORGANISMS:** Buyer, at Buyer's expense, may have the Property inspected by a Florida Certified Pest Control Operator ("Operator")
144 at least 10 days prior to Closing to determine if there is any visible active Wood Destroying Organism infestation or visible damage from Wood Destroying
145 Organism infestation, excluding fences. If either or both are found, Buyer may, within 5 days from date of written notice thereof, have cost of treatment of active
146 infestation estimated by the Operator and all damage inspected and estimated by an appropriately licensed contractor. Seller shall pay costs of treatment and
147 repair of all damage up to the amount provided in Paragraph XII(a). If estimated costs exceed that amount, Buyer shall have the option of canceling this Contract
148 within 5 days after receipt of contractor's repair estimate by giving written notice to Seller, or Buyer may elect to proceed with the transaction and receive a
149 credit at Closing on the amount provided in Paragraph XII(a). "Wood Destroying Organisms" shall be deemed to include all wood destroying organisms required
150 to be reported under the Florida Pest Control Act, as amended.
151 **E. INGRESS AND EGRESS:** Seller warrants and represents that there is ingress and egress to the Real Property sufficient for its intended use as described
152 in Paragraph VII hereof, and title to the Real Property is insurable in accordance with Standard A without exception for lack of legal right of access.
153 **F. LEASES:** Seller shall, at least 10 days before Closing, furnish to Buyer copies of all written leases and estoppel letters from each tenant specifying the nature
154 and duration of the tenant's occupancy, rental rates, advanced rent and security deposits paid by tenant. If Seller is unable to obtain such letter from each ten-
155 ant, the same information shall be furnished by Seller to Buyer within that time period in the form of a Seller's affidavit, and Buyer may thereafter contact ten-
156 ant to confirm such information. If the terms of the leases differ materially from Seller's representations, Buyer may terminate this Contract by delivering written
157 notice to Seller at least 5 days prior to Closing. Seller shall, at Closing, deliver and assign all original leases to Buyer.
158 **G. LIENS:** Seller shall furnish to Buyer at time of Closing an affidavit attesting to the absence, unless otherwise provided for herein, of any financing statement,
159 claims of lien or potential lienors known to Seller and further attesting that there have been no improvements or repairs to the Real Property for 90 days imme-
160 diately preceding date of Closing. If the Real Property has been improved or repaired within that time, Seller shall deliver releases or waivers of construction
161 liens executed by all general contractors, subcontractors, suppliers and materialmen in addition to Seller's lien affidavit setting forth the names of all such gen-
162 eral contractors, subcontractors, suppliers and materialmen, further affirming that all charges for improvements or repairs which could serve as a basis for a
163 construction lien or a claim for damages have been paid or will be paid at the Closing of this Contract.
164 **H. PLACE OF CLOSING:** Closing shall be held in the county wherein the Real Property is located at the office of the attorney or other closing agent ("Closing
165 Agent") designated by the party paying for title insurance, or, if no title insurance, designated by Seller.
166 **I. TIME:** In computing time periods of less than six (6) days, Saturdays, Sundays and state or national legal holidays shall be excluded. Any time periods provided
167 for herein which shall end on a Saturday, Sunday, or a legal holiday shall extend to 5 p.m. of the next business day. **Time is of the essence in this Contract.**
168 **J. CLOSING DOCUMENTS:** Seller shall furnish the deed, bill of sale, certificate of title, construction lien affidavit, owner's possession affidavit, assignments of leases,
169 tenant and mortgagee estoppel letters and corrective instruments. Buyer shall furnish mortgage, mortgage note, security agreement and financing statements.
170 **K. EXPENSES:** Documentary stamps on the deed and recording of corrective instruments shall be paid by Seller. Documentary stamps and intangible tax on
171 the purchase money mortgage and any mortgage assumed, mortgagee title insurance commitment with related fees, and recording of purchase money mort-
172 gage to Seller, deed and financing statements shall be paid by Buyer. Unless otherwise provided by law or rider to this Contract, charges for the following relat-
173 ed title services, namely title evidence, title examination, and closing fee (including preparation of closing statement), shall be paid by the party responsible for
174 furnishing the title evidence in accordance with Paragraph V.
175 **L. PRORATIONS; CREDITS:** Taxes, assessments, rent, interest, insurance and other expenses of the Property shall be prorated through the day before
176 Closing. Buyer shall have the option of taking over existing policies of insurance, if assumable, in which event premiums shall be prorated. Cash at Closing shall
177 be increased or decreased as may be required by prorations to be made through day prior to Closing, or occupancy, if occupancy occurs before Closing.
178 Advance rent and security deposits will be credited to Buyer. Escrow deposits held by mortgagee will be credited to Seller. Taxes shall be prorated based on
179 the current year's tax with due allowance made for maximum allowable discount, homestead and other exemptions. If Closing occurs at a date when the cur-
180 rent year's millage is not fixed and current year's assessment is available, taxes will be prorated based upon such assessment and prior year's millage. If cur-
181 rent year's assessment is not available, then taxes will be prorated on prior year's tax. If there are completed improvements on the Real Property by January
182 1st of year of Closing, which improvements were not in existence on January 1st of prior year, then taxes shall be prorated based upon prior year's millage and
183 at an equitable assessment to be agreed upon between the parties; failing which, request shall be made to the County Property Appraiser for an informal
184 assessment taking into account available exemptions. A tax proration based on an estimate shall, at request of either party, be readjusted upon receipt of tax
185 bill on condition that a statement to that effect is signed at Closing.
186 **M. SPECIAL ASSESSMENT LIENS:** Except as set forth in Paragraph XI(a), certified, confirmed and ratified special assessment liens imposed by public bod-
187 ies as of Closing are to be paid by Seller. Pending liens as of Closing shall be assumed by Buyer. If the improvement has been substantially completed as of

FIGURE 8.1   CONTRACT FOR SALE AND PURCHASE (Continued)

STANDARDS FOR REAL ESTATE TRANSACTIONS (CONTINUED)

188
189 Effective Date, any pending lien shall be considered certified, confirmed or ratified and Seller shall, at Closing, be charged an amount equal to the last estimate
190 or assessment for the improvement by the public body.
191 **N. INSPECTION, REPAIR AND MAINTENANCE:** Seller warrants that the ceiling, roof (including the fascia and soffits) and exterior and interior walls, founda-
192 tion, seawalls (or equivalent) and dockage of the Property do not have any visible evidence of leaks, water damage or structural damage and that the septic
193 tank, pool, all appliances, mechanical items, heating, cooling, electrical, plumbing systems and machinery are in Working Condition. The foregoing warranty
194 shall be limited to the items specified unless otherwise provided in an addendum. Buyer may inspect, or, at Buyer's expense, have a firm or individual special-
195 izing in home inspections and holding an occupational license for such purpose (if required) or an appropriately licensed Florida contractor make inspections
196 of, those items within 20 days after the Effective Date. Buyer shall, prior to Buyer's occupancy but not more than 20 days after Effective Date, report in writing
197 to Seller such items that do not meet the above standards as to defects. Unless Buyer timely reports such defects, Buyer shall be deemed to have waived
198 Seller's warranties as to defects not reported. If repairs or replacements are required to comply with this Standard, Seller shall cause them to be made and
199 shall pay up to the amount provided in Paragraph XII (b). Seller is not required to make repairs or replacements of a Cosmetic Condition unless caused by a
200 defect Seller is responsible to repair or replace. If the cost for such repair or replacement exceeds the amount provided in Paragraph XII (b), Buyer or Seller
201 may elect to pay such excess, failing which either party may cancel this Contract. If Seller is unable to correct the defects prior to Closing, the cost thereof shall
202 be paid into escrow at Closing. Seller shall, upon reasonable notice, provide utilities service and access to the Property for inspections, including a walk-through
203 prior to Closing, to confirm that all items of Personal Property are on the Real Property and, subject to the foregoing, that all required repairs and replacements
204 have been made and that the Property, including, but not limited to, lawn, shrubbery and pool, if any, has been maintained in the condition existing as of
205 Effective Date, ordinary wear and tear excepted. For purposes of this Contract: (1) "Working Condition" means operating in the manner in which the item was
206 designed to operate; (2) "Cosmetic Condition" means aesthetic imperfections that do not affect the Working Condition of the item, including, but not limited to:
207 pitted marcite or other pool finishes; missing or torn screens; fogged windows; tears, worn spots, or discoloration of floor coverings, wallpaper, or window
208 treatments; nail holes, scratches, dents, scrapes, chips or caulking in ceilings, walls, flooring, fixtures, or mirrors; and minor cracks in floors, tiles, windows,
209 driveways, sidewalks, or pool decks; and (3) cracked roof tiles, curling or worn shingles, or limited roof life shall not be considered defects Seller must repair
210 or replace, so long as there is no evidence of actual leaks or leakage or structural damage, but missing tiles will be Seller's responsibility to replace or repair.
211 **O. RISK OF LOSS:** If the Property is damaged by fire or other casualty before Closing and cost of restoration does not exceed 3% of the assessed valuation
212 of the Property so damaged, cost of restoration shall be an obligation of Seller and Closing shall proceed pursuant to the terms of this Contract with restora-
213 tion costs escrowed at Closing. If the cost of restoration exceeds 3% of the assessed valuation of the Property so damaged, Buyer shall either take the Property
214 as is, together with either the 3% or any insurance proceeds payable by virtue of such loss or damage, or receive a refund of deposit(s), thereby releasing Buyer
215 and Seller from all further obligations under this Contract.
216 **P. CLOSING PROCEDURE:** The deed shall be recorded upon clearance of funds. If the title agent insures adverse matters pursuant to Section 627.7841, F.S.,
217 as amended, the escrow and closing procedure required by this Standard shall be waived. Unless waived as set forth above the following closing procedures
218 shall apply: (1) all closing proceeds shall be held in escrow by the Closing Agent for a period of not more than 5 days after Closing; (2) if Seller's title is rendered
219 unmarketable, through no fault of Buyer, Buyer shall, within the 5 day period, notify Seller in writing of the defect and Seller shall have 30 days from date of receipt
220 of such notification to cure the defect; (3) if Seller fails to timely cure the defect, all deposits and closing funds shall, upon written demand by Buyer and within 5
221 days after demand, be returned to Buyer and, simultaneously with such repayment, Buyer shall return the Personal Property, vacate the Real Property and recon-
222 vey the Property to Seller by special warranty deed and bill of sale; and (4) if Buyer fails to make timely demand for refund, Buyer shall take title as is, waiving all
223 rights against Seller as to any intervening defect except as may be available to Buyer by virtue of warranties contained in the deed or bill of sale.
224 **Q. ESCROW:** Any Closing Agent or escrow agent ("Agent") receiving funds or equivalent is authorized and agrees by acceptance of them to deposit them
225 promptly, hold same in escrow and, subject to clearance, disburse them in accordance with terms and conditions of this Contract. Failure of funds to clear
226 shall not excuse Buyer's performance. If in doubt as to Agent's duties or liabilities under the provisions of this Contract, Agent may, at Agent's option, contin-
227 ue to hold the subject matter of the escrow until the parties hereto agree to its disbursement or until a judgment of a court of competent jurisdiction shall deter-
228 mine the rights of the parties, or Agent may deposit same with the clerk of the circuit court having jurisdiction of the dispute. An attorney who represents a
229 party and also acts as Agent may represent such party in such action. Upon notifying all parties concerned of such action, all liability on the part of Agent shall
230 fully terminate, except to the extent of accounting for any items previously delivered out of escrow. If a licensed real estate broker, Agent will comply with pro-
231 visions of Chapter 475, F.S., as amended. Any suit between Buyer and Seller wherein Agent is made a party because of acting as Agent hereunder, or in any
232 suit wherein Agent interpleads the subject matter of the escrow, Agent shall recover reasonable attorney's fees and costs incurred with these amounts to be
233 paid from and out of the escrowed funds or equivalent and charged and awarded as court costs in favor of the prevailing party. The Agent shall not be liable
234 to any party or person for misdelivery to Buyer or Seller of items subject to the escrow, unless such misdelivery is due to willful breach of the provisions of this
235 Contract or gross negligence of Agent.
236 **R. ATTORNEY'S FEES; COSTS:** In any litigation, including breach, enforcement or interpretation, arising out of this Contract, the prevailing party in such liti-
237 gation, which, for purposes of this Standard, shall include Seller, Buyer and any brokers acting in agency or nonagency relationships authorized by Chapter
238 475, F.S., as amended, shall be entitled to recover from the non-prevailing party reasonable attorney's fees, costs and expenses.
239 **S. FAILURE OF PERFORMANCE:** If Buyer fails to perform this Contract within the time specified, including payment of all deposits, the deposit(s) paid by
240 Buyer and deposit(s) agreed to be paid, may be recovered and retained by and for the account of Seller as agreed upon liquidated damages, consideration for
241 the execution of this Contract and in full settlement of any claims; whereupon, Buyer and Seller shall be relieved of all obligations under this Contract; or Seller,
242 at Seller's option, may proceed in equity to enforce Seller's rights under this Contract. If for any reason other than failure of Seller to make Seller's title mar-
243 ketable after diligent effort, Seller fails, neglects or refuses to perform this Contract, Buyer may seek specific performance or elect to receive the return of Buyer's
244 deposit(s) without thereby waiving any action for damages resulting from Seller's breach.
245 **T. CONTRACT NOT RECORDABLE; PERSONS BOUND; NOTICE; FACSIMILE:** Neither this Contract nor any notice of it shall be recorded in any public
246 records. This Contract shall bind and inure to the benefit of the parties and their successors in interest. Whenever the context permits, singular shall include
247 plural and one gender shall include all. Notice and delivery given by or to the attorney or broker representing any party shall be as effective as if given by or to
248 that party. All notices must be in writing and may be made by mail, personal delivery or electronic media. A legible facsimile copy of this Contract and any sig-
249 natures hereon shall be considered for all purposes as an original.
250 **U. CONVEYANCE:** Seller shall convey marketable title to the Real Property by statutory warranty, trustee's, personal representative's or guardian's deed, as
251 appropriate to the status of Seller, subject only to matters contained in Paragraph VII and those otherwise accepted by Buyer. Personal Property shall, at the
252 request of Buyer, be transferred by an absolute bill of sale with warranty of title, subject only to such matters as may be otherwise provided for herein.
253 **V. OTHER AGREEMENTS:** No prior or present agreements or representations shall be binding upon Buyer or Seller unless included in this Contract. No mod-
254 ification to or change in this Contract shall be valid or binding upon the parties unless in writing and executed by the parties intended to be bound by it.
255 **W. WARRANTY:** Seller warrants that there are no facts known to Seller materially affecting the value of the Property which are not readily observable by Buyer
256 or which have not been disclosed to Buyer.

FIGURE 8.2 EXERCISE OF OPTION

To: _____ _____, _____

This is to inform you that pursuant to the option agreement executed by us on the _____ day of _____ , _____, I hereby signify my intention to proceed with the purchase of the property therein described.

I am ready, willing and able to perform all of the terms and conditions of the agreement, and at such time and place designated by you, I will deposit the sum of _____ dollars ($ _____), in the form of a certified check, as payment in full of the purchase price. At that time, I am to receive a properly executed _____ deed of said property, along with all other necessary instruments and closing statements to consummate this transaction.

_____

(optionee)

DEFINE THESE KEY TERMS

abstract
bilateral contract
concurrency
contract
counteroffer
cross-defaulting clause
estoppel letter
executed contract
executory contract
exercised
express contract
fact of execution
FAR/BAR Contract for Sale
    and Purchase
FIRPTA
implied contract

option contract
paydown
performance
quasi-contract
rider
sales contract (contract for sale and
    purchase)
statute of frauds
time is of the essence
title insurance
unconscionable contract
unilateral contract
valid contract
voidable contract
void contract

CHAPTER 8 PRACTICE EXAM

1. Your neighbor promises to paint your house while you are on vacation. Responding to a question about the color desired, you answer "white." At that point, your neighbor and you have:
   a. an implied contract.
   b. no contractual agreement.
   c. an employment contract.
   d. an option contract.

2. A valid contract that creates a one-sided bargain, heavily weighted in favor of one party and against the interests of the other party, is termed a(n):
   a. voidable contract.
   b. quasi-contract.
   c. unilateral contract.
   d. unconscionable contract.

3. The FAR/BAR Contract for Sale and Purchase is *least* suitable for transactions involving the sale of a:
   a. single-family home.
   b. condominium dwelling unit.
   c. vacant residential site.
   d. business.

4. Before an optionee exercises his rights, an option contract is a(n):
   a. unilateral contract.
   b. bilateral contract.
   c. executed contract.
   d. implied contract.

5. When time is of the essence, failure of any party to perform within established time limits can result in automatic:
   a. cancellation of the contract.
   b. liability for damages.
   c. default by the tardy party.
   d. forfeiture of all contractual rights and deposits.

6. When a licensee verifies contract information, one of the preferred sources regarding the owner/seller and the legal description is:
   a. the MLS databank.
   b. a previous title insurance policy.
   c. the listing agreement.
   d. the latest appraisal report.

7. Which statement is *not* correct regarding a violation of the statute of frauds?
   a. It may not constitute an illegal act, but it invalidates a sales contract.
   b. It carries with it prescribed time frames for enforcement.
   c. It questions the contract's validity.
   d. It normally has to do with whether a contract is in writing.

8. What is FALSE about a valid real estate sales contract?
   a. It is legally enforceable in a court of law.
   b. It has five essential elements.
   c. It requires witnessing.
   d. It deals with the transfer of an interest in real property.

9. An adult contracting with a minor is an example of noncompliance with which of the following essentials of a real estate contract?
   a. Legal purpose
   b. Offer and acceptance
   c. Contractual capacity
   d. In writing and signed

10. Which one of the following statements is NOT correct regarding an option contract?
    a. It is an agreement.
    b. It must be in writing.
    c. It is a bilateral contract.
    d. It must contain all the essential elements of a contract.

11. A prospective buyer signs a sale and purchase contract form offering to pay the seller $175,000. When the listing sales associate presents the offer to the seller, the seller counteroffers for the full list price of $190,000. The buyer refuses the counteroffer and begins looking for another property. Later the seller agreed to the original contract. Which is correct?
    a. No enforceable contract exists. The counteroffer terminated the original offer.
    b. The contract is enforceable.
    c. The seller owes the broker a commission.
    d. The buyer owes the broker a commission.

12. Warren Janus has attempted to get a real estate license, but because of a prior conviction has been unable to do so. Warren has started buying options on property for a token consideration, then advertising and selling the property for a profit. One of the owners gives Warren an option on property at a price of $100,000. Warren sells and assigns the option to another person for $30,000, but the owner refuses to honor the option. Based on this information, which is correct?
    a. The owner must honor the option and sell to the option holder.
    b. The owner may sell for $130,000 but must pay Warren a commission.
    c. The owner need not honor the option; substantial valuable consideration did not exist.
    d. Warren could be disciplined by the FREC.

13. What is the classic test of the sufficiency of a legal description?
    a. It is the one used on the property tax bill.
    b. It is the one recorded in the clerk's office.
    c. It includes the address as shown by the U.S. Postal Service.
    d. A surveyor can locate the property by reference to the description.

14. The minimum description requirement in a contract for a platted subdivision does NOT include the:
    a. lot and block number.
    b. number of acres in the parcel.
    c. plat book and page number of recorded plats.
    d. county in which the property is located.

15. The date of the FAR/BAR contract is the date the:
    a. buyer signs the contract and gives the earnest money deposit.
    b. seller signs the contract.
    c. transaction will close.
    d. last one of the buyer or seller signs the contract and communicates it to the other.

16. If the buyer asks to have occupancy of a house before closing, what will best protect the seller?
    a. The purchase agreement should cover the early occupancy so that if the sale falls through, the buyer easily can be required to vacate.
    b. The early occupancy should require that both parties enter into a lease.
    c. The early occupancy should be avoided, if possible.
    d. Both b and c

17. An option contract is:
    a. bilateral and binds the optionor.
    b. bilateral and binds the optionee.
    c. unilateral and binds the optionor.
    d. unilateral and binds the optionee.

18. Calvin Goin, a sales associate, writes up a six-month option agreement for Ricky Field on property located on Capital Circle. Ricky puts up $2,000 in option money. Because Ricky is not sure about the terms of owner financing, Calvin writes, "Owner financing, terms of which will be agreed upon at the time this option is exercised." Five months later, Ricky exercises the option and sits down with the seller to work out financing. The seller wants a higher interest rate and a shorter loan term than Ricky will accept. In this case, which is correct?
    a. Ricky can sue and the court will force the seller to a lower interest rate.
    b. If Ricky sues, the court probably will decide that the option contract is not enforceable because it is too vague.
    c. The seller can sue Ricky and force him to close at the higher interest rate.
    d. The parties must go to binding arbitration.

19. Jimmy Padron purchases an option on property located on Dale Mabry Highway. He requires that the option contract be acknowledged and recorded. The seller asks June Cullars, his agent, about the best way to proceed. How should June answer?
    a. Option contracts cannot be recorded under Florida law.
    b. A release of option should be recorded in the event that the option is not exercised.
    c. The option should include a defeasance clause stating that the recorded option will automatically cease to be a lien on the property upon expiration of the exercise date.
    d. Either b or c

20. An insulation rider is required when the property:
    a. has residential improvements.
    b. has new residential improvements.
    c. was constructed before 1978.
    d. may be in an area with high levels of radon gas.

ACTION LIST

APPLY WHAT YOU'VE LEARNED!

The authors suggest the following actions to reinforce the material in *Section IV—Selling Real Property:*

- Preview at least five homes in your favorite price range. Try to see five each day for the next five days. Use a tape recorder to describe each home thoroughly, and try to match it with a prospective buyer or type of buyer.
- From your preview visits, list the best homes on the market. Pick your favorite home from that list.
- Describe every characteristic of *your* favorite home from your preview trips as if you were writing a book on the house. Try to remember colors, room sizes and arrangements, and garage size. Describe each room in as much detail as possible. If you can't do it, go back to the house again and make careful notes. Try to increase your observation powers every time you preview homes.
- When you visit a vacant home, thoroughly describe each room aloud as if your buyer were sight-impaired.
- Keep a tape recorder near your phone. The next time you answer a call from a prospective buyer, turn on the recorder. (You must observe the law, however; record only *your* side of the conversation.) When you have completed the call, listen to the tape. Make written notes about what you would change about your side of the conversation.
- Ride through a neighborhood you have not yet explored, describing into your tape recorder the details you see. Then do the same thing in the surrounding area to find shopping areas, libraries, car washes, schools, and churches.
- Write the features you think some close friends would like in a home. From memory, list the properties you would show them, and give reasons for your decisions. Make a buyer's cost statement based on a 90 percent conventional loan.
- Call your friends and tell them about the previous exercise. Ask whether they will let you show them the homes you chose for them. How well did you judge their tastes?

SECTION V

FINANCING REAL PROPERTY

Licensees often are asked for advice about the most appropriate type of loan for a buyer. This requires an understanding of the advantages and disadvantages of each mortgage type and the situations that make certain mortgages more suitable.

Sales associates must understand the loan application and underwriting process completely to effectively assist a buyer when dealing with lenders. This section will give licensees a better idea of the steps required to take a loan from application to closing.

CHAPTER 9—EXPLORING MORTGAGE ALTERNATIVES

LEARNING OBJECTIVES

Upon completion of this chapter, *you should be able to:*

1. describe the components of the lender's required annual percentage rate (APR) disclosures;
2. calculate the effective interest rate on 30-year, fixed-rate loans and on loans for shorter periods;
3. calculate the PITI payment for a borrower;
4. compare the interest savings on a 15-year, fixed-rate mortgage versus a 30-year, fixed-rate mortgage;
5. compare the interest savings on a biweekly mortgage versus a 30-year, fixed-rate mortgage;
6. discuss the pros and cons of an adjustable-rate mortgage (ARM);
7. explain the five components of an ARM;
8. explain the advantages of FHA interest rate caps over conventional ARM caps; and
9. calculate the interest rate adjustments on an ARM based on index changes.

CHAPTER 9

EXPLORING MORTGAGE ALTERNATIVES

1   The mortgage market has seen many significant changes in recent years. Twenty years
2   ago, more than 80 percent of home mortgages were originated by commercial banks
3   and savings associations. That share has dropped sharply, and today mortgage compa-
4   nies are the dominant factor in the market, originating more than 50% of all home
5   loans. Driven by market forces, lenders offer a wide variety of mortgage products tai-
6   lored to the needs of consumers. Experts expect the changes to accelerate in the future.

7   A general knowledge of these changes can enhance the opportunities available to the
8   realestate professional. Developing strong relationships with lenders who preapprove loans
9   for prospective buyers saves licensees time and can significantly increase their income.

STEPS BEFORE LOAN APPLICATION

11 Before buyers begin calling or visiting lenders, they should have a good understanding
12 of their own financial capabilities and housing objectives. Licensees should explain both
13 issues to their customers to help them understand the importance of prequalifying. This
14 is important because if a loan application is denied, the applicant may lose the oppor-
15 tunity to buy the desired home. In addition, some expense is involved in applying for a
16 loan. Fees may range from $150 to $500, depending on the property and circumstances.

Mortgage Shopping

18 In shopping for a mortgage, licensees should advise buyers to look for competitive rates
19 and a lender with a reputation for integrity and good service.

20 Surveys show that mortgage interest rates and closing costs vary in metropolitan mar-
21 kets for the same mortgage product. Comparing prices obviously is important, but it is
22 not an easy task. Lenders charge a variety of fees a borrower may be asked to pay when
23 she submits a loan application. Discount points, usually one of the largest fees lenders
24 charge, also vary from lender to lender in the same market area. The points change the
25 effective interest rate, and just two points more on a loan can mean significant addi-
26 tional expense to the borrower.

27 Licensees must learn which lenders can be trusted to act with speed and service to
28 borrowers. Licensees should use and recommend only those that provide good service.

Seller-Paid Closing Costs

30 A buyer must have the necessary income and debt ratios to afford a mortgage payment.
31 Coming up with enough cash to close is another big hurdle. The closing costs and

1 prepayments on a typical mortgage loan for $120,000 can reach $5,000 in addition to
2 the down payment. Many qualified buyers are forced to rent in order to accumulate the
3 savings necessary to close. Licensees who know lender standards on seller-paid closing
4 costs are able to sell to these buyers much sooner. The seller can pay part of the closing
5 costs for conventional, FHA, and VA mortgage loans. Figure 9.1 shows the current
6 allowed percentages.

7   A seller who could pay only 3 percent of the buyer's closing costs on a low down pay-
8 ment conventional loan for $120,000 would contribute $3,600. If a two-income family
9 is saving $300 per month, the home purchase could be made 12 months sooner.

DISCUSSION EXERCISE 9.1

Do you think most licensees guide potential borrowers to lenders with which they
have built relationships or to lenders that have the best mortgage rates on a given
day?

---

10 Annual Percentage Rate (APR)

11 The Truth-in-Lending Act requires that mortgage lenders disclose their annual per-
12 centage rates to potential borrowers. The **annual percentage rate (APR)** is a standard
13 expression of credit costs designed to give potential borrowers an easy method of com-
14 paring lenders' total finance charges. These financing costs include points and any
15 other prepaid interest or fees charged to obtain the loan in addition to the contract
16 interest cost. The APR must be, by law, the relationship of the total financing charge to
17 the total amount financed, and it must be computed to the nearest one-eighth of 1 per-
18 cent. Perhaps the best and most accurate definition of the APR is that it is the effective
19 interest rate for a mortgage loan repaid over its full term.

20   The law allows a lender three days after loan application to inform the applicant of
21 the APR. When a lender gives the borrower a good-faith estimate of the annual per-
22 centage rate, the consumer should be aware that this is not a legally binding document;
23 it is simply an estimate. Licensees should avoid lenders who frequently estimate a lower
24 APR than the rate available at closing.

25   Another feature of this act is that it assumes that borrowers will keep their loans for the
26 full number of years for which the loans are written. Records of mortgage lending, how-
27 ever, show that most borrowers either sell or refinance their homes in less than 12 years.
28 The actual (effective) interest rate paid depends on the number of years a loan is kept.

**FIGURE 9.1   MAXIMUM SELLER-PAID CLOSING COSTS THAT CAN BE
APPLIED TO BUYER'S CLOSING COSTS, PREPAID ITEMS, AND
RESERVES, EXPRESSED AS A PERCENTAGE OF THE PURCHASE PRICE**

Type of Loan	Percent
Conventional	
Less than 10% down payment	3
19% or greater down payment	6
FHA	6
VA	6

FIGURE 9.2 $100,000 30-YEAR FIXED-RATE MORTGAGE COMPARISON OF RATES AND DISCOUNT POINTS

	A. Interest rate	B. Discount Points	C. Principal and Interest Payment	D. Payment Difference from 7% Rate	E. Amount Paid in Discount Points	F. Months at Lower Rate for Points Payback (E ÷ D)
1.	7.000	0	$665.30	–	$0	0
2.	6.875	0.5	$656.93	$8.37	$500	59.7
3.	6.750	1.2	$648.60	$16.70	$1,200	71.9
4.	6.625	1.7	$640.31	$24.99	$1,700	68.0
5.	6.500	2.3	$632.07	$33.23	$2,300	69.2

Example: If the borrower expects to keep the loan for longer than 12 years, the points should be divided by 8, and the result added to the note interest rate. For example, if a lender has offered a first mortgage for 30 years at 7.5 percent and 3 points, the effective interest rate would be 7.875%, computed as follows:

$$\text{Note rate} + (\text{points} \div 8) = \text{Effective interest rate}$$
$$(7.5\% + (.03 \div 8) = 7.5\% + 0.375\%) = 7.875\%$$

When the lender gives a prospective borrower a rate quote, the borrower is often undecided about whether to pay discount points. Discount points can be considered prepaid interest that will reduce the interest rate on the note. In effect, a borrower has a "menu" of interest rates based on the amount paid as discount points. Figure 9.2 shows a sample market quote for a 30-year fixed-rate loan. Fluctuations in the market cause differences from day to day in the differential of discount points and yield.

From the example, it's obvious that a person who intended to occupy the property for three years should avoid paying points because it would take almost six years to break even. In some cases, a borrower should ask the lender to raise the interest rate not only to avoid discount points but also to avoid paying an origination fee.

If a person expected to remain in the property for the full 30-year period and would not be refinancing or making an early loan payoff, the savings could be worth paying points. At line 5, for instance, the borrower breaks even at 69 months. The difference in payments of $33.23 for the remaining 291 months would total $9,670, well worth paying the points.

Of course, the better way to analyze points is by considering the time value of money. Using the 6.5 percent rate on line 5, the borrower pays $2,300 in *today's* dollars (that could be invested to return some interest) to get a savings sometime in the *future*. A financial calculator approach shows the payback period is longer (87 months vs. 69.2 months):

Financial Calculator Keystrokes To Find Payback Period for $2,300 in Points with a 6.5 percent Yield

%I	PMT	PV	FV	Solve for:	N
.54167	33.23	2,300	0		87 months
Where:	%	=	*monthly* market interest rate: 6.5% ÷ 12 months =.54167		
	PMT	=	savings per monthly payment = $33.23		
	PV	=	Dollars paid in points = $2,300		
	FV	=	input zero for this problem = 0		
Solve for:	N	=	Number of months to pay back points		
			Solution is 87 months		

DISCUSSION EXERCISE 9.2

John has been transferred to Miami and expects to be in the location for about three years before being transferred again. He needs to borrow $200,000 for his new home. With no points, he can get a 7.5 percent fixed rate mortgage with principal and interest payments of $1,398.43. The lender offers him a 7.125 percent mortgage (payments of $1,347.44) with two points.

Should John take the lower interest rate mortgage?

Using simple math, how many months will it take John to break even by paying the points if he takes the lower interest rate?

---

1 ## PITI Payment

2 Customers often call on licensees to help them calculate the monthly mortgage payment
3 for a possible purchase or sale. Most lenders require an amount each month that
4 includes principal and interest plus escrow items—property taxes, homeowner's insur-
5 ance, and possibly mortgage insurance or homeowners'/condominium association
6 dues. This entire package of payments commonly is referred to as the **PITI payment.**

7   Principal and interest payments on the mortgage are the largest part of the monthly
8 PITI payment. Using the mortgage payment factor table shown in Table 9.1, multiply
9 the loan amount by the appropriate factor to get the principal and interest portion of
10 the payment.

11   For example, the payment factor for a 30-year mortgage at 8.5 percent is .0076891.
12 To calculate the monthly principal and interest for a 30-year loan of $98,000 at 8.5 per-
13 cent, use the following equation:

14 $$\$98,000 \times .0076891 = \$753.53$$

15   While the factor table has been included in this text so that all students can calculate
16 the monthly payment, most real estate licensees use a financial calculator to obtain the
17 monthly mortgage payment of principal and interest.

18   In the example shown above, the licensee with a financial calculator would solve the
19 problem as shown below:

N	**%I**	**PV**	**FV**	Solve for:	**PMT**
360	.70833	98,000	0		**$753.33**

20
21
22 Where: N   =   number of monthly periods in loan term
23   %I   =   interest rate (8.5% ÷ 12 months = .70833)
24   PV   =   loan amount
25   FV   =   input zero when solving for present value
26
27 Solve for: **PMT** =   **monthly mortgage payment**

28   A PITI worksheet that licensees can use in helping their clients and customers calcu-
29 late at the PITI amount for a potential loan is shown in Figure 9.3.

---

30 ## FIXED-RATE MORTGAGES

31 Any mortgage written to preclude change in the interest rate throughout the entire
32 duration of the loan is a **fixed-rate mortgage.** The term includes the traditional 30-year
33 mortgage, the 15-year mortgage, and the biweekly mortgage. The use of a due-on-sale

TABLE 9.1 MORTGAGE PAYMENT FACTOR TABLE

Multiply the mortgage principal times the factor to solve for the mortgage payment.

Term of Loan

Interest Rate	10 years	15 years	20 years	25 years	30 years
5.00%	0.0106066	0.0079079	0.0065996	0.0058459	0.0053682
5.25%	0.0107292	0.0080388	0.0067384	0.0059925	0.0055220
5.50%	0.0108526	0.0081708	0.0068789	0.0061409	0.0056779
5.75%	0.0109769	0.0083041	0.0070208	0.0062911	0.0058357
6.00%	0.0111021	0.0084386	0.0071643	0.0064430	0.0059955
6.25%	0.0112280	0.0085742	0.0073093	0.0065967	0.0061572
6.50%	0.0113548	0.0087111	0.0074557	0.0067521	0.0063207
6.75%	0.0114824	0.0088491	0.0076036	0.0069091	0.0064860
7.00%	0.0116108	0.0089883	0.0077530	0.0070678	0.0066530
7.25%	0.0117401	0.0091286	0.0079038	0.0072281	0.0068218
7.50%	0.0118702	0.0092701	0.0080559	0.0073899	0.0069921
7.75%	0.0120011	0.0094128	0.0082095	0.0075533	0.0071641
8.00%	0.0121328	0.0095565	0.0083644	0.0077182	0.0073376
8.25%	0.0122653	0.0097014	0.0085207	0.0078845	0.0075127
8.50%	0.0123986	0.0098474	0.0086782	0.0080523	0.0076891
8.75%	0.0125327	0.0099945	0.0088371	0.0082214	0.0078670
9.00%	0.0126676	0.0101427	0.0089973	0.0083920	0.0080462
9.25%	0.0128033	0.0102919	0.0091587	0.0085638	0.0082268
9.50%	0.0129398	0.0104422	0.0093213	0.0087370	0.0084085
9.75%	0.0130770	0.0105936	0.0094852	0.0089114	0.0085915
10.00%	0.0132151	0.0107461	0.0096502	0.0090870	0.0087757
10.25%	0.0133539	0.0108995	0.0098164	0.0092638	0.0089610
10.50%	0.0134935	0.0110540	0.0099838	0.0094418	0.0091474
10.75%	0.0136339	0.0112095	0.0101523	0.0096209	0.0093348
11.00%	0.0137750	0.0113660	0.0103219	0.0098011	0.0095232
11.25%	0.0139169	0.0115234	0.0104926	0.0099824	0.0097126
11.50%	0.0140595	0.0116819	0.0106643	0.0101647	0.0099029
11.75%	0.0142029	0.0118413	0.0108371	0.0103480	0.0100941

FIGURE 9.3 PITI WORKSHEET

Mortgage amount   \$ _____

Interest rate   _____%

Term of loan   _____ years

Mortgage payment factor   _____

Principal and interest payment: \$ _____

(\$ _____ × _____)

(mtg. amt.)   (factor)   _____

Property taxes: \$ _____ ÷ 12   _____

Hazard insurance: \$_____÷ 12   _____

Mortgage insurance:

\$ _____ × _____ ÷ 12

(mtg. amt.)   (premium rate)

TOTAL MONTHLY MORTGAGE PAYMENT (PITI)   \$ _____

SOURCE: Adapted by permission from Thomas C. Steinmetz, *The Mortgage Kit,* 4th ed. (Chicago: Dearborn Financial Publishing, Inc.®, 1998), 163.

clause in a fixed-rate mortgage reserves the lender's right to make an interest rate change if a transfer of ownership takes place. Practically all conventional mortgages issued since the early 1980s contain such a clause.

Traditional 30-Year Mortgage

The fixed-rate, fully amortizing mortgage loan has been the standard of the real estate finance industry for the past 50 years. A 30-year term provides a reasonably low payment for the amount borrowed, while the interest rate, payment amount, and repayment schedule are set permanently at the beginning of the loan period. Fixed-rate loans often are sold in the secondary market because they appeal to pension funds and other investors searching for a relatively safe investment with a known interest rate and a long duration.

Advantages of a 30-Year Mortgage. Monthly payments on the loan are spread over 30 years, offering the borrower protection against future increases in interest rates and inflation rates while providing for the orderly repayment of the amount borrowed. Household budgets are easier to manage when the borrower does not have to plan for changing payment amounts or interest rates.

Disadvantages of a 30-Year Mortgage. If overall interest rates drop, as they did in 2000-01, the rate on a fixed-rate mortgage will not go down with them. To take advantage of lower interest rates, the original loan must be repaid with the proceeds of a new loan taken out at the lower rate. This procedure, called **refinancing,** usually requires that the borrower pay substantial closing costs on the new loan.

15-Year Mortgage. The 15-year fixed-rate mortgage has become popular with both lenders and borrowers in recent years. It is just like a traditional 30-year loan, except that its monthly payment is higher, its interest rate typically is slightly lower, and it is paid off in 15 years. The 15-year mortgage saves the borrower thousands of dollars in interest payments.

The popular press sometimes compares the two mortgage plans, showing dramatic savings from the 15-year plan. The gross savings, however, usually are overstated. The higher payments on the 15-year plan have an opportunity cost. If the difference were invested, the return on the investment would reduce the net cost of the 30-year mortgage. The tax savings from mortgage interest deductions also would reduce the savings.

For many borrowers, the 15-year mortgage may be the best way to finance a home because in addition to the overall savings in total cost, it forces a monthly saving in the form of extra equity and allows a person who needs it a sense of confidence that her home will be paid off in 15 years. This is true for those planning in advance for retirement. Also, many in the baby boomer generation are in their 40s, with a growing number eager to conclude their mortgage payments and own their homes free and clear.

Licensees should point out, however, that the 15-year mortgage robs the borrower of some flexibility. A 15-year mortgage cannot be extended to 30 years, but a 30-year mortgage can be paid off in 15 years if the borrower accelerates monthly payments to create a 15-year loan or remits a lump-sum payment on principal each year. The borrower retains the right to decide when, or if, he will make extra payments. Borrowers must evaluate the benefits of the 15-year mortgage based on their personal situations.

Advantages of a 15-Year Mortgage.   Because lenders get their money back sooner than they do with traditional 30-year mortgages, they charge slightly lower rates for 15-year loans. Also, the loans are paid off faster, less money is borrowed for less time, and less total interest is paid over the lives of the loans—more than 50 percent less. As with a 30-year, fixed-rate loan, the interest rate on a 15-year mortgage does not change, and the monthly principal and interest payment does not go up. Finally, the higher monthly payment results in forced savings in the form of faster equity buildup.

Disadvantages of a 15-Year Mortgage.   The monthly payment on a 15-year loan is higher, and the borrower forgoes investment opportunities voluntarily for the extra dollars paid on the loan each month. Some income tax advantages related to home mortgages and investment opportunities are lost. Flexibility of mortgage payment is sacrificed, and any future increase in income tax rates could increase the 15-year mortgage's net costs.

Biweekly Mortgage.   The development of computer programs to service biweekly mortgages properly, the creation of a secondary market (Fannie Mae), increased familiarity with the product, and growing consumer demand all are combining to bring about a comeback for the biweekly mortgage. The **biweekly mortgage** alternative is a fixed-rate loan, amortized over a 30-year period, with payments made every two weeks instead of every month. Borrowers pay half the normal monthly payment every two weeks, which means a total of 26 payments each year, or the equivalent of 13 monthly payments. The extra month's payment each year reduces the principal faster and results in considerable savings in interest, as well as a reduction in the duration of the loan to between 19 and 21 years.

Normally, interest rates for biweekly mortgages are comparable to the rates charged for traditional 30-year mortgages. Most biweekly loans are scheduled to mature in 30 years even though the actual number of years to maturity depends on the interest rate. The higher the interest rate, the larger the monthly payment and the more that is applied to reducing mortgage principal. A biweekly mortgage with a 7 percent interest rate, for example, would be paid off in approximately 23 years, 9 months.

Consumer Reports Magazine analyzed several mortgage options and concluded that a $100,000 biweekly mortgage at 8 percent interest would save a borrower approximately $34,000 in interest, when compared with a traditional 30-year, fixed-rate mortgage at the same interest rate.

Table 9.2 compares the results of making scheduled payments on a traditional 30-year mortgage, of adding different amounts of additional principal payments each month, and of making scheduled payments on a biweekly mortgage amortized over 30 years.

TABLE 9.2   COMPARISON OF INTEREST COSTS FOR VARIOUS MORTGAGE PLANS FOR A $100,000 LOAN AT 8% INTEREST

Payment Pattern	Regular Payment Amount	Total Paid Each Year	Time Until Paid Off	Total Interest Paid
30-year Mortgage	$733.76	$ 8,805	30 years	$164,155
Added $25/month	758.76	9,105	26 yrs. + 6 mos.	141,286
Added $100/month	833.76	10,005	20 yrs. + 2 mos.	101,770
Biweekly Mortgage	366.88	9,539	22 yrs. + 10 mos.	117,804
15-Year Mortgage	$955.65	$11,468	15 yrs.	$72,017

Advantages of a Biweekly Mortgage.   A biweekly mortgage combines the benefits of the 30-year loan and the 15-year loan without the increased payments of the 15-year loan. It offers borrowers the affordability of the 30-year loan because the two biweekly payments come within a few pennies of the one monthly payment on a 30-year loan. Also, Fannie Mae requires that payments be deducted automatically from a borrower's checking or savings account every two weeks. Because more than half of the nation's workforce is paid on a biweekly basis, it is compatible with a large number of paychecks. Some lenders include a conversion clause that permits a borrower to change a biweekly mortgage to a traditional 30-year, fixed-rate, amortized mortgage at little or no cost with only 30 days' advance notice.

Disadvantages of a Biweekly Mortgage.   The biweekly mortgage has the same disadvantages as other fixed-rate mortgages. In addition, the biweekly loan threatens those borrowers who do not maintain stable checking or savings account balances. The biweekly mortgage also locks borrowers into payment plans that they could set up themselves, at their own discretion, with a traditional 30-year loan. Some lenders also charge a set-up fee.

DISCUSSION EXERCISE 9.3

If the biweekly mortgage combines the good features of both the traditional 30-year, fixed-rate mortgage and the 15-year, fixed-rate mortgage, why is it so seldom used, comparatively speaking, to finance residential purchases?

ADJUSTABLE-RATE MORTGAGES (ARMS)

The **adjustable-rate mortgage (ARM)** has become a widely accepted alternative to the traditional 30-year, fixed-rate, level-payment mortgage. The popularity of ARMs noticeably increases when interest rates rise, and they lose favor when interest rates fall. An adjustable-rate mortgage is, as the term implies, a financing instrument that allows the lender to increase or decrease the interest rate based on the rise or fall of a specified index.

Components of Adjustable-Rate Mortgages

The primary elements in determining the acceptability of an ARM from the borrower's viewpoint are the index, the lender's margin, the calculated interest rate, the initial interest rate, and the interest rate caps.

1   Lending institutions are permitted legally to link the interest rate of a conventional
2 ARM with any recognized **index** (indicator of cost or value) that is not controlled by the
3 lender and is verifiable by the borrower. The **margin,** also called the *spread,* is a per-
4 centage added to the index. The margin usually remains constant over the life of the
5 loan, while the selected index may move up or down with fluctuations in the nation's
6 economy. The calculated (or actual) interest rate is arrived at by adding the selected
7 index to the lender's margin (index plus margin equals calculated interest rate). This cal-
8 culated interest rate may be discounted during the initial payment period, but it is the
9 rate to which all future adjustments and caps apply.

10   To be competitive, lenders sometimes reduce the first year's earnings by discounting
11 the calculated interest rate, thus creating a lower initial interest rate. This helps to
12 qualify potential buyers at artificially low interest rates, which may or may not be a ser-
13 vice to the borrowers, and establishes the amount of the monthly loan payment during
14 the first time period of the loan. Be aware that many lenders now use the second year's
15 interest rate rather than the discounted rate as the qualifier. Both Fannie Mae and
16 Freddie Mac require borrowers with less than a 20 percent down payment on one-year,
17 adjustable-rate loans to be qualified at the initial interest rate plus 2 percent.

18   The main appeal of ARM loans is the lower-than-market initial interest rates offered
19 as inducements (teasers). But without some type of protection from unacceptable
20 increases in interest rates, borrowers would be in danger of being unable to make future
21 mortgage payments. To prevent this, most lenders and all federal housing agencies have
22 established standards calling for ceilings on increases. Three types of **caps** (ceilings)
23 limit increases in the calculated interest rates of ARM loans:

24   1. Amount of increase that can be applied at the time of the first adjustment (for
25   example, cap of 1 percent or 2 percent per adjustment period)
26   2. Amount of increase that can be applied during any one adjustment interval (for
27   example, no more than 2 percent during any one-year period)
28   3. Total amount the interest rate may be increased over the life of the loan (for exam-
29   ple, no more than 6 percent)

30   Borrowers should be cautious when payments are capped and interest rates are not
31 because of the probability that **negative amortization** will be involved in the loan. Neg-
32 ative amortization occurs when the monthly payment is not enough to pay the interest
33 on the loan. The shortfall is added to the mortgage balance.

34   Lenders must each provide potential borrowers with a worst-case example at loan
35 application. This disclosure must show the maximum possible payment increases if con-
36 ditions should warrant maximum interest rate increases at the earliest opportunities.

Conventional ARM

37

38   To help you better understand adjustable-rate versus fixed-rate mortgages, Table 9.3
39 compares two approaches to a $100,000 conventional mortgage using a worst-case sce-
40 nario for interest rate increases.

41   In this example, all monthly payment amounts are for principal and interest, and the
42 amounts are rounded to the nearest dollar. The upfront costs of points and fees will be
43 discussed later.

44   ARM loans have lower initial rates than fixed-rate mortgages, primarily because
45 lenders don't want the risk of interest rate changes for the full 30 years of the loan
46 period. ARM loans reduce the risk, so lenders don't need as much cushion for contin-
47 gencies. New ARM products are available that combine the ARM features of lower ini-
48 tial interest rate with a longer fixed-rate period between adjustments. For example,
49 three-year, five-year or ten-year ARMs are available at slightly higher initial rates than
50 one-year ARMs, but at lower rates than 30-year fixed mortgages.

DISCUSSION EXERCISE 9.4

In your opinion, do the lower initial rates offered on ARM loans cause borrowers to take on more mortgage debt than they can afford? Why or why not?

Interest Rates and Recognized Indexes.   The index to which a conventional ARM is tied can increase or decrease the volatility of interest rate changes. For example, an ARM tied to the cost-of-funds index prepared by the Federal Home Loan Bank 11th District is based on average interest rates paid on both long-term and short-term savings deposits. This index goes up and down relatively slowly. On the other hand, the more commonly used "constant maturity of the One-Year Treasury Security" index is based on current rates of interest offered at the U.S. Treasury's regular auctions of government paper. This index is much more volatile than the cost-of-funds index. The T-bill index, however, gives borrowers the full benefit of downward index movement, while upward movement is limited by caps in most ARMs.

Market observers feel that a correlation often exists between the interest rates and the indexes lenders choose. When rates are low, lenders prefer the T-bill index so that when rates rise, the index (and the borrowers' interest rates) reflects the rise more quickly. When rates are high, it is more common to see lenders use the cost-of-funds index because the index comes down more slowly than the more volatile indexes.

Lenders must provide consumers with details on conventional ARMs to assist them in comparison shopping. Potential borrowers must be informed of the index used, how often the loan will be adjusted, and the maximum amount of loan payment increase allowed.

When helping prospective borrowers sort through the many factors to be considered in selecting a conventional adjustable-rate loan, licensees should make sure the borrowers know:

- what rate will be used when interest rate caps are applied to an ARM loan;
- that the margin is one of the most important benchmarks in comparing lenders (most other ARM features are relatively similar, but the margins can vary considerably):
- to seek another lender if the one they are considering has policies that call for ARM increases exceeding the 2 percent annual cap or the 6 percent annual cap;
- not to consider loans that call for negative amortization;

TABLE 9.3 $100,000 MORTGAGE LOAN, 30-YEAR TERM, 8% FIXED-RATE VERSUS 5.5% ADJUSTABLE-RATE MORTGAGE (ANNUAL CAP 2%, LIFETIME CAP 6%)

Fixed Rate			Adjusted Rate		ARM Savings(Loss)	
Year	Payment	Rate	Payment	Rate	Monthly	Accumulated
1	$734	8%	$568	5.5%	$166	$1,992
2	734	8	699	7.5	35	2,412
3	734	8	841	9.5	(107)	1,128
4*	734	8	990	11.5	(256)	(1,944)

*ARM savings exhausted in fifth month of year 4.

1   • to compare upfront costs, such as underwriting fees, points, and origination fees,
2   because some lenders offer lower interest rates but make up for it with inflated
3   upfront costs;
4   • not to stretch their borrowing to the limit, as they could with a fixed-rate loan,
5   because the payments remain fixed and income should increase. Borrowing to the
6   limit can become a disaster when an ARM is involved. Prospective borrowers should
7   calculate their first-year payments at the initial interest rate plus 2 percent; otherwise,
8   the first adjustment could hurt them financially.

9   **Advantages of the ARM Loan.**   The ARM's low initial interest rate and the bor-
10   rower's ability to qualify for a larger mortgage top the list of advantages of adjustable-
11   rate mortgages. ARMs appear to be most appropriate for those who plan to hold the
12   mortgage loans for no more than four years. Also, anytime the interest rate gap between
13   a fixed-rate loan and an adjustable-rate loan reaches 3 percent in favor of the ARM, an
14   ARM loan with interest rate caps and a one-year Treasury bill constant maturity index
15   should make sense to homebuyers. Many ARMs are now written with conversion privi-
16   leges, allowing the mortgagors to convert to fixed-rate loans for a modest fee during a
17   specified period. This enables borrowers to take advantage of falling interest rates if
18   they desire to do so. One of the standard features of ARMs is no prepayment penalty.

19   *Longer Adjustment Periods Are Available.*   Many borrowers prefer an ARM loan
20   that won't adjust for periods longer than a year. For example, the low initial rate may
21   last for three, five, or seven years. If a buyer doesn't expect to live in the house any
22   longer than that, she may get the benefit of lower monthly payments.

DISCUSSION EXERCISE 9.5

Cindy has been transferred to Tampa, and is expecting to be in that location for about three years before being transferred again. She can get a 7½ percent fixed-rate mortgage with no discount points or a 5 percent one-year adjustable-rate mortgage with no points. The ARM has a 2 percent annual and a 6 percent lifetime cap. She asks for your recommendation.

What should Cindy do based on her situation?

What calculations did you use to make your recommendation?

---

23   **Disadvantages of the ARM Loan.**   ARM borrowers bet against the lenders that
24   interest rates will not rise to the extent that the maximum interest rate caps will be
25   needed. The main disadvantages of the ARM loan are the uncertain amounts of future
26   mortgage payments and the difficulty in calculating adjustments in interest rates as they
27   occur. Lenders, of course, do the actual calculation of adjustments, but they have been
28   known to make mistakes, and such mistakes can be expensive to the borrowers. Calcu-
29   lation details are spelled out in each loan document, but they are somewhat complicated
30   and require the use of either a financial calculator or a handbook of ARM payment
31   tables. For a borrower who wants to audit a lender's ARM adjustments without going to
32   the trouble of research and math calculations, Loantech, Inc., a Gaithersburg, Mary-
33   land, mortgage consulting firm (1-800-888-6781), will do a complete individual ARM
34   adjustment review for a fee, based on the terms of the loan document submitted.

35   ## FHA Adjustable-Rate Mortgage
36   Section 251 of the National Housing Act authorizes the Federal Housing Administra-
37   tion (FHA) to insure adjustable-rate mortgages on single-family properties. The interest

1   rate is the sum of the index and the margin. The index changes, but the margin will
2   remain the same over the life of the loan. The initial interest rate may be a result of com-
3   bining the current one-year Treasury bill index with the margin at the time the loan is
4   closed. This combination of components produces what is often called the **calculated**
5   **interest rate** or **contract rate.** Each FHA-approved lender is allowed to discount the cal-
6   culated interest rate to a lower figure if local competition requires it, or the calculated
7   interest rate may become the initial interest rate. The initial interest rate cannot be a
8   rate higher than the current index plus margin.

9   Once the initial interest rate is set, annual adjustments to FHA ARMs must be calcu-
10 lated. The first interest rate adjustment may not occur sooner than 12 months from the
11 due date of the first monthly payment or later than 18 months from that first designated
12 payment date. In other words, the first adjustment must be made during a six-month
13 period (six-month window) or it is forfeited. This time frame permits lenders to com-
14 plete the collection or pooling of many mortgages for sale to secondary market institu-
15 tions. Whatever date is designated as the initial interest rate adjustment date, all sub-
16 sequent rate adjustments must be made on the anniversary of that first adjustment date.

17   Unlike the conventional ARM choice of index, all FHA ARMs must use the published
18 "Constant Maturity of the One-Year Treasury Security" index, using the most recently
19 available figure that applied exactly 30 calendar days before the designated change date.
20 The new current index plus the constant margin rounded to the nearest one-eighth of
21 one percentage point is the new calculated interest rate. It is then compared with the
22 existing interest rate. If it is the same as the existing interest rate, no change is made to
23 the existing rate. If it is up to 1 percent higher or lower than the existing interest rate,
24 the new calculated interest rate becomes the new adjusted interest rate. If it is more than
25 1 percent higher or lower than the existing interest rate, the new adjusted interest rate
26 is limited to a 1 percent increase or decrease of the existing interest rate.

27   The new adjusted interest rate becomes effective on the designated change date and
28 is regarded as the existing interest rate until the next allowable change date. In no event
29 may any future combination of interest rate adjustments exceed five percentage points
30 higher or lower than the initial interest rate.

31   The FHA considers interest payable on the first day of the month following the month
32 in which the interest accrued. Therefore, adjusted monthly mortgage payments resulting
33 from the adjusted interest rate are not due until 30 days after the designated change date.
34 No negative amortization is allowed with FHA ARMs. The FHA requires that payments
35 be recalculated each year to provide for complete amortization of the outstanding princi-
36 pal balance over the remaining term of the loan at the new adjusted interest rate. Lenders
37 must give borrowers at least 30 days' notice of any increase or decrease in the monthly
38 mortgage payment amount. The adjustment notice must contain the date the adjustment
39 notice is given, the ARM change date, the new existing interest rate, the amount of the
40 new monthly mortgage payment, the current index used, the method of calculating the
41 adjustment, and any other information that may be required to clarify the adjustment.

42 **FHA Required Disclosure Statement.**   All approved lenders making FHA adjustable-
43 rate loans must provide each borrower with a mortgage loan information statement that
44 includes a worst-case example form. The borrower must receive this statement and be
45 given an opportunity to read the informative explanation before signing the borrower's
46 certification on the loan application. Licensees are urged to obtain personal copies of
47 the FHA adjustable-rate mortgage disclosure statement to use when counseling clients
48 or advising customers.

49 **Advantages of the FHA ARM.**   An FHA ARM has several advantages over a conven-
50 tional ARM. Often, an FHA ARM bears a slightly lower interest rate because of the gov-
51 ernment insurance provided the lender. In addition, the FHA commonly uses more
52 lenient qualification formulas. The down payment (required investment) also is lower

in many cases, and the interest rate increase each year is limited to 1 percent, with an overall cap of 5 percent (conventional caps usually are 2 percent per year, with a 6 percent over-all cap). FHA loans continue to be easier to assume than conventional loans, although the FHA has increased the requirements for assumption of FHA loans. The FHA now requires a review of the creditworthiness of each person seeking to assume an FHA-insured loan.

Disadvantages of the FHA ARM.   The FHA imposes a maximum loan amount that differs from region to region, depending on the cost of living in each region. Also, the FHA requires an upfront mortgage insurance premium (UFMIP) of 1.5 percent, although this cost may be financed along with the mortgage. If FHA loans are repaid early, mortgagors may apply for partial refunds of the mortgage insurance premiums.

MORTGAGE INSURANCE

Conventional lender usually require that the borrower pay for private mortgage insurance (PMI). PMI protects the lender if the borrower defaults on the loan. The *Homeowners Protection Act of 1998,* which became effective in 1999, established rules for automatic termination and borrower cancellation of PMI on home mortgages. These protections apply to certain home mortgages signed on or after July 29, 1999. These protections do not apply to government-insured FHA or VA guaranteed loans or to loans with lender-paid PMI.

For conventional home mortgages signed on or after July 29, 1999, PMI must, with certain exceptions, be terminated *automatically* when the borrower has achieved 22 percent equity in the home based on the *original property value,* if the mortgage payments are current. PMI also can be canceled when the borrower *requests it*—with certain exceptions—when the borrower achieves 20 percent equity in the home based on the original property value, if the mortgage payments are current.

There are three exceptions for which the PMI may continue:

1. If the loan is "high-risk"
2. If the borrower has not been current on the payments within the year prior to the time for termination or cancellation
3. If the borrower has other liens on the property

The FHA Homebuyer Savings Plan has also reduced mortgage insurance premiums on loans originated after January 1, 2001, to 1.5 percent of the original loan amount from 2.25 percent. FHA has also eliminated the .5 percent premium for borrowers who have achieved 22 percent equity in their house, based on the lower of the purchase price or the appraisal.

Web Links

www.fanniemae.com
Fannie Mae Home Page

www.freddiemac.com
Freddie Mac Home Page

www.hud.gov/fha/fhahome.html
U.S. Department of Housing and Urban Development: FHA

www.federalreserve.gov
Federal Reserve Board

www.va.gov
U.S. Department of Veterans Affairs

SUMMARY

Real estate licensees should assist their clients and customers in the initial two steps of prequalifying and shopping for a mortgage loan. Too often, the process begins instead with the loan application. Various proven tools and techniques exist for doing both before applying to a lender for a loan.

Fixed-rate mortgages remain popular. While the 30-year, fixed-rate mortgage is the most common, 15-year and biweekly mortgages are gaining in popularity. Adjustable-rate mortgages also are popular among lenders and borrowers. Conventional and FHA adjustable-rate mortgages are available. Each financing instrument has its own advantages and disadvantages, and licensees who understand the current and ever-changing mortgage market increase their chances for success in the business.

DEFINE THESE KEY TERMS

adjustable-rate mortgage (ARM)

annual percentage rate (APR)

biweekly mortgage

calculated interest rate

cap

contract rate

fixed-rate mortgage

index

margin

negative amortization

PITI payment

refinancing

CHAPTER 9 PRACTICE EXAM

1. The FHA-required disclosure statement indicates the initial interest rate for an FHA ARM loan may remain in effect for up to how many months?

   a. 12
   b. 18
   c. 24
   d. 30

2. The primary elements a borrower uses to determine whether to accept an adjustable-rate mortgage are the index, the lender's margin, and the:

   a. seller's income and credit history.
   b. housing expense ratio and total obligations ratio.
   c. calculated interest rate, initial interest rate, and interest rate caps.
   d. amount of the buydown and amount of negative amortization.

3. Of the recognized indexes used on ARM loans, which of the following is *least* volatile?

   a. Cost-of-funds index of the Federal Home Loan Bank, 11th District
   b. One-year Treasury bill index
   c. Six-month average Treasury bill index
   d. Prime rate charged by money center banks

4. Total interest rate increases on an FHA adjustable-rate loan may not exceed what percentage over the life of the loan?

   a. 5 percent
   b. 3 percent
   c. 2 percent
   d. 1 percent

5. On January 10, the one-year Treasury bill index was 7 percent. Southern Federal Savings Association used that index to write a new one-year adjustable-rate mortgage that included a 2 percent cap on annual interest rate increases. The margin was 2½ percent. What is the calculated interest rate contained in the new ARM loan above?

   a. 7 percent
   b. 9 percent
   c. 9½ percent
   d. 11 percent

6. Using the information in question 5, assume the index rose to 9½ percent in year two. What interest rate will be charged in year two?

   a. 11 percent
   b. 11½ percent
   c. 12 percent
   d. 9½ percent

7. Deidra takes out a $127,000, 30-year, fixed-rate mortgage at 9½ percent. The mortgage payment factor is .0084085. Taxes for the year are $2,400, and insurance is $600. What will Deidra pay in monthly PITI payments?

   a. $1,267.88
   b. $1,067.88
   c. $1,245.89
   d. $1,317.88

8. The component of an adjustable-rate mortgage that does *not* usually change is the:

   a. margin.
   b. index.
   c. points.
   d. calculated rate.

9. Jack purchased a new home at the FHA appraisal amount of $100,000 and financed it with an FHA mortgage loan. To what amount must he reduce the outstanding loan balance before he no longer has to pay the ½ percent annual mortgage insurance premium?

   a. $90,000
   b. $85,000
   c. $78,000
   d. $80,000

10. A borrower applies for a 30-year, fixed-rate mortgage with an interest rate of 8.75 percent plus three points. He plans to live in the mortgaged house for the rest of his life. Using only this information, what will be the effective interest rate for mortgage comparison purposes?

    a. 9.125 percent
    b. 9.25 percent
    c. 11.375 percent
    d. 9.875 percent

11. A borrower who is shopping for an acceptable ARM probably should reject a loan that has:

    a. annual caps of more than 2 percent.
    b. a lifetime cap greater than 4 percent.
    c. a margin greater than 2 percent.
    d. all of the above.

12. What is the maximum amount of a buyer's closing costs that can be paid by the seller under conventional lending standards when the borrower is making a 5 percent down payment?

    a. 6 percent of the purchase price
    b. 4 percent of the loan amount
    c. 3 percent of the purchase price
    d. 3 percent of the loan amount

13. Millie Proffit is buying a new home and will make a 10 percent down payment. The beginning interest rate on her ARM loan is 7 percent. Sara, her sales associate, prequalifies Millie based on a payments from the factor table at 7 percent, plus escrow items (PITI). Which is correct?

    a. Sara should have qualified Millie without the escrow items in the payment.
    b. Sara should have qualified Millie at a 9 percent payment factor plus escrow items.
    c. Millie can't get a 90 percent ARM loan; 80 percent is the maximum loan-to-value ratio.
    d. Sara should have qualified Millie at a 9 percent payment factor without escrow items.

14. Marian is shopping for a new $150,000 mortgage. She expects to live in her new home for about four years. She can get a 30-year, 7.75 percent fixed-rate mortgage with principal and interest payments of $1,074.62 with no points. She can also get a 7.25 percent mortgage loan (payments of $1,023.26) with three points. How many months will it take Marian to break even on the points if she takes the lower interest rate loan, using simple arithmetic?

    a. 48.5
    b. 58.6
    c. 87.6
    d. 89.2

15. ARM loans are more popular:

    a. than fixed-rate mortgages in most markets.
    b. when interest rates are low.
    c. for people who are risk-averse.
    d. when interest rates are high.

16. Mary Durrell is shopping for a new loan and has narrowed the field to two choices. One is a 30-year, fixed-rate loan that has principal and interest payments of $940 per month. The other is a biweekly mortgage. What is the difference in Mary's annual payments based on this information?

    a. $940
    b. No difference in payments but a big difference in interest saved
    c. No difference in payments and no difference in interest saved
    d. $470

17. When compared with a 30-year mortgage, a 15-year mortgage:

    a. is more flexible in repayment possibilities.
    b. has slightly higher interest rates.
    c. has slightly lower interest rates.
    d. has lower monthly payments.

18. Popular literature shows dramatic interest savings from a 15-year loan versus a 30-year loan. What is true about most of these analyses?

    a. Amounts saved usually are less because income tax effects are not factored in.
    b. Amounts saved usually are less because opportunity costs of the additional payments required are not considered.
    c. They usually show that the amounts of interest saved are not substantial.
    d. Both a and b are true.

19. Disclosure of the annual percentage rate of interest must:

    a. be given to the borrower within three days of loan application.
    b. be computed to the nearest one-eighth of 1 percent.
    c. show the total financing cost in relation to the amount financed.
    d. All of the above

20. Which is true about a loan's effective interest rate?

    a. Each point equals a ½ percent increase in the lender's yield.
    b. Origination fees should be added to the points charged in making the calculation.
    c. Each point equals one-eighth of a 1 percent increase in the lender's yield, even if the loan is in force for less than five years.
    d. Origination fees should not be considered.

CHAPTER 10—ACQUIRING FINANCING FOR THE PROPERTY

LEARNING OBJECTIVES

Upon completion of this chapter, *you should be able to:*

1. list three federal statutes that control the information a lender may obtain and consider when qualifying an applicant;
2. list the four basic loan processing procedures;
3. list two of the latest trends in mortgage lending due to computer technology;
4. describe the difference between qualifying the borrower and qualifying the property;
5. list the three major sections of a borrower's financial statement;
6. describe how lenders are using credit scoring to assist in the underwriting process;
7. itemize at least three sources of income that will be counted when qualifying a buyer;
8. explain what analyzing the title means and how it is accomplished;
9. list the components of a full title report;
10. list the two methods of obtaining assurance of good title; and
11. describe the differences between an owner's title insurance policy and a lender's title insurance policy.

CHAPTER 10

ACQUIRING FINANCING FOR THE PROPERTY

1   The origination of a home mortgage is subject to a number of federal statutes, particu-
2   larly the *Equal Credit Opportunity Act (ECOA)*, the *Consumer Credit Protection Act* (Title I:
3   Truth-in-Lending Act). and the *Real Estate Settlement Procedures Act* (RESPA). Together,
4   these laws control the information a lender may obtain and consider in qualifying con-
5   sumer mortgage loan applicants. They also dictate both the content and the form of
6   information lenders must present to borrowers, the procedure for closing mortgage
7   loan agreements, the documents to be used in closings, and the fees that may be
8   charged.

9   In today's environment, lenders are required by the Civil Rights Acts and amend-
10 ments to them not to discriminate against consumer mortgage loan applicants on the
11 basis of race, color, national origin, religion, sex, age, family status, or handicap. In addi-
12 tion, borrower rights have been better protected since passage of the Equal Credit
13 Opportunity Act and the *Federal Reserve Board of Governor's Regulation B,* which imple-
14 mented the act. The act requires fair consideration of consumer loan applications from
15 women, minority races, part-time employees, and others who may have suffered preju-
16 dicial treatment in the past.

17   As a result of increasing concern about protection of consumer rights, most mort-
18 gage lenders have developed specific guidelines for loan underwriters to follow to
19 ensure compliance with federal laws affecting consumer mortgage lending. Although
20 the guidelines are protective of consumers' rights, they do not interfere with the analysis
21 of an applicant's credit standing. The purpose of such guidelines is to prevent home-
22 buyers from being victimized, not to guarantee that a loan will be approved. In the final
23 analysis, good underwriting policies and practices by a lender combine compliance with
24 the continual search for financial safety and streamlined processing. Licensees can serve
25 themselves and their customers well by becoming knowledgeable about residential
26 mortgage loan processing and closing.

27   To accomplish the above-stated goals of government agencies and originating
28 lenders, four basic **loan processing procedures** have been developed:

29   1. Determining a borrower's ability to repay the loan
30   2. Estimating the value of the property being pledged as collateral to guarantee this
31   repayment
32   3. Researching and analyzing the marketability of the collateral's title
33   4. Preparing the documents necessary to close the loan transaction

34   Most lenders follow loan processing procedures that reflect a combined concern for
35 the borrower's credit ability and the collateral's value. Some loan transactions require

1   an emphasis of one factor over the other, but generally both borrower credit and collat-
2   eral value are essential determinants in the real estate finance loan processing equation.

3   **Loan underwriting** is the evaluation of the risks involved when issuing a new mort-
4   gage. This process involves qualifying the borrower and the property to determine
5   whether they meet the minimum requirements established by the lender, investor, or
6   secondary market in which the loan probably will be sold.

7 TRENDS IN THE MORTGAGE MARKET

8   The mortgage market is changing as rapidly as many other sectors of the real estate
9   industry, and technology is the engine of the change. The last two years have seen many
10   lenders migrating their loan programs to the Internet. Almost immediate loan approval
11   is possible on the Web. *Credit scoring,* discussed later in this chapter, is changing the way
12   mortgage interest rates are quoted. Appraisers can make restricted "drive-by" appraisals
13   when a loan application is strong.

14 Automated Underwriting

15   With **automated underwriting** a lender can enter loan application information into
16   Fannie Mae's Desktop Underwriter software and receive a decision almost immediately.
17   If the software determines that the buyer and the property are qualified, Fannie Mae is
18   required to purchase the loan from the originator.

19   Because of the huge growth of people using the Internet and the public's acceptance
20   of the technology, lenders are moving toward so-called **paperless mortgages.** For
21   example, a person who applies for a mortgage online can expect to take 15 minutes to
22   complete the application, and the applicant will get an automatic decision almost imme-
23   diately. This bypasses the need for a lender to take the application. How does all this
24   work? With **computer valuation** (appraisals) and credit scoring.

25 Automated Valuation

26   Some years ago, a consortium of lending organizations including Fannie Mae, Freddie
27   Mac, CitiBank, Countrywide Funding, and others formed an organization called the
28   *National Property Data Service.* The purpose was to reduce time and costs for both con-
29   sumers and lenders through **automated valuation.**

30   Each lender contributed all its residential appraisals to create a huge database of
31   property descriptions and sale prices. A review of the database might show, for example,
32   that 74 percent of all the homes in a given subdivision had been the subject of an
33   appraisal over a ten-year period.

34   An appraiser employs matched pair analysis using two or three pairs of properties to
35   estimate the value of a fourth bedroom, a swimming pool, or another feature. The
36   Desktop Underwriter uses multiple linear regression to do the same thing for that neigh-
37   borhood. It uses precise dollar adjustments and, depending on the buyer's credit score,
38   may allow an appraiser to do a "streamlined property inspection" (exterior only) to make
39   an estimate of value. When Fannie Mae uses this method, it has judged the reasonable-
40   ness of the sales price and has relied on the property value generated by the software.

41 QUALIFYING THE BORROWER

42   The framework for current real estate financing is the 30-year amortization schedule
43   and regular monthly payments of principal and interest. In addition, mortgagees cur-

FIGURE 10.1 MORTGAGE LOAN PROCESS

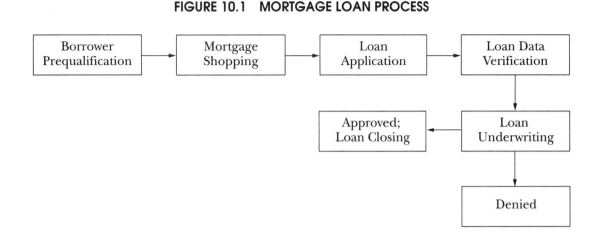

Source: Adapted by permission from Thomas C. Steinmetz, *The Mortgage Kit,* 4th ed. (Chicago: Dearborn Financial Publishing, Inc.®, 1998), 7.

1 rently can lend up to 100 percent of a property's value. High loan-to-value ratios com-
2 bined with long-term loan amortization payment schedules require a lender to look to
3 the credit of the borrower as the primary protection.

4   Even though lenders using insured or guaranteed programs of real estate finance do
5 not bear the risks of default directly, they still must follow the directions of their guar-
6 anteeing agencies and carefully screen loan applicants to derive some reasonable esti-
7 mate of the borrower's ability to pay and their inclinations to meet their contractual
8 obligations responsibly. Thus, a great effort is made to check and evaluate thoroughly
9 a potential mortgagor's credit history and current financial status to predict her future
10 economic stability. The mortgage loan process is shown in Figure 10.1.

Loan Application

Forms 12 When a licensee works with a buyer, one of the services the licensee can offer is that of
13 helping the buyer obtain financing. Before the buyer goes to the lender to make an
14 application, the licensee should provide a list of items the buyer will need. A sample list
15 is shown in the Forms-To-Go Appendix in the back of the book. Every formal real estate
16 loan processing operation begins with a lender completing a standardized loan applica-
17 tion form based on information the buyer provides. All loan applications are designed
18 to test a borrower's financial ability to meet the loan agreement's basic obligations. The
19 form in Figure 10.2 is the widely used Uniform Residential Loan Application, the
20 combined Fannie Mae/Freddie Mac form. It is used for conventional, FHA, and VA
21 loans secured by one-family to four-family properties. Lenders use this and similar
22 forms to obtain pertinent information from an applicant requesting a real estate loan.
23 The bulk of the application is devoted to securing personal information from the bor-
24 rower about family size and ages of dependent children, sources of income, and employ-
25 ment history, as well as a comprehensive financial statement. In addition, the property
26 is identified by its legal description.

27   The requirements of the national Real Estate Settlement Procedures Act apply when
28 the purchase is to be financed by a federally related mortgage loan involving a new first
29 mortgage for a one-family to four-family home. A Good-Faith Estimate of Borrower's
30 Settlement Costs must be prepared and given to the borrower at the time of loan appli-
31 cation or within three business days of application.

FIGURE 10.2   MORTGAGE LOAN APPLICATION

Uniform Residential Loan Application

This application is designed to be completed by the applicant(s) with the lender's assistance. Applicants should complete this form as "Borrower" or "Co-Borrower", as applicable. Co-Borrower information must also be provided (and the appropriate box checked) when ☐ the income or assets of a person other than the "Borrower" (including the Borrower's spouse) will be used as a basis for loan qualification or ☐ the income or assets of the Borrower's spouse will not be used as a basis for loan qualification, but his or her liabilities must be considered because the Borrower resides in a community property state, the security property is located in a community property state, or the Borrower is relying on other property located in a community property state as a basis for repayment of the loan.

I. TYPE OF MORTGAGE AND TERMS OF LOAN

Mortgage Applied for:	☐ VA ☐ FHA	☐ Conventional ☐ FmHA	☐ Other:	Agency Case Number		Lender Case No.	
Amount $	Interest Rate %	No. of Months	Amortization Type:	☐ Fixed Rate ☐ GPM	☐ Other (explain): ☐ ARM (type):		

II. PROPERTY INFORMATION AND PURPOSE OF LOAN

Subject Property Address (street, city, state, & zip code)   No. of Units

Legal Description of Subject Property (attach description if necessary)   Year Built

Purpose of Loan	☐ Purchase ☐ Refinance	☐ Construction ☐ Construction-Permanent	☐ Other (explain):	Property will be: ☐ Primary Residence ☐ Secondary Residence ☐ Investment

Complete this line if construction or construction-permanent loan.

Year Lot Acquired	Original Cost $	Amount Existing Liens $	(a) Present Value of Lot $	(b) Cost of Improvements $	Total (a + b) $

Complete this line if this is a refinance loan.

Year Acquired	Original Cost $	Amount Existing Liens $	Purpose of Refinance	Describe Improvements ☐ made ☐ to be made Cost: $

Title will be held in what Name(s)	Manner in which Title will be held	Estate will be held in: ☐ Fee Simple ☐ Leasehold (show expiration date)

Source of Down Payment, Settlement Charges and/or Subordinate Financing (explain)

III. BORROWER INFORMATION

Borrower	Co-Borrower
Borrower's Name (include Jr. or Sr. if applicable)	Co-Borrower's Name (include Jr. or Sr. if applicable)

Social Security Number	Home Phone (incl. area code)	Age	Yrs. School	Social Security Number	Home Phone (incl. area code)	Age	Yrs. School

☐ Married ☐ Separated ☐ Unmarried (include single, divorced, widowed)	Dependents (not listed by Co-Borrower) no. ages	☐ Married ☐ Separated ☐ Unmarried (include single, divorced, widowed)	Dependents (not listed by Borrower) no. ages

Present Address (street, city, state, zip code) ☐ Own ☐ Rent ____ No. Yrs.	Present Address (street, city, state, zip code) ☐ Own ☐ Rent ____ No. Yrs.

If residing at present address for less than two years, complete the following:

Former Address (street, city, state, zip code) ☐ Own ☐ Rent ____ No. Yrs.	Former Address (street, city, state, zip code) ☐ Own ☐ Rent ____ No. Yrs.

Former Address (street, city, state, zip code) ☐ Own ☐ Rent ____ No. Yrs.	Former Address (street, city, state, zip code) ☐ Own ☐ Rent ____ No. Yrs.

IV. EMPLOYMENT INFORMATION

Borrower	Co-Borrower
Name & Address of Employer ☐ Self Employed	Yrs. on this job	Name & Address of Employer ☐ Self Employed	Yrs. on this job

	Yrs. employed in this line of work/profession		Yrs. employed in this line of work/profession

Position/Title/Type of Business	Business Phone (incl. area code)	Position/Title/Type of Business	Business Phone (incl. area code)

If employed in current position for less than two years or if currently employed in more than one position, complete the following:

Name & Address of Employer ☐ Self Employed	Dates (from - to)	Name & Address of Employer ☐ Self Employed	Dates (from - to)
	Monthly Income $		Monthly Income $

Position/Title/Type of Business	Business Phone (incl. area code)	Position/Title/Type of Business	Business Phone (incl. area code)

Name & Address of Employer ☐ Self Employed	Dates (from - to)	Name & Address of Employer ☐ Self Employed	Dates (from - to)
	Monthly Income $		Monthly Income $

Position/Title/Type of Business	Business Phone (incl. area code)	Position/Title/Type of Business	Business Phone (incl. area code)

Freddie Mac Form 65 10/92   ITEM 7300 (9210)   Page 1 of 4 pages   Fannie Mae Form 1003 10/92

FIGURE 10.2 MORTGAGE LOAN APPLICATION (Continued)

V. MONTHLY INCOME AND COMBINED HOUSING EXPENSE INFORMATION

Gross Monthly Income	Borrower	Co-Borrower	Total	Combined Monthly Housing Expense	Present	Proposed
Base Empl. Income*	$	$	$	Rent	$	
Overtime				First Mortgage (P&I)		$
Bonuses				Other Financing (P&I)		
Commissions				Hazard Insurance		
Dividends/Interest				Real Estate Taxes		
Net Rental Income				Mortgage Insurance		
OTHER (before completing, see the notice in "describe other income," below)				Homeowner Assn. Dues		
				Other:		
Total	$	$	$	**Total**	$	$

*Self Employed Borrower(s) may be required to provide additional documentation such as tax returns and financial statements.

Describe Other Income *Notice:* **Alimony, child support, or separate maintenance income need not be revealed if the Borrower (B) or Co-Borrower (C) does not choose to have it considered for repaying this loan.**

B/C		Monthly Amount
		$

VI. ASSETS AND LIABILITIES

This Statement and any applicable supporting schedules may be completed jointly by both married and unmarried Co-Borrowers if their assets and liabilities are sufficiently joined so that the Statement can be meaningfully and fairly presented on a combined basis; otherwise separate Statements and Schedules are required. If the Co-Borrower section was completed about a spouse, this Statement and supporting schedules must be completed about that spouse also.

Completed ☐ Jointly ☐ Not Jointly

ASSETS Description	Cash or Market Value	Liabilities and Pledged Assets. List the creditor's name, address and account number for all outstanding debts, including automobile loans, revolving charge accounts, real estate loans, alimony, child support, stock pledges, etc. Use continuation sheet, if necessary. Indicate by (*) those liabilities which will be satisfied upon sale of real estate owned or upon refinancing of the subject property.	Monthly Payt. & Mos. Left to Pay	Unpaid Balance
Cash deposit toward purchase held by:	$	**LIABILITIES**		
		Name and address of Company	$ Payt./Mos.	$
List checking and savings accounts below				
Name and address of Bank, S&L, or Credit Union				
		Acct. no.		
		Name and address of Company	$ Payt./Mos.	$
Acct. no.	$			
Name and address of Bank, S&L, or Credit Union				
		Acct. no.		
		Name and address of Company	$ Payt./Mos.	$
Acct. no.	$			
Name and address of Bank, S&L, or Credit Union				
		Acct. no.		
		Name and address of Company	$ Payt./Mos.	$
Acct. no.	$			
Name and address of Bank, S&L, or Credit Union				
		Acct. no.		
		Name and address of Company	$ Payt./Mos.	$
Acct. no.	$			
Stocks & Bonds (Company name/number & description)	$			
		Acct. no.		
		Name and address of Company	$ Payt./Mos.	$
Life insurance net cash value	$			
Face amount: $				
Subtotal Liquid Assets	$			
Real estate owned (enter market value from schedule of real estate owned)	$	Acct. no.		
Vested interest in retirement fund	$	Name and address of Company	$ Payt./Mos.	$
Net worth of business(es) owned (attach financial statement)	$			
Automobiles owned (make and year)	$			
		Acct. no.		
		Alimony/Child Support/Separate Maintenance Payments Owed to:	$	
Other Assets (itemize)	$	Job Related Expense (child care, union dues, etc.)	$	
		Total Monthly Payments	$	
Total Assets a. $		**Net Worth (a minus b)** ► $	**Total Liabilities b.** $	

Freddie Mac Form 65 10/92   Page 2 of 4 pages   Fannie Mae Form 1003 10/92

FIGURE 10.2 MORTGAGE LOAN APPLICATION (Continued)

VI. ASSETS AND LIABILITIES (cont.)

Schedule of Real Estate Owned (If additional properties are owned, use continuation sheet.)

Property Address (enter S if sold, PS if pending sale or R if rental being held for income) ▶	Type of Property	Present Market Value	Amount of Mortgages & Liens	Gross Rental Income	Mortgage Payments	Insurance, Maintenance, Taxes & Misc.	Net Rental Income
		$	$	$	$	$	$
Totals		$	$	$	$	$	$

List any additional names under which credit has previously been received and indicate appropriate creditor name(s) and account number(s):

Alternate Name	Creditor Name	Account Number

VII. DETAILS OF TRANSACTION

a. Purchase price	$
b. Alterations, improvements, repairs	
c. Land (if acquired separately)	
d. Refinance (incl. debts to be paid off)	
e. Estimated prepaid items	
f. Estimated closing costs	
g. PMI, MIP, Funding Fee	
h. Discount (if Borrower will pay)	
i. Total costs (add items a through h)	
j. Subordinate financing	
k. Borrower's closing costs paid by Seller	
l. Other Credits (explain)	
m. Loan amount (exclude PMI, MIP, Funding Fee financed)	
n. PMI, MIP, Funding Fee financed	
o. Loan amount (add m & n)	
p. Cash from/to Borrower (subtract j, k, l & o from i)	

VIII. DECLARATIONS

If you answer "yes" to any questions a through i, please use continuation sheet for explanation.

	Borrower Yes	Borrower No	Co-Borrower Yes	Co-Borrower No
a. Are there any outstanding judgments against you?	☐	☐	☐	☐
b. Have you been declared bankrupt within the past 7 years?	☐	☐	☐	☐
c. Have you had property foreclosed upon or given title or deed in lieu thereof in the last 7 years?	☐	☐	☐	☐
d. Are you a party to a lawsuit?	☐	☐	☐	☐
e. Have you directly or indirectly been obligated on any loan which resulted in foreclosure, transfer of title in lieu of foreclosure, or judgment? (This would include such loans as home mortgage loans, SBA loans, home improvement loans, educational loans, manufactured (mobile) home loans, any mortgage, financial obligation, bond, or loan guarantee. If "Yes," provide details, including date, name and address of Lender, FHA or VA case number, if any, and reasons for the action.)	☐	☐	☐	☐
f. Are you presently delinquent or in default on any Federal debt or any other loan, mortgage, financial obligation, bond, or loan guarantee? If "Yes," give details as described in the preceding question.	☐	☐	☐	☐
g. Are you obligated to pay alimony, child support, or separate maintenance?	☐	☐	☐	☐
h. Is any part of the down payment borrowed?	☐	☐	☐	☐
i. Are you a co-maker or endorser on a note?	☐	☐	☐	☐
j. Are you a U.S. citizen?	☐	☐	☐	☐
k. Are you a permanent resident alien?	☐	☐	☐	☐
l. Do you intend to occupy the property as your primary residence? If "Yes," complete question m below.	☐	☐	☐	☐
m. Have you had an ownership interest in a property in the last three years?	☐	☐	☐	☐
(1) What type of property did you own - principal residence (PR), second home (SH), or investment property (IP)?				
(2) How did you hold title to the home - solely by yourself (S), jointly with your spouse (SP), or jointly with another person (O)?				

IX. ACKNOWLEDGMENT AND AGREEMENT

The undersigned specifically acknowledge(s) and agree(s) that: (1) the loan requested by this application will be secured by a first mortgage or deed of trust on the property described herein; (2) the property will not be used for any illegal or prohibited purpose or use; (3) all statements made in this application are made for the purpose of obtaining the loan indicated herein; (4) occupation of the property will be as indicated above; (5) verification or reverification of any information contained in the application may be made at any time by the Lender, its agents, successors and assigns, either directly or through a credit reporting agency, from any source named in this application, and the original copy of this application will be retained by the Lender, even if the loan is not approved; (6) the Lender, its agents, successors and assigns will rely on the information contained in the application and I/we have a continuing obligation to amend and/or supplement the information provided in this application if any of the material facts which I/we have represented herein should change prior to closing; (7) in the event my/our payments on the loan indicated in this application become delinquent, the Lender, its agents, successors and assigns, may, in addition to all their other rights and remedies, report my/our name(s) and account information to a credit reporting agency; (8) ownership of the loan may be transferred to successor or assign of the Lender without notice to me and/or the administration of the loan account may be transferred to an agent, successor or assign of the Lender with prior notice to me; (9) the Lender, its agents, successors and assigns make no representations or warranties, express or implied, to the Borrower(s) regarding the property, the condition of the property, or the value of the property.

Certification: I/We certify that the information provided in this application is true and correct as of the date set forth opposite my/our signature(s) on this application and acknowledge my/our understanding that any intentional or negligent misrepresentation(s) of the information contained in this application may result in civil liability and/or criminal penalties including, but not limited to, fine or imprisonment or both under the provisions of Title 18, United States Code, Section 1001, et seq. and liability for monetary damages to the Lender, its agents, successors and assigns, insurers and any other person who may suffer any loss due to reliance upon any misrepresentation which I/we have made on this application.

Borrower's Signature	Date	Co-Borrower's Signature	Date
X		X	

X. INFORMATION FOR GOVERNMENT MONITORING PURPOSES

The following information is requested by the Federal Government for certain types of loans related to a dwelling, in order to monitor the Lender's compliance with equal credit opportunity, fair housing and home mortgage disclosure laws. You are not required to furnish this information, but are encouraged to do so. The law provides that a Lender may neither discriminate on the basis of this information, nor on whether you choose to furnish it. However, if you choose not to furnish it, under Federal regulations this Lender is required to note race and sex on the basis of visual observation or surname. If you do not wish to furnish the above information, please check the box below. (Lender must review the above material to assure that the disclosures satisfy all requirements to which the Lender is subject under applicable state law for the particular type of loan applied for.)

BORROWER

☐ I do not wish to furnish this information

Race/National Origin: ☐ American Indian or Alaskan Native ☐ Asian or Pacific Islander ☐ White, not of Hispanic origin ☐ Black, not of Hispanic origin ☐ Hispanic ☐ Other (specify) _____

Sex: ☐ Female ☐ Male

CO-BORROWER

☐ I do not wish to furnish this information

Race/National Origin: ☐ American Indian or Alaskan Native ☐ Asian or Pacific Islander ☐ White, not of Hispanic origin ☐ Black, not of Hispanic origin ☐ Hispanic ☐ Other (specify) _____

Sex: ☐ Female ☐ Male

To be Completed by Interviewer

This application was taken by:

☐ face-to-face interview
☐ by mail
☐ by telephone

Interviewer's Name (print or type)	Name and Address of Interviewer's Employer
Interviewer's Signature	Date	
Interviewer's Phone Number (incl. area code)	

Freddie Mac Form 65 10/92   Page 3 of 4 pages   Fannie Mae Form 1003 10/92

Financial Statement. Most **financial statements** follow a standard format that lists all assets in a column on the left and all liabilities in a column on the right. This enables a lender to assess quickly and efficiently the applicant's current financial status.

Assets consist of all things of value the applicant owns, encumbered or not, with cash heading the list. Cash consists of money in hand, on deposit in checking and savings accounts, and given as a deposit on the property being purchased. Lenders place great weight on a borrower's cash position as a reflection of liquidity and money management habits. A strong cash balance develops a sense of confidence in a borrower's ability to make payments and meet other obligations, even in the event of temporary setbacks.

Next in the financial statement asset column are listed all monies invested in stocks and bonds, notes or accounts receivable, personal business ventures, and other real estate. The value of the applicant's automobiles, surrender value of life insurance policies, and worth of other personal property and assets are listed. All dollar amounts assigned to these items must reflect their realistic market values, not their purchase prices or some imagined values.

Liabilities consist of all the applicant's monetary obligations. Heading the list of liabilities are any notes payable because these are considered priority claims against cash assets. Next in order of importance are all installment accounts, such as charge accounts and automobile payments. Other accounts payable, such as medical bills or insurance premiums, follow the list of installment accounts. Remaining long-term liabilities are then listed: alimony and child support payments, any encumbrances on the real estate listed as assets, accrued and unpaid real estate property and income taxes, security obligations on personal property such as furniture, loans on the life insurance policies listed as assets, and any other debts for which the applicant is responsible.

The total of the assets should exceed the total of the liabilities, with the difference being the applicant's net worth. The amount of **net worth** is added to the total liabilities to balance both sides of the financial statement. A 2-to-1 ratio indicates that the applicant has twice as many assets as liabilities. In the event that total liabilities exceed an applicant's total assets, a loan probably would be denied and the file closed. Assuming an applicant has a positive net worth, a series of related actions begins.

Data Verification. The loan processor will verify the information included in the application by actually checking with the various references given, the banks where deposits are held, and the applicant's employer.

Deposits. The borrower must sign a separate deposit verification form for each bank account, authorizing the bank to reveal to the lender the current balance in the borrower's account. Under the *Federal Right to Privacy Act,* the bank cannot release such confidential information without a verification form. The knowledge that the loan processor can verify account amounts usually is enough incentive for the borrower to be truthful in reporting financial information. When the deposit balances are verified, the appropriate entries are made in the applicant's file.

Employment. The applicant also is required to sign an employment verification form authorizing the employer to reveal confidential information concerning the applicant's job status. Not only will the applicant's wages or salary and length of employment be verified but the employer also will be requested to offer an opinion of the applicant's job attitude and give a prognosis for continued employment and prospects for advancement. Employment may be checked again before closing.

Credit Report. Simultaneously with the gathering of financial and employment information, the loan processor sends a formal request for the borrower's credit report to a local company offering this service. The credit report is a central part of the loan

1   approval process, and the lender relies on it heavily. Of the two types of credit reports,
2   consumer credit and mortgage credit, the discussion here centers on the latter.

3   A credit report is the result of the compilation of information accumulated from a
4   thorough check of the creditors indicated on the loan application, as well as a check of
5   the public records to discover whether any lawsuits are pending against the applicant.
6   When completed, the credit search company sends the loan processor a confidential
7   report of its findings.

8   This report usually states the applicant's (and coapplicant's) age, address, status as a
9   tenant or owner, and length of residency at his current address and includes a brief
10 employment history and credit profile, both past and present. The credit profile item-
11 izes the status of current and past accounts, usually identified by industry, such as banks,
12 department and specialty stores, and finance companies. In addition, it indicates the
13 quality and dates of the payments made, and their regularity; delinquency, and any out-
14 standing balances also are reported. This payment history is the most important part of
15 the report because it indicates how well the applicant has managed debt over time.
16 Underwriters view a person's past behavior as the best indicator of future attitude
17 toward debt repayment. Research tends to reinforce these opinions, indicating that slow
18 and erratic payers generally retain those attitudes when securing new loans and that
19 prompt and steady payers also are consistent in meeting their future obligations. As a
20 result, lenders pay careful attention to the last section of a credit report, which indicates
21 an applicant's attitude toward debt and his payment pattern.

22   When a credit report is returned revealing a series of erratic and delinquent pay-
23 ments, the loan is usually denied at this point and the file closed. If an applicant is
24 denied a loan because of adverse information in a credit report, the applicant has the
25 right to inspect a summary of that report, to challenge inaccuracies, and to require cor-
26 rections to be made (see the most current RESPA-required brochure, *Settlement Costs: A
27 HUD Guide*). If one or two unusual entries stand out in a group of otherwise satisfactory
28 transactions, the applicant will be asked to explain these deviations.

29   As with many standardized procedures, credit reporting has become computerized,
30 dramatically shortening the time needed for completing a check. In exchange for time
31 efficiency, however, credit reporting bureaus risk sacrificing the borrower's confiden-
32 titality. The fraudulent use of credit reports is increasing now that information is so
33 easily accessed. Credit reports should be used only by the persons or institutions
34 requesting the information and only for the purposes stated. As a result of increased
35 seller financing, credit bureaus are receiving more requests from agents and sellers to
36 check the credit of potential purchasers. To protect a buyer's confidentiality, most
37 credit agencies insist on seeing the buyer's written permission before issuing any infor-
38 mation.

39   After the deposit and employment verifications are returned with acceptable infor-
40 mation and a favorable credit report is obtained, the lending officer makes a thorough
41 credit evaluation of the data collected before continuing with the loan process.

42 **Evaluation of Credit Ability.**   Despite the standardization of the detailed guidelines
43 used in the lending process, the one area allowing for the greatest amount of latitude
44 in interpretation is the analysis and evaluation of a borrower's credit ability. A degree
45 of subjective personal involvement may be introduced into an otherwise strongly objec-
46 tive and structured format by an evaluator's unintentional bias or by a loan company's
47 changing policies.

48   In addition, credit standards are altered periodically to reflect a lender's changing
49 monetary position. When money is scarce, standards are more stringent; when money
50 is plentiful, standards are lowered. An applicant who qualifies for a loan at one time may
51 not at another. Thus, although a credit analyst is governed by guidelines, rules and

regulations, the criteria fluctuate with the analyst's discretionary powers. In the long run, a lender's success is demonstrated by a low rate of default on approved loans and by the fact that no discrimination complaints have been filed.

Credit Scoring

One of the most significant changes on mortgage lending has been the use of credit scores to better evaluate a borrower's ability to repay. Many borrowers who would have been turned down for a loan five years ago can buy today, but at higher rates.

A major reason Fannie Mae and Freddie Mac lenders are willing to make immediate loan decisions is credit scoring. **Credit scoring** uses statistical samples to predict how likely it is that a borrower will pay back a loan. To develop a model, the lender selects a large random sample of its borrowers, analyzing characteristics that relate to creditworthiness. Each of the characteristics is assigned a weight based on how strong a predictor it is. Credit scores treat each person objectively because the same standards apply to everyone. Credit scores are blind to demographic or cultural differences among people.

The most commonly used credit score today is known as a **FICO score,** named after the company that developed it, Fair, Isaac & Co. FICO scores range from 300 to 850. The lower the score, the greater the risk of default. A recent study by the Federal Reserve Board found that borrowers with low credit scores accounted for 1.5 percent of new mortgages, but 17 percent of the delinquencies.

Freddie Mac has found that borrowers with credit scores above 660 are likely to repay the mortgage, and underwriters can do a basic review of the file for completeness. For applicants with scores between 620 and 660, the underwriter is required to do a comprehensive review. A very cautious review would be made for persons with credit scores below 620.

Subprime loans.   HSH Associates, Financial Publishers, has prepared a table using typical specifications for subprime loans, often called "B-C-D Credit," shown in Figure 10.3.

Is Credit Scoring Valid?   With credit scoring, lenders can evaluate millions of applicants consistently and impartially on many different characteristics. To be statistically valid, the system must be based on a big enough sample. When properly designed, the system promotes fast, impartial decisions.

Fair, Isaac has recently completed *NextGen*®, designed to more precisely define the risk of borrowers because it analyzes more criteria than the old model. Using the new model, lenders can evaluate credit profiles of high risk borrowers in terms of degrees, rather than lumping them into the same category.

What Information Does Credit Scoring Use?   The scoring models use the following information when evaluating a score:

- 35 percent of the score is determined by payment history with higher weight for recent history. If late payments, collections, and/or bankruptcy appear in the credit report they are subtracted from the score.
- Outstanding debt is very close in importance to payment history (30 percent of the total score). Many scoring models evaluate the amount of debt compared with the credit limits. If the amount owed is close to the credit limit, it affects the score negatively.
- 15 percent is the result of credit history. A long history is better if payments are always on time.
- 10 percent is very recent history and "inquiries" for new credit. If the applicant has applied for credit in many places recently, it will negatively affect the score.

FIGURE 10.3 SUBPRIME MORTGAGE LENDING*

Credit Score	Quality Level	Debt Ratio	Max LTV Ratio	Delinquencies			Typical Additional Requirements
				No. of Times	No. of Days	Within Last	
621+	A+ to A–	28/38	To 95%	0	–	24 mo.	Good/excellent credit during last 2 to 5 years
581–620	B+ to B–	50	75–85%	2–3	30	12 mo.	No 60-day mortgage lates
551–580	C+ to C–	55	75%	3–4	30	12 mo.	12-24 mo. since bankrupt discharge
521–550	D+ to D–	60	65–70%	2–6	60	12 mo.	Bankruptcy discharge within past 12 months
520–	E	65	50–65%	Poor payment record with a pattern of 30, 60, 90+ lates			Possible current bankruptcy, foreclosure; stable current employment

* This chart assumes purchase or refinance of a single-family house or condo unit valued at $100,000 by a person with reasonably stable employment (not self-employed) with fully documented income, assets, and liabilities.

Source: HSH Associates, Financial Publishers. Used with permission.

1   This problem occurs when a person goes car shopping. Sales associates at each car
2   lot will ask for the consumer's Social Security number in order to pull a credit report
3   ("no charge"). The shopper has no idea that as more reports are ordered, the shop-
4   per's credit rating declines.
5   • 10 percent is based on the mix of credit, including car loans, credit cards, and mort-
6   gages. Too many credit cards will hurt a person's credit score. In some models, loans
7   from finance companies or title loan companies will also hurt the score.

8   To improve the credit score, persons should pay bills on time, pay down outstanding
9   balances, and not take on new debt. It may take a long time to improve the score signif-
10   icantly.

11   **How Is Credit Scoring Being Used?**   Residential lenders now use credit scoring the
12   same way it is used in automobile financing and consumer loans. Interest rates on home
13   mortgages will be based on the credit score. In theory, a person with a very high score
14   should expect to get the best rate, but typically the rate is the same for anyone with a
15   FICO score higher than 620. Below the 620 line, several grades and interest rates have
16   resulted.

17   As an example, when an A+ borrower could obtain a 30-year fixed rate mortgage at
18   7 percent, the A– borrower paid 8.4%, the B borrower paid 8.7 percent, the C borrower
19   paid 9.15 percent, and the D borrower paid 9.95 percent. Before credit scoring, how-
20   ever, these borrowers might not have been able to get a loan at all.

21   Many people who go to subprime lenders have only slight credit problems and end up
22   paying 2 percent higher than they need to. Those borrowers may qualify for standard
23   rates, and should find out their credit scores before making a decision on a lender. If indi-
24   viduals cannot get their FICO score, E-Loan Corp. provides a credit score using basically

the same techniques. Individuals can get one free credit score by logging into E-Loan and requesting the information.

Web Links

www.eloan.com
E-Loan (for prequalifying and credit scores)

www.hsh.com
HSH Associates, Financial Publishers

www.fanniemae.com
Fannie Mae Home Page

www.freddiemac.com
Freddie Mac Home Page

www.hud.gov/fha/fhahome.html
FHA Home Page

www.federalreserve.go
Federal Reserve Board

www.va.gov/
U.S. Department of Veterans Affairs

www.fairisaac.com
Fair, Isaac & Company

The quantity and quality of an applicant's income are the two major considerations in determining ability to support a family and make the required monthly loan payments. Analysts consider the **quantity of income**–the total income–when they review a loan application. Not only is the regular salary of a family's primary supporter basic to the analysis but a spouse's full income usually is accepted. Extra sources of income also may be included in the analysis if circumstances warrant it.

Any bonuses will be accepted as income only if they are received on a regular basis. If commissions are a large part of an applicant's income base, the history of past earnings will be scrutinized to estimate the stability of this income as a regular source for an extended time period. Overtime wages are not included in the analysis unless they have been—and will be—earned consistently. Pensions, interest, and dividends are treated as full income, although it is recognized that interest and dividends fluctuate over time and could stop if an investment were cashed out.

A second job is accepted as part of the regular monthly income if it can be established that the job has existed for approximately two years and there is good reason to believe it will continue. Child support also can be included in the determination of monthly income, but only if it is the result of a court order and has a proven track record. Government entitlement funds must also be considered.

In addition to its total quantity, a loan analyst pays careful attention to the **quality of income.** An applicant's employer will be asked for an opinion of job stability and possible advancement. Length of time on the job no longer carries the importance it once did. Applicants whose employment records show frequent shifts in job situations that result in upward mobility each time will be given full consideration. Lenders will, however, be wary of an applicant who drifts from one job classification to another and cannot seem to become established in any specific type of work.

When the accumulated data strongly support a positive or negative decision, the loan underwriter's decision is easy, and minimal use of discretion is needed. However, numerous borderline cases make it difficult for a loan officer to form objective judgments. In such a case, the loan officer schedules an in-depth personal interview with the applicant during which questions regarding data appearing on the credit report

1 are clarified or mistakes in bank balances can be explained. More often, however, the
2 loan officer merely wishes to visit with the applicant to observe and probe her atti-
3 tudes regarding the purchase of the property and the repayment of the prospective
4 loan. Thus, although a person's credit character can be measured objectively, personal
5 character is subject to interpretation.

6   After reviewing all of the information provided in the application as well as the other
7 data collected, the loan officer decides either to approve or to disapprove the loan ap-
8 plication. If the officer judges a loan application to be unacceptable, he states the rea-
9 sons for the rejection, the parties to the loan are informed, and the file is closed.

DISCUSSION EXERCISE 10.1

You are a loan underwriter determining whether to approve a $140,000 conven-
tional loan application. The following monthly financial information applies:

Gross monthly income	$4,300
Mortgage principal and interest payment	931
Real estate tax escrow	150
Homeowner's insurance escrow	50
Private mortgage insurance	45
Car payment	250
Alimony or child support payment	225
Credit card payments (average)	50

The borrower's housing expense ratio is:_____

       Acceptable?_____

The borrower's total obligations ratio is: _____

       Acceptable? _____

What is your decision regarding the loan application?_____

---

10 QUALIFYING THE COLLATERAL

11 Despite the current trend toward emphasizing a borrower's financial ability as the loan-
12 granting criterion, real estate lenders and guarantors are practical and fully understand
13 that life is filled with events beyond one's control. Death is a possibility that can abruptly
14 eliminate a family's wage earner. Economic conditions can exert devastating financial
15 impact. Corporate downsizing and layoffs have resulted in hardship for many families.
16 Honest mistakes in personal decisions can result in bankruptcies, often damaging or
17 destroying credit.

18   To reduce the risk of loss, real estate lenders look to the value of the collateral (the
19 real property) as the basic underlying assurance for recovery of their investments in a
20 default situation.

21   Unique financing terms or an active local housing market in which the number of
22 potential buyers briefly exceeds the number of available properties may cause prices to
23 rise above actual market values. Therefore, each parcel of property pledged for collat-
24 eral must be inspected and appraised carefully to estimate its current market value
25 because this amount will be used as the basis for determining the mortgage loan
26 amount. Depending on the type of loan to be issued and its loan-to-value ratio, either

1 the amount determined through the formal or certified appraisal made as part of the
2 loan process or the purchase price, whichever is less, determines the loan's amount.

3   Some financial institutions maintain appraisers on their staffs, but most lenders
4 engage certified appraisers for estimates of value. All three approaches to estimating a
5 property's value are addressed. When an appraisal is completed, it is delivered to the loan
6 officer to aid in the final loan decision. As noted previously, a loan amount is based on
7 the lesser of either this appraised value or the purchase price of the property.

DISCUSSION EXERCISE 10.2

Which do you consider the more important factor in granting or denying a mortgage application: the borrower's ability to make the required payments or the
value of the collateral? Why?

---

8 ## ANALYZING THE TITLE

9 The assurance of good title is as essential to a loan's completion as are the borrower's
10 credit and the collateral's value. In anticipation of issuing a loan, the loan officer secures
11 a title report on the collateral property. The components of a full title report are a
12 survey, a physical inspection of the collateral, and a search of the records to determine
13 all the interests in a property. Normally, property interests are perfected through the
14 appropriate filing and recording of standard notices. A recorded deed notifies the
15 world that a grantee has the legal fee simple title to the property. A recorded construc-
16 tion lien, for example, is notice of another's interest in the property.

17   In Florida, two methods have been used to obtain assurance of good title: (1) the
18 abstract and opinion of title and (2) title insurance. Lenders prefer title insurance, but
19 whichever method is used, the title report should provide the loan officer and the
20 lender's attorney with all available information relevant to the legal status of the subject
21 property, as well as any interests revealed by constructive notice. This title search
22 requirement represents another effort by the lender to protect the loan investment.
23 Because title insurance is most lenders' and buyers' method of choice, it is discussed
24 here.

25 ### Title Insurance

26 Title insurance companies combine the abstracting process with a program of insurance
27 that guarantees the validity and accuracy of the title search. A purchaser of title insur-
28 ance can rely on the insurance company's assets to back up its guarantee of a property's
29 marketable title. This guarantee is evidenced by a policy of title insurance. Most finan-
30 cial institutions now require that a title policy be issued to them for the face amount of
31 a loan. Insurance is defined simply as coverage against loss.

32   When a title insurance policy is issued to a lender, it is usually in the American Land
33 Title Association (ALTA) form. While a standard title policy insures against losses over-
34 looked in the search of the recorded chain of title, an ALTA policy expands this stan-
35 dard coverage to include many unusual risks, such as forgeries, incompetency of parties
36 involved in issuing documents pertaining to the transfer of ownership, legal status of
37 parties involved in the specific loan negotiations, surveying errors, and other possible
38 off-record defects. Some additional risks can be and usually are covered by special
39 endorsements to an insurance policy. These could include protection against any unre-
40 corded easements or liens, rights of parties in possession of the subject property,

1   mining claims, water rights, and additional negotiated special items pertinent to the
2   property involved. Participants in the secondary mortgage market (Fannie Mae, Freddie
3   Mac, and Ginnie Mae) generally require the expanded ALTA policy for the added
4   protection it provides. Many lenders use the phrase "an ALTA policy" when describing
5   an extended-coverage policy.

Surveys

7   Whether the abstract and opinion of title method or the title insurance policy method
8   is used, a property's title is searched by an experienced abstractor who prepares a report
9   of those recorded documents that clearly affect the quality of ownership. In addition,
10 lenders usually require a survey of the collateral property as a condition for a new loan.
11 Although many properties are part of subdivisions that have been engineered and
12 described by licensed and registered surveyors and engineers, some owners might have
13 enlarged their homes or made additions to the improvements since the original survey.
14 These might not meet the various setback restrictions set forth in the local zoning laws.
15 Some properties might have been resubdivided, while others now might have encroach-
16 ment problems.

Defects

18 If a defect is found, sometimes called a *cloud on the title*, the loan process does not con-
19 tinue until this cloud is cleared to the lender's satisfaction. Such a cloud could be an
20 unsatisfied construction lien, an income tax lien, a property tax lien, an easement infrac-
21 tion, an encroachment, or a zoning violation. Sometimes a borrower's name is not cor-
22 rect on the deed, an error exists in the legal description, or the deed has a faulty
23 acknowledgment or lacks the appropriate signatures. Because of the many complexities
24 in a real estate transaction, there are possibilities for defects to appear in a title search
25 and property survey. It is the abstractor's responsibility to discover and report them.

26 In certain instances where clouds are difficult to remove by ordinary means, they
27 must be cleared by filing suits to quiet title. After appropriate evidence is submitted, a
28 judge removes or modifies an otherwise damaging defect in a title. The loan process can
29 continue when a clear chain of title is shown on the public records.

SUMMARY

The process of obtaining a real estate loan includes four steps: qualifying a borrower, evaluating the collateral, analyzing the title, and closing the loan transaction.

Beginning with an application to obtain a loan, the borrower's credit, financial condition, and personal attitudes are analyzed to determine her ability and willingness to honor debts and repay the loan as agreed. Current assets and employment are verified, a credit rating is obtained, and often a private interview is held between the borrower and loan officer to estimate certain credit characteristics. Other basic criteria used to determine the applicant's creditworthiness include gross monthly earnings of approximately four times the required monthly mortgage payment (sometimes higher for large loans), stability of earnings, and a good prognosis for continued employment and advancement.

Once the loan applicant's credit is accepted, either a staff appraiser or an independent fee appraiser analyzes the value of the real estate to be pledged as collateral. A certified appraisal report offering the appraiser's opinion of the subject property's value is submitted to the loan officer.

After the borrower's credit and the collateral's value are verified, the legal status of the property's title is examined and analyzed carefully, usually by a trained abstractor. The abstract is delivered to the lender's attorney for an opinion of accuracy and validity. Because of the growing activity of this nation's secondary mortgage market and its concurrent necessity for added protection, lenders generally require title insurance to guarantee the title search.

Finally, after approval of the borrower's credit, the collateral's value, and the title's marketability, the loan processor prepares the documents necessary for closing. With the delivery of the funds to the seller and the recording of the necessary papers transferring title, the loan transaction is completed.

DEFINE THESE KEY TERMS

assets	liabilities
automated underwriting	loan processing procedures
automated valuation	loan underwriting
computer valuation	net worth
credit scoring	paperless mortgage
FICO score	quality of income
financial statement	quantity of income

CHAPTER 10 PRACTICE EXAM

1. Qualifying the buyer has to do with income and assets. Qualifying the property has to do with the:

   a. income, credit report, and appraisal.
   b. appraisal, survey, and title report.
   c. appraisal, title report, and credit report.
   d. survey, title report, and income.

2. A lender, interested in evaluating an applicant's willingness to pay, reviews:

   a. income.
   b. assets.
   c. the credit report.
   d. all of the above.

3. A federally-related loan transaction is covered under RESPA guidelines if it:

   a. involves a 100-acre tract of land.
   b. involves an apartment complex of 60 units.
   c. involves a one-family to four-family home.
   d. All of the above

4. John has cash of $4,000, an automobile worth $8,000, and furniture worth $4,000. He owes $6,000 to the bank on the automobile, $2,500 on his Visa card, and $7,400 on a student loan. His income last year was $22,800. He wants to purchase a $58,000 home. What is John's net worth?

   a. $100
   b. $16,000
   c. $22,800
   d. $74,000

5. In question 4, what is John's ratio of assets to liabilities?

   a. 100-to-4
   b. 20-to-3
   c. 3-to-2
   d. 1-to-1

6. The cash surrender value of life insurance is listed as a(n):

   a. asset.
   b. liability.
   c. income item.
   d. expense item.

7. When Jim applies for a loan, he has more than enough income to qualify. His credit history also has been good. However, two late notices from creditors that have since been paid remain on the credit report. Under these circumstances, Jim's loan likely will be:

   a. denied.
   b. approved without further questions.
   c. approved after Jim explains the discrepancies.
   d. reduced to a maximum 80 percent loan-to-value ratio.

8. Joan earns $1,000 per week. Based on Fannie Mae's 28 percent housing expense ratio guidelines, what monthly payment would she qualify for?

    a. $1,213.33
    b. $1,120.00
    c. $1,000
    d. $867.33

9. Bonuses are acceptable as income on a loan application, provided that they:

    a. were actually collected.
    b. were a regular occurrence.
    c. exceeded $2,000 per year.
    d. totaled less than $2,000 per year.

10. A second job may be counted as a source of income on a loan application if it:

    a. pays more than $2,000 per year.
    b. is likely to continue.
    c. has been held for at least two years.
    d. is both b and c.

11. The guidelines for loan underwriting are tightly structured. The one facet that allows the most subjectivity on the part of the lender's evaluation is the:

    a. credit ability.
    b. amount of debt.
    c. asset valuation.
    d. income quantity.

12. The primary assurance to the lender if the borrower defaults on the loan, is the:

    a. borrower's income.
    b. borrower's assets.
    c. borrower's net worth.
    d. property value.

13. A title policy offering coverage over and above the standard coverage is which of the following types of policies?

    a. Mortgagor's
    b. Fannie Mae
    c. Owner's
    d. ALTA

14. When money is scarce, lender standards tend to be more:

    a. lenient.
    b. strict.
    c. relaxed in the evaluation of credit.
    d. relaxed in the evaluation of income.

15. When a loan officer evaluates a credit report, the most important part of the report is the:

    a. employment history.
    b. payment history.
    c. public records section.
    d. applicant's current address.

16. The employment verification is a check on the applicant's:

    a. length of employment.
    b. salary.
    c. prognosis for continued employment.
    d. All of the above

17. The components that together make a title report complete are a physical inspection of the collateral property, a search of the public records, and a(n):

    a. abstract of title.
    b. title insurance policy.
    c. satisfaction of previous mortgage document.
    d. survey of the property.

ACTION LIST

APPLY WHAT YOU'VE LEARNED!

The authors suggest the following actions to reinforce the material in *Section V–Financing Real Property:*

- Select a three-bedroom home that is currently for sale that you would like to own. Calculate the PITI payment, assuming you pay the listed price and make a 10 percent down payment. Use current interest rates.
- Find the Fannie Mae/Freddie Mae loan application included in this section. Fill it out as if you were the buyer of the three-bedroom home.
- Using a $100,000 mortgage amount with a 90 percent loan, calculate the PITI payment for the above property. Be conservative in your estimate.
- Based on the previous action, divide the PITI payment by the mortgage amount. This will give you the mortgage payment factor **including taxes, insurance, and PMI.** It will probably be just under 1 percent.
- Using the factor calculated above, quickly figure the payment for a $165,000 mortgage (1% × $165,000 = $1,650, quote just under that and estimate $1,634). Now quickly estimate the PITI payments for the following mortgage amounts:

Loan Amount	Payment (PITI)
$89,000	$_____
$138,000	$_____
$198,500	$_____
$212,000	$_____

- Write out a menu of interest rates and discount points to see how the rates can be bought down. Assume that the going rate with no points is 8 percent, and that each point paid reduces the rate by one-eighth of 1 percent.

Points	Interest Rate
0	8 %
1	___%
2	___%
3	___%
4	___%

SECTION VI

CLOSING THE TRANSACTION

The closing is often the most troublesome part of a real estate sale. This section is intended to give licensees information on how to reduce stress levels at closings and to make the licensees more efficient and professional. Many problems result from communication failures between cooperating brokers and sales associates. This section explores methods of tracking the necessary components of the closing to ensure that everything is completed on time.

Sales associates are expected to oversee closings and to review the closing documents, particularly the closing statement. A sales associate must understand each part of the statement. This section provides hands-on practice for the sales associate in preparing closing statements.

LEARNING OBJECTIVES

Upon completion of this chapter, *you should be able to:*

1. name the steps that a sales associate must follow after writing a contract to ensure a timely closing;
2. list the things that a sales associate should do after a closing;
3. describe the reasons why a licensee might not want to personally order repairs on a property and what steps can be taken to protect the sales associate from liability;
4. list at least four objectives of a preclosing inspection; and
5. describe the reasons a real estate sales associate should provide closing documents to the buyer and seller at least one day in advance of a closing.

CHAPTER 11

THE CLOSING PROCESS

CLOSING REAL ESTATE TRANSACTIONS

Once the real estate contract has been signed, the licensee's work has just begun. The parties to a transaction expect their sales associate personally to monitor and coordinate all the details of their closing. While the licensee may believe he has "passed the torch" to the next group of professionals (lenders and closing agents), the buyer and seller continue to look to their sales associate to coordinate all the details of the transaction. A smooth transition from contract to closing enhances the reputations of the firm and the sales associate. This section is intended to help licensees better understand the process and to follow the "road to closing" successfully. (See Figure 11.1.)

Some important steps a licensee may take to reduce problems with title closing include:

- disclosing everything to all parties that will affect their decisions before the buyer and seller sign the contract. Surprises after a contract is signed almost certainly will result in one party wanting to get out of the contract.
- writing the contract carefully and properly explaining it to the parties.
- recommending that buyers and sellers select lenders and title closing agents who are organized professionals able to meet deadlines.
- telling the loan officer and closing agent what the licensee expects in the way of communication and performance.
- preparation of a Property Sale Information Sheet similar to the one in the Forms-To-Go Appendix.
- giving the closing agent a copy of the prior title insurance policy, if possible.
- providing a complete legal description of the property to the closing agent.
- asking a lender and title agent to communicate by e-mail, speeding the process while also giving written documentation of the transaction.
- using a checklist of duties, such as the Closing Progress Chart, provided in the Forms-To-Go Appendix.
- asking the closing agent to close the buyer's and seller's sides separately to reduce confusion during the closing.

The Sales Information Sheet

To organize the work program, the sales associate needs to complete the Property Sale Information Sheet. It provides necessary data about the sale, the cooperating agent, the lender, the title company, and more. This form should be clipped inside the closing file and referred to as necessary when servicing the sale.

FIGURE 11.1   THE ROAD TO CLOSING

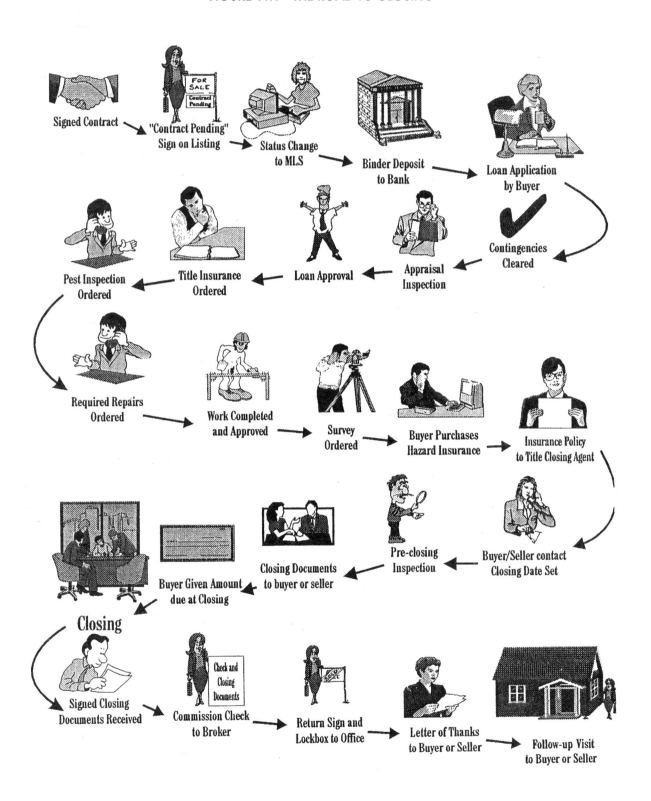

Establishing a Plan of Action.   One of the first steps after both buyer and seller sign the contract is to set up a plan for closing. This step is even more important if another sales associate is involved because miscommunication often delays closings and causes unnecessary problems. Organization and attention to detail are key to a successful closing.

THE CLOSING PROGRESS CHART

The Closing Progress Chart will help the licensee organize the details of the closing. If there is a cooperating licensee, the chart should be a joint effort so that licensees agree about which licensee will handle certain duties and when the tasks should be completed. Once agreement has been reached, each sales associate should place a copy of the chart in the closing file. Additionally, each date scheduled should be transferred to the sales associate's appointment book. As each task is completed, the sales associate should place a check mark in the appropriate row. An "X" in the chart indicates that comments have been made on the back of the form. A discussion of each item follows.

Preclosing Duties

"Sold" or "Sale Pending" Sign on Listing.   Placing a "sold" or "sale pending" sign on the listed property is a function of the listing sales associate. Until recently, FREC rules prohibited placing a "sold" sign on property until the sale had been closed, but that rule was repealed, and licensees now have their choice of signs. Some sellers prefer a "sold" sign so that prospective buyers are no longer escorted through the property, while others do not want to discourage activity until at least after the buyer's loan approval.

Notice of "Under Contract" to MLS.   Most MLS services require that all offices be notified of a listed property's status. Failure to change the status to "under contract" can result in agents from other offices appearing at the property with customers or clients. This wastes both the sales associate's and the prospective buyers' time, and reflects poorly on the listing office.

Binder Deposited in Bank.   A sales associate must give the earnest money deposit to the broker no later than the end of the next business day. FREC rules require that the buyer's good-faith deposit be placed in a bank no later than three business days after receipt of the funds. The broker might deposit the funds immediately or wait until the seller accepts the contract (in no case, however, may the broker wait longer than three days). If a title closing agent will hold the deposit, the broker must deliver the deposit to the title closing agent within the same time frames allowed by FREC for depositing the funds in a brokerage account. The broker should get a receipt for the funds.

Additional Binder Received, if Required.   If the contract requires the buyer to put up additional funds as a good-faith deposit, it is the sales associate's responsibility to ensure that the funds are received and deposited on a timely basis. The buyer's failure to comply with contract requirements is a default. The seller must be notified and the seller's instructions followed.

Loan Application Made by Buyer.   The FAR/BAR contract requires the buyer to make application for the loan by a certain date. The buyer's failure to comply with contract terms is a default, and the seller must be notified.

Contingencies Cleared in Writing.   The sales associate must ensure that **contingencies** are satisfied as soon as possible. Some normal contingencies include a home inspection, a soil test, a roof inspection, and financing. If a problem arises with one of the contingencies, the sales associate should do everything within her power to correct the problem, and all parties should be made aware of the situation.

Appraisal.   The appraisal normally is ordered and paid for at the time of loan application. The sales associate wants to be certain that the appraiser selected by the financial institution has complete cooperation, particularly with respect to access to the property. Failure to provide access wastes the appraiser's time and may delay the closing.

Loan Approval.   The FAR/BAR contract requires a loan commitment within a certain number of days from the contract's effective date. The licensee must monitor the lender's progress and provide to the lender without delay any information or documents requested. The lender's failure to provide the commitment within the required time may allow the buyer or the seller to void the contract.

Title Insurance Ordered.   Many lenders permit the sales associate to select the title closing agent, provided the company is on the lender's approved list. The seller or buyer also may have a preference in making the decision, based on who will pay for the policy. Many title companies prefer that the agent deliver the contract and financing information even before loan approval is obtained so that the title search can begin. Often little time is available from loan approval to closing, and the companies like a head start. If that is the case, the licensee must verify that the title company agrees to take the risk of a failed closing and that it will not charge a fee if the sale does not close.

The licensee should give the title closing agent the following items when a title insurance order is placed:

- A signed and dated sales contract.
- A previous title insurance policy on the property, if available.
- Enough information about the sellers, buyers, property, and lender to process and close the transaction, including:
  a. the sellers' and buyers' marital status;
  b. a complete legal description, for example, lot, block, subdivision name, phase or unit, recording information, and county;
  c. street address including ZIP code;
  d. terms of any purchase-money mortgage the title company must prepare;
  e. closing date and information about whether all parties will attend; and
  f. information on commission to broker and commission splits between brokers.

Wood-Destroying Organisms Inspection Ordered.   As soon as possible after loan approval, the wood-destroying organisms (WDO) inspection should be ordered. When it is completed, copies of the report should be delivered to the buyer, lender and title closing agent. If treatment or repairs are required, agents working with the buyer and seller should communicate and agree on the details. A sample report that indicates infestation is shown in Figure 11.2. If a structural inspection is required, a licensed contractor should be engaged to report on and estimate repair costs. Normally, the lender requires that treatment and repairs be completed satisfactorily before closing, so parties should act without delay in having the work performed.

Required Repairs Ordered.   Many contracts require repairs other than those covered by termite damage. The appraisal could show the need for a new roof, or the buyer may have made the contract contingent on the seller replacing a swimming pool vinyl liner, for example. As soon as loan approval is obtained, the work should be ordered.

A note of caution to licensees.   A licensee sometimes orders major repair items without the seller's authorization to do so. A failed closing can have adverse financial consequences for the sales associate aside from the loss of commission. While a sales associate might facilitate some of the legwork required in getting estimates, he should

FIGURE 11.2 WOOD-DESTROYING ORGANISMS INSPECTION REPORT

Section 482.226, Florida Statutes

Licensee name ___Mickey's Pest Control___ License number ___4411___
Licensee address ___2102 Village Rd.___
Inspector ___Luke Gast___ Inspection date ___1/15/95___ Identification Card No. _____
Requested by ___Arthur Cody___
(name) (address)
Property inspected ___180 Bliss St.___
(address)
Specific structures inspected ___Residence___
Structures on property NOT inspected ___None___
Areas of structure(s) NOT inspected ___① Attic ② Wood on or below ground.___
Reason NOT inspecting _____

SCOPE OF INSPECTION

"Wood-destroying organism" means arthropod or plant life which damages and can reinfest seasoned wood in a structure, namely termites, powder-post beetles, old-house borers, and wood decaying fungi.

THIS REPORT IS MADE ON THE BASIS OF WHAT WAS VISIBLE AND ACCESSIBLE AT THE TIME OF THE INSPECTION and is not an opinion covering areas such as, but not necessarily limited to, those that are enclosed or inaccessible, areas concealed by wall coverings, floor coverings, furniture, equipment, stored articles, or any portion of the structure in which inspection would necessitate removing or defacing any part of the structure.

THIS IS NOT A STRUCTURAL DAMAGE REPORT. A wood-destroying organisms inspector is not ordinarily a construction or building trade expert and therefore is not expected to possess any special qualifications which would enable him to attest to the structural soundness of the property. IF VISIBLE DAMAGE OR OTHER EVIDENCE IS NOTED IN THIS REPORT (ITEM NUMBER (3) OF THIS REPORT), FURTHER INVESTIGATION BY QUALIFIED EXPERTS OF THE BUILDING TRADE SHOULD BE MADE TO DETERMINE THE STRUCTURAL SOUNDNESS OF THE PROPERTY.

THIS REPORT SHALL NOT BE CONSTRUED TO CONSTITUTE A GUARANTEE OF THE ABSENCE OF WOOD-DESTROYING ORGANISMS OR DAMAGE OR OTHER EVIDENCE UNLESS THIS REPORT SPECIFICALLY STATES HEREIN THE EXTENT OF SUCH GUARANTEE.

REPORT OF FINDINGS

(1) Visible evidence of wood-destroying organisms observed: No ☐ Yes ☒ ___Sub-termites ② Carpenter bees___
(Common name of organisms)

Locations: ___① under back deck in debris___

(2) Live wood-destroying organisms observed: No ☐ Yes ☒ ___Siding left and right of sliding glass door. Trim left___
(Common name of organisms)

Locations: ___and right of sliding glass door. 2x4 under sliding glass door___

(3) Visible damage observed: No ☒ Yes ☐ _____
(Common Name of organisms causing damage)

Locations: _____

(4) Visible evidence of previous treatment was observed: No ☒ Yes ☐

Explain: _____

(5) This company has treated the structure(s) at time of inspection: No ☒ Yes ☐ . If YES: A copy of the contract is attached.

_____ _____
(Organisms treated) (Pesticide used)

(6) This company has treated the structure(s) No ☒ Yes ☐ . If YES: Date of treatment: _____

_____ _____
(Common name of organisms) (Common name of pesticide)

(7) A notice of this inspection ☒ and/or treatment ☐ has been affixed to the structure(s)

_____
(Location of notice(s))

COMMENTS: _____
_____
_____

Neither the licensee nor the inspector has any financial interest in the property inspected or is associated in any way in the transaction with any party to the transaction other than for inspection purposes.

SEND REPORT TO PERSON WHO REQUESTED THIS INSPECTION AND TO:
_____
_____

Signature of Licensee or agent ___Luke Gast___ Date ___1/15/01___

FIGURE 11.3   AREA OF TROPICAL STORMS AND HURRICANES THAT CAUSE INSURANCE DELAYS

Forms

1 not order the work without written approval. The seller or buyer, as appropriate, should
2 contract for the work. This also makes the contractor responsible to the appropriate
3 party if any warranty work is necessary later. A sample form is in the Forms-To-Go
4 Appendix.

5 **Required Repairs Completed and Approved.**   When the work has been com-
6 pleted, the appropriate party should inspect the work to be sure that it has been done
7 properly. A licensee who takes on this responsibility may be held responsible if defi-
8 ciencies are discovered later.

9 **Survey Ordered.**   The lender or the title closing agent often orders the survey after
10 loan approval. A licensee who orders the survey without written approval may be liable
11 for the fee if the sale does not close. In case of survey problems such as encroachments,
12 the sales associate must act quickly to help clear up the problems.

13 **Buyer Purchases Hazard Insurance.**   The buyer should purchase the insurance
14 policy as soon as possible in the transaction, especially during Florida's hurricane
15 season. If a hurricane or tropical storm develops anywhere within the "box," as shown
16 in Figure 11.3, insurance companies stop writing insurance until the danger has passed.
17 If there are several hurricanes at sea, the delay could be for a week or more, and could
18 cause significant delay of a closing.

19 **Buyer/Seller Contacted for Closing Appointment.**   Soon after loan approval,
20 the title closing agent should be able to set a closing date and time. The sales associate
21 should coordinate with the buyer and seller in setting a time agreeable to all. All parties
22 should be notified of the date, time, and place of the closing as far in advance as pos-
23 sible.

24 **Preclosing Inspection.**   The buyer should make a **preclosing walk-through inspec-
25 tion.** The inspection is to ensure that:

26 • the property is ready for occupancy;
27 • personal property the seller is required to leave remains on the property;
28 • all required repairs and maintenance have been completed; and

1   • the property has been maintained in the condition as it existed at the time of
2   contract, ordinary wear and tear excepted.

3   The sales associate should not conduct such an inspection because of the liability in-
4   volved. When the inspection has been completed to the buyer's satisfaction, the sales
5   associate should ask the buyer to sign a preclosing clearance form such as the one shown

Forms

6   in the Forms-To-Go Appendix.

Closing Papers Reviewed with the Buyer and Seller One Day before Closing.

8   A sales associate should attempt to work with lenders and title closing agents who under-
9   stand the sales associate's need to provide the highest level of service to his customers.
10 Those lenders and title agents work diligently to provide all documents for the closing
11 one day in advance. The sales associate must monitor all phases of the closing, including
12 a careful review of the closing statements. Many buyers and sellers attend their closings—
13 at which large sums of money are disbursed—without having seen any of the documents
14 beforehand. They are expected to sign all documents after a cursory review at the closing
15 table. This is not fair to the participants and can lead to embarrassment to their sales
16 associates. Often a sales associate gets little more than a dollar amount that the buyer
17 must bring in the form of a certified or cashier's check. This is simply not satisfactory to
18 the sales associate who wishes to handle the closing professionally.

19   Upon receiving the documents, the sales associate should arrange an appointment to
20 visit the buyer or seller and deliver copies of all documents that the person will sign. The
21 sales associate should review the closing statement carefully to ensure that all items are
22 correct and should explain each item to the buyer or seller at the appointment. The
23 sales associate working with the buyer should compare the closing statement to the
24 lender's good-faith estimate. The sales associate working with the seller should compare
25 the figures to those given to the seller on the approximate Seller's Net Proceeds Form.
26 The closing will go more quickly and pleasantly for the person who has reviewed all
27 documents the evening before.

28   Closing statements are covered in detail in the next chapter.

Buyer Given Figure for Certified Check for Closing.   This should be provided

30 to the buyer as soon as possible to allow him time to get a **certified check** for the proper
31 amount from his bank.

Binder Check Prepared to Take to Closing.   At least one day before closing, the

33 sales associate should get the binder check from the broker and clip it to the file folder
34 that will be taken to the closing. Also included in the folder will be the contract and
35 other related material, as well as copies of the inspection reports.

AT THE CLOSING TABLE

37 The closing normally includes the buyers, the sellers, and their respective licensees, if
38 any. Sometimes attorneys of the parties attend, and occasionally a lender's represen-
39 tative. The title closing agent conducts the closing.

Separate Closings

41 Many licensees prefer that the buyers and sellers close separately, rather than at the
42 same closing table. This reduces confusion and allows the title closing agent to focus
43 completely on each party as they close. It is appropriate if the parties have had a dispute
44 over some issue. Sometimes separate closings occur when there is a mail-away closing
45 package, or when the buyers or sellers live out of town.

Closing Disputes

The title closer is not an advocate for any of the parties. It is the title closer's job to close the transaction based on the contract and the lender's closing instructions. If there is a problem between the buyer and the lender, the closer gets them together on the phone. If there is a dispute between the buyer and the seller, the closer will often step out of the room until the dispute is settled and the parties are ready to close.

Truth-in-Lending Disclosure

If there is an institutional loan, the first document to be reviewed must be the Truth-in-Lending (TIL) disclosure. If the buyers were informed by the lender or the licensee when they applied for the loan that the annual percentage rate (APR) shown on the TIL would be higher than the interest rate on their note, this will not be a problem. If they were not informed, however, some buyers, upon seeing a 7.875 percent APR on the disclosure form say, "Wait a minute! I was supposed to be getting a 7½ percent loan!" The closer must explain that origination fees and discount points are included to calculate the APR, but the loan rate remains the same.

Loan Application

Usually the lender will want a typed loan application signed at closing, verifying the information given to the lender at the time of application.

Note

The closer presents the note for the buyer's signature. The note shows the principal balance, number of payments, and the dates and the amount of the payments. The amount will be for principal and interest only. The first payment date will normally be the first day of the second month after closing. The note is not witnessed or notarized. If a signature appears on the face of the note along with the borrower's signature, that person becomes a cosigner on the note.

Mortgage

The mortgage is the security for the note. It is the document that may require that the borrower pay $\frac{1}{12}$ of the ad valorem taxes, hazard insurance and mortgage insurance premium along with the principal and interest. It requires that payments be made on time, that taxes be paid, and that the property be covered by insurance and describes prepayment options. It also probably states that a transfer of the property will make the loan due immediately.

The Warranty Deed

The warranty deed is the most common deed, with the seller guaranteeing to the buyer that he has good title, without material defects or encumbrances, and will stand by the guarantee forever. Special attention should be given to the names and legal description and to any items in the "subject to" section, such as restrictive covenants and mortgages.

Other Documents

Some of the other documents the buyer may sign include an anticoercion statement that says the lender did not require the buyer to choose a certain insurance company. The lender and title insurance company will want a compliance agreement that the parties will do anything necessary to give the lender an acceptable loan package, such as signing new documents, if required. If the loan is above 80 percent of a home's value,

the lender will want an affidavit that the buyer will occupy the property. The seller will
be required to sign an affidavit that (1) she owns the property, (2) she has the right to
convey it and (3) it is not encumbered by any lien or right to a lien, such as a construction lien.

Disbursements at Closing

Everyone expects to be paid at closing. This is not always possible, and licensees should
be prepared to explain the problem to the sellers. Perhaps an example using a broker's
trust account is easier to understand. Many real estate brokers have hundreds of thousands of dollars in their escrow accounts. A broker who disburses from the escrow
account before making a deposit into the account, even if the future deposit would be
in certified funds, is guilty of a serious violation, because the broker would be using
funds that belong to others.

Title insurance companies are faced with a similar problem. Some title insurance
companies agree to disburse the proceeds at closing if the certified checks will be deposited by the close of business that day. (A real estate broker may never do this.) Many
title insurance companies will not disburse if the closing takes place too late to make a
same-day deposit or if the lender is holding the loan proceeds check until the loan
package is delivered.

Warehousing

Some companies are hesitant to insure title until the "gap" of time between the time of
the title commitment and the time of recording is checked. Any documents filed against
the property during the gap period may affect the title. A lot depends on whether the
title insurance company has any reason to suspect problems.

After the closing, all deposits are made by the title company, and the deeds and mortgages are copied for the lender's package before they are taken for recording. The
closing package would be prepared for the lender, awaiting only the recording information. The person who records the documents should ensure that the check amounts are
correctly calculated, that the documents are put in the correct recording order (deed
first, then mortgages), and that the "return to" address is properly entered. When the
documents are recorded, the information, including the date and time and the book
and page number, is entered into the final title insurance policy and the package is sent
to the lender.

When the recorded instruments are returned, the closing agent will send the buyer
the original deed with recording information, a copy of the mortgage (the lender gets
the original), and the title insurance policy.

Signed Closing Papers Received by Sales Associate.   The sales associate should
be careful that the office file is fully documented. This includes any walk-through clearance papers the buyer signs for the seller and the closing statements all parties must sign.
If disbursement is made at closing, the commission check also is received at this time.

Postclosing Duties

Commission Check to Broker.   Upon returning to the office, the sales associate
should give the closing file as well as the commission check to the broker.

Sign and Lockbox Picked up from Property.   The listing sales associate should
ensure that the sign and lockbox are removed from the property and returned to the
office. Often he does this just before closing. Many sales associates remove the lockbox
for security reasons immediately after the contract has been signed.

1 **Letter of Thanks to Buyer or Seller.**   The letter, which should include both the sales
2 associate's and the broker's signatures, will be appreciated by the customer, will foster
3 goodwill, and likely will result in future business. Many companies request that the
4 buyer or seller complete a questionnaire about the level of service provided in the trans-
5 action.

6 **Follow-up Visit to Buyer or Seller.**   The sales associate who calls on the customer
7 after the closing demonstrates the careful attention needed to ensure that all details of
8 the transaction have been completed satisfactorily.

9 **Notice of Closed Sale to MLS.**   Most MLS systems require that listing status
10 changes be submitted as soon as possible. This provides brokers and sales associates in
11 the area with the most current information about listing availability and comparable
12 sales information.

SUMMARY

The sales associate's job really is just beginning when the parties sign the contract. Much
work must be completed to ensure a successful closing. One of the first steps is to plan
for each required task and enter it on a timeline. Each sales associate and broker
involved should agree about what must be done, by whom, and when it must be done.

Licensees must complete tasks like attaching a "contract pending" sign, notifying the
MLS, making the binder deposit, helping the buyer with the loan application and taking
care of inspections and repairs. A major part of the sales associate's duties is reviewing
the closing documents with the buyer or seller before closing.

DEFINE THESE KEY TERMS

certified check   preclosing walk-through inspection
contingency   "sale pending" sign

CHAPTER 11 PRACTICE EXAM

1. When sales associate Shannon sells her listing, she places a "sold" sign on the property. In this situation, which of the following statements is correct?

   a. Shannon must put up a "contract pending" sign, by FREC rule.
   b. Shannon must put up a "sale pending" sign, by FREC rule.
   c. Shannon may not place the "sold" sign without the seller's approval.
   d. Shannon may place the "sold" sign without the seller's approval.

2. The preclosing walk-through inspection is to ensure that:

   a. personal property the seller is required to leave remains on the property.
   b. all required repairs have been completed.
   c. the property has been maintained in the condition as it existed at the time of the contract, ordinary wear and tear excepted.
   d. all of the above

3. Sales associate Brian listed the Brantly's home at 3217 Woodbrook Circle. Based on information the seller provided, Brian disclosed to the buyers, Jack and Helen Maxwell, that the pool liner was defective and needed replacement. The contract was written reflecting that the Maxwells would be responsible for the charges related to replacing the liner. After the sellers signed the contract, Brian contacted Pretty Pools Company and authorized the liner replacement at a cost of $1,750. The Maxwells were subsequently turned down for the required financing, and the sale did not close. Based on this information, Brian:

   a. is not liable to the pool company; the Maxwells are.
   b. is not liable to the pool company; the Brantlys are.
   c. might have to pay for the pool liner.
   d. may sue the Maxwells, because they defaulted.

4. The best way for a buyer to determine that the seller has moved out and the property is ready for occupancy is by:

   a. requiring a home inspection company to provide a report.
   b. reading a termite report.
   c. doing a preclosing walk-through inspection.
   d. asking the sales associate.

5. To expedite a closing, catch errors made in documents, and make the buyers feel more comfortable about documents they must sign, what should a sales associate do?

   a. Obtain a hold-harmless agreement from the title insurance company
   b. Limit the time for actually doing the closing
   c. Get the papers to the parties at least 24 hours in advance of the closing
   d. Have the lender sign an estoppel letter

6. When the title closing agent gave the buyer the Truth-in-Lending Disclosure showing the annual percentage rate was 7.62 percent, the buyer declared, "Wait, I was told the interest rate was going to be 7.25 percent. This is wrong!" What is the most likely reason for the discrepancy?

    a. Rates have gone up since the date of application.
    b. The lender is trying to make extra money, believing the borrower won't remember the original interest quote.
    c. While the note rate is probably 7.25 percent, the inclusion of lender fees such as discount points and origination fees has increased the annual percentage rate.
    d. The Federal Reserve Board mandates a ⅜ percent interest differential in mortgage loans.

7. A sales associate must give the earnest money deposit to the broker no later than the end of:

    a. the next business day.
    b. the second business day.
    c. the third business day.
    d. 15 days.

8. Contract contingencies should be cleared:

    a. within five days before closing.
    b. within five days after loan approval.
    c. within three days of contract.
    d. as soon as possible after the contract has been signed.

9. Jill listed a property for Sam, and he accepted an offer made on the property. The contract called for an additional binder to be deposited within ten days of the contract date. If the buyer failed to meet the contract's terms concerning the additional binder, the:

    a. contract is null and void.
    b. contract works like an option contract; the only remedy is the loss of the original binder.
    c. buyer has defaulted.
    d. contract should not have been accepted as written.

10. What would NOT be given to the title closing agent when the order is given?

    a. A signed and dated listing agreement.
    b. The seller's and buyer's marital status.
    c. A complete legal description.
    d. Property address, including zip code.

LEARNING OBJECTIVES

Upon completion of this chapter, *you should be able to:*

1. list the proration items paid in advance and those paid in arrears;
2. prorate rent, interest, and property taxes;
3. describe the methods lenders use to set up an escrow account for prepaid taxes, hazard insurance, and private mortgage insurance;
4. calculate prepaid interest for a new loan;
5. calculate the expenses on the closing statement; and
6. prepare and review a HUD-1 Settlement Statement.

CHAPTER 12

THE CLOSING STATEMENT

1   Buyers and sellers expect their sales associates to coordinate and monitor every step of
2   the closing process. The last step is the closing itself. A sales associate must be familiar
3   with the documents that will be presented to the parties at the closing table. One of the
4   most important documents, the HUD-1 Settlement Statement, relates to the financial
5   side of the transaction.

6   A closing statement is, in effect, the purchase and sales agreement reduced to
7   numbers. The sales associate must understand each number in the statement and be
8   able to explain it clearly to the buyer or seller. The material in this chapter is designed
9   to make the process easier.

PRORATIONS AND PREPAYMENTS

11   In every closing, property income and expenses should be prorated between the buyer
12   and the seller. Usually, the 365-day method is used for prorations of annual expenses.
13   The annual cost is divided by 365 days to get a daily rate. That rate is then multiplied
14   by the number of days involved to get the amount due. When calculating prorations
15   using the 30-day month method, the annual cost is divided by 12 months, then by
16   30 days to get the daily rate. That rate is then multiplied by the number of days in-
17   volved to get the amount due.

18   Proration calculations should be based on the last day of seller ownership. The day
19   of closing is charged to the buyer, although it is possible that, by negotiation or custom
20   in an area, the day of closing would be charged to the seller.

21   The most common items prorated on a closing statement are rents and security
22   deposits collected in advance by the seller, property taxes, and interest on assumed
23   mortgages. While insurance can be prorated between the parties, it is not recom-
24   mended and usually is not allowed by the insurer. The buyer should purchase a new
25   policy, and the seller should cancel the existing policy.

26   **Prorating Rent.**   If the property is an income property, the seller should pay the buyer
27   any rent that applies for the period after closing. The first step is to see the problem
28   graphically by drawing a timeline. The rental period is shown, as is the day of closing.
29   The following example illustrates the various aspects of prorations and prepayments. In
30   the example, if the seller had collected the rent in advance, the seller would owe the
31   buyer 16 days of the rent.

1 Closing date—April 15
2 Rent collected for April—$450

3   Beginning   **Closing date**   End
4   4/1   4/15   4/30

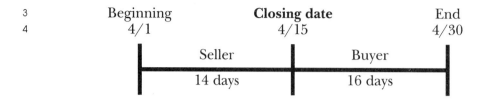

         Seller   Buyer
        14 days   16 days

5 Daily rate—$450 ÷ 30 days = $15
6 Proration—$15 × 16 days = $240

7 • Debit the seller, credit the buyer.

RENT PRORATION EXERCISE 12.1

Calculate the following rent prorations:

Closing Date	Rent Received	Debit	Credit	Amount
July 12	$760			$
November 12	900			$
January 6	425			$

---

8 **Prorating Property Taxes.**   Property taxes normally are paid in arrears by the buyer,
9 in which case they would be a debit to the seller and credit to the buyer. If the closing
10 occurs in November or December, it is possible that the seller has paid the tax bill
11 already, resulting in a credit to the seller and a debit to the buyer.

12 Closing date—April 15
13 Property taxes—$2,275

14   Beginning   **Closing date**   End
15   1/1   4/15   12/31

         Seller   Buyer
       104 days   261 days

16 Number of days from January 1 through April 15:

January	31
February	28
March	31
April	14
Total	**104**

17 Daily rate—$2,275 ÷ 365 days = $6.23288 per day
18 Proration—$6.23288 × 104 days = $648.22

19 • Debit the seller, credit the buyer.

PROPERTY TAX PRORATION EXERCISE 12.2

Do the following property tax prorations:

Closing Date	Taxes	Debit	Credit	Amount
September 12	$2,567.00			$
November 18	4,260.00 (Paid 11/3)			$
April 24	1,892.56			$

---

1 **Prorating Interest.** Interest is prorated between the parties when a loan is to be
2 assumed or when seller financing is involved. Interest usually is paid in arrears. For
3 example, when the mortgage payment is made on May 1, it pays the principal due on
4 May 1 and the interest for the month of April.

5 Closing date—April 15
6 Mortgage balance on April 1 is $67,125.
7 The interest rate is 8 percent.
8 Interest for April is $447.50 ($67,125 × .08 ÷ 12 months)

9 Daily rate—$447.50 ÷ 30 days = $14.91667 per day
10 Proration—$14.91667 × 14 days = $208.83

11 • Debit the seller, credit the buyer.

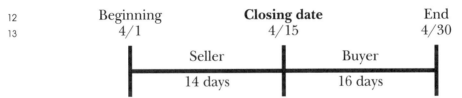

	Beginning 4/1	Closing date 4/15	End 4/30
	Seller	Buyer	
	14 days	16 days	

INTEREST PRORATION EXERCISE 12.3

Do the following interest prorations on these assumed mortgages:

Closing	Mortgage Bal.	Int. Rate	Debit	Credit	Amount
10/12	$137,500.00	9%			$
11/18	246,532.50	8.5			$
4/24	91,892.56	10			$

---

14   With seller financing, the first payment usually is set up so that the buyer pays on the
15 first of the month following closing. Because that first payment includes the interest
16 due for the entire month previous, the buyer should receive a credit for the portion of
17 that month owned by the seller. The proration would be handled the same way.

18 **Prepayments for New Loan.** When an institutional lender makes a new loan, and
19 if the loan-to-value ratio is greater than 80 percent, the lender likely will require that an
20 escrow fund for taxes, hazard insurance, and mortgage insurance be maintained. The
21 borrower must deposit a sum into a lender's escrow account so that adequate funds will
22 be available to make the payments when required. The amount of the specific charges
23 varies with the time of the year at which the loan is closed. Once the escrow account

1 is established, a monthly amount for taxes, insurance, and any required mortgage insur-
2 ance is added to the monthly principal and interest payment. These funds, placed in a
3 trust account, become the responsibility of the financial institution, which must pay
4 such items when they are due. Some of those prepaid items are discussed below.

5 **Prepaid Taxes.**   The lender normally collects taxes by adding the months of the year
6 through closing, then adding two or three more months. For instance, if the closing is in
7 April, the lender takes four months plus another three. In effect, the proration credit
8 for three-plus months that the buyer receives from the seller offsets the effect of the
9 lender's charge.

10 Closing date—April 15
11 Taxes—estimated at $2,275 for the year
12 Monthly taxes—$2,275 ÷ 12 = $189.58

13   The first payment will be on June 1. The lender will escrow seven months, so that
14 when November comes the lender will have sufficient funds to pay the property tax bill.

15   Monthly taxes $189.58 × 7 months = $1,327.06

16 • Debit the buyer for the amount of prepaid taxes.

17   The buyer has received a proration credit of $648.22 from the seller, so the net from
18 the buyer to set up the account is $678.84.

PREPAID TAX CALCULATION EXERCISE 12.4

Assuming the lender wants three extra months, calculate the amount of taxes to be
escrowed:

Closing Date	Taxes for the Year	Prepaid Amount
January 18	$2,400.00	$
July 3	4,842.30	$
September 30	1,453.89	$

---

19 **Prepaid Insurance.**   The buyer must pay the first year's policy in advance, plus
20 two months. For example, if the insurance policy is $1,160, the monthly payment is
21 $96.67 ($1,160 ÷ 12). Often the statement shows 14 months prepayment. In other cases,
22 if the buyer has paid the premium outside closing (POC), the statement shows only
23 two months.

24 • Debit the buyer for one year plus two months prepaid insurance.

PREPAID INSURANCE CALCULATION EXERCISE 12.5

Calculate the amount of insurance to be escrowed in the following example. The
lender wants it paid in advance plus two extra months.

Closing Date	Insurance for the Year	Prepaid Amount
January 18	$2,400	$
July 3	900	$
September 30	2,200 (POC)	$

Prepaid Interest. Because the first payment covers the interest for the previous month, interest is collected at closing for the days remaining in the closing month. There are two methods of calculating the daily rate of interest. One is to divide the annual interest by 12 months, then get a daily figure by dividing the actual number of days in the month into the monthly figure. This method is used for assumed loans. The other method (365-day method) divides the annual interest by 365 days to get the daily rate (most title closing agents and lenders use this method). This book uses the 365-day method.

Closing date—April 15
First payment on the mortgage—June 1

The first payment covers May interest. Interest must be collected on the day of closing from April 15 through April 30 (16 days).

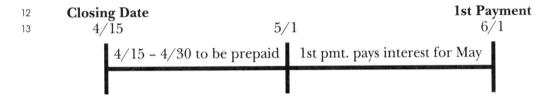

Closing Date		**1st Payment**
4/15	5/1	6/1
4/15 – 4/30 to be prepaid	1st pmt. pays interest for May	

$112,500 × .09 = $10,125 per year
$10,125 per year ÷ 365 days per year = $27.73973 per day
$27.73973 per day × 16 days = $443.84

• Debit the buyer $443.84 for prepaid interest.

PREPAID INTEREST CALCULATION EXERCISE 12.6

Calculate the interest prepayment for the new loans as follows:

Closing Date	Mortgage Loan Amount	Interest Rate	Prepaid Amount
September 12	$245,000	8.875%	$
January 17	92,500	8.75	$
December 29	127,000	9.0	$

Prepaid Mortgage Insurance. If mortgage insurance is required as part of an FHA or conventional mortgage loan, the borrower is charged for the coverage required.

The FHA requires homebuyers to pay two types of **mortgage insurance premiums (MIPs):**

1. Up-front MIP (UFMIP), which is a percentage of the mortgage amount
2. Annual premium, which is calculated on the unpaid principal balance

The VA does not charge for guaranteeing a loan; however, it imposes a **funding fee** based on the mortgage amount. This funding fee may be included as part of the amount borrowed or paid in one lump sum at closing. A lender also may require an amount in cash adequate to open an escrow account, plus 1 percent of the loan amount as a maximum placement fee. Under VA loan rules, the closing costs and placement fees cannot be included in the loan amount.

Conventional lenders require **private mortgage insurance (PMI)** when a loan-to-value (LTV) ratio is more than 80 percent. Premiums fall into two general categories.

In the first case, a single premium covers a lender's risk for a ten-year period. In the second case, a lender imposes a lower initial fee on the borrower and charges an insurance premium each year after that until the unpaid principal is reduced to a designated amount, normally 80 percent of appraised value. The first plan's one-time, single-premium charge or the second plan's lower initial cost is payable by the borrower at the time the loan closes. It should be noted that a PMI rate card must be used because of the different types of loans available and the different coverages required. The rates given in the following example do *not* apply to all loan types.

Assume a $112,500 (90 percent LTV) conventional mortgage has a first-year factor of .8 percent, with an annual factor in years two through ten of .34 percent. The up-front PMI would be $900 ($112,500 × .008), with a monthly PMI of $31.87 ($112,500 × .0034 ÷ 12).

Probably the best alternative is *not* to make a large up-front payment but instead make a higher monthly payment. In case of an early loan payoff, the premium is not refunded. The same PMI company has a factor of .54 percent for the monthly plan on this loan. The monthly payment using the alternate method would be $50.625 ($112,500 × .0054 ÷ 12).

- Debit the buyer $101.24 ($50.62 × 2 months) for prepaid mortgage insurance.

PREPAID PMI EXERCISE 12.7

Calculate the required prepayment for PMI on the following loans:

Mortgage Amount	Factor/Yr.	2 Months Prepaid
$350,000	.54%	$
125,000	.62	$
90,000	.73	$

DOCUMENTARY STAMP TAXES AND INTANGIBLE TAXES

Documentary stamp taxes are collected on the deed and the note. The seller normally pays for stamps on the deed, and the buyer pays for note stamps. The deed stamps are based on the sales price and are $.70 per $100 or fraction thereof. For example, if a property sells for $140,000, the documentary stamp taxes would be calculated as follows:

$$\$140,000 \div \$100 = 1,400 \text{ increments}$$
$$1,400 \times \$.70 = \$980$$

DEED STAMPS CALCULATION EXERCISE 12.8

Calculate the documentary stamp taxes on the deed for the following sales prices:

Sales Price	Doc. Stamp Amount
$325,000	$
127,415	$
93,000	$

Documentary stamp taxes on the new note are based on the amount of new or assumed mortgages and are $.35 per $100 or fraction thereof. No stamps are charged on notes taken subject to the mortgage because the buyer has not assumed any of the debt obligation. For example, if the note amount on a new mortgage is $112,500, the documentary stamp tax would be calculated on the note amount as follows:

$$\$112,500 \div \$100 = 1,125 \text{ increments}$$
$$1,125 \times \$.35 = \$393.75$$

Intangible tax on the new mortgage is calculated by multiplying the mortgage amount by .002. No tax is charged on existing recorded mortgages. The buyer normally pays this charge. For example, the intangible taxes on a new mortgage of $112,500 would be calculated as follows:

$$\$112,500 \times .002 = \$225. \text{ There is no rounding.}$$

NOTE STAMPS AND INTANGIBLE TAX CALCULATION EXERCISE 12.9

Calculate the documentary stamp taxes on the following note amounts:

Note Amount	Doc. Stamp Amount	Int. Tax Amount
$125,000	$	$
157,415	$	$
53,000	$	$

RESPA SETTLEMENT STATEMENT (HUD-1)

The HUD-1 settlement statement provides an itemized listing of the funds payable at closing. Closing agents must prepare the HUD-1 for the parties in a federally related mortgage loan. The HUD-1 is now used in nearly all residential closings, whether required or not. Each item in the statement is assigned a separate number within a standardized numbering system. The totals at the bottom of Page One of the HUD-1 statement show the seller's net proceeds and the amount due from the buyer at closing. A blank HUD-1 statement is included in the Forms-To-Go Appendix.

The HUD-1 statement has two pages. Page one shows the parties, the property description, the lender, the settlement agent, and a summary of the borrower's and seller's transactions. Page two (Section L) itemizes the settlement charges for each party, such as the broker's commission, loan closing costs, prepaid items, escrow account setup, title charges, and recording charges. The totals for each party on page two are transferred to the summary page on the front. When explaining the statement to the buyer and seller, the closing agents start at page two, then go to page one. A discussion of the lines on the statement follows.

Page Two

700. Sales/Broker's Commission. This section shows the total dollar amount of sales commission, usually paid by the seller. If more than one broker is involved, the split is shown on the next lines.

701–702. Division of Commission.   Cooperating brokers normally split commissions. This is only a disclosure item, and no actual charge is shown. The charge is listed on line 703.

703. Commission Paid at Settlement.   This is the total commission to be paid; it is charged to the buyer, the seller, or both.

800. Items Payable in Connection with Loan.   In this section, the fees the lender charges to process, approve, and make the mortgage loan are itemized.

801. Loan Origination.   The lender charges this fee for processing. It is often expressed as a percentage of the loan and varies among lenders and from locality to locality. Generally, the borrower pays the loan origination fee.

802. Loan Discount.   The loan discount is a one-time charge used to adjust the yield on the loan to what market conditions demand. It usually is expressed as points. Each point equals 1 percent of the mortgage amount. For example, if a lender charges two points on a $100,000 loan, this amounts to a fee of $2,000. On a 30-year loan, this fee increases the lender's yield by approximately one-fourth of 1 percent.

803. Appraisal Fee.   This fee is paid to a state-certified appraiser who prepares an estimate of value of the property that will be mortgaged. The borrower usually pays the appraisal fee, but either party may pay it as agreed in the sales contract.

804. Credit Report Fee.   This fee covers the cost of the credit report, which shows the lender the borrower's attitude and willingness to pay debt on time.

805. Lender's Inspection Fee.   This charge covers inspections, often of newly constructed housing, made by personnel of the lending institution or an outside inspector.

806. Mortgage Insurance Application Fee.   This fee covers processing of the application for private mortgage insurance, which may be required on certain loans.

807. Assumption Fee.   The assumption fee is charged for processing when the buyer takes over the seller's mortgage obligations.

900. Items Required by Lender To Be Paid in Advance.   This section lists prepaid items such as interest, mortgage insurance premium, and hazard insurance premium at the time of settlement.

901. Interest.   Lenders usually require that borrowers pay at settlement the interest on the mortgage from the date of closing to the beginning of the period covered by the first monthly payment. For example, if a closing takes place on August 12, and the first regular monthly payment is due October 1, the lender collects enough for interest from August 12 through August 31. September's interest is included in the October 1 payment.

902. Mortgage Insurance Premium.   Mortgage insurance protects the lender from loss if the borrower defaults. The premium may cover a specific number of months, a year in advance or the total amount. This type of insurance should not be confused with mortgage life, credit life, or disability insurance designed to pay off a mortgage in case of the borrower's disability or death.

903. Hazard Insurance Premium.   This prepayment is for insurance protection against loss due to fire, windstorm, and natural hazards. Lenders usually require payment of the first year's premium at closing.

904. Flood Insurance Premium.   If the property is located within a flood hazard area identified by Federal Emergency Management Agency (FEMA), the borrower may be required to carry flood insurance. The first year's premium must be paid in advance.

1000. Reserves Deposited with Lenders.   Lenders normally require **reserves** if the loan-to-value ratio is more than 80 percent. Reserves are escrow accounts the lender holds to ensure future payment for such recurring costs as real estate taxes, mortgage insurance, and hazard insurance. An initial amount for each of these items is collected to start the reserve account. Then part of each monthly payment is added to the reserve account.

1001. Hazard Insurance.   The lender determines how much money must be placed in the reserve to pay the next insurance premium when due. Normally, two months' premiums are collected.

1002. Mortgage Insurance.   The lender may require that part of the total annual premium be placed in the reserve account at settlement. Normally, two months' premiums are collected.

1003–1004. City/County Property Taxes.   The lender may require a regular monthly payment to the reserve account for property taxes. The lender pays the taxes in November, so a full year's taxes should be available in October. The lender collects an amount each month equal to one-twelfth of the estimated taxes.

1005. Annual Assessments.   This reserve item covers assessments that may be imposed by subdivisions or municipalities for special improvements (such as sidewalks, sewers, or paving) or fees (such as homeowners' association fees).

1009. Aggregate Analysis Adjustment.   This adjustment ensures that the lender has set up enough, but not too much, in reserves.

1100. Title Charges.   Title charges may cover a variety of services the closing agent performs.

1101. Settlement or Closing Fee.   This fee is paid to the closing agent, normally by the person who has agreed to pay for title insurance.

1102–1104. Abstract of Title Search, Title Examination, Title Insurance Binder.   These charges cover the costs of the search and examination of the public records to learn whether the seller can convey clear title to the property.

1105. Document Preparation.   This document fee covers preparation of final legal papers, such as a mortgage, deed of trust, note, or deed.

1106. Notary Fee.   If the notary charges for affixing her name and seal to various documents authenticating the parties' execution of these documents, the fee is shown here.

1107. Attorney's Fees.   The buyer and seller are advised to retain attorneys to check the various documents and to represent them at all stages of the transaction, including closing. If this service is not required and is paid for outside closing, the person conducting settlement is not obligated to record the fee on the settlement form.

1108. Title Insurance.   The total cost of the owner's and lender's title insurance is shown here. The borrower may pay all, a part, or none of this cost, depending on the terms of the sales contract or local custom.

1109. Lender's Title Insurance.   A one-time premium may be charged at closing for a lender's title policy that protects the lender against loss due to problems or defects concerning the title. The insurance usually is written for the amount of the mortgage loan and covers losses due to defects or problems not identified by title search and examination.

1110. Owner's Title Insurance.   This charge protects the buyer against losses due to title defects.

1200. Government Recording and Transfer Charges.   The seller usually pays the documentary stamp taxes on the deed. The borrower usually pays the recording fees for the new deed and mortgage (line 1201) and the documentary stamp and intangible taxes on the note and mortgage.

1300. Additional Settlement Charges.

1301. Survey.   Usually, the borrower pays the surveyor's fee, but it is sometimes paid by the seller, as shown in the contract.

1302. Pest and Other Inspections.   This fee covers wood-destroying organisms inspections. Fees for other inspections, such as for structural soundness, are entered on line 1303.

1400. Total Settlement Charges.   All the fees in the borrower's column entitled "Paid from Borrower's Funds at Settlement" are totaled here and transferred to line 103 of Section J, "Settlement charges to borrower," in the "Summary of Borrower's Transaction" on page one of the HUD-1 settlement statement. All the settlement fees the seller pays are transferred to line 502 of Section K, "Summary of Seller's Transaction," on page 1 of the HUD-1.

Page One

Section J summarizes the borrower's transaction.

100. Gross Amount Due from Borrower.

101. Contract Sales Price.   This ultimate closing cost is taken directly from the sales contract.

102. Personal Property.   The total price of items of personal property being sold to the buyer is entered on this line.

103. Settlement Charges to Borrower.   This total closing cost is carried forward from Page Two.

107. County Taxes.   This line is used only if the seller paid the annual taxes before closing.

108. Assessments.   This line is used if a seller prepaid a county or homeowners' association assessment.

120. Gross Amounts Due from Borrower.   This is a subtotal of the above items.

200. Amounts Paid by or in Behalf of Borrower.

201. Deposit or Earnest Money.   The buyer gets a credit for the binder deposit given at the time the contract was signed.

202. Principal Amount of New Loan.   The buyer is credited with the loan amount, which the lender gives to the closing agent.

203. Existing Loan(s) Taken Subject To.   If the buyer assumes or buys subject to a mortgage, the current principal balance is entered on this line.

211. County Taxes.   The amount due from the borrower is reduced by the amount of the seller's share of annual ad valorem taxes.

212. Assessments.   This line is used for amounts due to the buyer for assessments the seller has not paid.

220. Total Paid by/for Borrower.   This is the subtotal of lines 200 through 218.

300. Cash at Settlement to/from Borrower.   This section summarizes the transaction.

301. Gross Amount Due from Borrower (line 120).

302. Less Amounts Paid by/for Borrower (line 220).

303. Cash ❏ from ❏ to Borrower.   This is the grand total of the borrower's transaction.

   Section K summarizes the seller's transaction. Lines 400 through 420 are the seller's credits, which increase the amount due to the seller; lines 500 through 520 reduce the amount due to the seller; and lines 600 through 602 show the check due to the seller at closing.

400. Gross Amount Due to Seller.

401. Contract Sales Price.   The sum is taken directly from the sales contract.

402. Personal Property.   The total price of items of personal property being sold to the buyer is entered on this line.

407. County Taxes.   This line would be used only in the case where the seller had paid the annual taxes before closing.

408. Assessments.   This line would be used if a seller had prepaid a county or homeowner's association assessment.

420. Gross Amount Due to Seller.   This is a subtotal of the above items.

500. Reductions in Amount Due to Seller.

501. Excess Deposit.   If the buyer pays the earnest money deposit directly to the seller, not to the broker or title closing agent, it is shown on this line.

502. Settlement Charges to Seller.   This is the seller's total closing costs carried forward from page two.

503. Existing Loan(s) Taken Subject To.   If the buyer assumes or buys subject to a mortgage, the current principal balance is entered on this line.

504–505. Payoff of Mortgage Loan.   This is the balance due on the seller's mortgage that the closing agent must pay off.

511. County Taxes.   The amount due from the borrower is reduced by the amount of the seller's share of annual ad valorem taxes.

512. Assessments.   This line is used for amounts due to the buyer for assessments the seller has not paid.

520. Total Reductions in Amount Due Seller.   This is the subtotal of lines 500 through 519.

600. Cash at Settlement to/from Seller.   This section summarizes the transaction.

601. Gross Amount Due to Seller (Line 420).

602. Less Reductions in Amount Due Seller (Line 520).

603. Cash ❑ to ❑ from Seller.   This is the grand total of the seller's transaction.

CLOSING STATEMENT EXAMPLE

Anita Wilson purchases a home from Wendy Stratton. Closing date is April 15, with the day of closing charged to the buyer. The price of the property is $125,000, and Anita is financing the purchase with a new 7.5 percent loan for 90 percent of the purchase price. She gives the broker a $5,000 binder check. The seller will pay off the existing first mortgage. The payoff amount, including interest, is $74,298.60. The seller has agreed to give the buyer a $2,000 allowance for new carpeting. The lender has approved the allowance. Annual property tax, estimated at $1,750, is the only item to be prorated.

The lender requires that a hazard insurance policy be purchased and the premium paid for one year ($545). An escrow account is collected at closing for three months of taxes, two months of hazard insurance, and two months of private mortgage insurance. The first payment on the mortgage is due on June 1.

The buyer paid for the appraisal ($300) at the time of loan application. Other expenses to be entered on each line item are discussed below.

The seller pays a commission of 7 percent, an attorney's fee of $225, documentary stamp taxes on the deed, and other items as discussed below.

Based on the following information, complete the blank HUD-1 statement in the Forms-To-Go Appendix. Start on page two with the buyer's side.

Page Two

PAID FROM BORROWER'S FUNDS AT SETTLEMENT

ITEMS PAYABLE IN CONNECTION WITH LOAN

801	Origination fee—1% of the loan amount	?
	(Loan amount times the percentage: $112,500 × .01 = $?)	
802	Loan discount—1 point	?
	(Loan amount times points: $112,500 × .01 = $?)	
803	Appraisal fee POC* 300.00 buyer	
804	Credit report fee	55.00
807	Tax service fee	59.00

808	Underwriting fee	100.00
809	Document preparation fee	75.00
810	Courier fee	13.00

*POC on the statement means "paid outside closing."

ITEMS REQUIRED BY LENDER TO BE PAID IN ADVANCE

| 901 | Interest from 4/15/ to 4/30/ | ? |

(Loan amount times interest rate divided by 365 times number of days remaining in month of closing, counting the day of closing:

$112,500 × .075 = $8,437.48
$8,437.48 ÷ 365 = $23.1164 per day:

$23.1164 × 16 days = $369.86)

| 903 | Hazard insurance premium for 12 months to State Farm | 545.00 |

RESERVES DEPOSITED WITH LENDER

| 1001 | Hazard insurance 2 mo. @ $?/mo | ? |

(Annual insurance divided by 12 months times number of months required by lender: $545.00 ÷ 12 = $? per month; $? × 2 months = $?)

| 1002 | Mortgage Insurance 2 months @ $?/mo. | ? |

($300 per yr. divided by 12 months = $? per month:

$? per month × 2 months = $50.00)

| 1004 | County property taxes ($1,750) 7 mo. @ $?/mo. | 1020.81 |

(Annual taxes divided by 12 months times number of month's reserve required by lender: $1,750.00 ÷ 12 = $? per month; $? × 7 months = $?)

TITLE CHARGES

1101	Settlement or closing fee to Jones & Smith law firm	100.00
1102	Abstract or title search to Jones & Smith law firm	100.00
1103	Title examination to Jones & Smith law firm	75.00
1107	Attorney's fee to Jones & Smith law firm	300.00
1108	Title insurance to Jones & Smith law firm	725.00
1111	Florida 9 endorsement to Jones & Smith law firm	72.50
1112	ALTA 8.1 endorsement to Jones & Smith law firm	25.00

GOVERNMENT RECORDING AND TRANSFER CHARGES

| 1201 | Recording fee—deed $6.00; mortgage $60.00 | 66.00 |
| 1202 | Documentary stamp tax on note | ? |

		(Loan amount divided by 100, round up to next whole number, multiply by $.35)	
	1203	Intangible taxes on mortgage	225.00
		(Loan amount times .002)	
	1301	Survey to All Corners Surveyor	250.00
	1302	Pest inspection to All Pest Control	50.00
	1400	Total settlement charges (total, then enter on page one, line 103)	?

PAID FROM SELLER'S FUNDS AT SETTLEMENT

700, 701	Commission paid to Tillie Evans Realty	?
703	**(Sales price times commission rate of 7%)**	
1107	Attorney's fees to Jones & Smith law firm	?
1113	Courier fee for mortgage payoff to Jones & Smith law firm	20.00
1201	Satisfaction (release) recording fee	6.00
1202	Documentary stamp tax on deed	875.00
	(Sales price divided by 100, rounded to next higher whole number, times $.70)	
1400	Total settlement charges (total, then enter on page one, line 502)	?

Page One

SUMMARY OF BORROWER'S TRANSACTION

101	Purchase price	125,000.00
103	Settlement charges to borrower (from page two, line 1400)	?
120	Gross amount due from borrower	?
201	Deposit or earnest money	5,000.00
202	Principal amount of new loans	112,500.00
	(Price times loan-to-value ratio: $125,000 × .90 = $112,500)	
207	Carpet allowance to buyer	2,000.00
211, 511	Property taxes for the year (paid in arrears)—$1,750	?
	(Annual taxes divided by 365 days times number of seller days)	
220	TOTAL PAID BY/FOR BORROWER **(Sum of lines 201–219)**	?
301	GROSS AMOUNT DUE FROM BORROWER (Line 120)	?
302	LESS AMOUNTS PAID BY/FOR BORROWER (Line 220)	?
303	CASH FROM BORROWER	?

SUMMARY OF SELLER'S TRANSACTION

401	Purchase price	125,000.00
420	GROSS AMOUNT DUE TO SELLER	?

1	502	Settlement charges to seller (from page 2, line 1400)	?
2	504	Payoff of existing first mortgage (given)	74,298.60
3	507	Carpet allowance to buyer	2,000.00
4	511	Property taxes for the year (paid in arrears)–$1,750	?
5		**(See calculation for line 211)**	
6		TOTAL REDUCTION AMOUNT DUE SELLER **(Sum of lines 501-519)**	?
7	601	GROSS AMOUNT DUE TO SELLER (Line 420)	?
8	602	LESS REDUCTION AMOUNT DUE SELLER (Line 520)	?
9	603	CASH TO SELLER	?

DEFINE THESE KEY TERMS

documentary stamp taxes
funding fee
intangible tax

mortgage insurance premium (MIP)
private mortgage insurance (PMI)
reserves

FIGURE 12.1   HUD-1 SETTLEMENT STATEMENT

A. Settlement Statement

U.S. Department of Housing and Urban Development

OMB No. 2502-0265

B. Type of Loan

1. ☐FHA 2. ☐FmHA 3. ☐Conv. Unins.	6. File Number	7. Loan Number	8. Mortgage Insurance Case Number
4. ☐VA 5. ☒Conv. Ins.	EDODONNELL8LBM	12345678	

C. Note: This form is furnished to give you a statement of actual settlement costs. Amounts paid to and by the settlement agent are shown. Items marked "(p.o.c.)" were paid outside the closing; they are shown here for information purposes and are not included in the totals. WARNING: It is a crime to knowingly make false statements to the United States on this or any other similar form. Penalties upon conviction can include a fine and imprisonment. For details see: Title 18 U. S. Code Section 1001 and Section 1010.

D. NAME OF BORROWER: KYLE BYERS and KARI BYERS
ADDRESS: 1460 LIME DRIVE, TALLAHASSEE, FLORIDA 32301

E. NAME OF SELLER: JOHN SELLARS and SUSAN SELLARS
ADDRESS:

F. NAME OF LENDER: FIRST SOUTH BANK, A FEDERAL SAVINGS BANK
ADDRESS: 3020 HARTLEY ROAD, SUITE 330, JACKSONVILLE, FLORIDA 32257

G. PROPERTY ADDRESS: 1460 LIME DRIVE, TALLAHASSEE, FLORIDA 32301
LOT 8, ORANGE PARK SUBDIVISION

H. SETTLEMENT AGENT: SMITH, JONES AND ADAMS, P.A.
PLACE OF SETTLEMENT: 7889 Thomasville Rd, Tallahassee, Fl. 32308

I. SETTLEMENT DATE: 05/15/98

J. SUMMARY OF BORROWER'S TRANSACTION:		K. SUMMARY OF SELLER'S TRANSACTION:	
100. GROSS AMOUNT DUE FROM BORROWER		**400. GROSS AMOUNT DUE TO SELLER:**	
101. Contract sales price	120,000.00	401. Contract sales price	120,000.00
102. Personal Property		402. Personal Property	
103. Settlement charges to borrower (line 1400)	7,313.76	403.	
104.		404.	
105.		405.	
Adjustments for items paid by seller in advance		*Adjustments for items paid by seller in advance*	
106. City/town taxes		406. City/town taxes	
107. County taxes 05/15/98 to 12/31/98	1,329.04	407. County taxes 05/15/98 to 12/31/98	1,329.04
108. Assessments		408. Assessments	
109.		409.	
110.		410.	
111.		411.	
112.		412.	
120. GROSS AMOUNT DUE FROM BORROWER	128,642.80	**420. GROSS AMOUNT DUE TO SELLER:**	121,329.04
200. AMOUNTS PAID BY OR ON BEHALF OF BORROWER		**500. REDUCTIONS IN AMOUNT DUE TO SELLER**	
201. Deposit or earnest money	4,000.00	501. Excess Deposit (see instructions)	
202. Principal Amount of new loans	108,000.00	502. Settlement charges to seller (line 1400)	9,315.50
203. Existing loan(s) taken subject to		503. Existing loan(s) taken subject to	
204.		504. Payoff of First Mortgage Loan	45,452.65
		BARNETT BANK	
205.		505. Payoff of Second Mortgage Loan	
206.		506.	
207.		507.	
208.		508.	
209.		509.	
Adjustments for items unpaid by seller		*Adjustments for items unpaid by seller*	
210. City/town taxes		510. City/town taxes	
211. County taxes		511. County taxes	
212. Assessments		512. Assessments	
213.		513.	
214.		514.	
215.		515.	
216.		516.	
217.		517.	
218.		518.	
219.		519.	
220. TOTAL PAID BY/FOR BORROWER	112,000.00	**520. TOTAL REDUCTION AMOUNT DUE SELLER**	54,768.15
300. CASH AT SETTLEMENT FROM OR TO BORROWER		**600. CASH AT SETTLEMENT TO OR FROM SELLER**	
301. Gross amount due from borrower (line 120)	128,642.80	601. Gross amount due to seller (line 420)	121,329.04
302. Less amounts paid by/for borrower (line 220)	112,000.00	602. Less reduction amount due seller (line 520)	54,768.15
303. CASH FROM BORROWER	16,642.80	**603. CASH TO SELLER**	66,560.89

FIGURE 12.1   HUD-1 SETTLEMENT STATEMENT (Continued)

U.S. DEPARTMENT OF HOUSING AND URBAN DEVELOPMENT
SETTLEMENT STATEMENT

File Number: EDODONNELL8
PAGE 2

L. SETTLEMENT CHARGES		PAID FROM BORROWER'S FUNDS AT SETTLEMENT	PAID FROM SELLER'S FUNDS AT SETTLEMENT
700. **TOTAL SALES/BROKER'S COMMISSION** based on price $ 120,000.00 @ 7.000 = 8,400.00			
Division of commission (line 700) as follows:			
701. $ 8,400.00 to BIG BEND REALTY			
702. $ to			
703. Commission paid at Settlement			8,400.00
800. **ITEMS PAYABLE IN CONNECTION WITH LOAN**			
801. Loan Origination Fee 1.000 % FIRST SOUTH BANK		1,200.00	
802. Loan Discount 1.000 % FIRST SOUTH BANK		1,200.00	
803. Appraisal Fee to TALLAHASSEE APPRAISAL COMPANY (P.O.C.) 300.00 Buyer			
804. Credit Report to CREDCO		55.00	
805. Lender's Inspection Fee			
806. Mortgage Application Fee			
807. Assumption Fee			
808. AMORITIZATION SCHEDULE to FIRST SOUTH BANK		25.00	
809.			
810.			
811.			
900. **ITEMS REQUIRED BY LENDER TO BE PAID IN ADVANCE**			
901. Interest From 05/15/98 to 06/01/98 @$ 22.1917 /day 17 Days		377.26	
902. Mortgage Insurance Premium for to			
903. Hazard Insurance Premium for 12 to STATE FARM		840.00	
904.			
905.			
1000. **RESERVES DEPOSITED WITH LENDER FOR**			
1001. Hazard Insurance 2 mo. @ $ 70.00 /mo		140.00	
1002. Mortgage Insurance 2 mo. @ $ 45.00 /mo		90.00	
1003. City Property Taxes mo. @ $ /mo			
1004. County Property Taxes 8 mo. @ $ 175.00 /mo		1,400.00	
1005. Annual Assessments mo. @ $ /mo			
1009. Aggregate Analysis Adjustment			
1100. **TITLE CHARGES**			
1101. Settlement or closing fee to SMITH, JONES AND ADAMS, P.A.		100.00	
1102. Abstract or title search to SMITH, JONES AND ADAMS, P.A.		100.00	
1103. Title examination to SMITH, JONES AND ADAMS, P.A.		75.00	
1104. Title insurance binder			
1105. Document Preparation			
1106. Notary Fees			
1107. Attorney's fees			
(includes above items No:)			
1108. Title Insurance to SMITH, JONES AND ADAMS, P.A.		700.00	
(includes above items No:)			
1109. Lender's Coverage $ 108,000.00 - 25.00			
1110. Owner's Coverage $ 120,000.00 - 675.00			
1111. FL 9 to SMITH, JONES AND ADAMS, P.A.		70.00	
1112. ALTA 8.1 to SMITH, JONES AND ADAMS, P.A.		25.00	
1113. COURIER FEE to SMITH, JONES AND ADAMS, P.A.		20.00	20.00
1200. **GOVERNMENT RECORDING AND TRANSFER CHARGES**			
1201. Recording Fees Deed $ 10.50 ; Mortgage $ 42.00 ; Release $ 10.50		52.50	10.50
1202. City/County tax/stamps Deed $ 840.00 ; Mortgage $ 378.00		378.00	840.00
1203. State Tax/stamps Deed $; Mortgage $ 216.00		216.00	
1204.			
1205.			
1300. **ADDITIONAL SETTLEMENT CHARGES**			
1301. Survey to ALL CORNERS SURVEYOR		250.00	
1302. Pest Inspection to NO REQUIRED PER CONTRACT AND LENDER			
1303. MISC REPAIRS to FIX IT ALL, INC.			245.00
1304.			
1305.			
1306.			
1307.			
1308.			
1400. **TOTAL SETTLEMENT CHARGES** (enter on lines 103, Section J and 502, Section K)		7,313.76	9,515.50

CHAPTER 12 PRACTICE EXAM

As a sales associate with Big Bend Realty, you recently listed and sold a home. The closing is scheduled for May 15. You have just received the HUD-1 settlement statement from Jillian Winkle at Smith, Jones and Adams, P.A. (see Figure 12.1). Using the listing agreement, the sales contract, and the good-faith estimate of settlement costs given by the lender at the time of application, you begin the review. You intend to visit both the sellers and the buyers to go over the closing information before the closing.

As you review the sales contract, you trace certain items to the HUD-1 statement and check off each as you do so. Names of the buyers (Kyle and Kari Byers) are as listed on the contract. The sellers' legal names, John and Susan Sellars, were taken from their deed when you first took the listing. They are shown correctly. The property address on the contract is 1462 Lime Drive. The contract sales price is $120,000. The Byers gave a $4,000 earnest money deposit. The new mortgage is for $108,000 at 7.5 percent interest.

You know the lender charges 1 percent for discount points and 1 percent for the loan origination fee. The Byers paid an appraisal fee of $300 at the time of loan application (POC). The good-faith estimate of settlement costs given by the lender at the time of application shows a $55 credit report fee, $25 for an amortization schedule, $1,070 for title insurance, and $20 for courier services. The estimate also shows recording fees of $10.50 for the deed and $42 for the mortgage, the documentary stamp tax on the note, and intangible tax on the mortgage. The survey was estimated at $250.

The Byers must prepay interest on the loan from May 15 through May 31 because the first payment on the new mortgage is not due until July 1. The Byers also need to buy a one-year hazard insurance policy. They have chosen a State Farm policy with an annual premium of $840.

The lender requires that an escrow account be set up with two months' advance hazard insurance deposit, two months' advance mortgage insurance ($540 annual premium), and eight months' advance property taxes based on an estimate of $2,100 annually.

The payoff letter for the existing first mortgage requires $45,452.65, including interest. The Sellars have agreed to pay for recording the satisfaction of mortgage, and the $10.50 charge looks about right. The $20 courier fee to send the payoff check also seems OK. The Sellars have agreed to pay a bill from Fix It All, Inc., for $245 for miscellaneous repairs to the property. You calculate the documentary stamps on the deed and check your figures against the closing agent's figures. The Sellars' hazard insurance policy will be canceled. You review the listing agreement to see that the commission is 7 percent. It is not to be split with any cooperating brokerage firm.

If you find any errors on the statement, circle them and replace them with the correct figures. Totals on the statement may need to be changed. Once you have completed the review, answer the following questions:

1. Did you find any incorrect entries in the Byers' expenses in Section L?
   a. No
   b. Yes, the title insurance charges are wrong.
   c. Yes, the discount points and origination fees are incorrect.
   d. Yes, the documentary stamp taxes on the note are wrong.

2. Did you find any incorrect entries in the Sellars' expenses in Section L?

    a. No

    b. Yes, the commission is calculated incorrectly.

    c. Yes, the documentary stamp taxes on the deed are calculated incorrectly.

    d. Yes, the total at the bottom of the page is wrong.

3. Did you find any problems with the general information section of the statement?

    a. No

    b. Yes, the Sellars' names are spelled incorrectly.

    c. Yes, the Byers' names are incorrectly spelled.

    d. Yes, the address is incorrect.

4. Is the tax proration correct?

    a. Yes

    b. No, line 107 should be $1,329.04 and line 407 should show the difference, $770.96.

    c. No, the amount shown on lines 107 and 407 should be calculated from 1/1/98 through 5/15/98 ($770.96).

    d. No, the amount shown on line 107 should be calculated from 1/1/98 through 5/15/98 ($770.96) and be transferred to lines 211 and 511.

5. Did you find any other problems on the statement?

    I. No, I did not.

    II. Yes, many totals for the Byers and the Sellars are wrong.

    III. Yes, the expenses on line 502 are wrong.

    a. I

    b. II

    c. II and III

    d. III

Closing Statement Problem

Dawn Futch has purchased a duplex in Bradenton for $156,250 from William and Shannon Simmons. Dawn gave the broker a $10,000 binder check. The closing date is August 15, and the day of closing is charged to the buyer. Use the 365-day method for prorations. The new first mortgage loan is $125,000 for 30 years at an interest rate of 9 percent. Principal and interest total $1,005.78. The first payment is due on October 1. The sellers have a first mortgage with a payoff amount of $94,367.80 through August 15. The lender charges a one-point origination fee and a half-point discount. Taxes for the year are estimated to be $3,245. The lender requires an additional three months to be held in escrow. The seller has collected the $600 rent due from each side on the first of the month. The new insurance premium is $1,700, and the lender wants the policy paid in advance plus two months in escrow. Private mortgage insurance (PMI) is required on the loan. The annual PMI factor for paying on a monthly payment is .73 percent annually, and the lender requires two months in advance. The buyer will pay $900 for title insurance, $38.75 for recording the deed and mortgage, $180 for the survey, $300 for the appraisal (POC), and $75 in other loan costs. The seller will pay the broker's 7 percent commission, as well as documentary stamps on the deed. The seller's other miscellaneous expenses total $75. Complete the HUD-1 settlement statement in the Appendix Forms-To-Go, then answer the following questions:

6. How will the rent be handled on the closing statement?

    a. Debit seller, credit buyer $658.06
    b. Debit buyer, credit seller $658.06
    c. Debit seller, credit buyer $619.35
    d. Debit seller, credit buyer $329.03

7. How will taxes be handled on the closing statement?

    a. Debit seller, credit buyer $2,009.23
    b. Debit buyer, credit seller $2,009.23
    c. Debit seller, credit buyer $1,235.77
    d. Debit buyer, credit seller $1,235.77

8. If the lender requires a three-month cushion on the tax escrow, how much will be collected from Dawn at closing for prepaid taxes?

    a. $811.25
    b. $2,163.33
    c. $2,974.58
    d. $3,245.00

9. What is the amount of interest prepayment that will be required?

    a. $413.53
    b. $523.97
    c. $937.50
    d. $1,461.47

10. What is the prepayment required for insurance?

    a. $283.33
    b. $1,700.00
    c. $1,841.67
    d. $1,983.33

11. What is the prepayment for PMI?

    a. $76.04
    b. $152.08
    c. $912.50
    d. $1,825.00

12. What will Dawn's total monthly payments be?

    a. $1,005.78
    b. $1,417.87
    c. $1,493.91
    d. $1,495.00

13. What are the documentary stamp taxes on the deed?

    a. $437.50
    b. $547.05
    c. $1,093.75
    d. $1,094.10

14. What will Dawn pay in total for the documentary stamp tax on the note and the intangible taxes on the mortgage?

    a. $250.00
    b. $437.50
    c. $687.50
    d. $797.05

15. What will appear on Dawn's closing statement for origination fee and discount?

    a. $1,250.00
    b. $1,562.50
    c. $1,875.00
    d. $2,343.75

16. What is the amount of the brokerage fee to be paid by the Simmonses?

    a. $7,500.00
    b. $8,750.00
    c. $9,375.00
    d. $10,937.50

17. What is the amount due from Dawn in certified funds at closing?

    a. $27,972.92
    b. $39,458.12
    c. $47,108.31
    d. $109,141.69

18. What is the amount due to Mr. and Mrs. Simmons at closing?

    a. $27,972.92
    b. $47,108.31
    c. $109,141.69
    d. $165,640.21

19. What are the total debits on the Simmons' statement?

    a. $109,141.69
    b. $137,667.29
    c. $156.250.00
    d. $165,640.21

20. What is the grand total on Dawn Futch's statement?

    a. $109,141.69
    b. $137,667.29
    c. $156,250.00
    d. $165,640.21

ACTION LIST

APPLY WHAT YOU'VE LEARNED!

The authors suggest the following actions to reinforce the material in *Section VI–Closing the Transaction:*

- Ask a title closing officer to show you the entire closing process (usually the end of the month is a bad time for this). Ask to watch a title search to see what the title company looks for. Examine the closing officer's checklist for closings. See what an instruction package from the lender looks like. Watch as the closing officer enters information into the computer for the HUD-1 settlement statement.

- With your broker's approval, randomly select five file folders for closed transactions. Thoroughly review each file, and list every document in the file. Do some files seem more complete to you? Are there any that you believe are *not* complete? Note what documents you want in all *your* closed files.

- Start again at the first file folder. Inspect the contract, the good-faith buyer's estimate of settlement costs and payment amounts, and the HUD-1 form. Check to see whether the amount the sales associate estimated for the seller or buyer matched the actual amount on the HUD-1 form. Can you account for any material differences?

- Next, check every entry on the HUD-1 form for accuracy.

- If you have not yet had a closing, arrange with an associate to attend one of his closings. Remember, you should listen, not talk, at the closing.

SECTION VII

COMMERCIAL AND RESIDENTIAL INVESTMENT PROPERTY

Chapter 13.   Analyzing Real Estate Investments

Chapter 14.   Professional Property Management

A substantial part of our country's wealth has been generated by investments in real property. Chapter 13 shows some of the advantages and disadvantages of investing in income property, the pros and cons of different property types, and methods of evaluating the investment.

Because of the substantial amounts of capital required for real estate investments, most owners want the property managed professionally. Chapter 14 describes the relationship between owners and property managers, the employment of resident managers, and the marketing and maintenance of property.

CHAPTER 13—ANALYZING REAL ESTATE INVESTMENTS

LEARNING OBJECTIVES

Upon completion of this chapter, *you should be able to:*

1. list the three basic categories of changes and trends in the economy;
2. itemize the four phases of an economic cycle;
3. name four advantages of investing in real estate;
4. list at least four disadvantages of investing in real estate;
5. itemize five types of investment properties;
6. enter the major headings of an income property financial statement;
7. list and calculate four important income property ratios; and
8. itemize the three basic types of income tax deductions for investment property.

CHAPTER 13

ANALYZING REAL ESTATE INVESTMENTS

1 Investment in real estate has produced a substantial portion of the wealth of our
2 country and its citizens. Real estate licensees should be prepared to assist buyers and
3 sellers of investment real estate. Consumers expect their sales associates to have a basic
4 understanding of the fundamentals of investment. An investment study includes anal-
5 ysis of the national and local economies, specifically as they relate to real estate.

6 Investing in real estate has advantages and disadvantages, and each investor must
7 determine if an investment is suitable. This chapter focuses primarily on investment
8 opportunities in smaller income properties such as raw land and residential, office, and
9 commercial properties.

10 Basic investment ratios help buyers analyze properties to help reduce risk. Several
11 methods presented may help an investor use these ratios to determine the appropriate
12 amount to offer for a property.

13 While federal income taxes are an important consideration when weighing an invest-
14 ment in real estate, the property's operating economics are more important.

15 THE GENERAL BUSINESS ECONOMY

16 Timing is important in real estate investment. A good property purchased at the wrong
17 time may result in substantial losses to the investor. Many investors also understand that
18 a rapidly appreciating real estate market can make even marginal properties show
19 acceptable returns. Before deciding which type of real estate is right for him, the
20 investor must try to understand the current economic trends.

21 Trends in the business economy may either originate from or result in changes in the
22 real estate market. The condition of one directly affects the condition of the other.
23 Changes and trends in the general economy fall into three basic categories: seasonal
24 variations, **cyclic fluctuations,** and random changes.

25 Seasonal Variations

26 Changes that recur at regular intervals at least once a year are called **seasonal varia-**
27 **tions.** Such changes arise from both nature and custom. In the northern United States,
28 for example, construction stops during the winter months; this seasonal change affects
29 both the general economy and the real estate economy. Customs such as the nine-
30 month school year have a seasonal effect on residential sales. Each year, retired persons
31 fleeing cold weather swell Florida's winter population.

FIGURE 13.1 GENERAL BUSINESS CYCLE

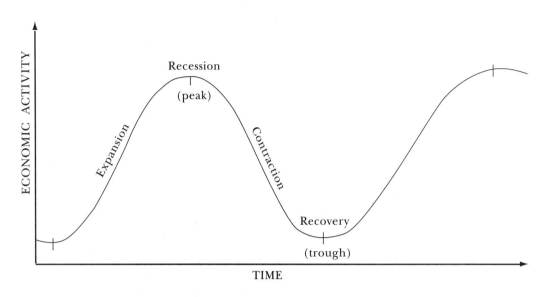

SOURCE: Adapted by permission from Robert C. Kyle and Floyd M. Baird, *Property Management*, 6th edition (Dearborn™ Real Estate Education, 1999, 25).

Cyclic Fluctuations

Business cycles usually are defined as wavelike movements of increasing and decreasing economic prosperity. A **cycle** consists of four phases: expansion, recession, contraction, and recovery. (See Figure 13.1.)

Production increases during **expansion** periods. High employment levels, wages, and consumer purchasing power increase demand for goods and services. Prices rise because of greater demand, and credit is easy, making more money available for purchasing.

Recession normally is defined as two successive quarterly declines in the **gross domestic product (GDP).** GDP is the sum total of goods and services produced by the United States. The four major components of GDP are: consumption, investment, government purchases, and net exports.

Contraction begins immediately after recession. Confidence in the economy is shaken, and consumers reduce spending in anticipation of lower earnings. Slower sales cause reduced production, worker layoffs, and unemployment. Prices are reduced to clear out inventories of unsold goods.

Recovery, defined as two successive quarterly increases in the GDP, begins when consumers, lured by lower prices, venture back into the market. As business activity increases, confidence begins to return. Slowly, production facilities gear up to meet the new consumer demand, capital begins to flow back into business enterprises, and additional employees are hired. Finally, as the gradual use in employment generates more spendable income and an increasing demand for more goods, the business cycle again enters the expansion phase.

Although business cycles technically consist of the four phases defined above, most discussions deal simply with expansion and contraction, measuring expansion from trough to peak and contraction from peak to trough. Business cycles are recurrent, but not periodic; that is, they vary in duration and timing. Economists have observed that a complete cycle in the general economy may vary from 1 to 12 years in length.

Specific Cycles. **Specific cycles** are wavelike movements similar to business cycles. They occur in specific sectors of the general economy, such as the real estate economy, and in individual sectors of the real estate economy, such as housing starts and real estate sales. Specific cycles do not always coincide with cycles of the general business economy, as the business cycle actually is a weighted average of all specific cycles.

Regardless of the state of the national economy, certain areas boom in recessions and stagnate in prosperous times because local demand runs counter to current broad economic trends. Northeastern manufacturing towns were in trouble in the early 1980s, for example, while an influx of new residents and industries into central Florida kept that area building and growing.

DISCUSSION EXERCISE 13.1

Review the following "Selected Headlines" from a major business newspaper. Then break into small groups to discuss what the likely effects will be on real estate investment properties, real estate brokerage firms, and other investment possibilities. Discuss which businesses will suffer in the near term and which will prosper.

SELECTED HEADLINES IN AN INFLATIONARY ECONOMY

"Strong business expansion under way, may lead to inflationary pressures on the economy"

"General Motors reports quarterly sales increase of 22%. Stock price surges!"

"Current rate of inflation is _____ %, expected to be at 9% within six months"

"Retail sales increase dramatically, paced by JC Penney, Wal-Mart, and The Limited"

"Federal Reserve Board raises discount rate ½%. Economists foresee higher interest rates soon"

"Travel industry sees bumpy road ahead if oil prices increase substantially"

"Mortgage interest rates anticipated to rise to the 12–14% rate in six months," warns CitiBank economist Wilton Smathers

"Inflation will continue for at least two years, according to Congressional Budget Office"

"Oil prices in the $35 price range within two months, according to industry sources"

Random Changes

Random changes are irregular fluctuations of the economy that may be caused by legislative and judicial decisions or by strikes, revolutions, wars, fires, storms, floods, and other catastrophes. These changes, impossible to predict or analyze, may affect one or more sectors of the aggregate economy. They may influence all industries in an area or one industry nationwide. Real estate activity, especially construction, is very vulnerable to labor strikes, political changes, and natural disasters. One example of a random

1   change in regard to real estate is a zoning ordinance change allowing undeveloped land
2   to be used for industrial purposes that would stimulate construction activity locally.
3   Government policy changes and changes in tax laws also can cause random changes in
4   real estate activity on a nationwide scale. Investors must be aware of what is
5   happening on both the national and local levels and have contingency plans to cope
6   with events as they occur.

THE REAL ESTATE ECONOMY

8   The real estate economy is an important component of the general business economy,
9   subject to the same four types of fluctuations. Specific cycles are the most pronounced
10 and important trends that appear in the real estate sector. They can be observed in
11 all phases of real estate: land development, building, sales, finance, investment, rental,
12 and redevelopment.

13   Most sectors of the real estate economy are subject to both long and short cycles.
14 Long-term cycles last from 15 to 22 years, and short-term cycles take about 3 years.

15   A controlling factor in the building cycle is the availability of money and credit in the
16 mortgage and construction markets. In general, when the economy is strong and prices
17 are rising, the Federal Reserve tightens the money supply to control inflation. The
18 resulting higher interest rates make real estate investment less attractive because
19 builders must either pass the higher costs on to consumers or accept lower profits.
20 Either situation slows the rate of construction. Conversely, interest rates decline during
21 a recession, making construction of new projects more feasible.

22   An extremely important indicator for forecasting the economy is the monthly report
23 of Housing Starts, published by the Census Department between the 16th to the 20th
24 of each month. Housing starts, along with auto sales, are the first to rise in an economic
25 recovery and the first to drop in a recession. Not only does new housing have a direct
26 effect on the market but housing-related purchases such as furniture and appliances
27 also fuel a rebounding economy.

28   Building permit data are released with the housing starts report. Because permits are
29 secured about a month ahead of construction starts, reviewing the increase or decrease
30 in building permits gives a pretty good idea of what housing starts will do next month.

31   Once investors have satisfied themselves that the general economic situation is sound,
32 it may be time to review the advantages and disadvantages of investment in real estate.

REAL ESTATE INVESTMENT ANALYSIS

34 Most of the wealthy people in this country amassed their great fortunes from real estate
35 investments. The most significant asset of most families is the equity in their homes.
36 Real estate may not be the right investment for everyone, however. Advantages and dis-
37 advantages exist, and should be evaluated by each individual.

Advantages of Investing in Real Estate

39 The advantages of investing in real estate include high leverage, good return, shelter
40 from federal income taxes, and personal control of the asset.

41 **Leverage.** **Leverage** is the use of other people's money to increase the investor's
42 return. Few other investments offer the high leverage real estate does. Stocks and bonds
43 typically require at least a 50 percent down payment; mutual funds want 100 percent

1 invested. Yet real estate investments can be made with 25 percent down payments and
2 less, in many cases. The following example of the benefits of leverage shows how impor-
3 tant it can be.

PRACTICE EXERCISE—LEVERAGE

Jack Gormley is considering the purchase of a duplex in an attractive neighborhood. He has reviewed the rental records for the previous four years that the property manager provided. The property's net income has increased about 4 percent
annually. Property values have increased at about the same rate. The property
value is $100,000, with a $20,000 down payment. Based on the new financing, Jack
anticipates before-tax cash flows of about $1,500 per year. He wants to compare
this investment with a mutual fund that has averaged a 10 percent return over the
previous five years. Assuming a holding period of five years and an annual property appreciation of 4 percent, how does the simple arithmetic look?

Property value at a 4% annual compound rate	$121,665
Less mortgage balance at year five	73,800
Equals increase in equity	$ 47,865
Plus $1,500 per year for five years	7,500
Equals total cash from investment	$ 55,365

The final figure averages $11,073 for each year. Divided by the original invest-
ment of $20,000, the average annual return is about 55 percent. The return
from annual cash flows was only 7.5 percent ($1,500 ÷ $20,000); and the balance
came from the increase in equity.

This type of analysis would be more accurate using the discounted cash flow approach, but the mutual fund returns would come in about the same pattern, making the comparison valid. Because of leverage, Jack's clear choice is the real estate.

---

4 **Good Returns.**   Many careful and astute investors achieve excellent returns, often
5 exceeding 20 percent.

6 **Income Tax Shelter.**   Most investment opportunities such as savings accounts, bonds,
7 stocks, and mutual funds require that the investor pay taxes on all current income (div-
8 idends). Real estate investments often provide tax-deferred cash flows, primarily
9 because of cost recovery deductions (depreciation). This allows the investor to avoid
10 paying taxes on the cash flows until she sells the property.

11   Exchanging and installment basis reporting are other ways to defer paying taxes.
12 They will be discussed later in this section.

13 **More Personal Control.**   Many investors are uncomfortable with the notion of
14 entrusting their assets to other persons or companies with little or no control over the
15 use of those assets. The purchase of real estate gives an investor much more control over
16 the investment's operation and management. This is true even if the investor employs
17 a property manager, as the manager is under the investor's control.

Disadvantages of Investing in Real Estate

19 Disadvantages of investing in real estate include management time, high capital require-
20 ments, poor liquidity, personal stress, and high risk.

Management Time.   Along with the advantage of personal control comes the disadvantage of the amount of time required to manage the property. Continuing review and management of an income property's operations is absolutely essential. A prudent investor takes an active role in overseeing management. The investor must seek a higher return on the investment to compensate for the time requirements.

High Capital Requirements.   Real estate requires a substantial capital investment. Not only does the investor need funds to acquire the property, he also must have reserve funds available to make major renovations when required or to cover unexpected events. If vacancy rates are high, the investor will find it difficult to sell the property and may need to inject more money into the real estate to pay its operating costs and debt service to carry him through the hard times.

Poor Liquidity.   Investment real estate is a complicated purchase, even in the best markets. Land-use requirements, environmental audits, maintenance inspections, lease reviews, and new financing all take a substantial amount of time. A seller must understand that it could be a year or more after putting the property on the market before a sale is closed. In bad markets, however, it can be close to impossible to sell property at a fair price because so many other properties are available. This is a significant disadvantage of investment real estate.

Personal Stress.   Many first-time real estate investors suffer rude awakenings when they discover that property management isn't just about cash flow projections and planning, but also about personal interaction with tenants. Because his first few properties usually are not large or profitable enough to justify hiring a manager, an owner is left with the task. When the mortgage payment is due, slow-paying tenants can become an irritation. Tenant complaints take time and interpersonal skills to resolve. Tenants sometimes leave a property in poor condition when they move, requiring a large contribution of time and money to restore the premises for the next tenant. Eviction is sometimes necessary and is usually distressing to both landlord and tenant.

High Risk.   It is said that the longer an asset is held, the greater the chance of catastrophe. Many examples exist of seemingly good real estate investments gone bad. It could result from overbuilding in the market, causing high competition and lower rents. Environmental laws also may require expensive retrofitting. Or a major employer may relocate to another area, causing widespread unemployment. Insurance does not cover this **dynamic risk.** To overcome dynamic risk, the investor must analyze a property carefully before purchasing, then manage it effectively.

   Static risk is risk that can be insured. Examples include fire, windstorm, accident liability, floods, appliance contracts, and workmen's compensation.

TYPES OF INVESTMENT PROPERTY

A wide range of property is available for investment, and the type of property suitable for an investor often depends on the investor's age, assets, and risk profile. Young investors usually are willing to take greater risks. This may be due partly to optimism that has not been dimmed by hard knocks and partly to higher energy levels. Older investors want to keep what they have because they don't have a lot of time to get it back if it is lost. They avoid high risk and are more likely to look for attractive current cash flows as opposed to speculative appreciation.

   Persons with very few assets have little to lose and are often risk-takers in their efforts to strike it rich. Persons who are financially comfortable usually are more conservative in their investment decisions.

Risk-averse investors ordinarily are not comfortable with industrial property, speculative land, or new construction of income property. They are more likely to want established income property with a proven record of income.

Types of investment property discussed below are raw land, residential income properties, office buildings, commercial properties, and industrial properties.

Raw Land. Investment in raw land can be extremely profitable if good research skills, good instincts, and good luck come together in one transaction. This type of property investment also can be extremely risky for the novice investor. Cities and counties in Florida, when trying to get a handle on growth guidelines, often change land uses in an area, which may have either wonderful or disastrous consequences for the investor. Income tax laws can change the feasibility of many projects. Raw land usually does not offer a cash flow to the investor and requires continuing infusions of funds to pay property taxes and interest on mortgages. Timing is important because the longer the property is held, the lower the rate of return tends to be.

The most important determinant of value for a vacant site is location. If land is planned for commercial use, it must have access and visibility from a major arterial road. Shopping centers should have easy access to expressways. Topography is important because it can affect building costs to correct for heavily sloping land.

Residential Income Properties. A single-family home usually is the investor's initial purchase. A single-family rental home provides the investor with a breakeven cash flow or a little income if the investor combines good management with good luck. It also has some limited tax advantages from depreciation. Because the margins are so slim, however, a vacancy for even a month can wipe out all the profit for the year.

As the investor's assets and borrowing power grow, her next investment may be a multifamily property. Larger properties benefit from the efficiencies of land use and management. Where single-family homes usually are breakeven propositions for the investors, larger properties can bring substantially higher yields. Because of the much larger investment required, a buyer should make a complete and detailed investment analysis.

Office Buildings. In the 1980s, office building construction was spurred on by the tax code and by infusion of capital into the market through limited partnerships. As a result, the office market became overbuilt in almost every major city, and vacancy rates of 25 percent were common. Many of the buildings were economically unsound, and there were many foreclosure sales. The market finally began to recover in the late 1990s, and developers are building again. Lenders, however, still are cautious and demand strong financial statements and tenant commitment to ensure reasonable occupancy rates when the buildings are complete.

Small investors must analyze the office building market carefully before committing their funds. What is the competition? How many new buildings are permitted? What's happening in the area economy? It is not enough to look at the overall occupancy rate. An investor should segment the market by age, location, and amenities. It is possible that vacancies are high in the older downtown buildings, while newer suburban office parks are nearly full. Prestige office buildings can be a trap for the investor. They're really pretty but often have low yields.

When analyzing the rent rates for competitive properties, the investor should pay careful attention to the services and tenant improvements included. Many buildings pay for utilities and janitorial service and give each tenant an initial allowance for buildout and partitioning.

Many investors prefer office buildings over residential apartments because tenants tend to occupy the properties longer, tenant complaints usually are made during business hours, and fewer collection problems occur. Smaller office buildings tend to have somewhat higher tenant turnover than buildings rented by national tenants.

Commercial Properties.   Many opportunities exist for small investors as well as shopping center developers to invest in commercial properties. Small strip shopping centers, because of their rectangular shape, lend themselves well to a variety of uses. They can be converted from storefronts to offices to restaurants with relatively little expense. A typical strip center consists of a 100' by 60' building with four 25' or five 20' wide bays. The market in many areas became very soft during the last economic downturn, making new construction loans difficult to obtain for some years. The market has improved in recent years, becoming attractive again to small investors.

Larger neighborhood shopping centers usually include a grocery store or a drug store as the anchor, along with some personal service stores such as dry cleaners, Laundromats, or restaurants.

Community shopping centers may include a Home Depot, K-Mart, or SteinMart as the anchor, along with a supermarket and other retailers, restaurants, and service companies. Management should try to arrange the mix of tenants so that each complements the others in the center and the overall effect is to generate additional traffic. Lease terms in these centers run longer than in strip centers. Professional property managers usually manage centers of this kind.

Regional shopping centers usually have three or more major department stores as anchors. They generally are located near expressways to draw more distant shoppers to the sites. The centers often have large numbers of general merchandise retailers. A professional manager is essential to enhance the value of this very large investment.

Industrial Properties.   Industrial properties usually are located near expressways, airports, seaports, or railroad lines. Investment in industrial property requires substantial research and carries significant risk. Most small investors should be wary about investment in this market. Many industrial properties serve special purposes and are subject to long periods of vacancy in market downturns. However, with a successful company as a tenant, an industrial property can achieve reasonable returns.

MARKET ANALYSIS

Once the investor has satisfied himself that the economy is sound and he begins to target the type of property for investment, a market study is the next necessary step. A regional market analysis should include demographic and economic information such as population statistics and trends, a list of major employers in the area, and income and employment data. It should explore the economic base of the city and prospects for the future in that locale. A neighborhood market analysis should assess five major factors:

1. **Boundaries and land usage.** Rivers, lakes, railroad tracks, parks, or major highways may help define the neighborhood's boundaries.
2. **Transportation and utilities.** Transportation and utilities are crucial to the success of income property. The investor should analyze the effect of major traffic artery changes, as well as proposed or scheduled widening of streets, opening or closing of bridges, or new highway construction, all of which may enhance or hurt a location.
3. **Economy.** The investor also should review the neighborhood's economic health. Rental rates in the neighborhood are a sound indicator of the real estate market's economic strength. The investor can obtain the most reliable current rental rate information by shopping the competition.

4. **Supply and demand.** A high occupancy rate indicates a shortage of space and the possibility of rental increases. A low rate, as evidenced by many "for rent" signs posted in the area, results in tenant demands for lower rents and other owner concessions.
5. **Neighborhood amenities and facilities.** The neighborhood's social, recreational, and cultural amenities can be important. Parks, theaters, restaurants, schools, and shopping centers attract potential tenants.

FINANCIAL ANALYSIS

After analyzing the market, the investor must examine the property's financial performance. This provides the basis for estimating the property's value, based on return criteria the investor establishes. Assembling the data is the most time-consuming part of the analysis process. The investor must review the property's financial history, as well as rent data, financial results, and amenities for competing properties. The first step after assembling the data is to prepare a one-year financial statement for the property.

Estimate Potential Gross Income (PGI). By multiplying the amount of space in the building by the base rental rate for that type of space, the investor can estimate rental income for each type of space found in the building. For example, the residential investor multiplies the number of studio, one-bedroom, and two-bedroom apartments by the rent for each type. The total of the estimated rent amounts from each type of space is the **potential gross income (PGI)** for the entire property.

Estimate Effective Gross Income (EGI). Effective gross income (EGI) is potential gross income minus vacancy and collection losses plus other income. Vacancy and collection losses are forecast from the experience of the subject property and of competing properties in the market, assuming typical, competent management. A good balance of supply and demand is a 95 percent occupancy rate. Occupancy rates change based on changing economic conditions, such as rising unemployment rates or overbuilding. Other income from sources such as vending machines and laundry areas is added to potential gross income *after* subtracting vacancy and collection losses.

Estimate Operating Expenses (OE). The next step is to calculate the property's **operating expenses (OE).** Operating expenses are divided into three categories: fixed expenses, variable expenses, and reserves for replacement (see below). Ad valorem taxes and property insurance are examples of fixed operating expenses. Their amounts normally do not vary with the level of the property's operation. Variable expenses include such items as utilities, maintenance, trash removal, supplies, janitorial services, and management. These expenses move in direct relationship with the level of occupancy. Regional norms for these expenses are available through trade journals and professional property management associations.

Establish Necessary Reserves for Replacement. If the level of expenses fluctuates widely from year to year, based on major maintenance and replacements of property components, it is difficult for the analyst to get a clear picture of typical expenses. To be meaningful, the expense figure must be stabilized. This is accomplished by establishing a **"reserves for replacement"** category of expenses. It is not a current cash outlay, but an annual charge that should account for future expenses. The most accurate way to establish reserves is to divide the cost of each item and piece of equipment by its expected useful life in years.

Estimate Net Operating Income (NOI). The **net operating income (NOI)** is obtained by deducting operating expenses (fixed, variable, and reserves) from effective gross income.

Determine Before-Tax Cash Flow. Income properties normally are purchased with mortgage financing, so owners must make mortgage payments from the NOI. When an annual mortgage payment is subtracted from NOI, the remaining amount is called **before-tax cash flow (BTCF),** sometimes called *cash throwoff.*

Constructing a Financial Statement for a Residential Investment

The following example describes the process of analyzing a residential investment. Sigrid Fleming is considering an investment in an apartment property located in southeast Tallahassee. The property, which is about seven years old and well-maintained, is located near some office buildings and shopping. Many of the tenants are employed in clerical and secretarial positions. The rental rates are very competitive in the area. Sigrid's broker has given her the bookkeeper's statements for the previous two years. Based on those statements and information from competing properties, she has constructed the operating statement shown in Figure 13.2.

Ratio Analysis. Sigrid's next step is to prepare a ratio analysis that helps her evaluate different investment opportunities. Some of the important ratios include capitalization rate, equity dividend rate, cash breakeven ratio, and debt coverage ratio. Use the statement on the Tallahassee Villas Apartments in Figure 13.2 to compute these ratios.

The Capitalization Rate. Capitalizing net operating income is a basic approach to estimating value. While an appraiser uses a rate determined by verified sales in the marketplace, an investor sets the rate that provides an acceptable return using subjective criteria the investor establishes. The capitalization rate is the one-year before-tax operating return on a real property investment without considering debt service on the property. If an investor pays all cash for a $300,000 investment and the net operating income is $30,000, the rate of return is 10 percent. This is calculated by dividing the net operating income by the value ($30,000 ÷ $300,000).

Assume, however, that the investor would not purchase the property unless it yielded 12 percent. By dividing the net operating income by the rate desired ($30,000 ÷ .12), the investor would agree to pay only $250,000.

DISCUSSION EXERCISE 13.2

What is the capitalization rate for the Tallahassee Villas Apartments?

If Sigrid desires a return of 14 percent, what will she pay for the property?

Equity Dividend Rate. The equity dividend rate differs from the capitalization rate when a mortgage is considered in the analysis. If no mortgage exists, the capitalization rate is the same as the equity dividend rate. To calculate the equity dividend rate, divide the before-tax cash flow by the equity (value minus the mortgage). Therefore, a property returning $14,000 after the owner makes the mortgage payment and having equity of $102,000 returns 13.7 percent on the equity ($14,000 ÷ $102,000). This percentage sometimes is called the **cash-on-cash return.**

FIGURE 13.2 Operating Statement for Residential Property

Tallahassee Villas Apartments
Operating Statement

Purchase Price: $1,000,000 / Mortgage $800,000

Potential Gross Income:	
25 units @ $425/mo.	$127,500
12 units @ $500/mo.	72,000
	$199,500
Less vacancy and coll. losses @ 5%	9,975
Effective Gross Income	$189,525
Operating Expenses:	
Property taxes	$ 8,700
Garbage collection	2,800
Pest control	4,500
Insurance	3,500
Maintenance	9,600
Management @ 5%	9,476
Resident manager's apt.	4,200
Reserves for replacements	30,000
Total Operating Expenses	$ 72,776
Net Operating Income	$116,749
Mtg. payment ($800,000 @ 10% for 25 years)	87,235
Before-Tax Cash Flow (cash throw-off)	$ 29,514

1 Many investors believe that the equity should return 50 percent more than current
2 mortgage rates. If mortgages are currently 8 percent, for example, the investor should
3 look for at least a 12 percent return.

4 Assume that the above investor will purchase only if the property returns 16 percent
5 on the equity. In that case, the investor would want to reduce the down payment from
6 $102,000 to $87,500, determined by dividing the cash flow by the desired return
7 ($14,000 ÷ .16). The price is determined by adding the down payment to the mortgage
8 calculated originally.

DISCUSSION EXERCISE 13.3

What is the equity dividend rate for the Tallahassee Villas Apartments?

If Sigrid desires a return of 16 percent, what down payment would she be willing to pay?

What price would she pay (add the down payment to the mortgage)?

1 ***Differences Between the Capitalization Rate and the Equity Dividend Rate.*** If
2 the equity dividend rate is higher than the capitalization rate, the investor has achieved
3 positive leverage. If the equity dividend rate is lower than the capitalization rate, nega-
4 tive leverage exists. Investors want positive leverage.

5   In the Tallahassee Villas Apartments, positive leverage exists. The capitalization rate
6 is 11.67 percent, and the equity dividend rate is 14.75 percent. The investor increased
7 her return by borrowing money with a favorable repayment rate. The repayment rate is
8 called the **annual mortgage constant,** with a symbol of *k*. The annual constant is calcu-
9 lated by dividing the annual debt service by the original mortgage balance. In the Talla-
10 hassee Villas, the annual debt service is $87,235, and the mortgage is $800,000; *k* is 10.9
11 percent (the interest rate is 10 percent, and principal amortization accounts for the bal-
12 ance.) The rule then becomes simple: *To achieve positive leverage,* k *must be lower than the*
13 *capitalization rate.*

14 ***Cash Breakeven Ratio.*** This ratio is extremely important to the investor because it
15 shows levels of occupancy required to generate enough revenue to make the required
16 payments for expenses and debt service. It is calculated by dividing the cash outflows
17 (expenses and debt service) by the potential gross income. The operating expenses
18 should show only those expenses required to be paid in cash. Reserves for replacements
19 usually are not a cash expense.

20   Assume that a small retail strip center has potential gross income of $100,000, annual
21 expenses of $40,000, including $4,000 in reserves for replacements, and annual debt
22 service of $47,000. What is the breakeven ratio? Divide the total cash expenses ($40,000
23 – $4,000 = $36,000) plus the debt service by the potential gross income.

24             $36,000 + $47,000 ÷ $100,000 = .83, or 83%

25   If all bays in the center rent for the same amount, the developer knows that the occu-
26 pancy rate must be greater than 83 percent or the developer will have to use his own
27 funds to make up the shortfall.

DISCUSSION EXERCISE 13.4

What is the cash breakeven ratio for the Tallahassee Villas Apartments? What will
be the impact on the owner if the vacancy rate is 20 percent?

---

28 ***Debt Service Coverage Ratio.*** A lender is concerned if a property has net oper-
29 ating income that is too low to allow the owner to make mortgage payments easily. The
30 lender wants a cushion so that even if vacancies or expenses increase, enough income
31 will remain to make the mortgage payment. The debt coverage ratio demonstrates the
32 amount of cushion. It is calculated by dividing the net operating income by the annual
33 debt service.

34   Assume the strip center discussed above has a 5 percent vacancy rate, the net oper-
35 ating income is $55,000, and the annual debt service is $47,000. The debt service cov-
36 erage ratio is 1.17. That means the net operating income is 117 percent of the amount
37 needed to cover the mortgage payment (a 17 percent cushion). A lender feels more
38 comfortable with a coverage ratio of at least 1.3.

39   The ratios discussed above should not be used solely to report on a property's status.
40 Astute investors use the ratios to help them determine the prices they would be willing
41 to pay based on income and cash flows. For instance, assume the seller's broker pro-

---

DISCUSSION EXERCISE 13.5

What is the debt service coverage ratio for the Tallahassee Villas Apartments?
Does it appear to be adequate?

---

1 vided the statement on the Tallahassee Villas Apartments. After Sigrid Fleming verifies
2 the statement for accuracy and prepares the ratio analysis as described above, she may
3 be prepared to make an offer on the property. The following format uses two calcula-
4 tions to assist in that process. The first calculation estimates the amount of mortgage
5 loan that would be available; the second determines how much down payment the
6 investor is willing to make. When the two figures are added, the result is the purchase
7 price.

8 **Estimating the Amount of Available Financing Based on Lender Standards.**   To
9 determine the financing, the investor needs to know the lender's requirements for the
10 debt service coverage ratio, and she needs to calculate the mortgage **loan constant** (k)
11 based on current lending rates. Dividing the NOI by the required debt coverage ratio
12 generates the allowed annual debt service. Dividing that figure by the loan constant
13 results in the available loan amount.

14   Assume that the mortgage market will allow a commercial building a 25-year loan at
15 a rate of 8 percent. The monthly payment factor is .00772 and the annual factor is
16 .09261. The second factor is k. With a net operating income of $55,000, a required debt
17 coverage ratio of 1.3 and an annual loan constant of .09261, the annual debt service can
18 be $42,308, as shown below:

19   1. Net operating income ÷ Debt coverage ratio = Annual debt service
20                        $55,000 ÷ 1.3 = $42,308

21   2. Annual debt service ÷ Mortgage loan constant = Mortgage loan amount
22                        $42,308 ÷ .09261 = $456,840

23 **Calculating the Down Payment Based on Investor Return Standards.**   The next
24 step is to calculate the maximum down payment. Once the mortgage amount is deter-
25 mined, the investor subtracts the annual debt service from the net operating income to
26 get before-tax cash flow. If the investor divides that figure by the required equity divi-
27 dend rate, the result is the down payment the investor is willing to make.

28   In the example above, we estimated that the debt service allowed by the lender is
29 $42,308. The net operating income is $55,000. Deducting the debt service of $42,308
30 results in a $12,692 cash flow. If the investor's required return is 15 percent, the down
31 payment would be $84,613, as shown below:

32   1. Net operating income – Debt service = Before-tax cash flow
33                        $55,000 – $42,308 = $12,692

34   2. Before-tax cash flow ÷ Required rate of return = Down payment
35                        $12,692 ÷ .15 = $84,613

36 **Calculating the Purchase Price.**   Once the above two steps are complete, the pur-
37 chase price is simply the addition of each figure. Continuing the above example, the cal-
38 culation is as follows:

39   Mortgage amount available from lender $456,837
40   Plus down payment from buyer   84,613
41   Equals purchase price offered $541,450

This technique for valuing income property is superior to simply capitalizing net income.

Other Financial Analysis Techniques. More sophisticated discounted cash flow techniques require the use of financial tables or a financial calculator and include the *net present value,* the *internal rate of return* and the *financial management rate of return.* In general, after-tax cash flows for future periods, including sales proceeds, are discounted back to the present value so that the pattern of receipts does not distort the analysis. While these techniques are important tools, they are beyond the scope of this text. The material is covered more fully in the broker's course and in commercial and investment real estate classes.

FEDERAL INCOME TAXES AND REAL ESTATE INVESTING

Real estate investors should not purchase property solely because of tax considerations. Many remember the large losses suffered by those who did so and were ruined financially by the 1986 Tax Reform Act. However, careful tax planning may help to maximize an investor's return on certain investments and should be considered when weighing alternative investments.

Income property owners enjoy certain tax advantages other investors do not. An owner is allowed three types of deductions from gross income when calculating taxable income from investment property: operating expenses, financing expenses and depreciation.

Operating expenses include those cash outlays necessary for operating and maintaining the property. Financing expenses include interest on indebtedness, as well as amortization of the costs of borrowing money, such as discount points.

Depreciation expense is not related to the depreciation used in appraising, which is based on realistic improvement lives. This is an arbitrary method of allowing the investor to recover the cost of improvements over a specified period. Costs of residential income property may be recovered over a life of 27½ years, and nonresidential income property may be written off over 39 years. For example, if a person bought a duplex three years ago for $125,000, paid closing costs of $5,000, and obtained an appraisal showing that the building was worth 80 percent of the total, what is the depreciation deduction?

To determine the deduction, first allocate the acquisition costs to the building and the land, then divide the building's acquisition costs by the applicable depreciable life. The $125,000 purchase price plus the $5,000 in closing costs equals the acquisition cost of $130,000. Because the building is worth 80 percent of value, the building's depreciable basis is $104,000. Residential property is depreciated over 27.5 years, so $104,000 divided by 27.5 years equals a deduction for this year of $3,781.81.

DISCUSSION EXERCISE 13.6

If closing costs on Tallahassee Villas Apartments are $12,000 and the improvements are estimated to represent 75 percent of the total value, what is the depreciation deduction?

The tax laws concerning capital gains taxes are covered in Chapter 2.

1   **Tax-Deferred Exchange.**   While the new capital gains rates are attractive, most inves-
2   tors attempt to defer (not eliminate) paying any taxes by exchanging the property for
3   "like" investment property. "Like" investment property includes real estate such as
4   vacant land, residential income property, commercial income property or industrial
5   income property.

6   The rules do not require a "barter" of property. A person may sell investment prop-
7   erty, escrow the proceeds out of his personal control, then identify another property to
8   buy within 45 days, closing within 180 days.

9   **Installment Basis Reporting.**   Taxes on the gain from the sale of a property need not
10 be paid at once if the seller does not receive her proceeds in the year of sale. The law
11 allows the taxpayer to pay taxes on the gain as the seller receives the proceeds. No min-
12 imum or maximum down payment is required. A loss on sale may not be reported using
13 installment basis reporting.

SUMMARY

Real estate licensees are quite active in marketing investment properties. Most small
investors concentrate initially on small residential properties but later may investigate
the opportunities in the office and commercial markets.

An understanding of the general business economy is helpful in timing investment
decisions. If the market is at the top of the cycle, buyers should be wary, but sellers
might wish to market their properties aggressively. Specific cycles are the most important cycles that affect the real estate market. Low interest rates are a critical component
to a strong real estate market.

Real estate investing offers many advantages, such as leverage, good returns, tax shel-
ters, and personal control. However, those advantages are tempered by problems with
stress, management time, risk, and poor liquidity.

After analyzing the market, an investor must prepare a careful financial statement,
together with meaningful ratios. The investor can use the ratios to help her determine
what price to offer for the property.

Licensees have an opportunity to help their customers take one of the most important steps of their lives—beginning a program of real estate investment.

DEFINE THESE KEY TERMS

annual mortgage constant
before-tax cash flow
contraction
cycle
cyclic fluctuation
dynamic risk
expansion
gross domestic product (GDP)
k
leverage
loan constant

net operating income (NOI)
operating expenses (OE)
potential gross income (PGI)
random changes
recession
recovery
reserves for replacements
seasonal variation
specific cycles
static risk

CHAPTER 13 PRACTICE EXAM

1. Funds set aside to prepare for the eventual replacement of worn-out appliances, carpeting and drapes are called:

   a. contingency funds.
   b. reserves for expenses.
   c. reserves for replacements.
   d. operating expenses.

2. Changes and trends in the general business economy fall into three categories—seasonal, random, and:

   a. expansion.
   b. recovery.
   c. periodic.
   d. cyclic.

3. Wavelike movements of increasing and decreasing economic prosperity in the general economy usually are called:

   a. random changes.
   b. cyclic fluctuations.
   c. seasonal variations.
   d. long-term movements.

4. The most pronounced and important economic changes and trends appearing in the real estate sector are the:

   a. seasonal fluctuations.
   b. specific cycles.
   c. expansion phases.
   d. random changes.

5. In general, when the economy is strong and prices are rising, the Federal Reserve Board tends to:

   a. loosen the money supply, causing interest rates to rise.
   b. loosen the money supply, causing interest rates to fall.
   c. tighten the money supply, causing interest rates to rise.
   d. tighten the money supply, causing interest rates to fall.

6. You are the property manager for a new, 60-unit garden apartment complex. The annual potential gross income is $291,000, other income is $480 per month, and vacancy and collection losses are 5 percent. What is the property's effective gross income?

   a. $276,450
   b. $276,930
   c. $281,922
   d. $282,210

7. Which of the following describes the debt service coverage ratio?

   a. Shows the level of occupancy necessary to pay all bills
   b. Important to lenders in showing how much net income exceeds the mortgage payment
   c. Indicates the length of time required to repay the mortgage based on current income rates
   d. Shows the amount of down payment the investor is willing to make

8. Changes that recur annually are called:

   a. familiar changes.
   b. long-term cyclic changes.
   c. random changes.
   d. seasonal variations.

9. An apartment property has potential gross income of $155,000, effective gross income of $150,000, operating expenses of $58,000, including reserves for replacement of $2,400, and debt service of $40,800. What is the property's net operating income?

   a. $48,800
   b. $51,200
   c. $92,000
   d. $94,600

10. Nonresidential income property may be depreciated over how many years?

    a. 15, with a 175% declining balance
    b. 27½
    c. 31
    d. 39

11. An investor obtains the best and most reliable information about rental rates in a neighborhood by checking:

    a. the Bureau of Labor Statistics' survey of sample cities.
    b. competing properties.
    c. classified ads in local newspapers that cover the past 18 to 24 months.
    d. current classified ads in local newspapers for advertisements of comparable space.

12. Total operating expenses include variable expenses, fixed expenses, and:

    a. debt-service expenses.
    b. management expenses.
    c. reserves for replacement.
    d. property taxes.

13. A problem many investors have with industrial properties is that:

    a. land boundaries are unstable.
    b. many properties serve special purposes and are difficult to rent once they are vacant.
    c. they rarely need proximity to airports.
    d. rates of return are always low.

debt coverage ratio

Use the following information to answer questions

Carolyn Bayer is considering an investment in an
She can secure a mortgage on the property as long
(1.3) times the new mortgage payment. She can get a
but has decided that she will not purchase unless he
Carolyn prepares an abbreviated financial statemer

Potential gross income	$1(
Less vacancy of 10%	10,000
Equals effective gross income	$90,000
Less operating expenses	36,000
Equals net operating income	$54,000
Annual debt service	
Before-tax cash flow	

14. What maximum annual debt service will the lender accept?

    a. $41,538
    b. $44,378
    c. $46,800
    d. $70,222

NOI / ● debt coverage ratio

15. What maximum amount will the lender loan to Carolyn, based on an annual
    constant of .096627?

    a. $429,880
    b. $440,345
    c. $475,000
    d. $503,000

annual debt service / Annual constant

16. What is the before-tax cash flow?

    a. $11,687
    b. $12,462
    c. $14,901
    d. $22,789

NOI − Annual debt service

17. What would Carolyn be willing to pay as a down payment based on the figures?

    a. $86,587
    b. $91,345
    c. $93,451
    d. $103,850

before-tax cash flow / rate of return

18. What total price would Carolyn be willing to pay based on the figures?

    a. $425,987
    b. $469,091
    c. $533,735
    d. $541,890

Amount lender will loan + downpayment

19. Is the leverage positive or negative?

    a. Positive
    b. Negative
    c. Neutral
    d. Not enough information to calculate

NOI / Total Price = 10% . dividend = 12%

A property has ~~doubt~~ NOI of 145,000
Lender agreed to 7% interest & requires
a debt coverage ratio of 1.5% Loan
will have a monthly mortgage

NOI / debt coverage ratio =

145,000 / 1.5 = 96,667 / 12

= 8056

CHAPTER 14—PROFESSIONAL PROPERTY MANAGEMENT

LEARNING OBJECTIVES

Upon completion of this chapter, *you should be able to:*

1. describe the general duties of professional property managers;
2. list the four major classifications of rental properties;
3. list at least six important elements of a management contract;
4. list the four major property maintenance categories;
5. describe the requirements that determine the need for an on-site maintenance staff, contract services, or a resident manager;
6. describe the differences between a property manager and a resident manager;
7. list at least three different advertising media that help to market rental property;
8. describe the uses and benefits of a show list;
9. identify at least five of the essential elements of a valid lease;
10. identify and explain the purpose of three of the financial reports an apartment building owner needs; and
11. identify those property managers who are exempt from the provisions of F.S. 475.

CHAPTER 14

PROFESSIONAL PROPERTY MANAGEMENT

Investors generally agree that professional property management is the key to maximizing their returns. The professional property manager must have a comprehensive understanding of the economic forces at work in the real estate market. He must be able to evaluate the property in terms of operating income, forecast its potential for the future, and construct a management plan that reflects the owner's objectives. The property manager must become a specialist skilled in space marketing, tenant psychology, the legal aspects of the landlord-tenant relationship, maintenance procedures, and accounting. This chapter examines these topics.

INTRODUCTION TO PROPERTY MANAGEMENT

A professional property manager may be an individual licensee, a member of a real estate firm specializing in property management, or a member of the property management department of a large full-service real estate company. She also may work within the trust department of a financial institution or within the real estate department of a large corporation or public institution. Regardless of their employment status, property managers pursue similar objectives and handle a wide variety of duties, including planning, merchandising, maintenance, and accounting. Although management duties vary according to the specific situation and particular property, a successful manager is competent in all of these areas.

The **Institute of Real Estate Management (IREM)** was created in 1933 by a group of property management firms as a subsidiary group of the National Association of REALTORS®. Currently, individuals wishing to join the institute must satisfy education and experience requirements, pass examinations given or approved by the institute, and adhere to a specific code of ethics. They are then awarded the prestigious designation **Certified Property Manager (CPM)** in recognition of their professional status as property managers.

CLASSIFICATION OF REAL PROPERTY

Real estate property managers manage four major classifications of real property: residential, commercial, industrial, and special-purpose. Each classification can be further subdivided and requires a different combination of property management knowledge and skills. This chapter introduces the field; it is not intended to be a complete discussion of property management. Residential property is emphasized in this introduction.

DISCUSSION EXERCISE 14.1

Relate a personal experience in renting or leasing residential property as a landlord or tenant.

Residential Property

Residential real estate is the largest source of demand for the services of professional property managers. Two principal categories of residential real estate exist: single-family homes and multifamily residences.

Single-Family Homes. Free-standing, single-family homes are the most popular form of housing in the United States. According to the Census Bureau, more than 60 percent of housing in this country is owner-occupied and does not require professional management. Although homes that are rented to other parties often are managed directly by the owners, there is a growing trend toward professional management of such properties, particularly condominiums and vacation homes. Many large corporations and their relocation companies hire property managers for homes vacated by employees who have been transferred.

Rising construction costs and a decrease in the availability of usable land have resulted in the growing popularity of town houses, condominiums, and cooperatives. Although each unit is a single-family residence, the individual owners of the units share certain responsibilities, such as maintenance of the roof, common walls, grounds, and common facilities, for the development as a whole. They usually employ professional managers to handle these jobs and maintain accounting records.

Multifamily Residences. The economy of design and land usage inherent in multifamily housing allows for a lower per-family cost of construction. Thus, multifamily residences are a rapidly growing segment of the national residential real estate market.

Multifamily residences can be held under various forms of ownership. Small properties of two to six units often are owner-occupied and owner-managed, whereas most large highrise apartment communities are professionally managed for their owners. Cooperative and condominium apartments usually are owner-occupied buildings governed by boards of directors the owners elect. These boards generally hire professional managers for their properties.

Multifamily residences can be classified as garden apartments, walk-up buildings, or highrise apartments. Each type is unique in its location, design, construction, services, and amenities.

Owner-Broker Relationship

Three basic relationships can exist between the individual or corporate owner of a building and the property manager: owner-broker, employer-employee, and trustor-trustee. Property managers in all categories are considered professionals, and their responsibilities are very similar. Because this section focuses on residential property management, only the principal-agent relationship is covered here.

Usually, when an owner engages a broker to be the property manager, the broker acts as a single agent for the owner. The principal-agent relationship is created by a written contract signed by both parties that empowers the property manager, as agent, to act on behalf of the owner, or principal, in certain situations. Specifically, the agent acts for the principal to bring her into legal relations with third parties. Implicit in this fiduciary relationship are the legal and ethical considerations that any agent must accord her principal. The property manager has the duties of skill, care and diligence, obedience, loyalty, accounting, disclosure, and confidentiality.

THE MANAGEMENT CONTRACT

Once the property manager and the owner (or owning body) have agreed on principles, objectives, and a viable management plan, it is in both parties' best interests to formalize their accord. The manager and the owner must work out the structure of their relationship, their specific responsibilities and liabilities, the scope of the manager's authority, management fees, and the duration of the management agreement. In addition, the owner must turn over management records and other information to the manager to facilitate the property's operation.

Whether the property involved is a duplex or a highrise complex, the responsibilities the manager assumes are of enough importance to warrant a written statement of intent. An agreement signed by both the manager and the owner defines the relationship between the parties, serves as a guide for the property's operation and helps prevent misunderstandings.

The terms of management contracts are as varied, but most share the following essential elements:

- Identification of the parties and the property
- The term of the contract
- Responsibilities of the manager
- Responsibilities of the owner
- Fees and leasing/sales commissions;
- Signatures of the parties

PROPERTY MAINTENANCE

Maintenance is a continual process of balancing services and costs in an attempt to please the tenants, preserve the physical condition of the property, and improve the owner's long-term margin of profit. Efficient property maintenance demands careful assessment of the status of the building's condition. Staffing and scheduling requirements vary with the type, size, and regional location of the property, so owner and manager usually agree in advance on maintenance objectives for the property. In some cases, the owner instructs that the manager reduce rental rates and expenditures for services and maintenance. Under this short-sighted policy, the manager may encounter management problems and the manager's reputation may be affected adversely. Properties can command premium rental rates if they are kept in top condition and operated with all possible tenant services.

Types of Maintenance

The successful property manager must be able to function effectively at four different levels of maintenance operations:

1. Preventive maintenance
2. Corrective maintenance
3. Routine maintenance
4. New construction maintenance

Preventive maintenance is aimed at preserving the physical integrity of the premises and eliminating corrective maintenance costs. Regular maintenance activities and routine inspections of the building and its equipment disclose structural and mechanical problems before major repairs become necessary.

Corrective maintenance involves the actual repairs that keep the building's equipment, utilities, and amenities functioning as contracted for by the tenants. Fixing a leaky faucet and replacing a broken air-conditioning unit are corrective maintenance activities.

Routine maintenance is the most frequently recurring type of maintenance activity. Common areas and grounds must be cleaned and patrolled daily. Also, cleaning and housekeeping chores should be scheduled and controlled carefully because such costs easily can become excessive.

New construction maintenance, linked closely with leasing and tenant relations, is designed to increase the property's marketability. This may be as elementary as new wallpaper, light fixtures, and carpeting. If the new construction is extensive, it might include new entryways, the addition of a swimming pool, conversion of space to a meeting room, or renovation of a previously occupied space. New construction often is performed at a tenant's request and expense. Sometimes a landlord redecorates or rehabilitates a space for a tenant as a condition of lease renewal.

Deferred maintenance is necessary maintenance which cannot or will not be performed. Deferred maintenance results in physical deterioration, unhappy tenants, and reduced rent collections.

On-Site Maintenance Staff. The manager's hiring policy for on-site maintenance personnel usually is based on the cost differential between maintaining a permanent building staff and contracting for the needed services. For example, the amount of construction activity stemming from alterations tenants require determines the hiring policy. It makes sense to hire outside contractors for major construction jobs or for small buildings that cannot support permanent staffs.

The Building Owners and Managers Institute (BOMI) sponsors instruction that leads to professional designations for maintenance personnel and supervisors. These courses are particularly instructive for on-site maintenance personnel. Property managers who wish to learn more about the technical and mechanical aspects of their properties will find these courses a good source of information.

Contract Services

Services performed by outside persons on a regular basis for specified fees are known as **contract services.** For the protection of both the manager and the owner, a service contract always should be in writing and contain a termination provision. The latter stipulation becomes important if service is not satisfactory or if the property is sold.

Before entering into any service contract, the manager should solicit competitive bids on the job from several local contractors. He can then compare the cost of contracting with the expense of using on-site personnel. The management agreement terms often set a ceiling on the service contracts the manager can execute without owner approval. Window cleaning, refuse removal, pest control, and security are services that usually can be performed more efficiently and inexpensively by outside contractors. The manager should check a contracting firm's references and work history before he employs them. The manager should determine whether the firm's employees are bonded and whether it has the necessary licenses or permits.

RESIDENT MANAGER—PROPERTY MANAGER RELATIONSHIP

Most properties of 20 units or more have a manager on the premises at all times. This **resident manager** is a salaried employee who usually coordinates rent collection, tenant relations, and maintenance work on the property. Obviously, these responsibilities increase with the building's size. The resident manager reports to the property manager. With this system, a single property manager can stay current with the operations of several large apartment properties without becoming consumed by the details. In addition to reviewing the reports submitted by resident managers, the property manager should visit each building regularly to gather information on necessary maintennce and repairs. Periodic inspections show the property manager how occupancy rates may be increased, indicate where operating costs can be cut, help improve tenant relations, and provide training and feedback reviews to the on-site manager.

In the past, building superintendents not only collected rents but also served as the maintenance staff. As the property management field grows more sophisticated and building equipment becomes more complicated, managers who perform all four maintenance functions have become the exception rather than the rule. Property managers are expected to recognize when maintenance is necessary and know where to turn for help with specific maintenance problems. While a property manager need not be a jack-of-all-trades, she should understand the basic operation of mechanical and electrical systems well enough to make intelligent decisions about their care and operation. The manager also must understand the economics, staffing, and scheduling involved in the smooth performance of maintenance tasks.

The hiring and firing of employees should be under the control of the property manager, not the resident manager. When screening a potential employee or making a decision to terminate an employee, the property manager should ask for the resident manager's opinion of the person's integrity, industry, and skills.

MARKETING THE SPACE

Two basic principles of marketing are "Know your product" and "Your best source of new business is your present customer base." Thorough preparation is required to give a suitable presentation of the premises as well as to determine such items as rental rates and advertising methods necessary to attract tenants. Maximum use of referrals from satisfied tenants is the best and least expensive method of renting property and is essential to any marketing effort.

It is the property manager's responsibility to generate the maximum beautification and functional utility per dollar spent. Items such as an attractive lobby, well-landscaped grounds, and the use of pleasant colors inside and outside the building may not create greater functional utility, but they may increase marketability and profitability.

Rental space is a consumer good that can be marketed with promotional techniques like those used to sell cars or homes. Because most apartment renter prospects come to the property as a result of a neighborhood search, attractive signage and strong curb appeal is essential. Each residential property should display a tasteful sign on the premises identifying the community, the management firm, the type of apartment, the person to call for further information, and a telephone number. However, walk-ins alone will not supply all the prospects needed. Other types of advertising also are necessary to attract qualified tenants.

Advertising and Display

Even if the property is priced at the appropriate market level, the premises are clean and attractive, and the property has a good location, the building still may experience an unacceptable vacancy rate if prospective tenants are not attracted to inspect the premises. The most common advertising is newspaper classified and display ads and apartment guides. The Florida Real Estate Commission (FREC) mandates that a broker's advertising must describe the property fairly and must not mislead. It also requires that the brokerage name appear in all advertising. Other agencies also impose restrictions on ads, particularly with respect to fair housing laws.

Classified Ads.   Newspaper classified advertising is the most important advertising medium for renting apartments. The property manager must keep the prospective tenant's needs in mind when composing the ad. For example, in a neighborhood where three-bedroom apartments are difficult to rent, an ad may appeal to a broader segment of the market if it offers a two-bedroom apartment with den. The classified advertisement should include the amount of rent, apartment size, property address, and manager's phone number. A brief summary of the property's major amenities also is very effective.

Display Ads.   More prestigious residential projects, especially when newly built, find it advantageous to use display advertisements. These larger ads attract immediate attention, appeal to potential tenants' desire for attractive living space, and demonstrate the many amenities a building offers. The specific rental rates often are omitted, with reference to a general range.

DISCUSSION EXERCISE 14.2

Bring to class a copy of the entire classified ad section of your local newspaper. Examine the sections dealing with display ads for large residential properties and compare various ads' effectiveness. Also, examine the help wanted sections for property and resident managers.

Apartment Guides.   Just as homes magazines are one of the most effective ways to market residential homes for sale, apartment guides appeal to potential tenants. Color photos make the property's presentation attractive and interesting. Many management firms report that the excellent response to ads in the guides is beginning to rival the effectiveness of newspaper classified advertising.

Broker Cooperation

While all selling activities have as their ultimate objective the closing of a sale or lease with the ultimate user, the property manager will want to take advantage of all opportunities for reaching customers. This means that sales efforts should be directed not only toward prospective buyers and tenants but also toward brokers and agents who can reach rental prospects.

Broker cooperation can be especially helpful when renting or leasing a new or very large development. Managers secure that cooperation by sending to key brokers brochures or newsletters describing available properties. Compensation usually is a split commission or referral fee. A manager also can make brokers aware of a property by making a personal presentation or by sponsoring an open house.

Rental Rate Strategy

Even when the space itself is clean, attractively decorated, and in good condition, market conditions may be such that some units cannot be leased. An alert manager quickly realizes which units are renting rapidly or are not moving fast enough and either adjusts the price or changes the method of advertising and display.

The goal in establishing a rental fee schedule is to realize the maximum market price for each unit. If each apartment type is priced correctly, all types will have the same rate of demand; that is, demand for studio, one-bedroom, and two-bedroom units will be equal, and the manager will be able to achieve a balanced occupancy rate for all three types. However, this level of demand is the exception in the real market. More often than not, the manager will have to raise the base rent on the unit types that are fully occupied and decrease the rate for those units less in demand. An optimal price structure assures the manager of a 95 percent occupancy level for all units. For this strategy to be economically sound, the revenue from the new 95 percent schedule must exceed the income that was collected when some types of units were fully occupied and others had tenant levels of less than 95 percent. The optimum rental rates in a local market are best determined by market analysis.

Show List

To establish a reasonable rental price schedule like the one outlined above, the manager must follow certain organizational procedures, such as compiling a **show list.** This show list should designate a few specific apartments in the building that are available currently for inspection by prospects. No more than three apartments of each type and size should be on the list at any one time; when a unit is rented, it should be replaced by another vacated apartment that is ready for rental.

The manager should use the show list both as a control guide for the marketing program and as a source of feedback on its success or failure. The features of particular units are itemized on the list so that the manager can do a better and more informed selling job. The maintenance staff will have no problem keeping a small number of vacant units on the list in top-notch condition. The limited number of show units also suggests that space is at a premium and that the prospective tenant must make her decision quickly.

The show list and traffic count should be reviewed weekly to determine which units are not moving. Particular units may not rent even after several showings to prospects. The manager then should inspect these units personally to find out why they are hard to rent. All curable flaws (for example, worn carpeting or obsolete fixtures) should be corrected. If poor curb appeal is the problem, painting or cleaning up entranceways, planting new landscaping, cutting grass, and trimming shrubs often works wonders.

It is important that fair housing laws be observed carefully. The limited show list must never be used as a method of illegal steering within the property.

Selling the Customer

The best advertising programs, landscaping, decorating, and maintenance may be in vain if the rental agent is unresponsive or unprofessional or does not properly show the property. Probably the most important ingredient of achieving occupancy targets is well-trained rental staff members who are personable, enthusiastic, and professional. Many large management organizations spend substantial time and money to ensure that rental agents have the technical knowledge and sales skills to best represent the property owner. The property manager should maintain records carefully, including guest books to record visitors' names. The rental agent should describe the result of each visit and record subsequent follow-up calls.

LEASES AND TENANT RELATIONS

Potential conflicts between property managers and tenants usually can be avoided when sound property management practices are employed. Sound management begins with negotiation between the property manager and the prospective tenant, the results of which should be in written form (the lease).

Essentials of a Valid Lease

The general requirements for a valid lease are similar to those for any legally enforceable contract:

- Complete and legal names of both parties (lessor and lessee)
- Legal description of the property
- Contractual capacity of the parties and legal purpose of the agreement
- Consideration or amount of rent
- Term of occupancy
- Use of the premises
- Rights and obligations of the lessor and lessee
- In writing and signed (if for more than one year)

Licensees may fill in the blanks on only the lease forms specifically approved by the Florida Supreme Court. Changing or adding to the terms of the approved forms or completing the blanks on any other lease form is considered unauthorized practice of law. Currently, there are two leases approved by the Supreme Court: the *Residential Lease for Single-Family Home and Duplex,* and a form developed by the Florida Bar.

The manager should explain the key points in the lease agreement. Rent collection policies should be covered. Tenants will usually pay rent promptly if the collection policy is efficient, effective, and reasonable. The manager should itemize other regulations that control the property and discuss the methods of enforcing them. The manager must be certain that the tenant understands maintenance policies and how responsibilities are divided between landlord and tenant. These policies and procedures are often outlined in a tenant brochure.

Most tenant-management problems center on maintenance service requests. When such a request is made, the tenant should be told immediately whether it will be granted. The tenant is the customer, not an adversary, and the staff should be reminded of that fact continually. Happy tenants remain in residence, eliminate expensive turnover, protect the owner's property (which lowers maintenance costs), and promote the property's reputation (which reduces vacancy losses and promotional expenses).

A tenant request for service should be entered on a standardized request form. The top copy and a copy to be left in the unit on completion of the work are assigned to the maintenance person answering the request. The manager keeps the third copy until the job is completed. An estimated completion date should be entered on the manager's copy for follow-up. The resident manager should contact the tenant to ensure that the work was completed properly.

Landlord and Tenant Act.   Chapter 83, F.S., the Florida Residential Landlord and Tenant Act, outlines the rights and duties of landlords and tenants, as well as the legal remedies available to both parties in case of noncompliance with lease terms. The intent was to create a reasonable balance between the two parties in their legal relationship. The law includes, among its many requirements, very specific rules for handling security deposits and advance rent. Florida licensees acting as residential managers must comply with the act. Those real estate licensees desiring to know more about this subject should obtain a current copy of this Florida law.

OPERATING REPORTS

Owners of residential rental apartments need current operating reports to measure the profitability of their investments. The annual operating budget, cash flow statement, and profit and loss statement give an owner the data necessary to evaluate his property and its management.

Operating Budget.   The property manager must prepare a meaningful annual operating budget that includes all anticipated income and expense items for the property. The starting point for this year's budget most often is based on the actual data from the previous year. The annual budget is helpful as a guide for overall profitability. It must, however, be broken down into monthly budgets if it is to be useful for controlling operations. There, the manager should produce monthly statements that compare actual and budgeted amounts and should be able to explain any significant variations.

Cash Flow Statement.   Probably the most important operating record is the manager's monthly **cash flow report** on receipts and disbursements. This report includes all operating income, such as the income from parking, washing machines, dryers, and vending machines, and all operating expenses as well as debt service. The reports show the owner how the property is doing on a cash basis. The report also can include the annual budget as well as the previous year's results, providing a budgetary control as well as a cash control. A sample cash flow statement is shown in the Appendix Forms-To-Go.

Profit and Loss Statement.   A **profit and loss statement** is a financial report of a property's actual net profit, which may differ from the cash flow. The full mortgage payment is not shown; only the interest payment is an expense. The manager usually prepares a profit and loss statement quarterly, semiannually, and yearly. Monthly income and expense reports provide the raw data for these statements. The more detail provided in the report, the better the opportunities for meaningful analysis.

Additional Reports.   Managers must be completely familiar with all phases of a property's operation. Other reports, such as vacancy ratios, bad-debt ratios, showings-to-rent ratios, and changes in tenant profiles, illustrate important trends that may require corrective action. Scrutiny of the budgets and actual expenditures per account from month to month and year to year can indicate the relative performance of management personnel.

LICENSING REQUIREMENTS IN FLORIDA

Property managers must be certain that the requirements of Chapter 475 of the Florida Statutes are followed carefully. The law requires that any person who rents or leases real property for another party for compensation to have a current, active license. Two exemptions exist:

1. Salaried employees of an owner, or of a registered broker working for an owner or for the properly licensed property manager of an apartment complex, who work in an on-site rental office of the apartment community in a leasing capacity
2. Salaried persons employed as managers of condominiums or cooperative apartment complexes who rent individual units, if the rentals arranged by the employees are for periods not exceeding one year

   These exemptions are granted under the law to unlicensed, salaried employees. They may not be paid a commission or any form of compensation on a transactional basis.

1   **Community Association Management.**   Property managers of certain community
2   associations must obtain community association manager licenses from the Department
3   of Business and Professional Regulation as discussed in detail in Chapter 2. Apartment
4   properties and commercial property are not affected by this law.

SUMMARY

When an owner hires a manager, the parties enter into one of three relationships: principal-agent, employer-employee, or trustor-trustee. Most management contracts share six basic characteristics and specify the duties and details of management operations that must be decided before responsibility for the property is transferred to the manager.

To handle the property's maintenance demands, the manager must know the building's needs and the number and type of personnel required to perform the maintenance functions. Staff and scheduling requirements vary with a property's type, size, and regional location.

Four types of maintenance operations exist: preventive maintenance, corrective maintenance, routine housekeeping, and new construction. Deferred maintenance is the term applied to accumulated postponed maintenance.

The hiring policy for on-site maintenance staff depends on the cost differential between maintaining a permanent building staff and contracting for needed services. A particular property's circumstances dictate which alternative is more efficient and economical.

Multifamily dwellings differ from one another in size, structure, location and number of amenities provided. These differences exert a direct influence on the advertising techniques used to market each type of space. A show list of units available for inspection also is important to a property manager's marketing program, as is newspaper advertising, the most widely used medium for renting space because it reaches a large audience.

In addition to leasing, supervising the resident manager, and inspecting the maintenance of the premises, the property manager must provide the owner with regular financial reports. Various financial statements provide the owner with the data necessary to evaluate the performance of the manager and the property itself.

Property managers in Florida must meet the requirements of Chapters 83, 468, and 475 of the Florida Statutes, unless specifically exempted.

DEFINE THESE KEY TERMS

cash flow report	new construction maintenance
Certified Property Manager (CPM)	preventative maintenance
contract service	profit and loss statement
corrective maintenance	resident manager
deferred maintenance	routine maintenance
Institute of Real Estate Management (IREM)	show list

Chapter 14 Practice Exam

1. A salaried, unlicensed manager of a resort condominium in Florida legally may rent individual condominium units if the rental periods do not exceed:

   a. one month.
   b. 90 days.
   c. six months.
   d. one year.

2. A person who provides services that require licensing under the Community Association Management Act must be licensed by the:

   a. Florida Real Estate Commission.
   b. Department of Administration.
   c. Department of Business and Professional Regulation.
   d. Department of Community Affairs.

3. Maintenance on a building that cannot or will not be performed when necessary is which of the following types of maintenance?

   a. Elective
   b. Deferred
   c. Corrective
   d. Routine

4. Maintenance services performed by a person or company outside the management company are called:

   a. service contracts.
   b. contract services.
   c. in-house maintenance.
   d. preventive maintenance.

5. The fastest-growing advertising medium for real estate residential rentals is:

   a. display advertising.
   b. apartment guides.
   c. homes magazines.
   d. classified advertising.

6. The major form of advertising used to rent apartments is:

   a. outdoor signs.
   b. television spot commercials.
   c. display ads.
   d. classified ads.

7. Apartments that are vacant and available for immediate rental are placed on the:

   a. floor list.
   b. up list.
   c. show list.
   d. cleared list.

8. According to the text, most tenant-management problems are related to:

   a. late or unpaid rent.
   b. maintenance service requests.
   c. conduct of tenants and their guests.
   d. handling of security deposits and advance rent.

9. The most important operating record for the property manager is probably the:

   a. vacancy and bad-debt report.
   b. after-tax cash flow analysis.
   c. annual profit and loss statement.
   d. monthly cash flow report.

10. Which of the following is *not* a category of property maintenance?

    a. Elective
    b. Preventive
    c. Routine
    d. Corrective

11. The individual responsible for the fiscal, physical, and administrative management functions for an investment property owner is the:

    a. resident manager.
    b. property manager.
    c. maintenance manager.
    d. residential property consultant.

12. What is NOT a requirement for a valid lease?

    a. Contractual capacity of the parties
    b. Amount of leasing commissions
    c. Term of occupancy
    d. Consideration

13. The starting point for most annual budgets is:

    a. what the manager thinks will happen.
    b. last year's actual results.
    c. this year's actual results.
    d. last year's budget.

14. Howard is an employee of a property management firm. He shows prospective tenants many of the duplexes the company manages around the city and writes up leases on the court-approved forms. Howard is paid $700 per month plus $50 per signed lease. Howard:

    a. must have a community association manager's license.
    b. must have a community association manager's license *and* a real estate license.
    c. must have a real estate license.
    d. need not be licensed because he is not paid a commission.

15. Wendy is the property manager for a new apartment community. She cannot seem to get occupancy up to budgeted levels, even with additional advertising. What else might be helpful?

    a. Additional training for the rental agents
    b. Soliciting broker cooperation
    c. Sprucing up the property's curb appeal
    d. All of the above

ACTION LIST

APPLY WHAT YOU'VE LEARNED!

The authors suggest the following actions to reinforce the material in *Section VII–Commercial and Residential Investment Property:*

- Select an apartment property in your area that has at least 30 units and learn the rental rate. Find out the typical vacancy rates in the area, then prepare a financial statement. Use an operating expense ratio of 40 percent.
- When you have completed the financial statement, capitalize the income at 10 percent to estimate a "ride-by" opinion of value.
- Call a lender and ask for information about what loans are available for properties of this type. Discuss loan-to-value ratios, debt coverage ratios, and interest rates.
- Based on this information, calculate the before-tax cash flow. Make sure the debt coverage ratio is at least what the lender requires. Using the before-tax cash flow, determine what an investor would be willing to pay in a down payment if she requires a 14 percent equity dividend rate.
- Travel on a thoroughfare, and visit at least three vacant commercial buildings. Make notes on the structures, and try to decide the highest and best uses. List three potential tenants for each site. Call the listing agent and get information on each property.
- Assume a potential buyer from out of town asks you to describe the local economy and estimate about what it will do in the next three years. Write your response as completely as possible. Get information from the local chamber of commerce, and compare your description with your classmates'.
- If you work in residential real estate, you often may encounter potential commercial customers. Ask your broker which commercial broker he recommends for referrals. Check with a licensee in that firm to see whether the referrals could go in both directions, with you getting her residential referrals.
- Visit several apartment properties in your area. List the ones you would recommend to a friend looking for an apartment.

APPENDIX I: RESOURCES

The following sources are selective and not exhaustive. Each is listed by section in the book and in the order recommended by the authors for further study. Numerous other available resources exist, including books, journals (e.g., FAR's Florida REALTOR® magazine), periodicals, newsletters, articles, legal cases, research studies, video programs, and seminars. Consult your broker, instructor, or local board librarian for further assistance.

SECTION I. LEGAL ISSUES IN REAL ESTATE PRACTICE

1. Reilly, John W. *Agency Relationships in Real Estate.* 1997 or later edition. Chicago: Real Estate Education Company®.
2. Crawford, Linda L., and Edward J. O'Donnell. *Florida Real Estate Broker's Guide.* 1st edition. Chicago: Real Estate Education Company®, 1999.
3. Gaines, George, Jr., David S. Coleman, and Linda Crawford. *Florida Real Estate Principles, Practices & Law.* 25th or later edition. Chicago: Real Estate Education Company®.
4. Lyons, Gail G., and Donald L. Harlan. *Buyer Agency: Your Competitive Edge in Real Estate.* 3rd or later edition. Chicago: Real Estate Education Company®.
5. *An Accidental Agency.* A videocassette tape program with discussion guide. Austin, Tex.: Texas Association of REALTORS®, 1988.
6. *The Alternative.* A quarterly newsletter. Ventura, Calif.: Who's Who in Creative Real Estate, Inc.
7. O'Donnell, Edward J. *Continuing Education for Florida Real Estate Professionals.* 2000-2001 edition. Chicago: Real Estate Education Company®, 1999.

SECTION II. PROFESSIONALISM IN REAL ESTATE

1. *Code of Ethics and Standards of Practice.* 2000 or later edition. Chicago: National Association of REALTORS®.
2. Pivar, William H. *Real Estate Ethics.* 3rd or later edition. Chicago: Real Estate Education Company®.

SECTION III. VALUATION AND LISTING

1. Gaines, George, Jr., David S. Coleman, and Linda Crawford. *Florida Real Estate Principles, Practices & Law.* 25th or later edition. Chicago: Real Estate Education Company®.
2. Galaty, Fillmore W., et al. *Modern Real Estate Practice.* 14th or later edition. Chicago: Real Estate Education Company®.

3. Reilly, John W. *The Language of Real Estate.* 4th or later edition. Chicago: Real Estate Education Company®.

4. Keane, Gerald B. *Florida Law: A Layman's Guide.* Englewood, Fla.: Pineapple Press, Inc., 1987.

5. Gibson, Frank, et al. *Real Estate Law.* 4th or later edition. Chicago: Real Estate Education Company®.

6. Ventolo, William L., Jr., and Martha R. Williams. *Fundamentals of Real Estate Appraisal.* 7th or later edition. Chicago: Real Estate Education Company®.

7. Crawford, Linda L., and Edward J. O'Donnell. *Florida Real Estate Broker's Guide.* 1st edition. Chicago: Real Estate Education Company®, 1999.

8. Smith, Halbert C. *Real Estate Appraisal.* 2nd or later edition. Worthington, Ohio: Century VII Publishing Company.

9. Ring, Alfred A., and James H. Boykin. *The Valuation of Real Estate.* 1986 or later edition. Englewood Cliffs, N.J.: Prentice-Hall, Inc.

SECTION V. FINANCING REAL PROPERTY

1. Sirota, David. *Essentials of Real Estate Finance.* 9th or later edition. Chicago: Real Estate Education Company®.

2. Crawford, Linda L., and Edward J. O'Donnell. *Florida Real Estate Broker's Guide.* 1st edition. Chicago: Real Estate Education Company®, 1999.

3. Steinmetz, Thomas C. *The Mortgage Kit.* 4th or later edition. Chicago: Real Estate Education Company®.

4. Mettling, Stephen R., and Gerald R. Cortesi. *Modern Residential Financing Methods.* 2nd or later edition. Chicago: Real Estate Education Company®.

5. Turner, R. J. *The Mortgage Maze.* 1982 or later edition. Arlington, Va.: Alexandria House Books.

6. Gaines, George, Jr., David S. Coleman, and Linda Crawford. *Florida Real Estate Principles, Practices & Law.* 25th or later edition. Chicago: Real Estate Education Company®.

7. O'Donnell, Edward J. *Continuing Education for Florida Real Estate Professionals.* 2000-2001 edition. Chicago: Real Estate Education Company®.

SECTION VI. CLOSING THE TRANSACTION

1. Sirota, David. *Essentials of Real Estate Finance.* 9th or later edition. Chicago: Real Estate Education Company®.

2. Crawford, Linda L., and Edward J. O'Donnell. *Florida Real Estate Broker's Guide.* 1st edition. Chicago: Real Estate Education Company®, 1999.

3. Steinmetz, Thomas C. *The Mortgage Kit.* 4th or later edition. Chicago: Real Estate Education Company®.

4. Mettling, Stephen R., and Gerald R. Cortesi. *Modern Residential Financing Methods.* 2nd or later edition. Chicago: Real Estate Education Company®.

5. Turner, R. J. *The Mortgage Maze.* 1982 or later edition. Arlington, Va.: Alexandria House Books.

6. O'Donnell, Edward J. *Continuing Education for Florida Real Estate Professionals.* 2001-2002 edition. Chicago: Real Estate Education Company,®.

7. Koogler, Karen E. *Closing Concepts–A Title Training Manual for Settlement Escrow Professionals.* 3rd Edition. Largo, Fla.: The Koogler Group, 1996.

SECTION VII. COMMERCIAL AND RESIDENTIAL INVESTMENT PROPERTY

1. Sirota, David. *Essentials of Real Estate Investment.* 6th or later edition. Chicago: Real Estate Education Company®.
2. Kyle, Robert C., and Floyd M. Baird. *Property Management.* 5th or later edition. Chicago: Real Estate Education Company®.
3. Crawford, Linda L., and Edward J. O'Donnell. *Florida Real Estate Broker's Guide.* 1st edition. Chicago: Real Estate Education Company®, 1999.
4. Downs, James C., Jr. *Principles of Real Estate Management.* 12th or later edition. Chicago: Institute of Real Estate Management.

Forms

This appendix is intended as a resource for real estate professionals. The forms included here have been carefully prepared and may be freely copied and used. While we believe the forms to be complete and accurate, we make no representations as to their legality. Before using these forms, licensees are cautioned to seek legal and other professional advice.

NO BROKERAGE RELATIONSHIP NOTICE

IMPORTANT NOTICE

FLORIDA LAW REQUIRES THAT REAL ESTATE LICENSEES PROVIDE THIS NOTICE TO POTENTIAL SELLERS AND BUYERS OF REAL ESTATE.

You should not assume that any real estate broker or sales associate represents you unless you agree to engage in a real estate licensee in an authorized brokerage relationship, either as a single agent or as a transaction broker. You are advised not to disclose any information you want to be held in confidence until you decide on representation.

NO BROKERAGE RELATIONSHIP NOTICE

FLORIDA LAW REQUIRES THAT REAL ESTATE LICENSEES WHO HAVE NO BROKERAGE RELATIONSHIP WITH A POTENTIAL SELLER OR BUYER DISCLOSE THEIR DUTIES TO SELLERS AND BUYERS.

As a real estate licensee who has no brokerage relationship with you, _____ (insert name of Real Estate Entity) and its Associates owe to you the following duties:

1. Dealing honestly and fairly;

2. Disclosing all known facts that materially affect the value of residential real property which are not readily observable to the buyer.

3. Accounting for all funds entrusted to the licensee.

Signature	Date
Signature	Date

SINGLE AGENT NOTICE

IMPORTANT NOTICE

FLORIDA LAW REQUIRES THAT REAL ESTATE LICENSEES PROVIDE THIS NOTICE TO POTENTIAL SELLERS AND BUYERS OF REAL ESTATE.

You should not assume that any real estate broker or sales associate represents you unless you agree to engage a real estate licensee in an authorized brokerage relationship, either as a single agent or as a transaction broker. You are advised not to disclose any information you want to be held in confidence until you make a decision on representation.

SINGLE AGENT NOTICE

FLORIDA LAW REQUIRES THAT REAL ESTATE LICENSEES OPERATING AS SINGLE AGENTS DISCLOSE TO BUYERS AND SELLERS THEIR DUTIES.

As a single agent, _____, *(insert name of Real Estate Entity)* and its Associates owe to you the following duties:

1. Dealing honestly and fairly;

2. Loyalty;

3. Confidentiality;

4. Obedience;

5. Full disclosure;

6. Accounting for all funds;

7. Skill, care, and diligence in the transaction;

8. Presenting all offers and counteroffers in a timely manner, unless a party has previously directed the licensee otherwise in writing; and.

9. Disclosing all known facts that materially affect the value of residential real property and are not readily observable.

_____   _____
Signature   Date

_____   _____
Signature   Date

TRANSACTION BROKER NOTICE

IMPORTANT NOTICE

FLORIDA LAW REQUIRES THAT REAL ESTATE LICENSEES PROVIDE THIS NOTICE TO POTENTIAL SELLERS AND BUYERS OF REAL ESTATE.

You should not assume that any real estate broker or sales associate represents you unless you agree to engage a real estate licensee in an authorized brokerage relationship, either as a single agent or as a transaction broker. You are advised not to disclose any information you want to be held in confidence until you make a decision on representation.

TRANSACTION BROKER NOTICE

FLORIDA LAW REQUIRES THAT REAL ESTATE LICENSEES OPERATING AS TRANSACTION BROKERS DISCLOSE TO BUYERS AND SELLERS THEIR ROLE AND DUTIES IN PROVIDING A LIMITED FORM OF REPRESENTATION.

As a transaction broker, *(insert name of Real Estate Firm)* and its Associates, provides to you a limited form of representation that includes the following duties:

1. Dealing honestly and fairly;

2. Accounting for all funds;

3. Using skill, care, and diligence in the transaction;

4. Disclosing all known facts that materially affect the value of residential real property and are not readily observable to the buyer;

5. Presenting all offers and counteroffers in a timely manner, unless a party has previously directed the licensee otherwise in writing.

6. Limited confidentiality, unless waived in writing by a party. This limited confidentiality will prevent disclosure that the seller will accept a price less than the asking or listed price, that the buyer will pay a price greater than the price submitted in a written offer, of the motivation of any party for selling or buying property, that a seller or buyer will agree to financing terms other than those offered, or of any other information requested by a party to remain confidential; and

7. Any additional duties that are entered into by this or by separate written agreement.

Limited representation means that a buyer or seller is not responsible for the acts of the licensee. Additionally, parties are giving up their rights to the undivided loyalty of the licensee. This aspect of limited representation allows a licensee to facilitate a real estate transaction by assisting both the buyer and the seller, but a licensee will not work to represent one party to the detriment of the other party when acting as a transaction broker to both parties.

_____   _____
Signature   Date

_____   _____
Signature   Date

CONSENT TO TRANSITION TO TRANSACTION BROKER

CONSENT TO TRANSITION TO
TRANSACTION BROKER

FLORIDA LAW ALLOWS REAL ESTATE LICENSEES WHO REPRESENT A BUYER OR SELLER AS A SINGLE AGENT TO CHANGE FROM A SINGLE AGENT RELATIONSHIP TO A TRANSACTION BROKERAGE RELATIONSHIP IN ORDER FOR THE LICENSEE TO ASSIST BOTH PARTIES IN A REAL ESTATE TRANSACTION BY PROVIDING A LIMITED FORM OF REPRESENTATION TO BOTH THE BUYER AND THE SELLER. THIS CHANGE IN RELATIONSHIP CANNOT OCCUR WITHOUT YOUR PRIOR WRITTEN CONSENT.

As a transaction broker,_____, provides to you a limited form of
            (insert name of Real Estate Firm and its Associates)

representation that includes the following duties:

1. Dealing honestly and fairly;

2. Accounting for all funds;

3. Using skill, care and diligence in the transaction;

4. Disclosing all known facts that materially affect the value of residential real property and are not readily observable to the buyer;

5. Presenting all offers and counteroffers in a timely manner, unless a party has previously directed the licensee otherwise in writing;

6. Limited confidentiality, unless waived in writing by a party. This limited confidentiality will prevent disclosure that the seller will accept a price less than the asking or listed price, that the buyer will pay a price greater than the price submitted in a written offer, of the motivation of any party for selling or buying property, that a seller or buyer will agree to financing terms other than those offered, or of any other information requested by a party to remain confidential; and

7. Any additional duties that are entered into by this or by separate written agreement.

Limited representation means that a buyer or seller is not responsible for the acts of the licensee. Additionally, parties are giving up their rights to the undivided loyalty of the licensee. This aspect of limited representation allows a licensee to facilitate a real estate transaction by assisting both the buyer and the seller, but a licensee will not work to represent one party to the detriment of the other party when acting as a transaction broker to both parties.

I agree that my agent may assume the role and duties of a transaction broker.
        [Must be initialed or signed]

_____   _____
Signature   Date

_____   _____
Signature   Date

DESIGNATED SALES ASSOCIATE NOTICE

DESIGNATED SALES ASSOCIATE NOTICE

Florida law prohibits a designated sales associate from disclosing, except to the broker or persons specified by the broker, information made confidential by request or at the instruction of the customer the designated sales associate is representing. However, Florida law allows a designated sales associate to disclose information allowed to be disclosed or required to be disclosed by law and also allows a designated sales associate to disclose to his or her broker, or persons specified by the broker, confidential information of a customer for the purpose of seeking advice or assistance for the benefit of the customer in regard to a transaction. Florida law requires that the broker must hold this information confidential and may not use such information to the detriment of the other party.

_____

Date

_____   _____

Signature optional   Signature optional

IMPORTANT NOTICE

FLORIDA LAW REQUIRES THAT REAL ESTATE LICENSEES PROVIDE THIS NOTICE TO POTENTIAL SELLERS AND BUYERS OF REAL ESTATE.

You should not assume that any real estate broker or sales associate represents you unless you agree to engage a real estate licensee in an authorized brokerage relationship, either as a single agent or as a transaction broker. You are advised not to disclose any information you want to be held in confidence until you make a decision on representation.

SINGLE AGENT NOTICE

FLORIDA LAW REQUIRES THAT REAL ESTATE LICENSEES OPERATING AS SINGLE AGENTS DISCLOSE TO BUYERS AND SELLERS THEIR DUTIES.

As a single agent, _____(insert name of Real Estate Entity) and its Associates owe to you the following duties:

1. Dealing honestly and fairly;
2. Loyalty;
3. Confidentiality;
4. Obedience;
5. Full disclosure;
6. Accounting for all funds;
7. Skill, care, and diligence in the transaction;
8. Presenting all offers and counteroffers in a timely manner, unless a party has previously directed the licensee otherwise in writing; and
9. Disclosing all known facts that materially affect the value of residential real property and are not readily observable.

_____   _____

Signature   Date

_____   _____

Signature   Date

GOALS WORKSHEET

1. During the next 12 months, I want to earn $_____

2. That works out to be monthly earnings of $_____
    (Line 1 ÷ 12)

3. Approximately 60% of my earnings should come from listings sold $_____
    (Line 2 × .60)

4. Approximately 40% of my earnings should come from sales made $_____
    (Line 2 × .40)

Achieving my listing income:

5. In my market area, the average listing commission amount is $_____
    (Get this amount from your broker.)

6. So I must have the following number of listings sold   _____
    (Line 3 ÷ Line 5)

7. If only 75% of my listings sell, I have to get this many listings: _____
    (Line 6 ÷ .75)

8. It may take this many listing appointments to get a listing: _____
    (Get this number from your broker.)

9. So I need to go on this many listing appointments   _____
    (Line 7 × Line 8)

10. It may take this many calls to get an appointment   _____
    (Get this number from your broker.)

11. So I have to make this many calls per month: _____
    (Line 9 × Line 10)

12. Which means this many calls per week   _____
    (Line 11 ÷ 4.3 weeks per month)

Achieving my sales income:

13. In my market area, the average sales commission is $_____
    (Get this amount from your broker.)

14. So I've got to make this many sales per month: _____
    (Line 4 ÷ Line 13)

15. It takes about this many showings to make a sale: _____
    (Get this number from your broker.)

16. So I must show this many properties per month: _____
    (Line 14 × Line 15)

FAIR HOUSING POSTER

U.S. Department of Housing and Urban Development

**EQUAL HOUSING
OPPORTUNITY**

We Do Business in Accordance With the Federal Fair Housing Law
(The Fair Housing Amendments Act of 1988)

It is Illegal to Discriminate Against Any Person Because of Race, Color, Religion, Sex, Handicap, Familial Status, or National Origin

■ In the sale or rental of housing or residential lots

■ In advertising the sale or rental of housing

■ In the financing of housing

■ In the provision of real estate brokerage services

■ In the appraisal of housing

■ Blockbusting is also illegal

Anyone who feels he or she has been discriminated against may file a complaint of housing discrimination with the:
1-800-424-8590 (Toll Free)
1-800-424-8529 (TDD)

**U.S. Department of Housing and
Urban Development
Assistant Secretary for Fair Housing and
Equal Opportunity
Washington, D.C. 20410**

Previous editions are obsolete   form **HUD-928.1** (3-89)

SOURCE: *Modern Real Estate Practice,* 15th Edition, by Galaty, Allaway and Kyle. Dearborn™ Real Estate Education.

SELLER'S REAL PROPERTY DISCLOSURE STATEMENT

SELLER'S PROPERTY DISCLOSURE

(IT IS SUGGESTED THAT COPIES OF THIS DISCLOSURE BE AVAILABLE AT THE PROPERTY)

STATEMENT

SELLER: _____

Property Address: _____

Date Property Purchased _____ If improved, year built_____

NOTICE TO SELLER: Every SELLER is obligated to disclose to a BUYER all known facts that materially and/or adversely affect the value of the property being sold. This disclosure statement is intended to assist SELLER in complying with disclosure requirements and to assist BUYER in evaluating the property being considered. The listing broker, the selling broker and their respective salespersons will also rely upon this information when they evaluate, market and present SELLER'S property to prospective BUYERS.

NOTICE TO BUYER: This is a disclosure of SELLER'S knowledge of the condition of the property as of the date signed by the SELLER and is not a substitute for any inspections that BUYER may wish to obtain. It is not a warranty of any kind by SELLER or a warranty or representation by the listing broker, the selling broker, or their salespersons.

• If this property is unimproved, complete sections 15 to 19 only.
• When explanations are needed please give details such as location, extent, date, and name of repair persons. Use extra sheets if necessary.

1. **OCCUPANCY**
   (a) Does SELLER currently occupy this property? ❑ Yes ❑ No
   (b) If not, when did SELLER vacate property?_____
   (c) If property is vacant, provide date it was vacated._____
   (d) Is the property tenant occupied? ❑ Yes ❑ No
   (e) If "Yes," is there a written lease? ❑ Yes ❑ No
   (f) Length of lease_____ Date lease ends: _____
   (g) Payment due under lease_____

2. **STRUCTURAL ITEMS**
   (a) Name of Contractor or Builder who built home, if known_____
   (b) Are you aware of any past or present movement, shifting, deterioration, structural damage or other problems with walls or foundations? ❑ Yes ❑ No
   (c) Are you aware of any past or present cracks or flaws in the walls, foundation or other parts of property? ❑ Yes ❑ No
   (d) Are you aware of any past or present water leakage or intrusion in the property? ❑ Yes ❑ No
   (e) Are you aware of any past or present problems with driveways, walkways, patios, or retaining walls? ❑ Yes ❑ No
   (f) Have there been any repairs or other efforts to control the cause or effect of any problem described above? ❑ Yes ❑ No
   (g) Has there ever been a fire in this property? ❑ Yes ❑ No ❑ Unknown
   (h) Are you aware of any problems with the fireplace? ❑ Yes ❑ No
   If any of your answers are "Yes," explain in detail: _____
   _____
   _____

3. **ADDITIONS / REMODELING**
   (a) Have you made any additions, structural changes, or other alterations to the property? ❑ Yes ❑ No
   (b) If "Yes," explain: _____
   (c) If "Yes," did you obtain all necessary permits? ❑ Yes ❑ No Was all the work in compliance with building codes? ❑ Yes ❑ No
   If your answer is "No," explain:_____
   (d) Did the previous owners make any additions, structural changes, or other alterations to the property that you are aware of?
   ❑ Yes ❑ No ❑ Unknown
   (e) If "Yes," explain: _____
   (f) Please provide the name of any Contractor or individual who did any additions, structural changes or other alterations to the property, if known._____

4. **ROOF**
   (a) Year roof put on_____
   (b) Has the roof ever leaked during your ownership? ❑ Yes ❑ No
   (c) Has the roof been replaced or repaired during your ownership? ❑ Yes ❑ No
   If "Yes," provide name of Contractor or individual who did the work and details of replacement/repair _____
   _____
   (d) Do you know of any problems with the roof or gutters? ❑ Yes ❑ No
   If any of your answers are "Yes," explain in detail: _____
   _____
   _____

SELLER'S REAL PROPERTY DISCLOSURE STATEMENT (Continued)

5. SIDING
(a) Exterior siding material(s)
    ❑ Brick   ❑ Wood   ❑ Vinyl   ❑ Stucco   ❑ Synthetic Stucco   ❑ Manufactured Siding
    ❑ Other_____   ❑ Unknown
(b) If manufactured siding, provide name of manufacturer, if known_____
(c) Do you know of any problems/defects with the siding? ❑ Yes   ❑ No
(d) Have you filed any claims with manufacturers in regards to the siding? ❑ Yes   ❑ No
If any of your answers are "Yes," explain in detail: _____
_____
_____

6. WINDOWS
(a) Are the windows insulated glass? ❑ Yes   ❑ No
(b) If "Yes," are there any fogged windows? ❑ Yes   ❑ No   ❑ Unknown
    If "Yes," which ones_____
(c) Are any windows broken or cracked? ❑ Yes   ❑ No   ❑ Unknown
(d) Do all operable windows open, stay open, close and lock properly? ❑ Yes   ❑ No   ❑ Unknown
(e) Are any screens missing or damaged? ❑ Yes   ❑ No   ❑ Unknown
If "Yes," which ones_____

Page 1 of 3   Initials _____ _____
_____ _____

7. HEATING AND AIR CONDITIONING
(a) Air Conditioning: ❑ Central Electric ❑ Natural Gas ❑ Window Units Number units included in sale_____
(b) Heating: ❑ Central Electric ❑ Central Electric Heat Pump ❑ Fuel Oil ❑ Natural Gas ❑ Other_____
Are you aware of any problems regarding these items? ❑ Yes   ❑ No
If "Yes," explain in detail: _____
_____
_____

8. ELECTRICAL SYSTEM
(a) Are you aware of any problems with the electrical system? ❑ Yes   ❑ No
(b) Who supplies electrical service: ❑ City of Tallahassee ❑ Talquin
(c) Average utility bill? $_____ month
(d) Number of people living in property_____
Comments:_____
_____

9. PLUMBING
(a) Are you aware of any problems with the plumbing system? ❑ Yes   ❑ No
(b) Are you aware of any leaks, back-ups, water, and sewer/septic tank problems? ❑ Yes   ❑ No
(c) What is your water supply source: ❑ Public   ❑ Community Well   ❑ Well on Property
(d) If your water is from a well, have there ever been repairs/replacements to the well or pump? ❑ Yes   ❑ No   ❑ Unknown
(e) Has the well water ever been tested? ❑ Yes   ❑ No   ❑ Unknown   Test Results:_____
(f) Do you have a water softener? ❑ Yes   ❑ No   If "Yes," is the system ❑ Owned   ❑ Leased
(g) What is the type of sewage system do you have? ❑ Public   ❑ Community Sewer   ❑ Septic Tank(s) How Many_____
    Location(s) _____ When was septic tank last pumped?_____
(h) Type of water heater? ❑ Gas   ❑ Electric   ❑ Solar   ❑ Number of gallons?_____ Is it on a timer? ❑ Yes ❑ No
If any of your answers are "Yes," explain in detail: _____
_____
_____

10. OTHER EQUIPMENT AND APPLIANCES INCLUDED IN SALE
Mark the items included in the sale of your property:
❑ Electric Garage Door Opener   Number of transmitters?_____

❑ Smoke Detector(s) How many?_____		
❑ Refrigerator	❑ Refrigerator w/ice maker	❑ Ice Maker
❑ Microwave Oven	❑ Dishwasher	❑ Garbage Disposal
❑ Trash Compactor	❑ Intercom	❑ Washer ❑ Dryer
❑ Ceiling Fan(s) Number of fans?_____	❑ Central Vacuum	
❑ Fireplace insert	❑ Sprinkler system	

❑ Oil/Propane Tanks   ❑ Owned   ❑ Leased, If leased, from whom _____ Cost _____
❑ Security System   ❑ Owned   ❑ Leased, If leased, from whom _____ Cost _____
❑ Other:_____
If any of these items have any defects, explain in detail: _____

SELLER'S REAL PROPERTY DISCLOSURE STATEMENT (Continued)

11. POOL / SPA / HOT TUB (Complete if applicable)

(a) ❑ POOL   year installed_____
     ❑ In ground: ❑ gunnite   ❑ fiberglass   ❑ vinyl   age of liner _____
     ❑ Above ground
(b) Pool heater: ❑ none   ❑ gas   ❑ electric   ❑ solar
(c) Pool pump: year installed_____   Filter type:_____   year installed_____
(d) Is pool equipment included? ❑ Yes   ❑ No
     If "Yes," itemize: _____
(e) ❑ SPA/HOT TUB   year installed_____
(f) Spa heater: ❑ none   ❑ gas   ❑ electric   ❑ solar
(g) Is Spa equipment included? ❑ Yes   ❑ No
     If "Yes," itemize: _____
If you are aware of any problems with any of the items above, please explain in detail:_____
_____
_____

12. EXCLUSIONS/LEASED SYSTEMS

(a) Is there anything on or about the property excluded from the sale? ❑ Yes   ❑ No
     If "Yes," itemize_____
     _____

(b) Are there any other leased systems that are not addressed elsewhere in the disclosure? ❑ Yes   ❑ No
     If "Yes," itemize:_____
     _____

13. CRAWL SPACES AND BASEMENTS (Complete if applicable)

(a) Has there ever been any water leakage, accumulation of water or dampness in the basement or crawl space? ❑ Yes   ❑ No
(b) Have there been any repairs or other attempts to control any water or dampness problems in the basement or crawlspace? ❑ Yes   ❑ No
If any of your answers are "Yes," explain in detail:_____
_____

14. WOOD DESTROYING ORGANISMS

(a) Have termites, wood destroying insects, or wood rot affected the property during your ownership? ❑ Yes   ❑ No
(b) Has there ever been any damage to the property caused by termites, wood destroying insects or wood rot during your ownership? ❑ Yes   ❑ No
(c) Is the property currently under bond for a wood destroying insect from a licensed pest control company? ❑ Yes   ❑ No
     What type of bond?_____What company?_____
(d) Do you know of any wood destroying organisms reports on the property in the last five years? ❑ Yes   ❑ No
If any of your answers are "Yes," explain in detail:_____
_____
_____

Page 2 of 3   Initials _____ _____
                         _____ _____

15. SOIL / DRAINAGE / BOUNDARIES

(a) Is there any fill or pipe clay on the property? ❑ Yes   ❑ No   ❑ Unknown
(b) Has there been any settling or earth movement on the property or in the immediate neighborhood? ❑ Yes   ❑ No   ❑ Unknown
(c) Is the property located in a flood hazard area? ❑ Yes   ❑ No   ❑ Unknown
     Flood zone, if known_____
(d) Is flood insurance required by your lender? ❑ Yes   ❑ No
(e) Have there been any past or present drainage or flood problems affecting the property or adjacent properties? ❑ Yes   ❑ No   ❑ Unknown
(f) Are there any encroachments, excroachments, boundary line disputes, or easements affecting the property? ❑ Yes   ❑ No   ❑ Unknown
(g) Are there any shared driveways, fences or joint use agreements? ❑ Yes   ❑ No
(h) Who owns any fences? _____
If any answers are "Yes," explain in detail:_____
_____

16. TOXIC SUBSTANCES

(a) Are you aware of any hazardous materials in, on or about the property? (Hazardous Materials may include but shall not be limited to: lead-based paint, asbestos materials, asbestos siding, and buried oil, fuel or other storage tanks) ❑ Yes   ❑ No
(b) Are you aware of the property ever being tested for radon or any other toxic substances? ❑ Yes   ❑ No
If any answers are "Yes," explain in detail:_____

SELLER'S REAL PROPERTY DISCLOSURE STATEMENT (Continued)

17. NEIGHBORHOOD

(a) Are you aware of any proposed change or condition in your neighborhood that could affect the value or desirability of the property?
❑ Yes ❑ No

(b) If "Yes," explain in detail: _____
_____

18. ASSOCIATIONS

(a) Is the property part of a ❑ homeowner's association ❑ condominium association ❑ other type of association _____

(b) Is the property subject to covenants, conditions and restrictions of the association? ❑ Yes ❑ No

(c) Are you aware if the property has any violations of the restrictive covenants? ❑ Yes ❑ No

(d) If "Yes," explain in detail: _____
_____

If the property is part of an association, complete the following:

(e) What is the annual fee? $ _____ How is it paid? _____ ❑ monthly ❑ yearly ❑ other _____

(f) What does the annual fee cover? _____

(g) Are fees current? ❑ Yes ❑ No

(h) Who is the contact person for the association? _____ Phone # _____

(i) Are there any defects, damages, legal actions, conditions or assessments that may affect the association or its fees? ❑ Yes ❑ No

(j) If "Yes," explain in detail: _____
_____

19. OTHER MATTERS

(a) Does anyone have a first right of refusal to buy or an option to buy to this property? ❑ Yes ❑ No

(b) Is there any existing or threatened legal action affecting the property? ❑ Yes ❑ No

(c) Are you aware of any zoning violation, non-conforming use, set back violations, or proposed zoning or road changes? ❑ Yes ❑ No

(d) Are you aware of any violations of local, state, or federal laws or regulations relating to this property? ❑ Yes ❑ No

(d) Is there anything else you feel you should disclose to a prospective buyer that may materially and/or adversely affect the value or desirability of the property? ❑ Yes ❑ No

(e) If "Yes," explain in detail: _____
_____
_____
_____

The undersigned SELLER represents that the information set forth in the foregoing property disclosure statement is accurate and complete to the best of the SELLER'S knowledge. SELLER does not intend this property disclosure statement to be a warranty or guaranty of any kind. SELLER hereby authorizes Listing Broker to provide this information to prospective BUYERS and to other real estate brokers and other agents.

SELLER understands and agrees that SELLER will immediately notify Listing Broker in writing if any information set forth in this property disclosure changes.

Seller: _____ Date: _____

Seller: _____ Date: _____

RECEIPT AND ACKNOWLEDGMENT BY BUYER

BUYER hereby acknowledges receipt of a copy of this property disclosure. BUYER furthermore acknowledges BUYER has been in and upon subject property. BUYER is strongly advised to obtain property inspection(s) as provided for in the Deposit Receipt and Contract for Sale and Purchase. BUYER should select professionals with appropriate qualifications to conduct inspections. BUYER is advised that some properties may have siding materials (such as, but not limited to, Louisiana Pacific and Synthetic Stucco) that have failed the manufacturer's warranties and/or have been known to have defects, and that inspection is one way to identify this and determine what conditions these materials may be in. BUYER is aware that this property disclosure is not intended as a warranty or guaranty of any kind by SELLER. The Brokers and their salespersons do not warrant or guarantee the condition of the property and are in no way responsible for the condition of the property. BUYER understands that the property is being sold in its present condition unless otherwise agreed upon in the Deposit Receipt and Contract for Sale and Purchase. BUYER acknowledges no representations concerning the condition of the property are being relied upon by BUYER except as disclosed herein or in the Deposit Receipt and Contract for Sale and Purchase.

Buyer: _____ Date: _____

Buyer: _____ Date: _____

DISCLOSURE OF LEAD-BASED PAINT AND LEAD-BASED PAINT HAZARDS

LEAD-BASED PAINT OR LEAD-BASED PAINT HAZARD ADDENDUM

It is a condition of this contract that, until midnight of _____ , Buyer shall have the right to obtain a risk assessment or inspection of the Property for the presence of lead-based paint and/or lead-based paint hazards* at Buyer's expense. This contingency will terminate at that time unless Buyer or Buyer's agent delivers to the Seller or Seller's agent a written inspection and/or risk assessment report listing the specific existing deficiencies and corrections needed, if any. If any corrections are necessary, Seller shall have the option of (i) completing them, (ii) providing for their completion, or (iii) refusing to complete them. If Seller elects not to complete or provide for completion of the corrections, then Buyer shall have the option of (iv) accepting the Property in its present condition, or (v) terminating this contract, in which case all earnest monies shall be refunded to Buyer. Buyer may waive the right to obtain a risk assessment or inspection of the Property for the presence of lead-based paint and/or lead based paint hazards at any time without cause.

*Intact lead-based paint that is in good condition is not necessarily a hazard. See EPA pamphlet "Protect Your Family From Lead in Your Home" for more information.

Disclosure of Information on Lead-Based Paint and Lead-Based Paint Hazards

Lead Warning Statement

Every Buyer of any interest in residential real property on which a residential dwelling was built prior to 1978 is notified that such property may present exposure to lead from lead-based paint that may place young children at risk of developing lead poisoning. Lead poisoning in young children may produce permanent neurological damage, including learning disabilities, reduced intelligence quotient, behavioral problems, and impaired memory. Lead poisoning also poses a particular risk to pregnant women. The Seller of any interest in residential real property is required to provide the Buyer with any information on lead-based paint hazards from risk assessments or inspections in the Seller's possession and notify the Buyer of any known lead-based paint hazards. A risk assessment or inspection for possible lead-based paint hazards is recommended prior to purchase.

Seller's Disclosure (initial)

_____ (a) Presence of lead-based paint and/or lead-based paint hazards (check one below):
  ❏ Known lead-based paint and/or lead-based paint hazards are present in the housing (explain).

  _____

  _____

  ❏ Seller has no knowledge of lead-based paint and/or lead-based paint hazards in the housing.
_____ (b) Records and reports available to the Seller (check one below):
  ❏ Seller has provided the Buyer with all available records and reports pertaining to lead-based paint and/or lead-based paint hazards in the housing (list documents below).

  _____

  _____

  ❏ Seller has no reports or records pertaining to lead-based paint and/or lead-based paint hazards in the housing.

Buyer's Acknowledgment (initial)

_____ (c) Buyer has received copies of all information listed above.
_____ (d) Buyer has received the pamphlet *Protect Your Family from Lead in Your Home.*
_____ (e) Buyer has (check one below):
  ❏ Received a 10-day opportunity (or mutually agreed upon period) to conduct a risk assessment or inspection for the presence of lead-based paint and/or lead-based paint hazards; or
  ❏ Waived the opportunity to conduct a risk assessment or inspection for the presence of lead-based paint and/or lead-based paint hazards.

Agent's Acknowledgment (initial)

_____ (f) Agent has informed the Seller of the Seller's obligations under 42 U.S.C. 4582(d) and is aware of his/her responsibility to ensure compliance.

Certification of Accuracy

The following parties have reviewed the information above and certify, to the best of their knowledge, that the information provided by the signatory is true and accurate.

Buyer: _____ (SEAL) Date _____
Buyer: _____ (SEAL) Date _____
Agent: _____ Date _____
Seller: _____ (SEAL) Date _____
Seller: _____ (SEAL) Date _____
Agent: _____ Date _____

Source: *Modern Real Estate Practice,* 15th Edition, by Galaty, Allaway and Kyle. Dearborn™ Real Estate Education, Chicago, 2000.

COMPARATIVE MARKET ANALYSIS

Comparative Market Analysis

Prepared by: _____

Date: _____

Prepared for: _____

Property Address: _____

Features: _____

Properties sold within the previous 12 months

Property Address	Sales Price	List Price	Days on Mkt.	Living Area	Features	Estimated Adjustment	Adjusted Sales Price	Comments

Percent sales price/list price _____ %   Median $ _____

Properties currently on the market

Property Address	List Price	Days on Mkt.	Living Area	Features	Estimated Adjustment	As Adjusted	Comments

Median $ _____

Properties which were listed but failed to sell during the previous 12 months

Property Address	List Price	Days on Mkt.	Living Area	Features	Estimated Adjustment	As Adjusted	Comments

Median $ _____

The suggested marketing range is $ _____ to $ _____

This information is believed to be accurate, but is not warranted.
This is an opinion of value and should not be considered an appraisal.

MORTGAGE LOAN APPLICATION CHECKLIST

Place personal and company information/logo here	Mortgage Lender: _____ Address: _____ Loan Officer: _____ Phone: _____ Date of Application: _____ Time: _____

Thanks for using our real estate firm to find your home. To assist you in making your mortgage loan application, we have prepared the list of items that may be needed by the lender. Additional information may be requested.

The Transaction:
- ❑ Copy of the signed purchase contract.
- ❑ If you have sold your present home, a copy of the HUD-1 closing statement. If the sale is not complete, a copy of the signed purchase contract.

Your Income:
- ❑ Original pay stubs for the latest 30-day period.
- ❑ Original W-2 forms for the previous two years.
- ❑ If you are self-employed or have commission income: a year-to-date profit and loss statement and balance sheet; copies of your last two years' personal and business signed federal tax returns.
- ❑ If you are using child support payments to qualify for mortgage: proof of receipt.

Your Assets:
- ❑ Original bank statements for all checking and savings accounts for the past three months. You should be able to explain all deposits not from payroll.
- ❑ Original statements from investment or brokerage firms for the last three months (if applicable).
- ❑ Original IRA or 401(k) statements (if applicable).
- ❑ List of real estate owned: address, market value, mortgage balance, name and address of mortgage company.
- ❑ List of life insurance policies with company name, face value, beneficiaries, and cash surrender value.
- ❑ List of automobiles, with make, model, value, amount owed, lender name, address and account number.
- ❑ Estimate of replacement value of household furniture and appliances.
- ❑ Value of other assets (collections, art, etc.)
- ❑ If you have sold a home in the past two years, a copy of the closing statement and a copy of the deed given.

Your Liabilties:
- ❑ Credit cards: name, address, account number, monthly payment; and present balance.
- ❑ Other liabilities: name, address, account number, monthly payment and present balance.

Payments for Housing:
- ❑ List of addresses for previous two years, along with names, addresses and phone numbers of landlords and/or mortgage companies where housing payments were made.
- ❑ Last 12 month's cancelled checks for housing payments (landlord or mortgage company).

If you are divorced:
- ❑ Copies of all divorce decrees, including any modifications or stipulations.
- ❑ Child support or alimony payments: amount, duration, and proof of payment for 12 months.

If you are applying for an FHA loan:
- ❑ Photocoy of driver's license or other acceptable photo ID.
- ❑ Photocopy of Social Security Card.

If you are applying for a VA loan:
- ❑ VA Certificate of Eligibilty.
- ❑ Form DD-214.

For in-service veterans or those discharged within the past two years.
- ❑ Statement of Service.
- ❑ Most recent Leave and Earnings Statement.

Other items:
- ❑ If you have graduated from high school or college within the previous two years, a copy of your diploma or transcripts.
- ❑ If you have a gap in employment for 30 days or more, include a letter explaining the reason.
- ❑ If part of your down payment is a gift, the lender will give you a gift letter for signature when you apply.
- ❑ If you have filed bankruptcy in the last seven years, give a letter explaining the reasons, a copy of the Petition Decree, a Schedule of Creditors, and the Discharge document.
- ❑ If you have rental property, a copy of the current lease and two year's signed income tax returns.

Your Check:
- ❑ Your check for the appraisal and application fee.

AUTHORIZATION FOR SALES ASSOCIATE TO ORDER WORK AND CUSTOMER'S AGREEMENT TO PAY

**AUTHORIZATION FOR SALES ASSOCIATE TO ORDER WORK AND
CUSTOMER'S AGREEMENT TO PAY**

Re: Property Address: _____

Responsible Person: _____ as ❑ Owner ❑ Buyer
Address: _____
Phone Number: _____
I hereby authorize _____ of
_____ to order on my behalf the item specified below and agree
to pay for said item upon demand as required by supplier regardless of the outcome of this property
transaction. I understand that these arrangements are being made by the sales associate as a courtesy
to me. I shall look to the supplier only for performance and workmanship and absolve sales associate
and the brokerage firm for the performance and workmanship of the supplier.

Item to be ordered by sales associate:

_____

_____

Supplier: _____   Price Quoted: _____

Signature: _____Date: _____

SUPPLIER AGREEMENT TO PROVIDE SERVICE AND
TO LOOK ONLY TO RESPONSIBLE PARTY FOR PAYMENT

Re: Property Address: _____
    City: _____

Supplier: _____
Phone Number: _____

I agree to provide the item/service specified below and agree to seek compensation from
"responsible party" shown above. I understand that these arrangements are being made by the sales
associate in this transaction as a courtesy to me. I agree to look to the "responsible party" only for
compensation and absolve sales associate and brokerage firm for the cost of the item/service.

Item to be ordered by sales associate:

_____

_____

Supplier: _____   Price Quoted: _____

Signature: _____Date: _____

PRECLOSING WALK-THROUGH INSPECTION RESULTS

Property Address: _____ Date of Inspection: _____

Seller: _____ Buyer: _____

I have made a walk-through inspection of the property. I acknowledge that the sales associate has accompanied me to the property to make it available, and not to conduct the inspection. I take complete responsibility for the inspection and agree to hold harmless the sales associate and the brokerage firm from any liability in connection with the inspection.

My inspection shows that:

1. personal property items required by the contract to
   be left are present in the property   ❑ Yes   ❑ No

2. required repairs, if any, have been completed   ❑ Yes   ❑ No

3. the property has been maintained in the condition as it
   existed at the time of the contract, reasonable wear and
   tear excepted.   ❑ Yes   ❑ No

Comments _____

_____

I accept the property as inspected and release the sellers, sales associates and brokers in this transaction of any further responsibilty for warranting the property. I have been notified of the benefits of having the property covered by a homeowner's warranty. If the seller has not provided such a warranty, I ❑ accept   ❑ decline to purchase coverage at a cost of $ _____.

Buyer: _____   Date: _____

Buyer: _____   Date: _____

PROPERTY SALE INFORMATION SHEET

Property Address: _____

Seller: _____   Buyer: _____

Contract Date: _____   Closing Date (Est.): _____

Seller	Buyer
Listing Broker: _____ Phone: _____ Fax: _____ Listing sales associate: _____ Home Ph.: _____ Office Ph.: _____ Mobile Ph.: _____	**Selling Broker:** _____ Phone: _____ Fax: _____ Selling sales associate: _____ Home Ph.: _____ Office Ph.: _____ Mobile Ph.: _____
Seller: _____ Old address: _____ New address: _____ City, State, Zip_____ Current Home Ph.: _____ Ofc.: _____	**Buyer:** _____ Present address: _____ City, State, Zip_____ Current Home Ph.: _____Ofc.: _____ Will buyer occupy new home? _____
Existing mortgage for Payoff (P) Assumption (A) 1st Mortgage holder:_____ 2nd Mortgage holder:_____	New Mortgage Lender: _____ Type (Fixed; ARM: FHA, VA, Conv.):_____ LTV Ratio: ____% Interest Rate: ____% Yrs: ____
Seller's Attorney:_____ Ph.: _____	Buyer's Attorney: _____ Ph.: _____

Lender:_____   **Loan Officer:** _____

Title Company:_____   **Closing Agent:**_____

Appraiser: _____

Date Scheduled to Close: _____

Service Providers:
    Pest inspection: _____   Ph.: _____
    Home inspection: _____   Ph.: _____
    Roof inspection: _____   Ph.: _____
    Contractor: _____   Ph.: _____
    Surveyor: _____   Ph.: _____

Buyer's Insurance Company: _____
    Agent: _____   Phone: _____

Property status: ❏ Occupied by seller   ❏ Occupied by tenant   ❏ Vacant

Key to property for inspection: ❏ At listing office   ❏ In lockbox at property   ❏ Call seller for appointment

CLOSING PROGRESS CHART

Property Address: _____

Seller: _____ Buyer: _____

Listing Sales Associate				**Closing Progress Chart**				**Selling Sales Associate**	
#	Sched Date	Actual Date	X	**Closing Duties**	Done √	X	Sched Date	Actual Date	
1				"Sale pending" sign on listing					
2				Notice of under contract to MLS					
3				Binder deposited in bank $_____					
4				Additional binder received, if rquired. $ _____					
5				Loan application made by buyer					
6				Contingencies cleared in wirting:					
7				Home inspection By: _____					
8				Soil test from: _____					
9				Roof inspection By: _____					
10				Other (describe): _____					
11				Appraisal By: _____					
12				Loan approval From: _____					
13				Title insurance ordered from: _____					
14				Pest inspection ordered (after loan approval) from:					
15				Report received and delivered to buyer					
16				Report received and delivered to lender					
17				Treatment ordered, if required					
18				Structure inspection ordered, if necessary					
19				Work completed and approved					
20				Required repairs ordered					
21				Required repairs completed					
22				Survey ordered (After loan approval)					
23				Survey completed. Results. . .					
24				Encroachments, survey problems cleared					
25				Buyer to get hazard insurance					
26				Insurance policy to title closing agent					
27				Buyer/seller contacted for closing appointment					
28				Pre-closing inspection					
29				Closing papers reviewed with buyer/seller 1 day prior					
30				Buyer given figure for certified check for closing					
31				Binder check prepared to take to closing					
32				Closing date					
33				Signed closing papers received by sales associate					
34				**Post-closing duties:**					
35				Commission check to broker					
36				Sign/lockbox picked up from property					
37				Buyer/seller letter of thanks					
38				Follow-up visit to buyer/seller					
39				Notice of closed sale to MLS					

SETTLEMENT STATEMENT FORM

A. **Settlement Statement**	U.S. Department of Housing and Urban Development	OMB Approval No. 2502-0265

B. Type of Loan

1. ☐ FHA 2. ☐ FmHA 3. ☐ Conv. Unins. 4. ☐ VA 5. ☐ Conv. Ins.	6. File Number:	7. Loan Number:	8. Mortgage Insurance Case Number:

C. Note: This form is furnished to give you a statement of actual settlement costs. Amounts paid to and by the settlement agent are shown. Items marked "(p.o.c.)" were paid outside the closing; they are shown here for informational purposes and are not included in the totals.

D. Name & Address of Borrower:	E. Name & Address of Seller:	F. Name & Address of Lender:

G. Property Location:	H. Settlement Agent:	
	Place of Settlement:	I. Settlement Date:

J. Summary of Borrower's Transaction		K. Summary of Seller's Transaction	
100. Gross Amount Due From Borrower		**400. Gross Amount Due To Seller**	
101. Contract sales price		401. Contract sales price	
102. Personal property		402. Personal property	
103. Settlement charges to borrower (line 1400)		403.	
104.		404.	
105.		405.	
Adjustments for items paid by seller in advance		**Adjustments for items paid by seller in advance**	
106. City/town taxes to		406. City/town taxes to	
107. County taxes to		407. County taxes to	
108. Assessments to		408. Assessments to	
109.		409.	
110.		410.	
111.		411.	
112.		412.	
120. Gross Amount Due From Borrower		**420. Gross Amount Due To Seller**	
200. Amounts Paid By Or In Behalf Of Borrower		**500. Reductions In Amount Due To Seller**	
201. Deposit or earnest money		501. Excess deposit (see instructions)	
202. Principal amount of new loan(s)		502. Settlement charges to seller (line 1400)	
203. Existing loan(s) taken subject to		503. Existing loan(s) taken subject to	
204.		504. Payoff of first mortgage loan	
205.		505. Payoff of second mortgage loan	
206.		506.	
207.		507.	
208.		508.	
209.		509.	
Adjustments for items unpaid by seller		**Adjustments for items unpaid by seller**	
210. City/town taxes to		510. City/town taxes to	
211. County taxes to		511. County taxes to	
212. Assessments to		512. Assessments to	
213.		513.	
214.		514.	
215.		515.	
216.		516.	
217.		517.	
218.		518.	
219.		519.	
220. Total Paid By/For Borrower		**520. Total Reduction Amount Due Seller**	
300. Cash At Settlement From/To Borrower		**600. Cash At Settlement To/From Seller**	
301. Gross Amount due from borrower (line 120)		601. Gross amount due to seller (line 420)	
302. Less amounts paid by/for borrower (line 220)	( )	602. Less reductions in amt. due seller (line 520)	( )
303. Cash ☐ From ☐ To Borrower		603. Cash ☐ To ☐ From Seller	

SETTLEMENT STATEMENT FORM (Continued)

L. Settlement Charges

		Paid From Borrowers Funds at Settlement	Paid From Seller's Funds at Settlement
700. Total Sales/Broker's Commission based on price $ _____ @ _____ % =			
Division of Commission (line 700) as follows:			
701. $ _____ to			
702. $ _____ to			
703. Commission paid at Settlement			
704.			
800. Items Payable In Connection With Loan			
801. Loan Origination Fee _____ %			
802. Loan Discount _____ %			
803. Appraisal Fee to			
804. Credit Report to			
805. Lender's Inspection Fee			
806. Mortgage Insurance Application Fee to			
807. Assumption Fee			
808.			
809.			
810.			
811.			
900. Items Required By Lender To Be Paid In Advance			
901. Interest from _____ to _____ @$ _____ /day			
902. Mortgage Insurance Premium for _____ months to			
903. Hazard Insurance Premium for _____ years to			
904. _____ years to			
905.			
1000. Reserves Deposited With Lender			
1001. Hazard insurance _____ months@$ _____ per month			
1002. Mortgage insurance _____ months@$ _____ per month			
1003. City property taxes _____ months@$ _____ per month			
1004. County property taxes _____ months@$ _____ per month			
1005. Annual assessments _____ months@$ _____ per month			
1006. _____ months@$ _____ per month			
1007. _____ months@$ _____ per month			
1008. _____ months@$ _____ per month			
1100. Title Charges			
1101. Settlement or closing fee to			
1102. Abstract or title search to			
1103. Title examination to			
1104. Title insurance binder to			
1105. Document preparation to			
1106. Notary fees to			
1107. Attorney's fees to			
(includes above items numbers: _____)			
1108. Title insurance to			
(includes above items numbers: _____)			
1109. Lender's coverage $			
1110. Owner's coverage $			
1111.			
1112.			
1113.			
1200. Government Recording and Transfer Charges			
1201. Recording fees: Deed $ _____ ; Mortgage $ _____ ; Releases $			
1202. City/county tax/stamps: Deed $ _____ ; Mortgage $			
1203. State tax/stamps: Deed $ _____ ; Mortgage $			
1204.			
1205.			
1300. Additional Settlement Charges			
1301. Survey to			
1302. Pest inspection to			
1303.			
1304.			
1305.			
1400. Total Settlement Charges (enter on lines 103, Section J and 502, Section K)			

SETTLEMENT STATEMENT FORM (Continued)

A. Settlement Statement   U.S. Department of Housing
                                 and Urban Development   OMB Approval No. 2502-0265

B. Type of Loan

| 1. ☐ FHA 2. ☐ FmHA 3. ☐ Conv. Unins. | 6. File Number: | 7. Loan Number: | 8. Mortgage Insurance Case Number: |
| 4. ☐ VA 5. ☐ Conv. Ins. | | | |

C. Note: This form is furnished to give you a statement of actual settlement costs. Amounts paid to and by the settlement agent are shown. Items marked "(p.o.c.)" were paid outside the closing; they are shown here for informational purposes and are not included in the totals.

D. Name & Address of Borrower:	E. Name & Address of Seller:	F. Name & Address of Lender:

G. Property Location:	H. Settlement Agent:	
	Place of Settlement:	I. Settlement Date:

J. Summary of Borrower's Transaction		**K. Summary of Seller's Transaction**	
100. Gross Amount Due From Borrower		**400. Gross Amount Due To Seller**	
101. Contract sales price		401. Contract sales price	
102. Personal property		402. Personal property	
103. Settlement charges to borrower (line 1400)		403.	
104.		404.	
105.		405.	
Adjustments for items paid by seller in advance		**Adjustments for items paid by seller in advance**	
106. City/town taxes to		406. City/town taxes to	
107. County taxes to		407. County taxes to	
108. Assessments to		408. Assessments to	
109.		409.	
110.		410.	
111.		411.	
112.		412.	
120. Gross Amount Due From Borrower		**420. Gross Amount Due To Seller**	
200. Amounts Paid By Or In Behalf Of Borrower		**500. Reductions In Amount Due To Seller**	
201. Deposit or earnest money		501. Excess deposit (see instructions)	
202. Principal amount of new loan(s)		502. Settlement charges to seller (line 1400)	
203. Existing loan(s) taken subject to		503. Existing loan(s) taken subject to	
204.		504. Payoff of first mortgage loan	
205.		505. Payoff of second mortgage loan	
206.		506.	
207.		507.	
208.		508.	
209.		509.	
Adjustments for items unpaid by seller		**Adjustments for items unpaid by seller**	
210. City/town taxes to		510. City/town taxes to	
211. County taxes to		511. County taxes to	
212. Assessments to		512. Assessments to	
213.		513.	
214.		514.	
215.		515.	
216.		516.	
217.		517.	
218.		518.	
219.		519.	
220. Total Paid By/For Borrower		**520. Total Reduction Amount Due Seller**	
300. Cash At Settlement From/To Borrower		**600. Cash At Settlement To/From Seller**	
301. Gross Amount due from borrower (line 120)		601. Gross amount due to seller (line 420)	
302. Less amounts paid by/for borrower (line 220)	( )	602. Less reductions in amt. due seller (line 520)	( )
303. Cash ☐ From ☐ To Borrower		**603. Cash ☐ To ☐ From Seller**	

SETTLEMENT STATEMENT FORM (Continued)

L. Settlement Charges

		Paid From Borrowers Funds at Settlement	Paid From Seller's Funds at Settlement
700. Total Sales/Broker's Commission based on price $ @ % =			
Division of Commission (line 700) as follows:			
701. $ to			
702. $ to			
703. Commission paid at Settlement			
704.			
800. Items Payable In Connection With Loan			
801. Loan Origination Fee %			
802. Loan Discount %			
803. Appraisal Fee to			
804. Credit Report to			
805. Lender's Inspection Fee			
806. Mortgage Insurance Application Fee to			
807. Assumption Fee			
808.			
809.			
810.			
811.			
900. Items Required By Lender To Be Paid In Advance			
901. Interest from to @$ /day			
902. Mortgage Insurance Premium for months to			
903. Hazard Insurance Premium for years to			
904. years to			
905.			
1000. Reserves Deposited With Lender			
1001. Hazard insurance months@$ per month			
1002. Mortgage insurance months@$ per month			
1003. City property taxes months@$ per month			
1004. County property taxes months@$ per month			
1005. Annual assessments months@$ per month			
1006. months@$ per month			
1007. months@$ per month			
1008. months@$ per month			
1100. Title Charges			
1101. Settlement or closing fee to			
1102. Abstract or title search to			
1103. Title examination to			
1104. Title insurance binder to			
1105. Document preparation to			
1106. Notary fees to			
1107. Attorney's fees to			
(includes above items numbers:)			
1108. Title insurance to			
(includes above items numbers:)			
1109. Lender's coverage $			
1110. Owner's coverage $			
1111.			
1112.			
1113.			
1200. Government Recording and Transfer Charges			
1201. Recording fees: Deed $; Mortgage $; Releases $			
1202. City/county tax/stamps: Deed $; Mortgage $			
1203. State tax/stamps: Deed $; Mortgage $			
1204.			
1205.			
1300. Additional Settlement Charges			
1301. Survey to			
1302. Pest inspection to			
1303.			
1304.			
1305.			
1400. Total Settlement Charges (enter on lines 103, Section J and 502, Section K)			

PROPERTY MANAGEMENT CASH FLOW STATEMENT

Your firm logo here

PROPERTY CASH FLOW STATEMENT

Owner: _____   Report period: _____

Property location: _____   Prepared by: _____

Item	%	Actual	Budget	Comments
Cash Receipts				
Gross rents collected				
Other:				
Other:				
Total cash collected		$	$	
Cash Disbursements				
Accounting & Legal				
Advertising				
Insurance				
Management fee				
Payroll				
Property taxes				
Repairs and maintenance				
Services: janitorial lawn pest control trash				
Supplies				
Utilities: electric gas & oil water & sewer				
Other:				
Other:				
Other:				
Other:				
Monthly mortgage payment				
Total cash disbursements		$	$	
Cash flow (deficit)		$	$	

REQUEST FOR CHANGE OF STATUS

DBPR RE-2050-1 – Request for Change of Status
REV 12/01

Florida's Future...
RightHere:
RightNow.

STATE OF FLORIDA
DEPARTMENT OF BUSINESS AND PROFESSIONAL
REGULATION
1940 North Monroe Street
Tallahassee, FL 32399-0783

CHECK ACTION REQUESTED
Transaction Type: ❑ Become Active – no charge ❑ Become Inactive – no charge ❑ Add/Delete Trade Name – no charge ❑ Become Sole Proprietor – no charge ❑ Change Broker/Owner Employer – no charge ❑ Terminate Employee – no charge ❑ Add/Delete PA - $30.00 fee required ❑ Request for Multiple License - $95.00

SALESPERSON INFORMATION
License Number
Applicant Name

BROKER OR CORPORATION INFORMATION	
Broker License Number	Corporation/Partnership License Number
Broker or Corporation Name	
Trade Name (if applicable)	
Are you now or with the issuance of this license an officer or director of any corporation or partnership which acts as a broker? Yes ❑ No ❑	
If yes, please list name of entity	

ATTEST STATEMENT REQUIRES SIGNATURE OF EMPLOYING BROKER (EXCEPT FOR ADD/DELETE PA - WHICH MAY BE SIGNED BY THE LICENSEE)
I affirm that I have provided the above information completely and truthfully to the best of my knowledge. Sign Here:_____ Date: _____

Mail this form to:

Division of Real Estate
Hurston North Tower
Suite N309
400 West Robinson Street
Orlando, FL 32801

PRACTICE FINAL EXAM

Before you take the end-of-course examination, test your readiness by completing this 100-question, multiple-choice practice exam that is similar to the course exam. The questions are drawn from the 14 chapters in this book; they are of the same type and in the same form with a similar degree of difficulty to the end-of-course exam questions. If you score 75 or higher without using any reference material (in other words, if you simulate exam conditions), you are in a strong position to pass the course exam. Circle or otherwise mark your answers; your instructor can discuss the correct answers to each question. Be certain to review those subject areas you miss.

1. Which brokerage relationship requires that a licensee disclose all known facts that materialy affect the value of residential property?

   I. Nonrepresentation
   II. Single agency
   III. Transaction broker
   a. I only
   b. I and II
   c. I, II, and III
   d. I and III

2. Where the agreement of the parties is contrary to any of the provisions or standards in a preprinted sales contract, it is best to:

   a. line out the particular provision or standard affected.
   b. insert one or more special clauses in an addendum to the contract.
   c. renegotiate the contrary item(s) with the parties to the contract.
   d. prepare a nonstandard contract.

3. A homeowner is willing to pay $400 for a written, detailed appraisal of her home. To do the appraisal legally and collect the fee, an individual must follow the Uniform Standards of Professional Appraisal Practice, and be licensed as a(n):

   a. active real estate sales associate.
   b. active real estate broker.
   c. a state certified appraiser.
   d. Any of the above

4. Which duty is owed by the broker to a principal in a single agency relationship that is *not* owed to a customer in a transaction broker relationship?

   a. Skill, care and diligence
   b. Dealing honestly and fairly
   c. Loyalty
   d. Accounting for all funds

5. John is a single agent for the seller, and will not be representing buyers to whom he shows the property. What must he do?

   a. He must give the buyer an oral notice of his status.
   b. He may not work with buyers unless he is their single agent or transaction broker.
   c. He must give the buyers a No Brokerage Relationship Notice before showing the property
   d. He must give the buyers a Transaction Broker Notice before showing the property.

6. A licensee who has limited representation duties in a real estate transaction is called a(n):

   a. disclosed dual agent.
   b. transaction broker.
   c. single agent.
   d. attorney-in-fact.

7. Yesterday, Broker Bono concluded a 90-day listing contract with a seller. The contract contains a self-renewing provision extending the agreement an additional 60 days after expiration unless either party cancels in writing. The listing contract is:

   a. void.
   b. unconscionable.
   c. valid.
   d. implied.

8. Broker Javits was a transaction broker in the sale and purchase of an office building. He felt an obligation to tell the buyer about the seller's need to sell quickly. As a balance, he helped the seller get a better price from the buyer because of some comments the buyer made during the property inspection. What is correct?

   a. Because the disclosures were balanced and both buyer and seller were treated fairly, no violation has occurred.
   b. Disclosure of such information violates Chapter 475.
   c. While an ethical violation has occurred, no statutory violation has taken place.
   d. While the broker may disclose motivation information, he may not discuss specifically what price a seller might accept or the buyer might pay.

9. The increased popularity of town houses, condominiums, and cooperatives can best be attributed to:

   a. rising construction costs and a younger, more mobile population.
   b. a decrease in usable land and a gradually declining average household size.
   c. increased single-family home construction costs and higher costs for desirable land.
   d. an increase in the number of households.

10. To reduce liability from residential property defects, a listing sales associate should:

    a. request the seller to complete and sign a property condition disclosure statement.
    b. do a complete house inspection, including attic and crawl space.
    c. rely on the seller's verbal assurance that everything is in good condition.
    d. warn all prospective buyers that the property may or may not have material defects.

11. Any contract that appears to create a one-sided bargain in favor of one of the principals and at the expense of another is in danger of being declared:

    a. unconstitutional.
    b. voidable.
    c. void.
    d. unconscionable.

12. Sales tax must be collected on personal property sold as part of a real estate transaction when it is:

    a. depreciated for income tax purposes.
    b. itemized and valued in the sales contract.
    c. mentioned in the contract.
    d. used to determine the broker's compensation.

13. The best way to acquire product knowledge is to:

    a. be in the marketplace.
    b. read the many books available through NAR.
    c. give on-the-job training classes.
    d. attend a class at the community college.

14. The most probable price a property should bring in an arm's-length transaction in a competitive and open market is called the:

    a. market price.
    b. market value.
    c. exchange value.
    d. sales price.

15. The point where the business cycle, at its highest point, levels off and begins to fall is called:

    a. expansion.
    b. recession.
    c. contraction.
    d. recovery.

16. A buyer has agreed to pay a broker to help locate a specific type of property, but he refuses to create a principal-agent relationship with the broker. The listing agent did not offer subagency. The term below that best describes the broker's status is:

   a. nonrepresentative or transaction broker.
   b. buyer's broker.
   c. buyer's subagent.
   d. seller's subagent.

17. The law requiring that certain types of contracts be written to be enforceable is:

   a. Chapter 455, F.S.
   b. the statute of frauds.
   c. the statute of limitations.
   d. the "Little FTC Act."

18. To ensure maximum future value of the properties, subdivision restrictions rely on the principle of:

   a. contribution.
   b. substitution.
   c. conformity.
   d. competition.

19. What is NOT correct about listing agreements in Florida?

   a. Listing contracts for less than one year are covered by the statute of frauds.
   b. All written listings must have definite expiration dates.
   c. Oral listing contracts are enforceable.
   d. Listings are personal service contracts.

20. John is working on a CMA for a three-bedroom, two-bath home with a swimming pool and a two-car garage. He finds comparables as follows:

Comparable #1	Comparable #2	Comparable #3
$126,000	$121,000	$124,000
four bedrooms	three bedrooms	four bedrooms
pool	no pool	no pool
one-car garage	two-car garage	two-car garage

   The extra bedroom contributes $3,000 to the price, the pool contributes $4,000, and the difference between a one-car and a two-car garage is $2,000. Based strictly on this information, what is the subject's estimated value?

   a. $121,000
   b. $124,000
   c. $125,000
   d. $126,000

21. The entire process of evaluating the risks involved in issuing a new real estate mortgage is commonly called:

    a. buyer/borrower qualification.
    b. loan risk evaluation.
    c. buyer/borrower prequalification.
    d. loan underwriting.

22. What is most important in a sales contract?

    a. Seller's marital status
    b. Serial number on each major appliance
    c. Buyer's maiden name
    d. Subject property's legal description

23. In the comparable sales approach:

    a. the subject property must have sold recently in the same neighborhood.
    b. adjustments for differences are always made to the subject property.
    c. adjustments for differences are always made to the comparable property.
    d. the appraiser must know construction costs to complete this approach.

24. What is NOT a good reason to make a preclosing walk-through inspection?

    a. To determine that no encroachments exist
    b. To determine that the property has been maintained in the same condition it existed in at closing, reasonable wear and tear excepted
    c. To ensure that all required repairs have been made
    d. To determine that all items of personal property are on the real property

25. In an adjustable-rate mortgage, the component that does not change from year to year is the:

    a. margin.
    b. index.
    c. calculated rate.
    d. rate charged.

26. Which ad would NOT trigger Truth-in-Lending dislcosures?

    a. "Beautiful home. Save $48,567 in interest with a 15-year mortgage."
    b. "Four bedroom home close to downtown. 5% down, no closing costs."
    c. "New home in Kendall. $895 monthly payment."
    d. "Three bedroom home with pool. Easy financing terms."

27. The optimum rental price for standard space in a local area is determined by:

    a. market analysis.
    b. property analysis.
    c. neighborhood analysis.
    d. surveys of past, current, and projected tenant population figures.

28. Joining Toastmasters is one of the most effective ways to improve which of the following types of skills?

    a. Written communication
    b. Verbal communication
    c. Nonverbal communication
    d. Product knowledge

29. Brokers must notify the FREC and follow the prescribed escrow settlement procedures in case of conflicting demands EXCEPT when a buyer cancels the contract because:

    a. the home inspection showed flaws and there was a home inspection contingency clause.
    b. the property was a condominium and the buyer delivers written notice within the allowed time period to cancel.
    c. the licensee did not provide the required homeowners' association notice.
    d. the selling sales associate did not have a current, active license.

30. The fiduciary duties of care, skill, and diligence require that a licensee be knowledgeable concerning all of the following *except:*

    a. Florida license laws.
    b. a property's quality of title.
    c. a property's physical characteristics.
    d. the meaning of important clauses.

31. When calculating a property's net operating income, such items as depreciation, income taxes and property financing costs are:

    a. included in variable operating costs.
    b. included in fixed operating costs.
    c. considered as funds reserved for operations or replacements.
    d. excluded from consideration.

32. When annual debt service is subtracted from net operating income, the resulting amount is the:

    a. after-tax cash flow.
    b. before-tax cash flow.
    c. cash flow.
    d. net spendable income.

33. Broker Wilson committed a minor violation three years ago, and has not been disciplined since that time. If Broker Wilson wants the violation removed from public inspection, she may:

    a. request an informal hearing before the FREC.
    b. post a surety bond for $10,000 guaranteeing no further violations.
    c. pay a $5,000 fine to the DBPR.
    d. petition the Department to classify the violation as inactive.

34. A person who authorizes another person (the agent) to represent her in a real estate transaction is the:

    a. customer.
    b. prospect.
    c. principal.
    d. third party.

35. What is a contract that may be terminated at the option of one of the parties?

    a. Voidable
    b. Implied
    c. Option
    d. Dual representation

36. The monthly Housing Starts report is:

    a. an extremely important economic indicator.
    b. a lagging economic indicator.
    c. not able to be forecast by the previous month's building permit data.
    d. prepared by the Department of Veterans Affairs.

37. What is the difference between effective gross income and net operating income?

    a. Before-tax cash flow
    b. Vacancy
    c. Operating expenses
    d. Cash throwoff

38. A mortgage note normally shows the amount required to pay monthly:

    a. principal and interest only.
    b. principal, interest, and one-twelfth of annual property taxes.
    c. principal, interest, and one-twelfth of annual hazard insurance.
    d. principal, interest, and one-twelfth of annual taxes and insurance.

39. How many days does a broker have to place an earnest money deposit in her escrow account?

    a. One
    b. Three
    c. Five
    d. Ten

40. An agreement that is unenforceable under the law because it does not contain the essential elements is which of the following types of contracts?

    a. Unconscionable
    b. Option
    c. Void
    d. Illegal

41. A bilateral agreement spelling out the complete terms between a buyer and a seller for the transfer of a parcel of real property is a(n):

    a. representation agreement.
    b. sales contract.
    c. option contract.
    d. wraparound mortgage.

42. The principle of value that says improvement to a property is worth only what it adds to the property's market value, regardless of actual cost, is called the principle of:

    a. substitution.
    b. conformity.
    c. contribution.
    d. competition.

43. Most conventional residential mortgage lenders have adopted the Fannie Mae suggested housing expense ratio and the total long-term obligations ratio calculated from gross income amounts for underwriting loans. The Fannie Mae ratios for housing expense (HER) and total obligations (TOR) currently range from:

    a. 3 to 1 (HER) and 4 to 1 (TOR).
    b. 25% to 28% (HER) and 33% to 36% (TOR).
    c. 10% to 30% (HER) and 20% to 30% (TOR).
    d. 25% to 40% (HER) and 25% to 40% (TOR).

44. The three components of a full property title report are a physical inspection of the property, a search of the public records, and a(n):

    a. survey.
    b. legal description.
    c. valid conveyance from all previous owners.
    d. abstract or opinion of title.

45. How does the appraisal cost usually appear in the HUD-1 settlement statement when a new institutional mortgage has been used for the purchase?

    a. Debit to the seller
    b. Credit to the buyer
    c. Debit to the buyer
    d. POC

46. If a broker provides limited representation to the parties in a transaction, the broker would be considered a:

    a. transaction broker.
    b. disclosed dual agent.
    c. single agent for both buyer and seller.
    d. nonrepresentative.

47. The relationship between supply and demand for a particular type of multifamily property at its current rental level is reflected by the:

    a. rental market's equilibrium.
    b. turnover of tenants whose leases expire.
    c. area's location quotient.
    d. occupancy rate for that type of property.

48. A basic principle of value stating that a property's maximum value tends to be set by the cost of producing an equally desirable property is known as the principle of:

    a. anticipation.
    b. conformity.
    c. increasing returns.
    d. substitution.

49. What is the best method for estimating a property's value based on its net operating income?

    a. Income capitalization
    b. Rule-of-thumb
    c. Cost-depreciation
    d. Time value of future income

50. If a single agent residential seller's broker wishes to provide limited representation to a buyer, what must the broker do?

    a. Have the seller sign the Consent to Transition to Transaction Broker Notice and have both parties sign the Transaction Broker Notice.
    b. Have the buyer sign the Consent to Transition to Transaction Broker Notice and have both parties sign the Transaction Broker Notice.
    c. Have both the seller and buyer sign the Transaction Broker Notice.
    d. Become a single agent for the buyer also.

51. An agreement between a seller of real property and a real estate broker that authorizes the broker to sell the property on specified terms in return for a sales commission if the broker is successful is a(n):

    a. single agency contract.
    b. sales contract.
    c. option contract.
    d. listing contract.

52. In real estate appraisal, a loss in an improvement's value for any reason is called:

    a. disintermediation.
    b. depreciation.
    c. discounting.
    d. disclosure.

53. A sales associate who has been licensed for eight years did not renew his license last March 31 as required. What is his status?

   a. Void.
   b. Suspended.
   c. Voluntary inactive.
   d. Involuntary inactive.

54. In doing a CMA, you find a comparable property that sold two months ago for $138,000. It has four bedrooms (the subject property has three) and is 160 square feet larger as a result. You decide that the additional room/space makes an $8,000 difference. The subject is newer and in slightly better condition, so you estimate a difference of $5,000. Due to the difference in square footage and bedrooms, you make a:

   a. plus $8,000 adjustment to the comparable.
   b. plus $8,000 adjustment to the subject.
   c. minus $8,000 adjustment to the subject.
   d. minus $8,000 adjustment to the comparable.

55. Using the information in the previous question, you adjust for size and physical condition. The resulting net adjustment for these property characteristics is:

   a. plus $3,000.
   b. minus $3,000.
   c. plus $5,000.
   d. minus $5,000.

56. Using the information from the previous two questions, the adjusted sales price of the comparable property is:

   a. $143,000.
   b. $138,000.
   c. $135,000.
   d. $130,000.

57. Trees, landscaping, driveways, fences, pools, and other improvements of a home should be valued by the listing sales associate at:

   a. their original cost.
   b. their original cost, less their physical depreciation.
   c. their contribution to value.
   d. the seller's best representation of their value.

58. The relationship between a property's net operating income and its present value is the:

   a. cash throwoff.
   b. debt service.
   c. capitalization rate.
   d. return on investment.

59. An agreement to hold open for a set time period an offer to sell or lease real property is a(n):

    a. contract for deed.
    b. option contract.
    c. installment contract.
    d. agreement for deed.

60. Which contract does the seller warrant appliances to be in working order?

    a. Quasi
    b. Executory
    c. FAR/BAR
    d. Implied

61. A real estate contract given to one broker as sole agent for the sale of an owner's property, with a commission going to that broker regardless of who actually sells the property during the contract period, is a(n):

    a. unilateral agreement.
    b. exclusive-representation agreement.
    c. exclusive-agency listing.
    d. exclusive-right-to-sell listing.

62. A method for estimating a property's market value based on the value of the site plus the expense of constructing a new building on the site is which of the following approaches?

    a. Comparable sales
    b. Cost-depreciation
    c. Future income capitalization
    d. Rule-of-thumb

63. John and Bill are sales associates working for Southland Commercial brokers. Their broker allows John to act as a single agent for the buyer and Bill to act as a single agent for the seller. Both the buyer and seller have assets of more than $1 million and each agrees to this form of representation. The situation describes a:

    a. transaction broker relationship.
    b. single agency.
    c. dual agency.
    d. designated sales associate.

64. In the FAR/BAR contract, if a survey shows an encroachment, the:

    a. encroachment will be treated as a title defect.
    b. encroachment will be a breach of contract on the seller's part.
    c. seller must pay damages to the buyer for any delays due to the problem.
    d. buyer is responsible for any expenses associated with curing the problem.

65. The best and least expensive method of renting or leasing residential properties is the use of:

    a. referrals from satisfied tenants.
    b. newspaper classified ads.
    c. radio ads of 30 seconds or less.
    d. short, relatively inexpensive television commercials.

66. On a financial statement, the value remaining after deducting liabilities from assets is:

    a. cash flow.
    b. net operating income.
    c. effective gross income.
    d. net worth.

67. Under RESPA, a lender must provide to a buyer, within three days of the loan application, a:

    a. lock-in letter guaranteeing the interest rate for at least 60 days.
    b. good-faith estimate of settlement costs.
    c. closing statement that includes prorations.
    d. commitment letter.

68. A person wishing to avoid liability under the Comprehensive Environmental Response, Compensation and Liability Act of 1980, claiming innocent purchaser status, must:

    a. pay for an insurance bond issued by the Department of Environmental Regulation.
    b. require the seller to obtain an insurance bond issued by the Department of Environmental Regulation.
    c. exercise due diligence by investigating the property, usually in the form of an environmental audit.
    d. obtain certifications from the local planning commission that the property never has been used as a gas station or dry cleaning establishment.

69. A property is sold by a married couple who file jointly and who have owned and occupied their personal residence for three years. Which statement is true about their tax liability?

    a. They must pay taxes at a 20 percent rate on the amount that the property's adjusted sales price exceeds the property's new price.
    b. They may exclude up to $600,000 of any gain before becoming liable for taxes.
    c. They may exclude up to $500,000 of any gain before becoming liable for taxes.
    d. Their maximum capital gains rate is reduced to 10 percent because it was a personal residence.

70. Which is NOT a type of operating expense?

    a. Fixed expenses
    b. Reserves for replacements
    c. Depreciation
    d. Variable expenses

71. The practice of representing either the buyer or the seller but never both in a real estate transaction is called:

    a. customer-level service.
    b. single agency.
    c. subagency.
    d. customer-level representation.

72. John sells an investment property he has owned for five years and has a capital gain of $125,000. His ordinary income tax rate is 28 percent. Using just this information, how much will his taxes be for this transaction?

    a. He may exclude up to $500,000 of the gain before calculating taxes.
    b. $12,500
    c. $18,750
    d. $35,000

73. Under the Coastal Zone Management Act, a seller must provide to a buyer, at or before closing, a(n):

    a. written warranty that the property may be used for single-family housing.
    b. survey or performance bond.
    c. performance bond or affidavit concerning the CCCL.
    d. affidavit or survey delineating the CCCL unless the buyer waives it in writing.

74. Under Florida's Growth Management Act:

    a. it is more difficult to subdivide parcels inside the urban services area.
    b. concurrency means that schools must provide evidence of being in the upper quartile of performance before new construction can commence.
    c. a county may not designate a land-use plan without a referendum.
    d. it is more difficult to subdivide parcels outside the urban services area.

75. A Florida licensee who sells time-share units for a commission without having an active license is subject to:

    a. mandatory suspension for one year.
    b. mandatory revocation.
    c. mandatory fine of $1,000 per violation.
    d. no penalty.

76. When selling his property, Fred Goldman failed to disclose the fact that a person died of AIDS in the home. Fred:

    a. and his broker are legally liable to the buyer for damages.
    b. and his broker are subject to disciplinary action by FREC.
    c. and his broker can have the court dismiss the suit.
    d. is liable; the broker is not.

77. Any active real estate licensee is entitled to be paid for providing an appraisal and appraisal services *except* when:

    a. the property is involved in a federally related transaction.
    b. he does not represent himself as being a certified, licensed, or registered appraiser.
    c. he does not represent his report as being a certified, licensed, or registered appraisal.
    d. he is not listing or selling the property.

78. A sales associate hires a licensed personal assistant. The personal assistant's contract requires a salary of $1,000 per month and 15% of the sales associate's share of commissions. Which is correct?

    a. The broker must pay both the salary and the commission to the personal assistant.
    b. The sales associate may pay both the salary and the commission to the personal assistant.
    c. The salary may be paid by either the sales associate or the broker. The broker must pay the commission to the personal assistant.
    d. Sharing commissions with a licensed personal assistant is a violation of Florida license law.

79. Properties that should be rejected as comparable for determining a subject property's value include all properties *except* those:

    a. sold within the previous six months.
    b. that differ in quality of construction.
    c. that are much different in size.
    d. in which the buyers and sellers were relatives.

80. Paula is purchasing a new residence with an 8.75 percent loan in the amount of $125,000. The closing date is October 15, and the first payment on the new loan is due on December 1. What is the amount of prepaid interest to be collected at closing?

    a. $419.52
    b. $479.52
    c. $509.42
    d. $928.94

81. When an investment property is sold for a gain, the seller may be required to pay taxes on the gain, plus taxes on the depreciation taken during the time of ownership. What is that tax rate on the depreciation?

    a. 20%
    b. 25%
    c. 28%
    d. 31%

82. A lead-based paint hazard disclosure must be made if the house being sold was built before:

    a. 1998.
    b. 1978.
    c. 1975.
    d. 1963.

83. The ratio of monthly housing expenses to monthly income is the:

    a. housing expense.
    b. income and expense.
    c. total obligations.
    d. total consumer credit.

84. A licensee should work hard to clear contract contingencies:

    a. within five days before closing.
    b. within five days after loan approval.
    c. within three days of contract.
    d. as soon as possible after the contract has been signed.

85. The FAR/BAR contract requires that the seller warrant appliances, heating and cooling systems, and plumbing systems to be in working order:

    a. at closing.
    b. on the date of contract.
    c. as of ten days before closing.
    d. as of three days before closing.

86. At the time a listing agreement is negotiated, the listing broker should discuss with the seller all of the following subjects *except* the:

    a. pros and cons of subagency.
    b. seller's religious preference.
    c. use of the local MLS.
    d. seller's attitude toward the broker sharing the sales commission with a cooperating broker.

87. Marilyn is searching for a new apartment. When she drives through the entrance of The Fountains, she gets a wonderful impression and decides to rent if the price is right. Marilyn's first impression is called:

    a. market value.
    b. eye invitation.
    c. curb appeal.
    d. comparative market analysis.

88. Comparable properties should be adjusted so that they reflect:

    a. the monetary difference in features between the subject property and the comparable property.
    b. the subject property's characteristics.
    c. the price the subject property should sell for.
    d. current market influences.

89. Richard expects to live in his new home for about five years. He is shopping for a new $100,000 mortgage. With no points, he can get a 30-year 8 percent fixed rate mortgage with principal and interest payments of $733.76. Another lender has a 7.75 percent mortgage (payments of $716.41) with one point. How many months will it take Richard to break even on the points if he takes the lower interest loan, using simple arithmetic?

    a. 48.5
    b. 57.6
    c. 68.6
    d. 69.2

90. The FAR/BAR Contract for Sale and Purchase is NOT suitable for:

    a. contracts for deed.
    b. single-family dwellings.
    c. unimproved properties.
    d. condominium units.

91. Carolyn, a licensed sales associate, has an unlicensed personal assistant who is salaried. The personal assistant hands out brochures at an open house but does not do any selling, nor does she write contracts. Which is correct?

    a. Carolyn and her assistant have both committed a violation of Chapter 475.
    b. This is allowed under the rules of the Commission.
    c. If the sales associate collects a commission, this is illegal.
    d. The broker, Carolyn, and her assistant have all committed a violation of Chapter 475.

92. Within five days after transfer of the property, sellers who have been cited for a building code violation must give to the code enforcement agency a:

    a. $500 administrative fee for transferring the information to the buyer's name.
    b. contractor's affidavit that the building code violations were corrected before the property was transferred.
    c. document stating the existence and nature of the violation.
    d. notice of the name and address of the new owner.

93. Jack is a buyers' broker working with the Smiths. The Smiths become interested in a home where Jack is the single agent for the seller. What should Jack do before showing his listing to his buyers?

    a. Have both parties agree to his becoming a transaction broker, have them each sign a Consent to Transition to Transaction Broker Notice, and ask them each to sign the Transaction Broker Notice
    b. Become a designated sales representative for both parties
    c. Provide a dual agency disclosure statement and have it signed by both parties
    d. Nothing; he may not sell his own listing

Use the following information to answer questions 94 through 100.

Susan Rigsby lists her home with broker William Merritt for $90,000 on March 16. On August 1, Henry Hart makes an offer of $85,000, accompanied by a binder deposit of $5,000, and asks the seller to pay points on a new loan of $80,000. Susan counters at a price of $87,500 and agrees to pay four points on a loan of $82,500. Henry accepts.

Henry qualifies for the loan at an interest rate of 9 percent and agrees to pay a 1 percent origination fee. The monthly payment for principal and interest is $663.81. Henry also will be charged for prepaid interest for the balance of the month of closing. Closing date is September 15, and Henry is charged for the day of closing.

Henry will purchase an insurance policy for $720. City and county taxes are $760. Susan agreed to pay her own attorney's fees of $125. Hart must pay $130 for attorney's fees, $56 to record the mortgage, $6 to record the deed, and $640 for title insurance.

The payoff on Susan's existing mortgage will be $64,455.16 on the day of closing. Broker William's fee is 6 percent. Doc stamps and intangible taxes are paid according to custom. Use the 365-day method for prorations.

94. How are the points to be handled on the closing statement?

    a. Credit Henry $3,500.
    b. Debit Susan $3,500.
    c. Debit Susan $3,300; credit Henry $3,300.
    d. Debit Susan $3,300.

95. If the lender wants a three-month tax escrow plus the number of months through the day of closing, what is the amount of prepaid taxes the lender collects at closing?

    a. $190.00
    b. $696.67
    c. $760.00
    d. $773.33

96. What is the proration of taxes between the seller and the buyer?

    a. Debit Henry; credit Susan $535.12.
    b. Debit Henry; credit Susan $224.88.
    c. Debit Susan; credit Henry $535.12.
    d. Debit Susan; credit Henry $224.88.

97. What is the amount of documentary stamp taxes on the note?

    a. $288.75
    b. $306.25
    c. $577.50
    d. $612.50

98. Using the 365-day method and the exact number of days in the month, how will prepaid interest be handled on the closing statement?

    a. Henry must pay $325.48 in prepaid interest at closing.
    b. Susan must pay $325.48 in prepaid interest at closing.
    c. Henry must pay $330.00 in prepaid interest at closing.
    d. Henry must pay $535.12 in prepaid interest at closing.

99. How are the documentary stamp taxes on the deed handled on the closing statement?

    a. Credit Henry $612.50.
    b. Debit Susan $612.50.
    c. Debit Henry $306.25.
    d. Debit Susan $306.25.

100. Assuming the mortgage insurance premium is $50.18 per month, what is the total monthly payment (PITI) on the mortgagee?

    a. $663.81
    b. $725.89
    c. $787.14
    d. $837.32

GLOSSARY

A

abstract. A history of a property shown by the public records used to give an opinion of title. Less frequently used today than title insurance.

adjustable-rate mortgage (ARM). A loan that allows the borrower's interest rate to fluctuate based on some external index beyond the control of the lender.

adjustments. Method used by brokers and appraisers to account for differences in comparable properties. If a subject property is superior, the appraiser would make a dollar adjustment increasing the sale price of the comparable. If the subject property is inferior to the comparable property, a negative adjustment would be made.

after-tax cash flow. The amount remaining to an owner of income property after all expenses, debt service and income taxes have been paid.

agency. The relationship of agents and their principals.

agent. A person who represents another person in a fiduciary relationship.

ambiguity. A statement that is unclear, or may have several meanings.

annual mortgage constant. The factor that, if multiplied by the original loan balance, will result in the annual mortgage payment; the mortgage payment's percentage of the original loan.

annual percentage rate (APR). An expression of credit costs over the life of a loan, taking into account the contract interest rate plus lender fees for originating, processing and closing a mortgage loan.

antitrust. Federal law that prohibits monopolistic practices such as price fixing.

appraisal. An unbiased estimate of a property's market value.

appraising. The process of estimating the market value of property.

arm's-length transaction. A business transaction in which the parties are dealing in their own self interest, not being under the control of the other party. One of the requirements before a comparable sale should be used in an appraisal.

assets. Things of value owned by a person or organization.

automated underwriting. The evaluation of a mortgage loan application using predetermined formulas and credit scores. Fannie Mae's *Desktop Underwriter* performs automated underwriting.

automated valuation. The use of computers and linear regression formulas to calculate the market value of property based on large numbers of comparable sales.

B

before-tax cash flow. The amount of spendable income from an income property after paying operating expenses and debt service, but before the effect of income taxes.

bilateral contract. A contract that requires both parties to perform, such as a sales contract.

biweekly mortgage. A mortgage that requires the borrower to make payments every two weeks (26 payments per year). The payment is calculated by dividing the monthly mortgage payment by two. The effective result is that the borrower makes 13 monthly payments per year.

blockbusting. The illegal act of a licensee who frightens homeowners into selling by raising fears that minority homeowners are moving into a neighborhood.

body language. Nonverbal communication expressed by the position of the body, hands, arms, legs, or facial expressions.

browser. A software program that makes access to Web pages possible. *Netscape* and *Internet Explorer* are examples.

buyer brokerage agreement. An agreement between a buyer and a broker for the broker to provide services to a buyer for compensation. The broker may be acting as a single agent, a transaction broker, or a nonrepresentative.

buyer agency. The fiduciary relationship between a buyer and the buyer's single agent broker.

C

calculated interest rate. The interest rate in an adjustable rate mortgage that is calculated by adding the margin to the index.

canvassing. Prospecting for buyers or sellers by telephoning or walking door-to-door.

cap. The maximum amount that an interest rate can increase per year, or during the life of a loan.

capitalization rate. The net operating income divided by the property value. A percentage representing the return on the investment, assuming the property was purchased for cash.

cash flow report. A property manager's monthly report to the owner, showing cash receipts and cash disbursements of an income property.

certified check. A check issued by a bank guaranteeing payment. The buyer is usually required to bring a certified check to closing by most title closing agents to speed disbursement at closing.

Certified Property Manager (CPM). A professional designation awarded by the Institute of Real Estate Management (IREM) to a property manager who has successfully completed required education and experience.

closing statement. A detailed accounting of charges and credits for the buyer and the seller in a real estate transaction.

Coastal Construction Control Line (CCCL). An imaginary line established by Florida counties a specified distance from the mean high water mark of the Atlantic Ocean or the Gulf of Mexico that prohibits construction seaward from the line.

collateral. Something of value given as security for a debt. In real estate, the mortgage pledges the property as collateral for the repayment of the loan.

commission.   Compensation for professional services that is usually calculated as a percentage of the property's sales price.

community association manager.   An individual licensed by the Department of Business and Professional Regulation who is paid to perform certain functions for a residential homeowner's association.

community association.   A residential homeowner's association in which members own a residence in a development authorized to impose a fee that may become a lien on the parcel. Also defined in Chapter 468, F.S. as any association "greater than 50 units or with an annual budget greater than $100,000."

compact disc (CD) drive.   A part of the computer that allows the user to access information or programs on a compact disc.

comparable property.   A similar property in the same market area that may be used to help estimate the value of the property being appraised.

comparable sales approach.   A method used to estimate a property's value by comparing sales prices of similar properties, making dollar adjustments for differences.

comparative market analysis (CMA).   Similar to the comparable sales approach used by appraisers, but usually less detailed. Used by brokers and sales associates to estimate the most likely selling price of properties they are listing or selling.

computer valuation.   The use of computers and linear regression formulas to estimate the market value of property based on large numbers of comparable sales.

computer-assisted design (CAD).   Software program that assists the user in making technical drawings.

concurrency.   A state law requiring that infrastructure such as roads, sewers, schools, etc. be in place as development occurs.

Consent to Transition to Transaction Broker Notice.   A disclosure form that allows a single agent to become a transaction broker. The notice must be signed by the principal before the broker can make the change.

contingency.   A condition in a contract that, unless satisfied, may make the contract voidable by one of the parties.

contract.   An agreement between two or more parties to do or not do a specific act.

contract service.   A property maintenance service that is done by an individual or company not in the employ of the property manager.

contraction.   The phase of a business cycle that begins after a recession when economic conditions worsen.

cooperative sale.   Sale of a property by a broker who is not the listing broker. Normally, commissions are split between the two brokerage firms.

corrective maintenance.   The repairs to a building's structure and equipment following breakdown.

cost-depreciation approach.   The approach to value in appraising that estimates the cost to reproduce a building, subtracts accumulated depreciation and adds land value.

counteroffer.   A substitution for the original offer made by the offeree who changes the price or terms offered, sending it back to the offeror. The original offer is terminated. The original offeree becomes the offeror.

crash. The termination of a software program on a computer so that all unsaved data in random access memory is lost. Usually, the computer must be restarted.

credit scoring. A method of credit reporting using a numeric score. A higher score reflects a person with better credit history.

curb appeal. The impression, good or bad, that is made when a person first looks at a house from the street.

customer. A person who works with a sales associate or a broker. The usual definition is that the broker is either a transaction broker, or has no brokerage relationship with the person.

cycle. Periodic fluctuations of the overall economy, or any part of the economy, between good times and bad. The four parts of a general cycle are expansion, recession, contraction and recovery.

cyclic fluctuation. Part of an economic cycle.

D

database. A listing of information in a form that allows easy manipulation and reporting. It is also the name for a software program that makes the organization of information easier.

deferred maintenance. Maintenance that needs to be done, but for some reason, usually economic, has not been done.

designated sales associate. A sales associate who is appointed by a broker to be a single agent for a buyer or seller in a nonresidential transaction when another sales associate in the firm has been appointed to be the single agent for the other party in the transaction. Both buyer and seller must have assets of at least $1 million and agree to the arrangement.

digital camera. A camera that does not use conventional film, but instead stores images in a memory chip in the camera, ready to be loaded into a computer for display or printing.

disclosure. The revelation of information important to a transaction.

documentary stamp taxes. A tax on a real estate transaction that may be levied on the sales price of a property, or on the amount of a mortgage note.

dual agent. An illegal arrangement whereby the broker tries to represent both the buyer and the seller in the same transaction.

dynamic risk. Uninsurable risk, such as that of an economic downturn.

E

effective gross income. The amount of rent and other income actually collected by the owner. When preparing an income statement, vacancy and collection losses are deducted from potential gross income, and other income such as vending machine collections are added.

e-mail. Electronic mail that is sent over the Internet.

equity. The amount of the owner's portion of the property value after deducting mortgages and other liens.

ethical. The right thing to do. Usually a higher standard than legality.

exclusive-agency listing.   A listing that requires the owner to pay the listing broker if the property is sold by any broker, but allows the owner to personally sell the property without being liable for a commission.

exclusive-right-of-sale listing.   A listing that requires the owner to pay the listing broker no matter who sells the property. The broker is automatically the procuring cause of the sale.

executed contract.   A contract in which nothing else remains to be done. All requirements have been performed by the parties.

executory contract.   A contract in which part of the agreement remains to be done. It has not yet "closed."

exercised.   Used in connection with an option contract. An option contract is a unilateral contract until the optionee agrees to purchase, and is said to have "exercised" the option.

expansion.   The phase of a business cycle that begins after a recovery when economic conditions improve.

express contract.   An oral or written agreement where the words specifically describe the intent of the parties.

F

fact of execution.   The acceptance of an offer. The offeree or his licensee must communicate the fact of execution to the offeror in order to make a valid contract.

Fair Housing Act.   The federal law that prohibits discrimination in housing based on race, color, religion, sex, national origin, familial status and handicap.

fall-back list.   A list of properties similar to the property being advertised that can be used by the licensee if the advertised property does not appeal to the person responding to the ad.

false or misleading statement.   In real estate, a statement made by a licensee or party in a real estate transaction that is not factual.

FAR/BAR Contract for Sale and Purchase.   The most widely used contract in Florida, prepared and updated regularly the Florida Association of Realtors® and the Florida Bar.

federally related transaction.   A real estate transaction financed by a lender insured by the federal government, or a loan insured or guaranteed by the federal government that requires the services of an appraiser.

fee.   Compensation, either as a fixed dollar amount or a percentage of the sale price.

FICO score.   A proprietary numeric credit score used to evaluate a prospective borrower, developed by Fair, Isaacs & Co.

fiduciary relationship.   A relationship of trust and confidence between an agent and principal.

Foreign Investment in Real Property Tax Act (FIRPTA).   A federal law for aliens and alien corporations for U.S. income tax requiring the buyer to withhold a percentage of the sale price as taxes on the gain from the sale of a real property interest located in the United States.

fixed-rate mortgage.   A loan secured by real estate that has the same rate of interest for the life of the loan.

funding fee.   A charge levied by the Department of Veteran's Affairs to veterans who use VA loans.

G

gross domestic product (GDP).   The sum total of goods and services produced by the United States. The four major components of GDP are: consumption, investment, government purchases, and net exports.

H

hardware.   Tangible computer equipment that runs programs, called software.

http.   A prefix for Web site addresses, meaning "hypertext transport protocol."

hyperlink.   A link on a Web page that, when clicked, transports the user to another Web page.

hypertext.   The text, usually colored blue and underlined, in a Web page that is the hyperlink to another Web page.

I

implied contract.   An agreement not spelled out in words where the agreement of the parties is demonstrated by their acts and conduct.

income capitalization approach.   A method for estimating a property's value calculated by dividing the net operating income of a property by the capitalization rate experienced by similar properties that have been sold.

index.   An indicator beyond the control of a lender to which the interest rate on an adjustable rate mortgage is tied.

infrastructure.   The system of public works for a country, state or region, such as roads, schools, sewers, water treatment facilities, etc.

inkjet printer.   A printer that uses an ink spray for black and color printing.

innocent purchaser status.   An amendment to the Comprehensive Environmental Response, Compensation and Liability Act (CERCLA) that exempts landowners from liability who made reasonable inquiries about hazardous substances before purchasing the property.

Institute of Real Estate Management (IREM).   A national organization of property managers affiliated with the National Association of Realtors®.

intangible tax.   A tax of 2 mils (.002) levied on the amount of new mortgage indebtedness.

Internet.   The global network of computers connected by cable and phone lines.

Internet service provider.   A company or organization that acts as the portal for a user to gain access to the Internet.

J

jargon.   A word or expression related to a specific vocation that a layperson may not understand.

K

k.   The symbol for the annual mortgage constant, calculated by dividing the annual payment of principal and interest by the original amount of the loan.

keysafe.   A lockbox holding the key to the home, usually attached to a door handle allowing licensees who are members of the MLS easy access to the property.

L

laptop. A small computer designed for travel, that can run on battery power.

laser printer. A printer using a toner bonded to the paper by laser and heat.

latent defects addenda. A disclosure by the seller that informs the seller of a duty to disclose known property defects and to hold the licensee harmless for the seller's failure to disclose.

leverage. The use of borrowed money with the intent to increase the investor's return on the cash invested. If the return on the investment is greater than the interest rate paid by the borrower, the owner has positive leverage.

liabilities. Amounts owed by a person.

listing agreement. An agreement between a seller and a broker whereby the seller agrees to pay the broker a commission if the broker is successful in selling the property.

loan underwriting. The evaluation of risk when a lender makes a mortgage loan to reduce the lender's exposure to loss.

loan processing procedures. Steps taken by a lender to ensure that underwriting and documentation of a mortgage loan are done in a manner that reduces the lender's exposure to loss.

loan constant. Calculated by dividing the annual payment of principal and interest by the original amount of the loan.

lockbox. A secure box holding the key to the home, usually attached to a door handle allowing licensees who are members of the MLS easy access to the property by using a special access key to the box.

M

margin. The additional percentage added to the index on an adjustable rate mortgage, resulting in the calculated interest rate.

marketing knowledge. A licensee's knowledge of the sales process, including the psychology of selling, advertising, personal marketing, and prospecting.

material fact. An important fact that may affect a buyer's decision to buy, or a seller's decision to sell. Licensees must disclose facts that materially affect the value of residential property.

misrepresentation. A false or misleading statement made intentionally or unintentionally, or the failure to disclose a material fact.

modem. A device allowing a computer to communicate with other computers by phone lines or cable.

mortgage insurance premium (MIP). The amount paid by a borrower for insurance that protects the lender against loss in case of the borrower's default. FHA mortgage insurance is called MIP.

mutual recognition. An agreement between states to recognize a licensee's education obtained in another state. Florida has mutual recognition agreements with several states that exempts licensees in those states from taking a Florida prelicense course if the licensee can pass a 40-question test on Florida real estate law.

N

negative amortization.   A situation occurring, usually under a graduated payment mortgage, where the payment on the loan is less than the amount required to pay the accrued interest. The unpaid interest is added to the principal balance of the loan, and the loan balance gradually increases.

net operating income (NOI).   The income from an investment property remaining after operating expenses have been paid from the effective gross income.

net worth.   The amount remaining when liabilities are subtracted from assets.

new construction maintenance.   Work done on an income property designed to enhance the property's appeal to tenants. Includes adding new wallpaper, carpeting, and light fixtures.

No Brokerage Relationship Notice.   A disclosure that must be given by a licensee who does not represent a buyer or seller before entering into an agreement or showing a property.

nonverbal communication.   Unspoken communication expressed by the position of the body, hands, arms, legs, or facial expressions, commonly called body language.

O

open listing.   A nonexclusive agreement in which a seller agrees to pay a broker if the broker sells the property. The broker is not paid if the seller or another broker sells the property.

operating expenses (OE).   Costs of operating an income property such as property taxes, maintenance, insurance, payrolls and reserves for replacements.

opinion of value.   A broker's price opinion, usually based on a comparative market analysis.

option contract.   An agreement that allows one party to buy, sell or lease real property for specified terms within a specified time limit.

P

paperless mortgage.   A mortgage that is "signed" electronically, using digital signatures.

performance.   The completion of a contract's requirements.

PITI payment.   The payment required of a borrower that includes principal, interest, taxes and insurance.

planned unit development (PUD).   A residential development designed to have mixed land uses and a high residential density.

point.   A lender's charge to the borrower that increases the lender's yield. One point is equal to one percent of the loan amount.

potential gross income (PGI).   The total annual income a property would produce if it is 100 percent occupied, with no vacancy or collection loss.

preclosing walk-through inspection.   An inspection of the house by the buyer, done sometime before the sale closes, to determine that the property is in the same condition as it existed when the contract was signed, and to ensure that all required repairs have been completed.

prequalification.   The preliminary process during which a prospective lender evaluates the buyer's ability to obtain a mortgage loan. Most licensees want a buyer to be prequalified or preapproved before showing properties.

preventive maintenance.   A work program designed to preserve the physical integrity of the premises and eliminate the more costly corrective maintenance.

previewing properties.   The activity a licensee uses to stay abreast of the market and to find specific properties to show to a prospective buyer.

principal.   1) The person who enters into a fiduciary relationship with a single agent licensee. 2) The amount of money remaining due on a mortgage loan.

prioritize.   To set up a list of activities in an order based on their importance.

private mortgage insurance (PMI).   The amount paid by a borrower for insurance that protects the lender against loss in case of the borrower's default. Conventional lenders use the term private mortgage insurance; FHA mortgage insurance is called MIP.

product knowledge.   A licensee's familiarity with the real estate market and specific properties available for sale.

professional ethics.   A body of accepted codes of behavior for a specific industry.

profile sheet.   A form designed to organize the gathering and input of property listing information into the Multiple Listing Service.

profit and loss statement.   A detailed report of the income and expenses of an investment property over a stated period of time.

property condition disclosure.   A form designed for disclosure to a buyer of any property defects. The form is normally signed by the seller, and the buyer signs a receipt that the buyer has received the disclosure.

property characteristics.   The features of a property that are used as a basis of comparison in an appraisal or comparative market analysis.

Q

qualifying.   The process used by a licensee to determine whether to spend time working with a buyer or seller. For example, a buyer would first be qualified financially, then based on motivation to buy.

quality of income.   A lender's analysis of factors that reveal the likelihood of the borrower's income continuing over a long period of time.

quantity of income.   The total amount of a borrower's income from all sources.

quasi-contract.   A contract that is imposed by law to prevent unjust enrichment. For example, if a person's bank made an error in the person's favor, the quasi-contract invented by the courts would require the person to repay the bank.

R

radon gas.   A colorless, odorless gas occurring from the natural breakdown of uranium in the soil. Many experts believe radon gas to the be the second leading cause of lung cancer.

random access memory (RAM).   Dynamic memory in a computer that disappears when the computer is turned off. Information in the RAM would be lost if it were not saved on the hard drive.

random changes.   Irregular fluctuations of the economy that may be caused by legislative and judicial decisions, wars, weather, etc.

recession.   Two successive quarterly declines in the Gross Domestic Product (GDP). This is the point at which economic activity has peaked and will be followed by a contraction.

reconciliation.   The final step in the appraisal process before the report is prepared. The correlation of property values derived from each of the three appraisal approaches into a single estimate of value.

recovery.   Two successive quarterly increases in the Gross Domestic Product (GDP). This is the point at which economic activity has bottomed and will be followed by expansion.

redlining.   A lender's refusal to loan money in an area based on illegal discrimination.

refinancing.   Placing a new mortgage on a property to replace another mortgage.

Regulation Z.   The part of the Truth-in-Lending Act that requires lenders to calculate and disclose the effective annual percentage rate to the consumer.

reserves for replacements.   A portion of an investment property's income that is set aside to pay the cost of replacing major building components when necessary.

resident manager.   A salaried individual employed for specific management functions for a single investment property.

Real Estate Settlement Procedures Act (RESPA).   A federal law requiring disclosure of loan closing costs in certain real estate financial transactions.

rewritable CD drive (CD-RW).   A computer device that writes information, graphics, or music onto a compact disc.

rider.   An attachment to a contract.

routine maintenance.   The most common maintenance performed on an investment property, such as grounds care and housekeeping.

S

sales contract (contract for sale and purchase).   A bilateral agreement in which a buyer agrees to purchase a seller's property at a specified price and terms.

scanner.   A computer device that allows the user to copy a document or picture and for use in a computer.

search engine.   A Web site that has indexed millions of Web pages, allowing users to locate information by entering key words.

seasonal variation.   Changes in the economy (for example, winter tourism in Florida) that recur at regular intervals at least once a year.

seller agency.   The relationship of a single agent and his principal, the seller.

seller's net proceeds form.   A form used to show the seller's equity, expenses and pro-rations, as well as the net amount the seller is estimated to receive as proceeds from the sale of the property.

servicing the listing.   The actions of a licensee who stays in touch with a seller regularly, getting feedback from licensees who have shown the property, sending the seller copies of advertisements, and generally keeping the seller informed of the marketing efforts.

show list.   A selected inventory of apartments that are available for inspection by prospective tenants.

single agent. A broker who represents either the seller or the buyer in a real estate transaction, but not both.

Single Agent Notice. A disclosure form informing the principal of the duties of his single agent.

software. Computer programs designed specifically to perform specialized functions.

specific cycles. Wavelike movements similar to business cycles that occur in specific sectors of the general economy, such as the real estate market.

spreadsheet. A software program using columns and rows that allows the user to create formulas that act on the numbers stored in the spreadsheet. A change in one amount will change other numbers or totals in the spreadsheet, making "what-if" scenarios simple.

static risk. Risk that is quantifiable and insurable. For example, the risk of fire is a static risk. Fire insurance will transfer the risk from the owner to the insurance company.

statute of frauds. A body of law that requires certain contracts, such as those for the sale of real property, to be written.

steering. The illegal, discriminatory act of a sales associate who brings buyers into an area based on the racial or ethnic makeup of the neighborhood.

subject property. The property being appraised.

surfing. The actions of a person using the Internet who visits many Web sites.

T

technical knowledge. The knowledge needed by licensees to properly conduct their business that relates to filling out contracts, preparing seller's proceeds estimates, doing comparative market analyses, etc.

thumbnail. A picture reduced in size to save loading time that, when clicked on in a Web page, is converted to full size.

time management. The organization of a person's day to maximize efficiency. It includes planning, scheduling and prioritizing.

time is of the essence. A contract clause that requires strict compliance with all dates and times specified in the contract. If a party fails to perform some act by time specified, the person may be in default.

title insurance. A guarantee to reimburse a loss arising from defects in title or liens against real property.

"to-do" list. A daily list, usually designed in priority order, of tasks to be completed that day.

transaction broker. A licensee who has limited representation to the buyer and/or the seller in a transaction. Instead of being an advocate for the buyer or the seller, the licensee is working for the contract.

Transaction Broker Notice. A disclosure form disclosing the transaction broker's duties to buyers and sellers.

transactional characteristics. The factors related to a real estate transaction itself, such as time of sale, and financing terms.

Truth-in-Lending Act. A federal law that requires lenders to inform consumers of exact credit costs before they make their purchases.

U

unconscionable contract.   An agreement that a court may declare unenforceable because it would be grossly unfair to one party if enforced.

Uniform Resource Locator (URL).   A specific Web site address, such as http://www.dearborn-fla.com

Uniform Standards of Professional Appraisal Practice (USPAP).   Strict requirements for appraisers interpreted and amended by the Appraisal Standards Board. Florida appraisers and brokers who prepare appraisals must follow the guidelines.

unilateral contract.   A contract in which only one of the parties is required to perform, such as an option contract. The optionor must sell if the optionee exercises the option, but the optionee is not required to buy.

V

valid contract.   An agreement that complies with all the essentials of a contract and is binding on all parties.

verbal communications skills.   The ability to speak effectively one-on-one or in a group presentation.

void contract.   An agreement that is not binding on either party.

voidable contract.   An agreement that may be canceled by the party who would be damaged if the contract were enforced.

W

warranty of owner.   A hold harmless clause in a listing agreement whereby the seller warrants that all information given to the broker is correct.

World Wide Web.   A collection of millions of documents on the Internet.

written communication skills.   The ability to communicate effectively in letters, e-mails and other documents.

INDEX

Post-Licensing Education for Real Estate Sales Associates
Student Feedback Survey

Thank you for using this text to complete your post-licensing education requirement. We would appreciate your taking time to help make this a better course. We will use your comments to make this text current, relevant and useful.

Date:_____

A. At what school did you take this course? _____

B. When did you complete the course? Month: _____ Year:_____

C. Overall, I found the textbook to be: ❏ excellent   ❏ good   ❏ fair   ❏ poor

D. What new subject areas do you think should be added to future editions of the book?

_____

E. Is your license active or inactive?   ❏ active   ❏ inactive

F. Other comments concerning this text:

_____

_____

Thank you for your comments.

We will give them careful consideration when planning the next edition.

Post-Licensing Education for Sales Associates
Fifth Edition

NOTE: This page, when folded over and taped,
becomes a postage-free envelope that has been
approved by the United States Postal Service.
It has been provided for your convenience.

Important—Please Fold Over and Tape Before Mailing

Important—Please Fold Over and Tape Before Mailing

Return Address:

_____

_____

_____

BUSINESS REPLY MAIL

FIRST CLASS MAIL   PERMIT NO. 88176   CHICAGO, IL

POSTAGE WILL BE PAID BY ADDRESSEE:

 Dearborn
Real Estate Education
30 South Wacker Drive, Suite 2500
Chicago, Illinois 60606-7481

Attn: Editorial Department

Post-Licensing Education for Real Estate Sales Associates
Student Feedback Survey

Thank you for using this text to complete your post-licensing education requirement. We would appreciate your taking time to help make this a better course. We will use your comments to make this text current, relevant and useful.

Date:_____

A. At what school did you take this course? _____

B. When did you complete the course? Month: _____ Year:_____

C. Overall, I found the textbook to be: ❏ excellent   ❏ good   ❏ fair   ❏ poor

D. What new subject areas do you think should be added to future editions of the book?

_____

E. Is your license active or inactive?   ❏ active   ❏ inactive

F. Other comments concerning this text:

_____

_____

Thank you for your comments.

We will give them careful consideration when planning the next edition.

NOTE: This page, when folded over and taped, becomes a postage-free envelope that has been approved by the United States Postal Service. It has been provided for your convenience.

Important—Please Fold Over and Tape Before Mailing

Important—Please Fold Over and Tape Before Mailing

Return Address:

_____

_____

_____

BUSINESS REPLY MAIL

FIRST CLASS MAIL   PERMIT NO. 88176   CHICAGO, IL

POSTAGE WILL BE PAID BY ADDRESSEE:

Real Estate Education

30 South Wacker Drive, Suite 2500

Chicago, Illinois 60606-7481

Attn: Editorial Department